THE NEGRO AND
EMPLOYMENT OPPORTUNITY
Problems and Practices

THE NEGRO AND EMPLOYMENT OPPORTUNITY
Problems and Practices

Edited by

Herbert R. Northrup

Professor of Industry and
Chairman, Department of Industry
Wharton School of Finance and Commerce
University of Pennsylvania

and

Richard L. Rowan

Assistant Professor of Industry
Wharton School of Finance and Commerce
University of Pennsylvania

BUREAU OF INDUSTRIAL RELATIONS
Graduate School of Business Administration
The University of Michigan
Ann Arbor

FOREWORD

The Labor Relations Council of the Wharton School was established in 1946 and, except for a one-year interval, its programs have been an integral part of the school's program. Through the Council, a close cooperation has been maintained over the years between the Industry Department faculty and executives of the member companies. In the monthly seminars, attended by faculty and company members of the Council, many subjects of mutual interest have been discussed. The roster of guest speakers is an imposing one. The monthly seminars have been the heart of the Labor Relations Council, but we believe that other parts of the program have been very important.

Council funds have been used primarily to sponsor research in the field of labor-management relations by faculty members and graduate students. The results have been frequently made available in the form of articles published in numerous journals. The Council has also issued publications under its own auspices. They include the monograph series on Industry-Wide Collective Bargaining published in 1948, the Labor Arbitration Series published in 1952, and the book entitled *New Concepts in Wage Determination* published by McGraw-Hill Book Company, Inc., in 1957.

There is a third facet of Council activities. Whenever it has seemed that some particular problem of national importance might be clarified by public discussion, the Council has conducted public conferences. For example, in November, 1960, at the beginning of what seemed to be a period of economic growth and adjustment to technological change, a conference was held on "Industrial Relations in the 1960's — Problems and Prospects." The demand for the Conference Proceedings has been great. Serious consideration for holding another public conference was not given until early in 1964 when it became apparent that the most critical and the most perplexing issue of employer-employee relations had become the provision of equal job opportunities regardless of color. It seemed not only timely but urgently necessary to bring together a group of outstanding men whose experience made them eminently qualified to discuss not only the nature of the problem but the ways and means for resolving it. A public conference on "Equal Opportunity — The Job Aspect" was held on November 13, 1964. Dr. Herbert Northrup, Chairman of the Industry Department of the Wharton

School, had the primary responsibility for arranging the program.

We believe that the papers presented at the November 13, 1964 conference constitute a significant contribution to an understanding of the problem of providing equal job opportunity to which this nation is increasingly dedicating itself. Along with several other papers which the editors believed to be important additions, those manuscripts presented at the conference are now made available in this volume. It represents, we believe, a significant addition to the publications sponsored by the Labor Relations Council of the Wharton School.

GEORGE W. TAYLOR, Chairman,
Labor Relations Council and
Harnwell Professor of Industry

INTRODUCTION

As Dr. Taylor remarked in the foreword, this book developed from a conference sponsored by the Labor Relations Council of the Wharton School of Finance and Commerce, University of Pennsylvania, that was held in November, 1964. When the conference was being developed, it was determined to bring together the leading scholars in the field and representatives of those companies that had done the most effective job of integration over a long period of time. After the conference was completed, the material looked so promising that plans were made to publish it. Additional contributors were secured in order to make the book more comprehensive.

Part I of the book deals with general problems. In the introductory essay, Professor Ray Marshall of the University of Texas analyzes the job problems of Negroes from an overall point of view. He stresses the need for an increase in economic growth and an attack on the special structural problems of unemployment if progress is to be made toward equal opportunity. Dr. Marshall thus attempts to bridge the gap between the apostles of "growthmanship" and those of structural analysis as means of alleviating the overall situation.

Dr. Marshall's essay is followed by an unusual contribution by Professor Lowell Gallaway of the Wharton School. Dr. Gallaway uses hitherto unpublished data compiled by the Social Security Administration to analyze the differential between Negro and white income. His gloomy conclusion is that as the Negro grows older, he tends to go backward rather than forward in comparative earnings. Unfortunately, this is all too true. Scholars and practitioners alike will find in Dr. Gallaway's data additional proof of the difficult job ahead if equal opportunity is to be created.

In Part II, two views of equal rights and equal opportunity legislation are presented. Mr. George Schermer, a long-time practitioner in the field and now a consultant, discusses the effectiveness of equal opportunity legislation from the point of view of the administrator. He finds that the effectiveness is sometimes overplayed and that there is a limited effect of such legislation. Dr. Northrup covers much of the same ground, but more from the point of view of the impact on companies and unions. He emphasizes that neither this legislation nor equal pay laws have any extended opposition from management or labor, but that nevertheless their effectiveness is likely to be slight except for small companies because larger companies have already put their houses in order. The issue is training and competence, not equal employment. (Training is discussed in many of the papers in Parts IV, V, and VI.) In addition, Dr. Northrup calls attention to numerous potential conflicts between Title VII of the Civil Rights Act and already existing legislation.

In Part III, unusual analyses of individual company performance are presented by representatives of the companies. These are unusual because of their objectivity and also because they present experiences of some of the companies that have done the best job over the longest period of time. International Harvester, for example, has been practicing effective fair employment for more than twenty-five years. Lockheed-Georgia has done an exceptionally thorough job in a Southern atmosphere. Honeywell, General Motors, Western Electric, and General Electric all contribute to our knowledge by reciting their experience, the problems that they have had, and the problems that endure. Of particular note is the fact that each and every one of these companies stresses the need for a strong company policy effectively backed at the top. Moreover, they emphasize that, while they make unusual efforts to obtain minority group applicants, once the man is on the job, he receives no special treatment. The need to establish policies and adhere to them — not vary from them — would seem to be the most important lesson from these outstanding case experiences.

In Part IV, union policies are discussed. Professor Marshall provides insight into union racial practices using data collected over a long period of time and covering union activity in many parts of the country. Mr. James H. Jones, chairman of the Human Rights Committee of the Philadelphia AFL-CIO and International Representative of the United Steelworkers of America, tells of the very interesting work of the Human Rights Committee. Special problems in the printing and electrical trades and in the construction industry are analyzed by Messrs. Theodore W. Kheel and Joseph B. Meranze. These are industries, of course, in which union hiring policies are the dominant factor.

In Part V, community approaches to equal employment opportunity are highlighted. Professor Richard L. Rowan of the Wharton School presents an analysis of chamber of commerce and employer association activities. The tremendous range of these policies is shown by his survey, and a comparison is made between the activities of employer associations in the East, South, and Mid-West. Mr. Frank H. Cassell of Inland Steel Company summarizes the very fascinating Illinois study and its implications. Here was an unusual undertaking by a tri-partite committee appointed by the Governor of Illinois. Its results indicate the problems that big cities face in this regard. Such problems are discussed further in Part VI.

The remainder of Part V is composed of two articles dealing with a study made in Lancaster, Pennsylvania, by Dr. Walter Gershenfeld of Temple University and Dr. Rowan. The Lancaster study was sponsored by the Chamber of Commerce there. It has led to an action program designed to improve Negro employment opportunities, but it also raised some very interesting implications that Dr. Gershenfeld discusses. In particular, the Lancaster study demonstrates that high employment is not by itself the solution to Negro job opportunities, although certainly it is essential if such problems are to be mitigated. This case study confirms the general analysis of Professor Marshall that appears in Part I.

The vexing problems of our major cities insofar as race relations and Negro and minority group employment are concerned were touched upon in previous sections, particularly Part V. But so important is this problem to the future of equal opportunity in employment that a special section, Part VI, is devoted to it. The general problem of employing Negroes in a typical urban labor market — Philadelphia — is realistically analyzed by Mr. Walter H. Powell, Vice-President of International Resistance Company. Mr. Powell's company has been a leader in equal employment in practice, and yet the discouraging problems that the equal opportunity employer must overcome are revealed in his analysis. Dr. Arthur B. Shostak of the Wharton School further traces out some of the significant issues pertinent to the Negroes' advancement in the large urban areas.

On the bright side is the dropout program that has been developed by Carson, Pirie Scott and analyzed by its president, Mr. C. V. Martin. That dropouts with low I. Q.'s can be developed into useful citizens is proved by his experience and the additional work in Newark, New Jersey, that Bamberger's, a division of R. H. Macy, has pioneered so well. Mr. Charles W. Garrison, Vice-President of Bamberger's, discusses this experience.

It is natural, of course, that an urban-based university like the University of Pennsylvania would be keenly interested in the problems of its urban area. Philadelphia is the unique laboratory to analyze and learn about the problem of minority group employees. Approximately thirty per cent of the population is Negro, and it is growing very fast in relation to the white population. Professor Leonard Rico of the Wharton School gives a profile of the Negro worker in Philadelphia. Dr. Howard E. Mitchell, head of the University's Human Resources Project, explains what is being done by

the university to rescue dropouts. It is a pleasure to add here that
the Wharton School has established a center for the study of the
economic problems of minorities and is continuing the type of work
of which Dr. Rico's article is a product.

   The final section of the book is devoted to business and professional jobs and Negro leadership. Professor William Gomberg of
the Wharton School discusses the problems of Negro entrepreneurs
and the need for a greater interest in the Negro community in
establishing business. In this section, the speeches of Mr. M. J.
Puryear, Associate Director of the National Urban League, and
Mr. Roy Wilkins, Executive Secretary of the National Association
for the Advancement of Colored People, are reproduced also. They
discuss the problems of Negro job opportunities as seen by their
organizations with particular reference on the part of Mr. Puryear
to white collar professional workers.

   The editors would like to thank all of those who contributed
essays to this volume, and a special word of praise goes to Mrs.
Margaret E. Doyle and Mrs. Helen White — excellent typists and
faithful assistants.

HERBERT R. NORTHRUP
RICHARD L. ROWAN

Philadelphia
January 26, 1965

CONTENTS

PART VI

DROPOUTS, TRAINING, AND OTHER
URBAN INDUSTRIAL PROBLEMS

PART VII

BUSINESS AND PROFESSIONAL JOBS
AND NEGRO LEADERSHIP

PART I

An Overall Look at the Job Problems of Negroes

1

THE JOB PROBLEMS OF NEGROES

Ray Marshall *

Negro job problems have assumed added significance since World War II. The problems are not new, of course, but the migration of Negroes out of the rural South and the intensity of the civil rights crisis during the 1950's and 1960's caused more attention to be given the Negro's economic as well as his political and social conditions. What was formerly mainly a problem of the South has now become a national problem of major proportions. We have learned, moreover, that the economic impact of discrimination is not restricted to Negroes. For example, the Council of Economic Advisers estimated in September 1962 that the economic loss from racial discrimination in employment might well be as much as $13 billion a year,[1] which represented about 2.5 per cent of Gross National Product. And in 1963 the National Urban League estimated the direct national income loss from discrimination to be $14.3 billion. The League put the indirect loss at an additional $13.7 billion.[2]

Although there are important noneconomic causes of racial tension, there can be little doubt that job opportunities are central concerns of Negroes and whites. The white workers' hostility toward Negroes is caused in part by a fear of job competition. But the impact of inadequate jobs is much more serious for Negroes. And the problem is not only in terms of dollars, but also in terms of poor health, broken families, high rates of crime, squalid housing, personal degradation and misery. Indeed, Negroes apparently consider their most important problems to be economic. In a July, 1964 survey of Negro districts in New York City, for example, 54 per cent of those interviewed listed economic complaints (jobs, welfare, high cost of living, low pay, etc.) as being the "biggest problems that Negroes . . . have to worry about." Only 16 per cent listed civil rights (freedom, discrimination) as the Negroes' biggest worry.[3]

---

*Professor of Economics, University of Texas.

1

This paper will discuss some of the causes of the increased militancy of Negroes, outline and discuss the reasons for Negro job patterns, and conclude with a discussion of some of the public policy measures designed to overcome the Negroes' job disadvantages.

Industrialization and Race Relations

Although we have no way of really knowing what was behind the increased militancy of the civil rights movement during the 1950's and early 1960's, technological and economic changes undoubtedly were fundamental. And although the Negroes' deteriorating economic position[4] was undoubtedly the immediate cause of some of this increased militancy, I would guess that the more fundamental factors relate to long-run changes in the economy, particularly industrialization and urbanization, which have *improved* rather than *worsened* the Negroes' economic and political welfare. There can be little question, for example, that the migration of Negroes out of the rural South has increased their political and economic power as well as their level of expectations. Nor is this surprising or unusual, because industrialization logically causes disadvantaged groups to demand full citizenship rights and equal educational and job opportunities as means of advancement in an industrial society.[5] Although most Negroes remain at the bottom of the economic ladder, the civil rights movement apparently is led by Negroes, particularly relatively well-educated young people, who have already advanced a little but who find further betterment blocked by racial discrimination. They realize, therefore, that there are problems that all Negroes must overcome if the favored few are to make additional progress. But in the United States the pattern of Negro protest also is conditioned by the constitutional guarantees of civil rights, which have been deferred in many areas since the Civil War.

Industrialization and urbanization have had other important influences on the civil rights movement. They have led to better communications, which focuses instant worldwide attention on the mistreatment of minorities, a significant factor in the cold war contest for the allegiance of the world's nonwhite majority. Since Negroes have more influence with the federal government than with many of the states, the growing power of the federal government, which is partly the product of the growing complexity of society, increases the Negroes' power to effect changes in states where they have little political power.

But industrialization also produces more direct changes in areas like the South. Economic development tends to dissolve regional differences and to make the South's political and economic leaders more vulnerable to pressures from civil rights groups. Particularly significant is the South's intense desire to industrialize as a means of overcoming the region's economic disadvantages. Negroes and whites learned from Little Rock, if they did not know it earlier, that racial unrest and violence will repel industry. Many Southerners also realize that the industrial society's emphasis on education is incompatible with an educational system weakened by the necessity of supporting a dual school system.

Moreover, the South's preoccupation with the preservation of racial segregation caused it to develop strained relations with the federal government which impeded economic development.[6] Industrialization not only has weakened this traditional position, but it also has led to growing political diversity which enhances Negroes' political power. Southern Democrats realize, for instance, that the emerging Republican Party will split the white vote and give Negroes more political power. Their dilemma is that industry tends to breed Republicans, and they cannot figure out how to get the former without the latter.

Labor Relations and Civil Rights

The Negroes' demands for equal employment opportunities and an end to discrimination by unions have important implications for labor relations. And, because of their training and experience, industrial relations specialists have a responsibility to interpret the civil rights movement to the business community. Many of the traditional tools of the behavioral sciences are applicable to racial employment problems, and there are many similarities between the civil rights and labor movements.

We should not press the analogy too far, however, because there also are important differences between the civil rights and industrial relations problems which require imaginative policies and new procedures. The race problem has many more noneconomic dimensions, and it is difficult to see how negotiations between civil rights organizations and business firms can be regularized as they were in the industrial relations field. When confronted with competing demands for union recognition, for example, it is possible to settle the conflict by holding representation elections. But in cases where civil rights groups demonstrate against business firms to get more jobs, it sometimes is difficult to determine who speaks for Negroes, making it difficult for demonstrations to lead to fruitful negotiations.

NEGRO EMPLOYMENT PATTERNS

Although an increasing proportion of Negroes are in the white collar and skilled categories, Negroes still are concentrated disproportionately in unskilled, menial occupations, are rarely promoted to supervisory positions over whites, and have occupied skilled jobs mainly in Negro communities or occupations traditionally reserved for Negroes. In 1962, for example, only 16.7 per cent of nonwhites but 47.2 per cent of whites were in white collar occupations. Other noticeable differences in the patterns are the much higher proportion of nonwhite farm and service workers and the lower proportion of nonwhite foremen and craftsmen. However, the National Planning Association's projections shown in Table 1 suggest a gradual reduction of these differences by 1972.

Significant gains were made by nonwhites in the 1955-1962 period in such professional categories as hospital, medical, and other health services, welfare and religious institutions, and business and repair services. The relative increase of nonwhites in these occupations was 70 per cent, about twice that of whites. Nonwhites also have gained relatively faster than whites in the educational services field and in government employment.[7]

Tables 3 and 4 show the relative changes in the distribution of white and nonwhite males between 1940 and 1960. The influence of the sustained period of wartime labor shortages on nonwhite males is shown in Table 4. The nonwhite proportion of total male employment increased in every category except farming during the war. Similarly, in every case except craftsmen, foremen, operatives and kindred workers, nonwhite proportions declined after the war.

Tables 5 and 6 indicate some of the changes in the skilled trades categories between 1950 and 1960 by regions. Nonwhites increased at a slightly faster rate than whites (29 per cent as compared with 28 per cent) in the South for all of these categories, but increased much faster than whites in the non-South (69 per cent as compared with 24 per cent). These overall results undoubtedly reflect the influence of migration of skilled nonwhites out of the South as well as the improvement in their positions in the non-South. These tables also suggest the importance of the supply of Negro labor as a factor in job opportunities. For example, Negro construction craftsmen in the South have been sufficiently numerous to supply the needs of contractors who are boycotted by whites and have therefore been able to protect their positions. Nonwhite construction craftsmen increased their proportion in the South from 10.19 per cent to 11.37 per cent and 65.2 per cent of nonwhite construction craftsmen resided in the South in 1950 as compared with 67.2

per cent in 1960. The proportion of all nonwhite craftsmen residing in the South declined from 55.3 per cent in 1950 to 48.6 per cent in 1960. The proportion of all nonwhites living in the South declined from 64 per cent to 57 per cent between these dates.

Expected Changes in Nonwhite Employment by 1972

Some of the main characteristics of the expected change in employment by 1972 are as follows:

	White (Millions)	Nonwhite (Millions)
Total change	12.5	1.8
Change in age 25-54	4.5	1.0
Change in Females	4.2	.8
Change in Males	8.3	1.0
Change in Blue Collar Workers	1.5	.4
Change in White Collar Workers	10.7	.9
Change in Service Workers	1.6	.5
Change in Farmers	— .7	— .1

Tables 7 and 8 contain other projections. It will be observed that significant differences are expected in the 25-54 age bracket. Over 50 per cent of the nonwhite, but only 25 per cent of the white, increase is expected to be in this age group.

Incomes and Participation Rates

Although Negroes have improved their income positions over the long run, depressed economic conditions during the 1950's and 1960's eroded the Negro's overall economic position relative to whites faster than it was improved by migration out of agriculture, falling racial barriers, and better training and education. Negroes had improved their median family incomes to 56.8 per cent of whites at the postwar relative high in 1952, as compared with 51.2 per cent in 1958 and 53 per cent in 1962. In order to maintain even these relative positions, however, nonwhites have had a larger number of wage-earners per family than whites. The civilian labor force participation rates in 1962 were 60.0 per cent for nonwhites and 56.1 per cent for whites. Significantly, the nonwhite male participation rate (76.4 per cent) was *lower* than the white male rate (78.6 per cent), but the nonwhite female rate (45.6 per cent) was much higher than the white female rate (35.6 per cent). The participation rates for both nonwhite males and females were higher in 1948 (84.8 per cent and 44.4 per cent) than the rates for whites (84.2 per cent and 30.6 per cent). These rates tend to support the argument by some observers that much of the unrest in Negro communities is attributable to the deterioration in the economic opportunities of Negro males.

The Problem of Unemployment

The deterioration in the nonwhite employment picture after 1953 is indicated by the following unemployment rates:

	Per cent White	Per cent Nonwhite
1951	2.8	4.8
1952	2.4	4.6
1953	2.3	4.1
1954	4.5	8.9
1955	3.6	7.9
1956	3.3	7.5
1957	3.9	8.0
1958	6.1	12.6
1959	4.9	10.7
1960	5.0	10.2
1961	6.0	12.5
1962	4.9	11.0
1963	5.1	10.9

Source: U. S. Dept. of Labor, Bureau of Labor Statistics.

Table 9 shows that unemployment rates for nonwhites were generally over twice those of whites but that the rates varied with occupations for both racial categories.

Is Negro Unemployment Structural or Cyclical?

Although unemployment rates of nonwhites are about twice those of whites, and have increased markedly since 1953, between 1956 and 1963 nonwhite unemployment did not increase relative to total unemployment or as a proportion of total unemployment, as indicated by the following figures:

	Ratio of unemployment in each group to national unemployment rate		Percentage of total national unemployment in each group	
	White	Nonwhite	White	Nonwhite
1956	.87	1.98	78.5	21.5
1959	.88	1.95	78.8	21.2
1962	.87	1.97	78.1	21.9
1963	.89	1.91	78.8	21.2

Source: R. A. Gordon, "Has Structural Unemployment Worsened," *Industrial Relations,* May 1964, p. 71.

Actually, these figures, which are selected for years which minimize the importance of the business cycle, show that nonwhite unemployment rates *improved* slightly relative to the totals between 1956 and 1963, suggesting that the *increases in* Negro unemployment rates are more cyclical than structural. This does not mean, of course, that the higher rates in 1956 and 1963 were not due to structural factors, or that we would get the same results if we compared 1953 with these other years. In addition, unemployment of nonwhite teenagers increased by about 60 per cent between 1955 and 1962 as compared with only 30 per cent for white teenagers.

Negro Employment and Economic Growth

In recent years, Negro unemployment rates seem to change at about twice the rate of total unemployment, whether the latter is rising or falling. With respect to longer trends, a recent study of Negro and white employment patterns during economic development found no relationship between changes in Negro female and total employment but concluded: [8]

> In expanding fields Negro male employment has tended to grow at a faster rate than white male or total employment. . . . Even in slowly growing fields the employment of Negro men has nevertheless tended to increase at a faster rate than total employment or that of white men. . . . In rapidly declining fields, however, employment of Negro men has tended to decline more rapidly than that of white men both nationally and in the South.

This suggests that Negroes would gain relatively from sustained growth as well as full employment. If the general unemployment rate could be reduced to 4 per cent, the nonwhite rate might be cut to less than 8 per cent. And if this rate could be sustained while the rate of economic growth increased and measures were taken to upgrade nonwhites, the income and employment gap between whites and nonwhites could be narrowed still further.

Factors Responsible for Racial Employment Patterns

Although the patterns of racial employment are relatively clear, it is not as easy to determine the factors responsible for these patterns. This is because the patterns are due to a complex of interrelated causes, in addition to racial discrimination, making it very difficult to determine the contribution to the total pattern made by each factor. However, although it is not possible to assign precise weights to each of these causes, the main factors responsible for the total pattern are discernible.

An important impediment to the Negro's ability to improve his occupational position is undoubtedly his easy identification and the image of inferiority stamped upon him by slavery. Not having worked in a variety of skilled, technical operations, Negroes have become stereotyped for certain jobs by employers, white workers, and even themselves. Since the Negro has been regarded as inferior by many whites, those who would perpetuate a feeling of superiority for their crafts or occupations often seek to exclude Negroes.

Negroes also are restricted in their employment opportunities by a host of cultural and social factors. Since Negroes usually live in segregated neighborhoods, they rarely learn about jobs with few or no Negroes in them, and they apply for the kinds of jobs they know they can get. Since aspirations are conditioned by one's associates, few Negroes are motivated to apply for jobs from which they have been excluded.

Negroes also are prepared inadequately through education and training to compete on an equal basis with whites. While the educational level of nonwhites is improving, the median is still 2.6 years below that of whites. Since education is related to income, the Negro's position is in some sense self-perpetuating. The median incomes of heads of families and their educational attainments in 1961 were as follows:

Education	White	Nonwhite	Ratio of Nonwhite to White (Percentages)
Elementary	$4,378	$2,539	58.0
Less than 8 years	3,656	2,294	62.7
8 years	4,911	3,338	68.0
High school	6,186	3,863	64.2
1 to 3 years	5,882	3,449	58.6
4 years	6,390	4,559	71.3
College	8,288	6,444	77.8
1 to 3 years	7,344	5,525	74.2
4 years or more	9,315	7,875	84.5

Source: U. S. Bureau of the Census.

These figures indicate that, as a general rule, the ratio of nonwhite to white income increases with the level of education.

The percentage educational distributions of whites and non-whites for various years were as follows:

Education	White				Nonwhite			
	1952	1957	1959	1962	1952	1957	1959	1962
Elementary:								
Less than 5 years	5.2	4.3	3.7	3.3	26.7	21.2	17.9	15.5
5 to 8 years	29.3	25.8	23.6	21.4	38.7	34.9	34.3	29.8
High School:								
1 to 3 years	18.7	19.0	19.4	18.8	15.9	19.3	20.6	23.2
4 years	28.3	30.8	32.0	33.5	10.8	14.8	15.8	21.0
College:								
1 to 3 years	8.8	9.0	9.7	11.3	3.7	3.9	4.5	5.7
4 years or more	8.5	9.7	10.2	11.8	2.6	3.4	3.9	4.8
Median years completed	11.4	12.1	12.1	12.2	7.6	8.4	8.7	9.6

Source: U. S. Bureau of the Census and Bureau of Labor Statistics.

These figures reveal a great decline in the proportion of nonwhites who had less than five years of education and a significant increase in the proportion of nonwhites attending high school.

While there are some examples of improved job opportunities for Negroes, for some reason nonwhite high school graduates do not fair as well as white dropouts. For example, 15 per cent of white male dropouts, but only 10 per cent of Negro boys *who graduated* from high school in October 1962 found employment as craftsmen or kindred workers.[9] Moreover, nonwhites have much more difficulty being absorbed into the labor force. Of the white high-school graduates who last attended school in 1959, for instance, only 5.3 per cent remained out of work 2.5 years after graduation as compared with 14.5 per cent of nonwhite high school graduates. Of the 1959 dropouts, 10.2 per cent of the whites and 18 per cent of the nonwhites were unemployed two years later.[10]

The Negroes' inadequate vocational and apprenticeship training also tend to perpetuate their employment in traditional jobs. In the South it has been customary to have segregated vocational schools where Negroes were trained only for traditional occupations. While there are some excellent Negro vocational training schools associated with Negro colleges, many Negroes are barred from these as well as apprenticeship programs because they are not high school graduates. Moreover, even the graduates of these schools have not been able to acquire additional apprenticeship training to become journeymen because of discrimination in apprenticeship training programs.

The National Institute of Labor Education has launched a Youth Employment Program in cooperation with the Department of Labor and various union-management apprenticeship programs to prepare dropouts for apprenticeships. Such programs are underway in Newark, the District of Columbia, Baltimore, and Norfolk. Although it is too early to evaluate these programs, they have to date produced many problems but some hopeful results. It would be a mistake, however, to expect apprenticeship training to do very much to overcome the occupational disadvantages of Negroes. There has probably been a tendency for civil rights groups to exaggerate the importance of this type of training because of the virtual absence of Negroes from many apprenticeship programs and the fact that apprenticeship, while not too significant in the overall manpower picture, is the gateway to employment in many of the skilled trades, particularly in the construction industry.

It could be argued, however, that the present level of apprenticeship training is inadequate for the manpower needs of the future. Apprenticeship training is important for the expanding skilled trades because vocational training alone has rarely given students sufficient practical and theoretical training to equip them to become well-rounded craftsmen. Apprenticeship also has important advantages over other means of acquiring skilled trades (armed forces, "picking-it-up," and upgrading within plants) and assumes greater importance as technological innovations increase the need for well-trained craftsmen. In the past, the United States has relied heavily on immigrants as a source of skilled manpower. But, with the relatively high levels of prosperity in many European countries, this flow of skilled workers has virtually dried up.

Although it is estimated that apprenticeship training will furnish a relatively small proportion of the projected needs of skilled building tradesmen by 1970 unless something is done to increase the number of apprentices, perhaps as many as 7,000-8,000 Negroes a year could complete apprenticeship training programs if they attained the same relative proportion as whites. Apprenticeship training furnished only 70,000-80,000 of the 500,000 skilled craftsmen needed each year during the 1950's and 1960's.[11]

Management Attitudes

Although unions have important influences in employment patterns in some of the building trades and other casual occupations, management usually makes the basic employment decisions. Management prejudices and stereotypes will therefore influence the extent to which Negroes can be upgraded within plants and are hired in traditional or nontraditional categories. There is ample evidence that management has usually considered Negroes to be suitable only for certain low-status jobs. For example, one management official, sympathetic to the upgrading of Negroes, described a common employer view as follows:

> Negroes, basically and as a group, with only rare exceptions, are not as well trained for higher skills and jobs as whites. They appear to be excellent for work, usually unskilled, that requires stamina and brawn — and little else. They are unreliable and cannot adjust to the demands of the factory.[12]

Other observers have confirmed the prevalence of this attitude.[13]

In addition to its prejudices, however, management has practiced racial discrimination because of fears of reaction from white workers and the white community.

The Negro and Organized Labor

In discussing the effects of unions on Negro employment opportunities, it is necessary to distinguish the various kinds of unions and the forms of racial policies adopted by each.[14] Since they control the supply of labor in their trades, for example, craft unions can influence Negro employment opportunities by barring them from their unions and imposing closed shop conditions which require the employer to get his labor from the union, so if the union bars Negroes from membership they are effectively barred from the unionized sector of the trade. In some cases, there have been "gentlemen's agreements" that Negroes would be permitted to work only in certain areas of a trade, such as in Negro neighborhoods or on lower-paying jobs, while unionized whites retained the more desirable jobs. This has been the pattern among many building trades unions, for example, where craft unions like the Plumbers, Electricians, and Sheet Metal Workers have either barred Negroes from membership or restricted them to certain kinds of work. Railroad brotherhoods have had the most rigid forms of discrimination. The historical pattern has been for these unions to bar Negroes from membership and from the jobs.

Although no precise statistics are available, there have been some significant changes in union racial practices since the 1930's. Formal racial restrictions in constitutions or rituals have declined from at least twenty-two in 1930 to only two in 1964. In addition, in most of the major cities outside the South and in a few cases in the South some Negroes have gained entry to unions from which they were excluded by informal means. Of course, in most of these cases union and civil rights leaders are likely to disagree over the significance of the changes that have taken place.

There has also been a great decline in the number of segregated local unions. A number of unions have moved to merge segregated locals in the South under pressure from the President's Committee on Equal Employment Opportunity and in the North because segregation violated the state FEP laws. The National Labor Relations Board has also taken measures to discourage segregated locals by holding segregated job quotas to be unfair labor practices and by holding that where segregation exists an existing contract would not bar a new representation election. In general, therefore, in the last ten years segregated local unions have become relatively unimportant.

Job Segregation

Industrial unions were more concerned with the exclusion of Negroes from employment in manufacturing industries and with job segregation within those industries than with exclusion or segregated locals. Although unions were not responsible for these employment patterns, because they existed before industrial unions were significant, white workers have used the strike threat to perpetuate job discrimination.

Union Efforts to Abolish Discrimination

It would be a mistake to conclude that the impact of unions on Negro job opportunities has been mainly negative, because on balance the union movement probably has done much more to promote than to retard Negro job opportunities. At the national level, the labor movement has contributed substantially to the fight for more equal opportunities for Negroes and has been indispensable in the movement for civil rights, improved education, and other social legislation. Moreover, the AFL-CIO, and its predecessors, the AFL and the CIO, adopted equalitarian racial policies. In addition, most of the CIO unions protected the Negro's employment rights after he was hired and on some occasions even sought to force employers to sign nondiscrimination agreements covering the *hiring* of workers. Nondiscrimination agreements, which existed in about one-fifth of all major collective bargaining contracts in 1961, became especially significant during the racial ferment of the 1950's and 1960's.[15] Vigorous antidiscrimination drives have been undertaken by the United Packinghouse Workers and the Retail, Wholesale and Department Store Union in the South, and nondiscrimination agreements were reached between the United Auto Workers and the Ford, General Motors, Chrysler, and American Motors companies in 1961 and between the Steelworkers and eleven major steel companies in 1964, including Armco, Bethlehem, Colorado Fuel &

Iron, Great Lakes Steel, Inland, Jones & Laughlin, Pittsburgh Steel, Republic, United States Steel, Wheeling, and Youngstown Sheet & Tube.

In addition, the mere presence of a certified union has given Negro workers rights they would not otherwise have had. Not only can Negroes sue for violation of specific contract rights, but, as will be shown later, the union is required by the courts, and more recently by the National Labor Relations Board, to follow non-discrimination policies with respect to all workers in the bargaining unit.

Finally, unions have promoted Negro interests as a part of the very equalitarian policies upon which American unions are founded. Unions are weakened if they fail to promote equal seniority, wage and other benefits for all workers, regardless of race. Moreover, fringe benefits and the elimination of occupational wage differentials help Negroes — who are concentrated in lower job categories.

This does not mean, of course, that all labor organizations have protected the Negro's seniority rights because they realized that to do otherwise would weaken the unions. Some unions have violated the Negro's seniority rights in spite of the knowledge that this not only weakened seniority, but also gravely damaged the reputation of the whole labor movement and jeopardized the informal Negro-labor political coalitions built up since the 1930's. But the fact that discrimination *tends* to weaken seniority is a factor *undermining* discrimination by unions. Moreover, if the Negro workers' seniority rights are violated, they have a legal cause of action against the union and the employer for violating the contract.

But just as employers do not always follow merit employment practices, even though to do so might be more rational, many international unions and the federations have permitted discrimination to continue at the local level even though they were opposed to it. Since the AFL, the CIO, and the AFL-CIO were voluntary associations, they sometimes had inadequate power to compel their affiliates to comply with their equalitarian racial policies. Since much racial discrimination is at the local level, local union leaders, who are elected to their positions, have been reluctant to vigorously oppose discrimination where this might cost them their jobs. Moreover, unions, like employers, have feared that equalitarian policies would jeopardize their positions in the South.

NEGRO EMPLOYMENT AND PUBLIC POLICY

There has been a noticeable increase in public policy measures against racial discrimination in employment since the 1930's. Especially important are the Committee on Fair Employment Practices (FEPC) created by President Roosevelt in 1941, the various government contract committees created by every president since the New Deal, the FEP laws passed in twenty-five states and a number of municipalities, court rulings and NLRB decisions which require unions to represent Negroes fairly, and the Civil Rights Act of 1964. Since these measures have been discussed a great deal and their uses and limitations are relatively well known, we can limit our observations to some of their more controversial aspects.[16]

The President's Committee on Government Contracts established by President Eisenhower was used by civil rights groups to get jobs for Negroes in many cases where they had not previously been employed. But the PCGC was limited by its indirect approach through the contracting agencies and the fact that its power was restricted to recommending the revocation of contracts. There seems to have been a prevailing conviction, which proved accurate, moreover, that the PCGC really would not cause contracts to be revoked. The influence of the PCGC also was limited by the committee's lack of power over unions, because labor organizations were not parties to government contracts. Contract revocation is not an effective device in many cases because the contract frequently is as important to the contracting agency as it is to the company.

Many of these limitations also applied to the President's Committee on Equal Employment Opportunity created by President Kennedy and continued under President Johnson. However, the PCEEO took a more aggressive approach and was extended to include federally-assisted construction projects and all of a firm's activities, not just those plants with government contracts. By threatening to cancel or deny contracts to four relatively small contractors, the PCEEO created the impression that it would in fact revoke contracts. The PCEEO also was partly responsible for the adoption of nondiscrimination provisions in federal apprenticeship standards, which were put into effect in January, 1964 over the heated objections of some building trades union leaders. Finally, the so-called "Plans for Progress" (PFP) to get companies and unions voluntarily to comply with nondiscrimination programs reached areas (like unions) that were beyond the jurisdiction of the government contract provisions. As a result of these plans and the increasing militancy of the civil rights movement, many unions and employers intensified their antidiscrimination programs.

Compulsory vs. Voluntary Nondiscrimination Plans

Although they are sometimes viewed as competitive, compulsory nondiscrimination measures tend to induce and strengthen voluntary programs. There is something about the threat of prosecution that seems to make the voluntary programs work much better. There is no denying, for example, that the PFP program has produced results. There is no denying that this program has been adopted. This program originated in May, 1961, and of 91 companies reported on as of July, 1963, total employment had increased by 12.4 per cent and nonwhite employment 14.7 per cent, or by 27,180 employees.[17] In addition, PFP companies increased their employment by 60,000 between September and November, 1963, and 25 per cent of these were nonwhite. In comparable periods before the PFP program, nonwhite employment would have increased by about 3 per cent.[18] These job increases are important when it is considered that much effort is required to produce additional jobs for nonwhites.[19]

We should not conclude, however, that the voluntary programs by themselves would have produced these results. It is significant that the "voluntary" plans came at a time of increasing militancy by civil rights groups. Equally significant, all but one of the 35 largest government defense contractors in 1962 were among the first 91 companies to sign plans for progress. Indeed, defense contracts accounted for over half of the total sales for 17 of these 35 largest companies in 1962.[20] The Lockheed Aircraft Corporation, for example, had the largest volume of prime military contracts in 1962 of any U.S. company. Indeed, its award of approximately $1.42 billion dollars was 81.27 per cent of its total sales and was greater than the value of military contracts awarded in 22 states. This undoubtedly helps explain why Lockheed was willing to pioneer in the PFP program. The only one of the largest 35 defense contractors not among the first 91 companies in the Plans for Progress was Standard Oil of New Jersey, which was the 28th largest recipient of defense contracts. Standard of New Jersey's defense contracts in 1962 amounted to only $180,000, however, and accounted for only 1.89 per cent of its sales — the lowest proportion of sales of any of the largest 35 contractors.

Conclusions on State FEP Laws

Since so many other factors were at work influencing racial employment patterns besides the state FEP laws, it is difficult to determine their impact. A careful study of these laws concludes, however, that they have definitely improved the employment opportunities of minorities, particularly in places like New York, New Jersey, and Philadelphia, which have relatively well-financed and well-staffed enforcement agencies.[21] An examination of the records of these commissions reveals that they have caused many companies, unions, and employment agencies to alter their discriminatory practices and opened the door to employment in thousands of cases. Union referral systems have been regularized and a number of the most recalcitrant craft unions in the building and railroad trades have been forced to admit Negroes or abolish discriminatory provisions in their constitutions. Indeed, one of the main factors causing unions to remove the formal restrictions in their constitutions was the passage of the New York, New Jersey, and Connecticut FEP laws.

In spite of these accomplishments, however, civil rights groups have become very critical of the effects of these laws. It is significant that the racial demonstrations in Northern cities during 1963 and 1964 were in states and municipalities with the most active FEP commissions. Negroes are dissatisfied with the rate of change in racial employment patterns, partly because they probably expected too much from the commissions where the case-by-case approach is bound to produce results only slowly. Moreover, it is not always easy to prove discrimination where Negroes think it exists. Large percentages of the cases are found to be without merit. Sometimes the practices complained of were very complicated and operated to restrict employment to a particular group. Moreover, during times of growing unemployment, racial employment patterns will change very slowly because of limited changes in total employment.

The Courts

Negroes have also used the courts to overcome discrimination by unions and employers. However, most court cases have dealt with unions because, in the absence of legislation or contract provisions to the contrary, employers have had no legal obligation to follow nondiscrimination policies. The same is not true of unions, however, because they acquire legal rights and duties as a result of the National Labor Relations and Railway Labor Acts. The U. S. Supreme Court has ruled, therefore, that the Constitution imposes upon the unions which acquire the privilege of exclusive bargaining rights under these acts the duty to represent all members of the bargaining unit fairly.[22] Some federal courts also have held that employers are jointly liable with unions for the duty of fair representation,[23] and aggrieved minorities have brought suit against unions for damages resulting from violation of their legal rights. Although court action requires a great deal of time, is uncertain as to its outcome, and has rarely resulted in damages to the plaintiffs, lawsuits are valuable to aggrieved minorities as a threat to discriminating employers and unions, and injunctions have been used to make it possible for Negroes to retain their jobs.[24]

The NLRB

The disadvantage of court cases could be avoided if there were effective administrative remedies, but the National Labor Relations Board traditionally has been much more cautious than the courts in interpreting and applying its power to prevent discrimination by unions. Though the Board has entertained ". . . grave doubt whether a union which discriminatorily denies membership to employees on the basis of race, may nevertheless bargain as the exclusive representative in an appropriate unit composed of members of the excluded race,"[25] the Board has repeatedly permitted unions which excluded Negroes to participate in elections covering bargaining units containing Negroes.[26] Indeed, the Board ruled that

> Neither exclusion from membership nor segregated membership per se represents evasion on the part of a labor organization of its statutory duty of "equal representation." But in each case where the issue is presented the Board will scrutinize the contract and conduct of a representative organization and withdraw certification if it finds the organization has discriminated against employees in the bargaining units through its membership restrictions or otherwise.[27]

The Hughes Tool decision,[28] handed down by the NLRB the same day President Johnson signed the Civil Rights Act of 1964, raises some important questions and, if sustained in the federal courts, could have important consequences for union racial practices. Specifically reversing the NLRB's previous position, the Board ruled for the first time that a violation of the duty of fair representation is also an unfair labor practice. Previously, the NLRB had interpreted its authority in such cases as limited to the relatively weak penalty of revoking a union's certification. But if the union's violation of the duty of fair representation is also an unfair labor practice, the Board can issue cease and desist orders enforceable in the federal courts. The Hughes Tool theory would in effect give the aggrieved person an administrative remedy for the duty of fair representation, making it no longer necessary for him to seek relief in the courts.

The Civil Rights Act of 1964

If it is sustained by the U. S. Supreme Court, the Civil Rights Act of 1964 will undoubtedly prove to be the most important anti-discrimination act yet passed. Title VII of the act bans discrimination in employment because of race, color, religion, national origin, or sex. Title VII will become effective one year after July 2, 1964, and covers unions and enterprises in industries affecting commerce, including employment agencies, union hiring halls, employers with 100 or more employees, and unions with 100 or more members. By 1968, minimum coverage will be reduced to 25 employees or members. The act is administered by a bipartisan Equal Employment Opportunities Commission (EEOC), established to investigate and adjudicate complaints.

Evaluation

Although the Civil Rights Act could have important effects in the South, it is likely to have limited effect elsewhere. In the first place, the Hughes Tool doctrine, if sustained by the Supreme Court, in many ways gives more effective relief for unionized employees than the Civil Rights Act. With all of the uncertainties of the EEOC procedures, an aggrieved individual would probably get faster relief through the NLRB, which does not have to wait for one to three years to take action. If the Hughes Tool doctrine is not sustained, however, the Board's power would be limited to the revocation of certification, which is not a very potent remedy. The law also will have apparently little influence in those states and municipalities which have antidiscrimination laws.

SOME PUBLIC POLICY CONTROVERSIES

Are antidiscrimination laws necessary?

Some observers who claim to favor merit employment nevertheless feel that legislation is unnecessary because the market tends to eliminate discrimination and because laws interfere with the employer's ability to make rational choices. For instance, Milton Friedman argues that "it is a striking historical fact that the development of capitalism has been accompanied by a major reduction in the extent to which particular religious, racial, or social groups have operated under special handicaps in respect of their economic activities; have, as the saying goes, been discriminated against."[29] This is true, according to Friedman, because ". . . there is an economic incentive in a free market to separate economic efficiency from other characteristics of the individual."[30] Professor Friedman therefore believes that FEP legislation "clearly involves interference with the freedom of individuals to enter into voluntary contracts with one another."

If Professor Friedman is talking about an idealized world which does not exist, we may grant his conclusions. But if he means by "historical fact" that such an idealized world exists, it is difficult to agree with him. Indeed, he recognizes that capitalists might discriminate against Negroes not because of prejudice, but because they "may simply be transmitting the tastes of the community." Thus, in a perfectly rational economic world, it is possible that noneconomic considerations, like social pressures, might counteract economic tendencies. We might grant, for example, that there is a long-run tendency for industrialism or a market economy to eliminate racial discrimination. But on grounds for legislation one might still be dissatisfied with the *rate* at which these market forces produce equality. Even assuming that employers have no prejudices and are motivated entirely by *pecunious rex,* it might be that employers are blocked from making more rational economic decisions because they fear community reaction or because they see no compelling reason to take a chance when there are plenty of white workers available. In this case, obviously, an individual employer would be unwilling to adopt equalitarian practices for fear of being boycotted by the community. But if the law forced all employers to take this action, there would be no possibility of boycott. In this case, far from being a force for "irrationality," the law would free the employer from irrational community reactions by permitting him to neutralize community pressure effectively. Of course, if we lived in a perfect world where ". . . the appropriate recourse of those of us who believe that a particular criterion such as color is irrelevant [was] to persuade our fellows to be of like mind, not to use the coercive power of the state to force them to act in accordance with our principles," then laws would indeed be unnecessary. But those of us who believe that there are many decisions that the market is not likely to make with sufficient rapidity or precision, and that rational discourse is not likely to persuade many bigots to change their ways, will favor legislation to achieve this end. Indeed, many of us are convinced that attitudes are more likely to be molded by actions than vice versa.

This is not to argue, however, either that legislation will do much by itself to change racial employment patterns or that the implementation of laws cannot produce more harm than good. Unless proper safeguards are imposed, for example, it might be possible for innocent employers to be forced by civil rights agencies to hire unqualified Negroes. There are some employers who would conclude that it would be better to hire an unqualified worker than to suffer the embarrassment of public hearing. If we can judge by the state FEP commission, however, there is little reason to believe that this will be an important problem.

With respect to the Civil Rights Act of 1964, a number of safeguards have been included to protect the interests of those charged with discrimination. Sec. 706 (g) provides that a federal district court can enjoin respondents only if it finds that they have "intentionally engaged . . . in an unlawful employment practice charged in the complaint." The same section also provides that the court cannot require the reinstatement of any individual, or award back pay to him, if he is discharged for some reason other than discrimination because of race, color, religion, sex, or national origin. The act also makes exceptions where employment because of religion or national origin is a bona fide business necessity. Section 703 (h) provides that it shall not be unlawful for an employer to use seniority, merit, or testing systems in order "to apply different standards of compensation, or different terms, conditions or privileges of employment" where these are not intended or designed to be used for discriminatory practices forbidden by the act.

The Civil Rights Act also protects the employer by making it clear that "nothing in this title shall be interpreted to require any employer, employment agency, labor organization, or joint labor-management committee . . . to grant preferential treatment to any individual or to any group because of race . . . on account of an imbalance which may exist with respect to the total number or percentage of" such persons hired, referred, or accepted into membership. Clearly, however, the act does not *prohibit* preferential treatment, and therefore any protection given to employers by the act might not prohibit coercive tactics to require racial quotas.

Section 705 (g) (4) gives the Equal Employment Opportunity Commission power "upon the request of any employer, whose employees or some of them, or any labor organization, whose members or some of them, refuse or threaten to refuse to cooperate in effectuating the provisions of this title, to assist in such effectuation by conciliation or such other remedial action as is provided by this title." This "other remedial action" presumably includes court orders against the offending individuals.

Although it remains to be seen how these provisions are interpreted, our tentative conclusion is that the Civil Rights Act probably contains adequate safeguards for respondents. Indeed, respondents are much more carefully protected by the act than by many of the state laws — and there apparently have been few complaints concerning the latter. We noted that an unprotected area for employers is the threat of coercive activities by civil rights groups even though the employer is in complete compliance with the law. And there is a possibility that even this activity would fall within the scope of the act. It might be argued, for example, that civil rights groups are labor organizations within the act's definition: ". . . any organization of any kind, any agency, or employee representation committee group, association, or plan so engaged . . . which exists for the purpose, in whole or in part, of dealing with employers concerning grievances, labor disputes, wages, rates of pay, hours, or other terms or conditions of employment . . ." Certainly some civil rights groups undertake to accomplish these things for minorities and would therefore fall within the scope of the act. Section 703 (c) (3) makes it an "unlawful employment practice" for a labor organization "to cause or attempt to cause an employer to discriminate against an individual in violation of this section," and Section 703 (c) (2) makes it an unlawful employment practice for a labor organization to limit the employment opportunities of any individual "or otherwise adversely affect his status as an employee or as an applicant for employment" because of his race, etc. Thus, if civil rights organizations insisted on activities that would cause employers to discriminate against whites, they might violate these provisions of the law, though we might here be encroaching on that prerogative of judges to stretch the law to make it say what we would like for it to say.

Relative Importance of Nondiscrimination Policies

Although major attention has been given to antidiscrimination legislation, it would seem that measures to improve the operation of the labor market and promote more rational manpower policies would, at this juncture, do more to improve Negro job conditions. This is not to infer, of course, that no attention should be paid to antidiscrimination laws and policies. Nor do we mean to infer that discrimination is no longer a problem. Our concentration on "success stories" among the larger and more conspicuous unions and employers — who are also likely to depend heavily on defense contracts — should not blind us to the prevalence of discrimination in every section of the country as evidenced by the slowness with which the labor market absorbs even educated Negroes. At the same time, however, at the national level the policy of no discrimination in employment has been established, and there are many complaints from unions and employers concerning the shortage of qualified Negro applicants. If we are to prevent token breakthroughs in employment from remaining just that, it will be necessary to improve the operation of the labor market through better job information and projections, improved public education, better job counseling, and measures to overcome unemployment and promote economic growth.

Retraining Programs

Since they are designed to aid workers who are unemployed because of technological and long-term economic changes, the Manpower Development and Training Act (MDTA) and Area Development Act (ARA) programs offer some hope for improving the lot of
minority groups. Although not as many nonwhites as whites were
being trained for the higher-paying jobs in 1963, Table 11 reveals
that nonwhite representation was higher in the MDTA clerical,
sales, skilled, and semiskilled categories than nonwhite employment
distribution. The proportion of nonwhites in training under the
MDTA program in June 1963 was 20.3 per cent, which was about
twice their representation in the work force and about equal their
proportion of the unemployed.

Nevertheless, the MDTA and ARA programs have certain limitations from the standpoint of improving Negro employment opportunities. The programs are administered in cooperation with
the states, and the requirement that programs be integrated apparently has restricted the participation of several Southern states
with large Negro concentrations. In 1961, for instance, the most
ambitious single ARA plan undertaken in its first two years — a
program to train some 1200 equipment operators in the Yazoo Delta
of Mississippi, where over 50 per cent of the males were unemployed
— had to be canceled for this reason. Louisiana refused to cooperate for the first two years of the program.[31]

In addition, very few Negroes actually have been trained under
these programs. By June, 1963, for example, after about a year,
only 43,491 trainees had enrolled in MDTA programs, 8,700 of
whom were nonwhites. Of course, it could be that more trainees
will be enrolled as the program matures, but this will not make
much of an impact on the 750,000 nonwhites who are unemployed.
Indeed, since nonwhites have had more difficulty getting placed
than whites when they complete retraining, not all of these 8,700
trainees will get jobs. In a hospital training program in San Francisco, for instance, 89 per cent of whites but only 63 per cent of
nonwhites who completed the course were able to find jobs. Similar
results were found in a study of the retraining program launched by
Armour and Company, the Packinghouse Workers, and the Amalgamated Meat Cutters in connection with the closing of the company's Fort Worth, Texas plant in 1962. Although placement
from the program was aided by an unemployment rate of less than
5 per cent, and although retrainees had many fewer unemployment experiences than nonretrainees, of the Negro men who finished
training by November, 1963, 60 per cent were in jobs unrelated to
their training, as compared with only 20 per cent for white male

retrainees.[32] On the average, however, Negroes and Latins fared better than whites in acquiring jobs after they were retrained, although the wages of Negroes were significantly below those of whites. This suggests that, although Negroes will have more difficulty getting jobs than whites after they are trained, retraining helps them get some kinds of jobs even though their wages will be less than those of white retrainees.

Programs which do not bar participation of workers because of education or aptitude will obviously do more to reduce nonwhite unemployment. The impact of the MDTA program on unemployment is therefore limited because budget restrictions have caused it to concentrate on training younger, better-educated workers.[33]

Public vs. Private Job Training

Although public *education* programs are very important, public *job training* is likely to be less significant than private programs. The President's 1963 Manpower Report to the Congress suggests, for example, that well over three million workers were in private training programs in the spring of 1962. These programs naturally place heavy emphasis on training for specific jobs and are designed for the most capable and trainable workers. Nonwhites will therefore do much more to improve their job chances if they seek to gain greater participation in these private training programs than by concentrating on public programs. Since private training is likely to be much more important than public programs, public policy measures might be designed to encourage the growth of, and nonwhite participation in, these private programs, perhaps through tax relief or outright subsidies. Public programs also might be designed to supplement private programs by training older, less well-educated workers and by encouraging the extension of general education.

Wage Policy

Another problem which should be studied very carefully by civil rights groups is the effect of wage policy on minority employment opportunities. Although the evidence is incomplete, it suggests that as long as employers are prejudiced against Negro workers, equalization of wages will tend to cause unemployment among Negroes. It is possible, however, that protection through nondiscrimination programs or collective bargaining can prevent unemployment which results from wage equalization.

The effect of uniform minimum wages on minority employment opportunities also deserves careful study. Because they are concen trated in low-wage industries, Negroes probably have experienced more unemployment than whites because of legal minimum wages. Although the evidence suggests that federal minimum wage laws have caused unemployment, the problem has not been too great because the minimum rates have been relatively low and have gone into effect when employment was rising. Now, however, when the rates are relatively high and unemployment is a problem, further extension of minimum wages might lead to more unemployment among low-wage workers. More flexible, rather than uniform, minimum wages would probably help the unemployment problems of older, less-educated workers. Higher minimum wages, at this juncture, probably would worsen rather than help the economic conditions of nonwhite workers.

Preferential Treatment for Disadvantaged Minorities

Some civil rights groups advocate that minorities be given preferential treatment to compensate for the cumulative influences of discrimination. These demands are based upon the realization that, even with nondiscriminatory employment policies, Negroes would not be able to change their employment patterns very rapidly.

Although preferential treatment is usually condemned by employers, union leaders, and most government agencies, it has been surprisingly common. Indeed, when Negroes have brought pressures for more jobs or official positions in unions, formal or informal racial quota arrangements have seemed the logical compromises to settle these disputes. The federal government also has sanctioned quota systems in the past and has at least left the impression that it expects government contractors to give preferential treatment to minorities. For example, in the Labor Department's apprenticeship training standards, it is specified that one of the nondiscriminatory policies that could be adopted is "the taking of whatever steps are necessary, in acting upon application lists developed prior to this time, to remove the effects of previous practices under which discriminatory patterns of employment may have resulted." Although the standards specifically bar quota systems, construction union critics of these standards insist that they contemplate preferential treatment in the selection of nonwhites. Some employers also argue that the PCEEO'S standards for compliance strongly imply that preferential treatment should be given nonwhites in order to improve the manpower profiles which they are required to submit annually as "proof of affirmative action." It would also be very unlikely that, in the absence of preferential treatment, nonwhite blue collar employment by government contractors would have increased, while total blue collar employment was declining, as it did between 1961 and 1962. In addition, companies signing Plans for Progress with the PCEEO agree to "vigorously seek qualified minority group applicants for all job categories, and . . . make particular efforts to increase minority group representation in occupations at the higher levels of skill and responsibility." During the construction of the National Aeronautics and Space Administration's Michaud plant in New Orleans, one of the prime contractors, the Boeing Company, announced in 1963 that it was importing Negro craftsmen from the North because it was bound by its government contract to "maintain balance between the races."[34] The PCGC also checked on quota systems to determine whether discrimination existed in Atomic Energy Commission construction work in Tennessee.

The Legality of Preferential Treatment of Minorities

Although quota systems seem to have been specifically banned by most state antidiscrimination commissions and by the NLRB, the Civil Rights Act of 1964 is not clear with respect to the legality of these practices. As noted earlier, the act simply declares that preferential treatment and quota systems are not required by Title VII. Presumably preferential treatment would be legal, though not required. However, in order to be consistent with other provisions of the act, preferential treatment which discriminates against whites presumably would be unlawful, but preferential treatment which does not deprive whites of established rights would probably be lawful.

The NLRB's recent decision in the Brownsville ILA case dealt with the legality of a racial quota system. In this case, which involved Locals 1367 (white) and 1368 (Negro) of the International Longshoremen's Association in Brownsville, Texas, the NLRB ruled that by maintaining a quota system which distributed work 75-25 among Locals 1367 and 1368 "based on race and union membership" and by prohibiting Negro and white gangs from working together, the South Atlantic and Gulf Coast District of ILA and Local 1367 "failed to comply with their duty as exclusive bargaining representative to represent all employees in the bargaining unit fairly and impartially and thereby violated Section 8 (b) (1) (A) of the Act."[35] The Board's majority relied upon their reasoning in the Hughes Tool case.

Quota systems have existed among Southern longshoremen since the Civil War, and have been buttressed by racially segregated local unions. On the Gulf and South Atlantic ports, longshoremen's jobs have been held exclusively by Negroes, but in New Orleans and the Western Gulf ports there are segregated locals and racial quota systems. With few exceptions, clerks' jobs are held exclusively by whites.

Negro longshoremen have been able to retain their positions mainly because they have had sufficient supplies of labor to prevent whites from freezing them out. The international union apparently has used its influence to maintain racial balance.

Although quota systems preserve some jobs for Negroes, many colored longshoremen have inferior job conditions relative to whites. During the 1962-1963 contract year, for example, the 9,930 non-white dock workers in New Orleans worked an average of only 537 hours, while 3,296 whites worked an average of 863 hours. About half of the nonwhites, but only a fifth of whites, worked less than 100 hours. Over 10 per cent of whites, but less than one per cent of nonwhites, worked 2000 hours or more. In longshore jobs, 5,977 nonwhites worked an average of 529 hours while 1,430 whites worked an average of 908 hours. Although all of the 2,176 carloaders were nonwhites, the 1,110 wharf clerks were whites.

While nonwhite longshoremen worked shorter hours on the average, they worked a total of more hours than whites, as indicated by the following:

	White	Nonwhite
Total hours worked in all jobs	2,844,448	5,332,410
Total hours in longshoring jobs	1,298,440	3,160,833

Thus, nonwhites worked 65 per cent of all jobs and constituted about 75 per cent of all employees. Nonwhites got 71 per cent of the general longshoremen's jobs and had about 81 per cent of the employees. Since the Negro ILA locals in New Orleans control their own memberships, they could increase the average number of hours worked, though there are many more Negroes than whites looking for work as longshoremen. It might also be observed that the Brownsville, Texas complaint to the NLRB in the case discussed above was not against the quota system but for an increase in the share of jobs going to Negroes.

Conclusions on Preferential Treatment of Minorities

Preferential treatment for Negroes is opposed, of course, because it might deprive whites of rights they already enjoy and therefore would be discrimination in reverse. But *special* programs for Negroes need not take the form of quota systems and need not deprive whites of existing rights. For example, companies and unions that have not recruited among Negroes in the past and that have no Negro employees or members might make special efforts to recruit

Negroes or to help them acquire training. This would be special treatment to include Negroes in the recruitment pattern, but it would not be preferential treatment because it would extend to Negroes benefits which whites already enjoy.

Preferential treatment of Negroes can also be conducted in such a way as not to deprive whites of existing rights. For example, if a Negro and a white applicant were about equally qualified, it would be preferential treatment if the Negro were hired in order to advertise to the Negro community (or government agencies) that the company had lowered its racial barriers. In this case, the white applicant was not deprived of pre-existing rights. Of course, what most critics apparently have in mind is the form of preferential treatment where Negroes are hired regardless of their qualifications when more qualified whites are available, or when Negroes actually displace whites. The latter form of preferential treatment understandably leads to racial unrest. Preferential treatment which destroys the pre-existing rights of whites is based on the theory (in my judgment, mistaken) that whites as a race are collectively responsible for the disadvantages suffered by Negroes and that whites should be penalized now in order to compensate Negroes for their present historically-conditioned disadvantages. It seems to be just as unfair to hold all whites responsible for the Negroes' conditions as it is to consider all Negroes inferior to all whites.

Although the whole question of preferential treatment needs to be studied at greater length, especially some detailed studies of situations where preferential treatment has been used, the available evidence seems to support the following tentative conclusions:

1. Quota systems have usually been established as a result of pressure by Negroes to get jobs, which were sometimes accompanied by race riots, and have been maintained only because Negroes have had sufficient economic power to enforce the quota requirements or have been able to get help from the federal government to enforce quotas on government projects.

2. Quota systems are usually informal and are used mainly in casual occupations. They obviously would destroy seniority systems and are rarely used where seniority applies. However, in the South quota systems have frequently supplemented seniority arrangements by informal "gentlemen's agreements" over the division of jobs.

3. Although quota systems apparently have given Negroes inferior job opportunities on the average, these arrangements have made it possible for Negroes to get jobs they would have had difficulty retaining in the absence of quotas imposed by unions or the federal government. However, it seems that racial quotas are not justified where nondiscrimination policies have been established.

4. In those very rare cases where a Negro and a white worker are equally qualified, hiring the Negro might conceivably be considered discrimination against the white worker because of his race. However, the white worker is not deprived of an established right, although a technical difference might arise where the employer advertises for workers as compared with the intentional recruitment of qualified Negro workers. In this case, it is proposed that the decision be left entirely to the employer.

CONCLUSIONS

In conclusion, it seems to me that Negro job opportunities depend mainly on general economic and technological forces. Although discrimination will remain an important problem for some time, at this juncture discrimination, as well as other structural defects, are more like bottlenecks in the mainstream of the economy than fundamental determinants of job patterns. It is important to keep the stream open, but it is more important to keep it flowing freely. The flow will be determined mainly by the general level of economic activity and by the efforts made by individuals to prepare themselves to take advantage of the opportunities opened up. The supply of labor is important because, to a degree, a supply of trained workers can create their own demand. There are things governments can do to keep the economy moving at a healthy pace, but the basic decisions are likely to be made by private employers and workers who are motivated to create, prepare for, and seek jobs. The most effective government policies will therefore be those which influence private decisions through incentives and penalties, although the former will be more important than the latter. Public policy must encourage the creation of jobs as well as the training of workers qualified to fill those jobs. But in those cases where workers cannot be made to fit jobs, it will be necessary to create jobs to fit the workers. Surely there are enough things that need to be done in the way of public improvements that employment can be created for workers who are untrainable.

Finally, it is hard to create jobs and even harder to create jobs for Negroes. The prospects are not good, but there are a lot of things that can be done to make them better.

APPENDIX TABLES

TABLE 1

OCCUPATIONAL DISTRIBUTION OF THE CIVILIAN
LABOR FORCE BY COLOR
1957, 1962, AND PROJECTIONS FOR 1972
(PERCENTAGES)

Occupational Group	1957		1962		1972	
	White	Non-white	White	Non-white	White	Non-white
White collar workers	43.9	13.3	47.2	16.7	53.4	24.2
Professional, technical	10.7	4.0	12.6	5.3	17.0	8.7
Managerial, props.	11.2	2.4	11.9	2.6	12.1	2.9
Clerical	15.1	5.5	15.8	7.2	16.8	10.4
Sales	6.9	1.4	6.9	1.6	7.5	2.2
Blue Collar Workers	37.9	41.1	35.3	39.5	31.0	35.7
Craftsmen, foreman	14.3	5.4	13.6	6.0	12.9	7.3
Operatives	19.0	20.5	17.4	19.9	14.9	19.2
Laborers	4.6	15.2	4.3	13.6	3.2	9.2
Service workers	9.3	32.1	10.7	32.8	11.1	32.5
Private household	1.9	14.8	2.1	14.7	1.8	13.0
Other	7.4	17.3	8.6	18.1	9.3	19.5
Farmers	8.9	13.5	6.8	11.0	4.5	7.6
Total	100.0	100.0	100.0	100.0	100.0	100.0

Source: Statement by Sidney Sonenblum to U. S. Senate Subcommittee on
Manpower and Employment, September, 1963, *Hearings,* Part 5,
p. 1400.

TABLE 2

EMPLOYED PERSONS, BY OCCUPATION GROUP
AND COLOR, 1948, 1955, AND 1962[1]
(PER CENT DISTRIBUTION)

Major Occupation Group	White			Nonwhite		
	1962	1955	1948	1962	1955	1948
Total employed						
Number (thousands)	60.7	56.7	53.4	7.1	6.5	5.9
Per cent	100.0	100.0	100.0	100.0	100.0	100.0
White collar workers	47.3	42.1	39.1	16.7	12.0	9.0
Professional and technical workers	12.6	9.8	7.2	5.3	3.5	2.4
Managers, officials, and proprietors, except farm	11.9	11.1	11.6	2.6	2.3	2.3
Clerical	15.8	14.2	13.6	7.2	4.9	3.3
Sales	7.0	6.9	6.7	1.6	1.3	1.1
Blue collar workers	35.4	39.0	40.5	39.5	41.8	39.7
Craftsmen and foremen	13.6	14.1	14.6	6.0	5.2	5.3
Operatives	17.5	20.2	21.0	19.9	20.9	20.1
Laborers, except farm and mine	4.3	4.7	4.9	13.6	15.8	14.3
Service workers	10.6	9.0	7.9	32.8	31.6	30.3
Private household workers	2.1	1.8	1.5	14.7	14.8	15.6
Other service workers	8.5	7.2	6.4	18.1	16.8	14.7
Farm workers	6.8	9.9	12.4	11.0	14.5	21.0
Farmers and farm managers	4.0	6.0	7.8	2.7	5.0	8.5
Laborers and foremen	2.8	3.9	4.6	8.3	9.5	12.5

[1]Data for 1948 and 1955 not adjusted to reflect changes in definition of unemployment adopted in 1957

Note: Because of rounding, sums of individual percentages may not equal 100.

Source: M. A. Kessler, "Economic Status of Nonwhite Workers, 1955-62," *Monthly Labor Review,* July, 1963, p. 2.

TABLE 3

PER CENT DISTRIBUTION OF EMPLOYED MALES,
BY COLOR
1940, 1950, AND 1960

Occupational Group	Nonwhite			White		
	1960	1950	1940	1960	1950	1940
			Per cent Distribution			
Total Employed Men	100.0	100.0	100.0	100.0	100.0	100.0
Professional, Technical and Kindred	3.9	2.2	1.9	11.0	7.9	6.6
Mgrs., Officials, & Proprietors, except Farm	2.3	2.0	1.6	11.5	11.6	10.6
Clerical & Kindred Workers	5.0	3.4	1.2	7.1	6.8	6.5
Sales Workers	1.5	1.5	1.0	7.4	6.6	6.8
Craftsmen, Foremen & Kindred Workers	10.2	7.6	4.4	20.5	19.3	15.9
Operatives & Kindred Workers	23.5	20.8	12.4	19.5	20.0	18.7
Private Household	0.7	0.8	2.3	0.1	0.1	0.1
Service except Private Household	13.7	12.5	12.3	6.0	4.9	5.2
Laborers, except Farm & Mine	19.4	23.1	21.3	5.6	6.6	7.6
Other	8.4	1.3	0.6	4.2	1.2	0.7
Total Nonfarm	88.5	75.2	58.9	92.1	85.1	78.8
Farmers & Farm Mgrs.	4.4	13.5	21.1	5.6	10.5	14.2
Farm Laborers & Foremen	8.1	11.3	20.0	2.3	4.4	7.0
Total Farm	11.5	24.8	41.1	7.9	14.9	21.2

Source: U.S. Bureau of the Census

TABLE 4

PROPORTION OF NONWHITE TO TOTAL MALES IN
EACH OCCUPATIONAL GROUP 1940-1959[1]
(PERCENTAGES)

Occupational Group	1959	1952	1950	1948	1944	1940
Total Employed Men	9.2	8.9	8.3	8.4	9.8	9.0
Professional, Technical and Kindred	3.0	2.5	2.6	2.6	3.3	3.1
Mgrs., Officials & Proprietors, Except Farm	1.5	1.6	1.9	1.8	2.1	1.5
Clerical and Kindred Workers	6.5	3.4[2]	2.8[2]	2.3[2]	2.8[2]	1.6
Sales Workers	1.8					1.4
Craftsmen, Foremen & Kindred Workers	4.2	4.0	3.9	3.7	3.6	2.7
Operatives and Kindred Workers	10.7	10.4	8.5	10.1	10.1	6.1
Private Household	37.7	31.6	51.3	53.7	75.2	61.8
Service, except Private Household	20.6	21.7	21.4	20.7	21.9	17.4
Laborers, except Farm and Mine	29.5	26.9	21.4	23.6	27.6	21.2
Farmers and Farm Managers	8.2	10.7	10.5	9.8	11.0	13.1
Farm Laborers and Foremen	24.0	16.2	19.8	15.8	21.1	22.5

[1]April of selected years
[2]Includes Sales 1944-1952
Source: U.S. Bureau of the Census

TABLE 5

NONWHITE MALE CRAFT EMPLOYMENT[1] – SOUTH[2]
AND NON-SOUTH[3]
AND SOUTHERN NONWHITE SHARE OF TOTAL U.S.[4]
NONWHITE EMPLOYMENT – 1950 & 1960

	SOUTH				Per cent Nonwhite of South	
Classification	Total		Nonwhite[5]			
	1950	1960	1950	1960	1950	1960
Foremen (n.e.c.)[6]	185,697	277,369	3,544	5,504	1.90	1.98
Mechanics & Repairmen[7]	439,312	617,538	34,660	53,051	7.88	8.59
Metal Craftsmen[8]	157,671	178,465	9,670	8,153	6.13	4.57
Construction Craftsmen[9]	750,027	787,727	76,416	89,552	10.19	11.37
Other Craftsmen[10]	259,629	429,503	18,900	28,352	7.28	6.60
TOTAL	1,752,406	2,290,602	143,190	184,612	8.17	8.06

[1]Figures compiled from Census of the Population: 1950, U.S. Department of Commerce, Bureau of the Census, Vol. II, General Social and Economic Characteristics, By State, Table 77 – "Detailed Characteristics – Role and Class of Worker of Employed Persons, by Occupation and Sex, for the [each one individually] State and for Standard Metropolitan Areas of 100,000 or more"; 1950 Census of Population; U.S. Department of Commerce Bureau of the Census, Vol. III – General Social and Economic Characteristics, By State, Table 58 – "Occupation Group of Employed Persons By Color and Sex, for the State, Urban and Rural: 1960."

[2]South is defined as including Alabama, Arkansas, Delaware, District of Columbia, Florida, Georgia, Kan., Louisiana, Maryland, Miss., North Carolina, Oklahoma, So. Carolina, Tenn., Texas, Virginia, and West Va.

[3]Non-South is defined as including all other states except Alaska and Hawaii.

[4]U.S. is defined as including all states except Alaska and Hawaii.

[5]Nonwhite includes Negro, Indian, and Oriental.

[6]Same as 1940 census – foremen "not elsewhere classified" (n.e.c.)

[7]Same as 1940 census.

[8]Includes blacksmiths, forgemen, hammermen, boilermakers, machinists and job setters, millwrights, molders, tinsmiths, coppersmiths, sheet metal workers, toolmakers, die makers, and setters. 1960 figures also include heat treaters, metal rollers and roller hands, which were classified in the 1950 "other" category.

[9]Includes masons, tile setters, carpenters, electricians, painters, paperhangers, plasterers and cement finishers, plumbers and pipefitters, and structural metal workers. Cranemen, hoistmen, and construction machine operators have been substituted in the 1950 figures for the 1960 classification of excavating, grading, and road machine operators. Glaziers and stone cutters, included under "construction" in 1950, are found in the category of "other craftsmen" in 1960.

TABLE 5 — continued

NONWHITE MALE CRAFT EMPLOYMENT[1] — SOUTH[2]
AND NON-SOUTH[3]
AND SOUTHERN NONWHITE SHARE OF TOTAL U.S.[4]
NONWHITE EMPLOYMENT — 1950 & 1960

NON-SOUTH				Per cent Nonwhite of Non-South		TOTAL U.S. Nonwhite		Per cent Southern of Total U.S. Nonwhite	
Total 1950	1960	Nonwhite 1950	1960	1950	1960	1950	1960	1950	1960
548,481	815,177	5,768	12,365	1.05	1.52	9,312	17,869	38.1	30.8
1,180,857	1,568,041	38,194	71,513	3.23	4.56	72,854	124,564	47.6	42.6
798,258	919,087	17,295	28,980	2.17	3.15	26,965	37,133	35.9	22.0
1,553,677	1,600,813	37,331	47,782	2.40	2.98	113,747	137,334	67.2	65.2
836,622	1,254,405	17,030	34,732	2.04	2.77	35,930	63,084	52.6	44.9
4,917,895	6,157,523	115,618	195,372	2.35	3.17	258,808	379,984	55.3	48.6

[10]Includes bakers, compositors and typesetters, locomotive engineers and firemen, pressmen, bookbinders, cabinet makers, engravers, furriers, goldsmiths, inspectors, jewelers, lens grinders and polishers, log and lumber scalers and graders, millers, motion picture projectionists, opticians, piano and organ tuners and repairmen, shoemakers (except in factories), silversmiths, tailors, telegraph and telephone linemen and servicemen, upholsterers, watchmakers, and window dressers. The 1950 figures also include heat treaters, annealers and temperers, metal rollers and roll hands, roofers and slaters, craftsmen and kindred workers (not elsewhere classified), and members of the armed forces whereas the 1960 figures contain cranemen, derrickmen, electrotypes, glaziers, lithographers, loom fixers, plate printers, stereotypes, stone carvers, and stone cutters.

TABLE 6

PERCENTAGE CHANGE IN CRAFT EMPLOYMENT BY CATEGORY AND RACE SOUTH,[2] NON-SOUTH,[3] AND UNITED STATES[4] 1950-1960[1]

Classification	SOUTH White			Nonwhite[5]			1950
	1950	1960	1960/ 1950	1950	1960	1960/ 1950	
Foremen (n.e.c.)[6]	182,153	271,865	149	3,544	5,504	155	542,713
Mechanics & Repairmen[7]	404,659	564,487	139	34,660	53,051	153	1,142,663
Metal Craftsmen[8]	148,001	170,312	115	9,670	8,153	84	789,963
Construction Craftsmen[9]	673,611	698,175	104	76,416	89,552	117	1,516,346
Other Craftsmen[10]	240,792	401,151	167	18,900	28,352	150	819,502
TOTAL	1,649,216	2,105,990	128	143,190	184,612	129	4,802,277

[1] (Same as #1, Table 5)
[2] (Same as #2, Table 5)
[3] (Same as #3, Table 5)
[4] Includes figures for all states except Alaska and Hawaii
[5] (Same as #5, Table 5)
[6] (Same as #6, Table 5)
[7] (Same as #7, Table 5)
[8] (Same as #8, Table 5)
[9] (Same as #9, Table 5)
[10] (Same as #10, Table 5)

TABLE 6 — continued

PERCENTAGE CHANGE IN CRAFT EMPLOYMENT
BY CATEGORY AND RACE
SOUTH,[2] NON-SOUTH,[3] AND UNITED STATES[4]
1950-1960[1]

| NON-SOUTH | | | | | UNITED STATES | | | | | |
| White | | Nonwhite | | | White | | | Nonwhite | | |
1960	1960/ 1950	1950	1960	1960/ 1950	1950	1960	1960/ 1950	1950	1960	1960/ 1950
802,812	148	5,768	12,365	214	724,866	1,074,677	148	9,312	17,869	192
1,496,528	131	38,194	71,513	187	1,547,322	2,061,015	133	72,854	124,564	171
890,107	114	17,295	28,980	168	928,964	1,060,419	114	26,965	37,133	138
1,553,031	102	37,331	47,782	128	2,189,957	2,251,206	103	113,747	137,334	121
1,219,673	149	17,030	34,732	204	1,060,384	1,620,824	153	35,930	63,084	176
5,962,151	124	115,618	195,372	169	6,451,493	8,068,141	125	258,808	379,984	147

TABLE 7

PROJECTED CHANGES IN CIVILIAN LABOR FORCE
BY COLOR AND AGE GROUP, 1962-1972

Age Group	1962				1972			
	Whites		Nonwhites		Whites		Nonwhites	
	Millions	Per cent	Per cent	Millions	Per cent	Millions	Per cent	Millions
	64.0	89.2	10.8	7.9	88.7	76.5	11.3	9.7
14 - 19	5.6	7.8	1.0	.7	8.7	7.5	1.0	1.0
20 - 24	6.2	8.6	1.3	.9	11.1	9.6	1.4	1.2
25 - 54	40.6	56.5	7.1	5.1	52.3	45.1	7.0	6.1
55 and over	11.7	16.3	1.5	1.1	16.6	14.3	1.6	1.4

TABLE 8

PROJECTED CHANGES IN LABOR FORCE
BY COLOR AND SEX, 1962-1972

	1962		1972		1962-1972
	Millions	Per cent of Labor Force	Per cent of Labor Force	Millions	Change (Millions)
Labor Force	71.9	100.0	100.0	86.2	14.3
Whites	64.0	89.0	88.7	76.5	12.5
Nonwhites	7.9	11.0	11.3	9.7	1.8
Females	24.5	34.1	35.3	30.5	6.0
White	21.3	29.6	30.7	26.5	4.2
Nonwhite	3.2	4.5	4.6	4.6	.8
Males	47.4	65.9	64.6	55.7	8.3
White	42.7	59.4	58.0	50.0	7.3
Nonwhite	4.7	6.5	6.6	5.7	1.0

Source: Statement of Sidney Sonenblum to U.S. Senate Subcommittee on Manpower and Employment, *Hearings*, September, 1963, Part 5, p. 1393.

TABLE 9

UNEMPLOYMENT RATES OF EXPERIENCED WORKERS[1]
BY COLOR AND MAJOR OCCUPATION GROUP
1955 and 1962

Major occupation group	White		Nonwhite		Nonwhite as percent of white	
	1962	1955	1962	1955	1962	1955
All occupation groups[2]	4.9	3.5	11.0	7.7	224	208
Clerical and sales workers	3.8	3.2	7.7	7.0	203	219
Craftsmen and foremen	4.8	3.9	9.7	8.8	202	226
Operatives	6.9	5.5	12.0	8.4	174	153
Private Household workers	3.1	3.0	7.1	5.6	229	187
Other service workers	5.3	5.2	10.8	8.8	204	169
Farm laborers and foremen	3.9	3.0	5.8	6.3	149	210
Laborers, except farm and mine	11.0	9.8	15.8	12.1	144	123

[1]The base for the unemployment rate includes the employed, classified according to their current jobs, and the unemployed, classified according to their latest civilian job, if any; excludes the unemployed persons who never held a full-time civilian job.

[2]Includes the following groups not shown separately: Professional and technical workers; managers, officials, and proprietors; and farmers and farm managers.

Source: "Economic Status of Nonwhite Workers, 1955-62," From the *Monthly Labor Review*, July, 1963, United States Department of Labor, Bureau of Labor Statistics.

TABLE 10

UNEMPLOYMENT RATES
BY COLOR, AGE, AND SEX, 1962

	Unemployment Rates			
	Males		Females	
Age Group	White	Nonwhite	White	Nonwhite
	Per cent	Per cent	Per cent	Per cent
14 and over	4.6	11.9	5.5	11.1
14 - 19 years	12.3	20.7	11.5	28.2
20 - 24 years	8.0	14.6	7.7	18.2
25 - 34 years	3.8	10.5	5.4	11.5
35 - 44 years	3.1	8.6	4.5	8.9
45 - 54 years	3.5	8.3	3.7	7.1
55 years and over	4.1	10.1	3.5	3.6

Source: M. A. Kessler, "Economic Status of Nonwhite Workers, 1955-1962," *Monthly Labor Review*, July, 1963, p. 3.

TABLE 11

MDTA TRAINEES AND TOTAL NONWHITE
EMPLOYMENT BY OCCUPATION

| Occupational Group | Per cent MDTA Trainees* | | Per cent Nonwhite Employment (1962) |
| | Total | Nonwhite | |
	100.0	100.0	100.00
Professional, management	8.6	7.9	7.9
Clerical, sales	23.0	19.0	8.8
Skilled	30.8	26.9	6.0
Semiskilled	25.4	29.6	19.9
Service	10.2	14.2	32.8
Other	2.0	2.3	24.6

*June, 1963
Source: Statement by Seymour Wolfbein, Deputy Manpower Administrator, U. S. Dept. of Labor before Senate Subcommittee on Manpower and Employment, June 6, 1963.

FOOTNOTES

1. U. S. Congress, 88th, 2d Session, Joint Economic Committee, Congress of the United States, *1964 Joint Economic Report*, Senate Report No. 931, p. 61.

2. Defined as the ". . . amounts which the nation pays out to help support the dependent Negro who, were he not denied equal opportunity, would be self-supporting. They are the amounts which the nation pays out for a higher-than-necessary crime rate, for the support and rehabilitation of blighted housing areas, for needless property damage created by racial violence, and for a host of equally expensive situations which would not exist except for race discrimination." National Urban League, *Industry's Most Underdeveloped Resource*, New York, n.d., n.p.

3. *New York Times*, July 27, 1964.

4. While median nonwhite incomes have increased steadily from $1,614 in 1947 to $3,330 in 1962, with the exception of 1960-1961 when there was a slight decline, the nonwhite median was only 53 per cent of whites in 1962 as compared with 57 per cent in 1952.

5. See Clark Kerr, John T. Dunlop, Charles Myers, and Frederick Harbison, *Industrialism and Industrial Man* (Cambridge: Harvard University Press, 1960), p. 35.

6. See William H. Nicholls, *Southern Tradition and Economic Progress* (Chapel Hill: University of North Carolina Press, 1961).

7. Mathew A. Kessler, "Economic Status of Nonwhite Workers, 1955-62," *Monthly Labor Review*, July, 1963, pp. 2-3.

8. Dale E. Hiestand, *Economic Growth and Employment Opportunities of Minorities*, New York Columbia University Press, 1964, pp. 110-111.

9. Statement of Samuel Ganz, Assistant Director for Manpower and Automation Research, Office of Manpower, Automation and Training, U. S. Department of Labor to the U. S. Senate Subcommittee on Employment and Manpower of the Committee on Labor and Public Welfare, September 10, 1963.

10. *Ibid.*

11. The estimates of the proportions to be supplied to various crafts by 1970 at the present rate of apprenticeship training range from a low of 3 per cent for electricians. 1961 United States Commission on Civil Rights Report, *Employment*, Table 16, p. 232. See also Louis Ruthenburg, "The Crisis in Apprenticeship Training," *Personnel*, July/August, 1959; U. S. Department of Labor, *Our Manpower Implications* (Washington, D. C.: U. S. Govt. Printing Office, 1957); National Manpower Council, *A Policy for Skilled Manpower* (New York: Columbia University Press, 1954), p. 228; Eli Ginzberg, *The Negro Potential* (New York: Columbia University Press, 1956).

12. J. J. Morrow, "American Negroes, A Wasted Resource," *Harvard Business Review*, January-February, 1957, p. 69.

13. See, for example, Connecticut Commission on Civil Rights, *Training*

of *Negroes in the Skilled Trades,* Hartford, Conn., 1954, p. 56; Irving Babow and Edward Howden, *A Civil Rights Inventory of San Francisco,* Part I — "Employment," Council for Civic Unity, San Francisco, California, 1958 p. 109; Lanston T. Hawley, "Negro Employment in the Birmingham Metropolitan Area," Case Study No. 3 in *Selected Studies in Negro Employment in the South,* National Planning Association, Committee of the South, Report No. 6, 1955; E. William Noland and E. Wight Bakke, *Workers Wanted: A Study of Employer Hiring, Policies, Preferences and Practices* (New York: Harper Brothers, 1949), pp. 32, 59; Bernard Rosenberg and Penny Chapin, "Management and Minority Groups: A Study of Attitude and Practices in Hiring and Upgrading," in *Discrimination and Low Incomes,* New York State Commission Against Discrimination, 1949.

14. See my *The Negro and Organized Labor* (New York: Wiley, 1965).

15. Leon E. Lunden, "Antidiscrimination Provisions in Major Contracts, 1961," *Monthly Labor Review,* June, 1962, p. 643.

16. See Paul Norgren and Samuel Hill, *Toward Fair Employment* (New York: Columbia University Press, 1964) and Ray Marshall, *The Negro and Organized Labor* (New York: Wiley, 1965).

17. Employment of salaried workers increased by 13.8 per cent but nonwhite employment in these categories increased by 23.5 per cent. Of these nonwhite salaried employees, 3,266 were placed in management, professional, sales, and technical jobs and 2,884 as clerical and office employees. The increase in nonwhite hourly employment was distributed as follows:

Craftsmen	1,964
Operatives	17,557
Service	971
Laborers	538

(Report to the President, The President's Committee on Equal Employment Opportunity, November, 1963, p. 116.)

18. PCEEO, Committee Reporter, November, 1963.

19. For example, in spite of all of the demonstrations in New York during the summer of 1963, by December, 1963, only 111 Negroes and Puerto Ricans gained entry into unions as journeymen or apprentices. (*New York Times,* December, 1963.) And in spite of much agitation after 1953 to eliminate job segregation in the Southern petroleum refining industry, a study of 11 companies revealed that by 1960 only about 550 Negroes had been promoted. Of these, 364 promotions were in two companies and 24 were temporary appointments. (See Ray Marshall, "Some Factors Influencing the Upgrading of Negroes in the Southern Petroleum Refining Industry," *Social Forces,* December, 1963.)

20. U. S. Senate, Subcommittee on Manpower and Employment, *Hearings on the Nation's Manpower Revolution,* Part 9, 1963, pp. 3134-3145.

21. Paul Norgren and Samuel Hill, *Toward Fair Employment,* Chs. II and III.

22. Steele v. L. & N. R. R., 323 U. S. 192; Archibald Cox, "The Duty

of Fair Representation," *Villanova Law Review,* January 1957; Benjamin Aaron, "Some Aspects of the Union's Duty of Fair Representation," *Ohio State Law Journal,* Winter, 1961, p. 39; Wallace Corp. v. NLRB, 323 U. S. 248.

23. Central of Georgia Ry. v. Jons, 229 F. 2d 648, Cert. denied 352 U. S. 848; Richardson v. Texas & New Orleans Ry. Co., 242 F. 2d 239; 77 S. Ct. 230.

24. See Hunter v. Atcheson Topeka and Santa Fe Ry. II Race Relations Law Reporter 996.

25. Bethlehem Alameda Shipyard Cases, R-5963-94 (1943).

26. Carter Manufacturing Company, 59 NLRB 803.

27. NLRB, *Tenth Annual Report,* 1945, p. 18.

28. 147 NLRB no. 166.

29. Milton Friedman, *Capitalism and Freedom* (Chicago: University of Chicago Press, 1962), p. 108.

30. *Ibid.,* p. 109.

31. Statement by Sar Levitan, "Training Under the Area Redevelopment Act," to the U. S. Senate Employment and Manpower Subcommittee, June 7, 1963.

32. George P. Schultz, "The Fort Worth Project of the Armour Automation Committee," *Monthly Labor Review,* January, 1964, p. 56.

33. Indeed, in June, 1963, it was reported that only 2.7 per cent of the MDTA's trainees but 20.1 per cent of the unemployed in 1962 had less than eight years of education, and 60.9 per cent of MDTA trainees and only 37.1 per cent of the unemployed were high school graduates. Moreover, only 10 per cent of MDTA trainees but 30 per cent of the unemployed were over 45 years of age.

34. *New York Times,* July 13, 1963, p. 7.

35. Local 1367, ILA, Case No. 23-CB-467, 148 NLRB No. 44, September 14, 1964.

2

THE ANATOMY OF THE NEGRO-WHITE INCOME DIFFERENTIAL*

Lowell E. Gallaway**

Two developments of the past few years have created increased interest in the income levels of Negro members of the American community: (1) the renewed drive against discriminatory practices in the United States and (2) the sudden revival of interest in the question of the extent of poverty in the American economy. The first of these suggests an explanation for the observed low levels of Negro income while the latter is concerned with the effects of such levels of income. There can be no disputing the existence of marked income differentials between whites and Negroes in the United States: the 1960 decennial census shows that median family income for nonwhites (mostly Negroes) was $3,161 while that for whites was $5,893. Thus, nonwhite median family income is 53.6 per cent of white median family income. The divergence between white and nonwhite income, in turn, is the ultimate basis for the various statements pointing out that one-fifth to one-fourth of America's families with poverty levels of income are nonwhite despite their making up only about one-tenth of the total population.[1]

The data detailing the absolute levels of white and nonwhite income are primarily cross-sectional in character; i. e., they describe the distribution of income at a particular point in time. However, little evidence of the dynamics of the income distribution process as it relates to the movements of whites and nonwhites between income classes through time is available. In this paper data from

---

*The major part of this research was conducted while the author was a member of the staff of the Social Security Administration. It was in this capacity that the special tabulations of Social Security Administration data were made available to him.

**Associate Professor of Industry, Wharton School of Finance and Commerce, University of Pennsylvania.

the records maintained by the Social Security Administration in the course of its administering the old-age, survivors, and disability insurance (OASDI) program will be used to shed some light on this aspect of the white-nonwhite income differential. The character of these data will be described in more detail in a later section of the paper.

INCOME DISTRIBUTION AS A DYNAMIC PROCESS

Some inferences about the dynamics of the income-distribution process as it affects different racial groups can be drawn from the existing cross-sectional data. In order to develop these, let us initially describe the way in which income is distributed in terms of a simple probability process.[2] For example, assume that there are two income classes in the economy: "high" and "low." Also, assume that the probabilities that individuals will move beween these classes is given by the matrix:

$$(1) \qquad P = \begin{Vmatrix} p_{11} & p_{1h} \\ p_{h1} & p_{hh} \end{Vmatrix}$$

in which the subscripts l and h refer to low and high, respectively. Now, if it is assumed that these probabilities are applicable to any and all individuals in the particular income class, the operation of these probabilities will describe the distribution of individuals among the two income classes at any moment in time. As a case in point, the pattern of transition among income classes between an initial point in time (t_0) and a point two periods later (t_2) is given by P^2 (the square of the matrix P), which may be thought of as a two-period transition matrix. Similarly, a transition matrix may be generated for any number of time periods so that the movement of individuals between income classes over the interval t_0 to t_n is always describable by such a matrix (equal to P^n). Now, as n grows larger, P^n approaches an equilibrium state in which all the elements in a particular column of the matrix are equal to one another. Once the equilibrium position is achieved, the distribution of income into the various income classes remains unchanged so long as the initial probability matrix (P) remains unchanged.

Quite obviously, this approach to conceptualizing the process of income distribution places its major emphasis on the nature of the transition probabilities between income classes (i. e., on the matrix P). In the simple illustrative case, the larger the term p_{11}, *ceteris paribus*, the greater will be the proportion of individuals who in equilibrium are in the low income group. Similarly, the larger the value p_{hh}, *ceteris paribus*, the greater will be the proportion who in equilibrium find themselves in the high income class.

In our simple case the relative numbers of individuals in each income class at time t_0 do not affect the final distribution between high and low income classes. This enables us to reach an initial conclusion with respect to the character of the income transition probabilities of whites and Negroes; for even though discrimination against Negroes upon their initial entry into the labor market forced a disproportionate number of them into low income classes, the possession of similar income transition probabilities by this group would tend to eliminate the impact of the discrimination. Therefore, the observable difference in the levels of income of whites and Negroes (particularly across all age classes)[3] is indicative of differences in the income transition probabilities of these groups. This points up the fact that the relative income position of Negroes is more than the product of an initial disadvantage in job opportunities; in addition, it is the result of a relative inability on the part of Negroes to advance from income class to income class. This difference in their income transition probabilities may be the result of several factors:

1. A lack of job qualifications which would permit upward movement through the various income classes. In particular, this is likely to be the result of differences in levels of educational attainment of whites and Negroes.
2. Differences in the relative proximity of Negroes to jobs with higher levels of remuneration; e. g., the geographical concentration of the Negro in the relatively low-wage South.
3. A consistent pattern of white exercise against Negroes of what Becker calls a "taste for discrimination."[4]
4. Differences in the extent to which whites and Negroes are able to acquire on-the-job training and experience.
5. Differences in the impact on whites and Negroes of the normal processes of economic change in the American economy.

The relative strength of each of these factors is difficult to assess but through the use of the aforementioned Social Security Administration data a tentative exploration of the phenomenon of differential income transition probabilities will be attempted.

NATURE OF THE DATA

It is possible to obtain information from the Social Security Administration records describing the patterns of movement between income classes over time for a sample of those who earn income in employment covered by the old-age, survivors, and disability insurance system. These data are derived from the 0.1 per cent Continuous Work History Sample maintained by the Social Security Administration. While these data are useful for this purpose, they do possess certain shortcomings. For one thing, the types of income for which records are available are wage and self-employment income and, consequently, provide no information regarding income from nonemployment sources (i.e., property income). Secondly, the data provide only fragmentary information regarding movement between income classes because data are not available describing levels of employment income in excess of the taxable limit for social security purposes. As a result no information on the behavior of individuals in the higher income groups is available.

While these shortcomings in the data should not be completely ignored, neither should the useful features of the data be disregarded. After all, there is available from this source information relating to the employment income patterns of a reasonably representative sample of the working population of the United States. Specifically, data describing these patterns for the years 1955-58 by sex, race, and age will be employed in this paper. These should prove quite useful from the standpoint of increasing our understanding of the nature of the differences in income opportunities for whites and Negroes.

AGGREGATE WHITE-NEGRO INCOME TRANSITION PROBABILITIES

The data referred to group individuals into four different income classes for the years 1955-58: $1-1049, $1,050-2,099, $2,100-3,149, and $3,150 and over. We will designate these income classes by the numbers 1, 2, 3, and 4, respectively. The individuals included in the sample are restricted to male wage earners in 1959 who had earnings credits under the OASDI system in all the years 1955-58. From these data aggregate income transition matrices for the period 1955 through 1958 were calculated for white and Negro members of the sample (Table I).[5] These show a definite pattern: in the three lowest income classes there is a pronounced tendency for Negroes to have less of an opportunity to advance to a higher income class while in the highest income class it is more difficult for Negroes to remain in this class than it is for whites.

TABLE I

INCOME TRANSITION MATRICES 1955-58, 1959
MALE WAGE WORKERS, BY RACE

Income Class	White Matrix[1]				Negro Matrix[2]			
	Income Class				Income Class			
	1	2	3	4	1	2	3	4
1..............	.310	.280	.169	.241	.470	.298	.159	.073
2..............	.157	.269	.237	.337	.224	.393	.278	.105
3..............	.065	.128	.284	.523	.103	.136	.390	.371
4..............	.017	.031	.044	.908	.064	.066	.097	.773

[1]Sample of 27,851.
[2]Sample of 2,707.
Source: Social Security Administration, 0.1 per cent Continuous Work
  History Sample.

On two counts these data are not surprising. After all, they are in agreement with the inference concerning racial income transition probabilities that was drawn from the cross-sectional estimates of income levels by race. But, beyond that, they can be anticipated from one aspect of the work which has been done in connection with the permanent income hypothesis.[6] According to the permanent income thesis, the further one's income lies from its normal level, the greater the likelihood of its returning to that level in some future period. For example, an individual with a normal income of $3,000 a year whose income this year is $1,000 has a greater probability of having an income of $3,000 next year than he would if this year's income were $2,000. The significance of this for the data of Table I is clear. Since the same dollar income intervals are used in defining the income classes for both whites and Negroes, whites in income class 1 are likely to be further removed from their normal income level than Negroes in income class 1 (remember the difference between white and Negro median incomes). Consequently, whites in income class 1 would be expected to have a greater probability of advancing out of that class than Negroes.

No matter what the source of the differences shown in Table I, the conclusion the data suggests is that Negroes have less opportunity to improve their levels of income than whites. A quantitative measure of the impact of the differences in the transition rates of Table I upon the income opportunities of Negroes can be constructed by means of the following simple statistic:

$$(2) \qquad \sum_{\substack{i \\ i < j}} \sum_{j} P_{ij} - \sum_{\substack{i \\ i > j}} \sum_{j} P_{ij}$$

Very simply, this statistic provides a measure of the net gain in terms of improvement in income position for the group possessing the income transition matrix in question. For the white matrix this statistic has a value of $+ 1.345$ while for the Negro it is $+ .594$. Thus, the net opportunities (in a probability sense) for improvement in income status over this period are more than twice as great for whites than for Negroes. A more sophisticated measure of income opportunity can be obtained by weighting each of the P_{ij}'s by the number of income classes moved. This produces a statistic which, in addition to measuring the opportunity for advancement, takes into account differing magnitudes of advancement. In this form the income opportunity statistic is

$$(3) \qquad \sum_{\substack{i \\ i \neq j}} \sum_{j} (j - i) \, P_{ij}$$

The calculated values for the statistic are $+ 2.203$ for the white matrix and $+ .707$ for the Negro indicating that Negroes have a substantially smaller opportunity of achieving an income advancement of a given amount than do whites.

REGIONAL TRANSITION MATRICES

The opportunity statistics calculated from the transition matrices of Table I are suggestive of various kinds of discrimination against Negroes (such as discrimination in job opportunities, education, etc.). However, it is conceivable that they reflect nothing more than regional differences in income opportunity combined with a differing geographic distribution of whites and Negroes. To be more specific, larger percentages of Negroes than whites are found in low-income regions of the United States. Thus, the income opportunities prevalent in these low-income regions receive greater weight in the Negro transition matrix than in the white and may account

for a substantial part of the observed difference in income opportunity between the two racial groups.

This difficulty could be overcome if it were possible to classify
the individuals in the sample by region. Unfortunately, such information is not available. However, we can attack the problem
indirectly. Consider our initial 2x2 income transition matrix (with
the numbers 1 and 2 substituted for the subscripts 1 and h):

$$
\text{(1a)} \qquad P = \left\| \begin{matrix} P_{11} & P_{12} \\ \\ P_{21} & P_{22} \end{matrix} \right\|
$$

Now, any element of P can be defined as a weighted average
of the following type:

$$
\text{(4)} \qquad P_{ij} = \sum_{k=1} \alpha_{ik} (P_{ij})_k
$$

where α_{ik} represents the appropriate weights to be attached to
the P_{ij} of various regions and k is a subscript denoting region.[7]

In addition, by definition:

$$
\text{(5)} \qquad \sum_{j=1} (P_{ij})_k = 1
$$

Together, expressions (4) and (5) define six constraints on the
P_{ij} of k regions.[8] This is not sufficient to permit solving for the
P_{ij} of even two regions (which would total eight). One additional
constraint can be obtained from the relationship:[9]

$$
\text{(6)} \qquad \rho_j = \sum_{i=1} \sum_{k=1} \lambda_{ik} (P_{ij})_k
$$

where ρ_j represents the percentage of individuals in the jth income
class and λ_{ik} denotes the appropriate weights to be attached to the
various P_{ij} $(\sum_{i=1} \sum_{k=1} \lambda_{ik} = 1)$. [10]

The addition of a seventh constraint makes it possible to solve
the following set of simultaneous equations for a 2x2 income
transition matrix:

$$
\begin{aligned}
\alpha_{1m}(P_{11})_m + \alpha_{1n}(P_{11})_n \cdots\cdots\cdots \quad\cdots\cdots\cdots \quad\cdots\cdots\cdots &= \overline{P}_{11} \\
\cdots\cdots\cdots + \alpha_{1m}(P_{12})_m + \alpha_{1n}(P_{12})_n \cdots\cdots\cdots \quad\cdots\cdots\cdots &= \overline{P}_{12} \\
\cdots\cdots\cdots \quad\cdots\cdots\cdots + \alpha_{2m}(P_{21})_m + \alpha_{2n}(P_{21})_n \cdots\cdots\cdots &= \overline{P}_{21} \\
\cdots\cdots\cdots \quad\cdots\cdots\cdots \quad\cdots\cdots\cdots \quad\cdots\cdots\cdots + \alpha_{2n}(P_{22})_n &= \overline{P}_{22} - \alpha_{2m}(P_{22})_m \\
(P_{11})_m \quad + (P_{12})_m \cdots\cdots\cdots \quad\cdots\cdots\cdots \quad\cdots\cdots\cdots &= 1 \\
\cdots\cdots\cdots \quad\cdots\cdots\cdots + (P_{21})_m \cdots\cdots\cdots \quad\cdots\cdots\cdots &= 1 - (P_{22})_m \\
\lambda_{1m}(P_{11})_m + \lambda_{1m}(P_{11})_n + \lambda_{2m}(P_{21})_m + \lambda_{2n}(P_{21})_n \cdots\cdots\cdots &= \rho_1
\end{aligned}
$$

where the $\overline{P}_{ij}$ denote the transition probabilities of the aggregate transition matrix and the subscripts m and n denote two different regions.

Note that the absence of an eighth constraint makes it necessary to express the solutions for the various P_{ij} in terms of one of the P_{ij}'s. In this case the P_{ij} treated as a parameter is $(P_{22})_m$. Estimates of the other parameters were obtained from the 1960 population census and the sample data used in calculating the matrices of Table I (see Appendix for a detailed explanation of sources of the estimates of the parameters). The regions used were the South (consisting of the South Atlantic, East South Central, and West South Central states) and the non-South (the remainder of the continental United States). For the Negro income transition matrix, the results of solving the set of simultaneous equations are as follows:

Negro Matrices

Non-South (m)

Income Class

Income Class	1	2
1	$-.609 + 1.522\,(P_{22})_m$	$1.609 - 1.522\,(P_{22})_m$
2	$1 - (P_{22})_m$	$(P_{22})_m$

South (n)

Income Class

Income Class	1	2
1	$1.267 - .672\,(P_{22})_m$	$-.267 + .672\,(P_{22})_m$
2	$-1.067 + 1.505\,(P_{22})_m$	$2.067 - 1.505\,(P_{22})_m$

Disaggregating the white matrix in this fashion produces:

White Matrices

Non-South (m)

Income Class

Income Class	1	2
1	$.202 + .474\,(P'_{22})_m$	$.798 - .474\,(P'_{22})_m$
2	$1 - (P'_{22})_m$	$(P'_{22})_m$

South (n)

Income
Class

Income Class

	1	2
1	$1.107 - .880 (P'_{22})_m$	$-.107 + .880 (P'_{22})_m$
2	$-2.250 + 2.505 (P'_{22})_m$	$3.250 - 2.505 (P'_{22})_m$

An examination of the computed regional income transition matrices reveals that there are definite limits on the range of the values $(P_{22})_m$ and $(P'_{22})_m$ (the prime symbol is here used to distinguish the white from the Negro matrix). For example, the calculated value of $(P_{21})_n$ (which must be $\geqslant 0$) implies that $(P_{22})_m \geqslant .709$. Similarly, the calculated value of $(P'_{21})_n$ implies that $(P'_{22})_m \geqslant .898$. Of course, the maximum values for $(P_{22})_m$ and $(P'_{22})_m$ are equal to unity. From this knowledge it is possible to compute income opportunity statistics of the type shown in expression (2) for the extreme values of $(P_{22})_m$ and $(P'_{22})_m$. With a 2 x 2 transition matrix the opportunity statistic is simply

(7) $$P_{12} - P_{21}$$

which is a linear relationship for all the estimated regional transition matrices. Consequently, by estimating (7) for the extreme values of $(P_{22})_m$ and $(P'_{22})_m$ we define the entire set of regional opportunity statistics. These are shown graphically in Figure I.

The graphic display of Figure I yields startlingly clear conclusions with respect to the possibility that the observed difference in the income opportunity statistics calculated from the aggregated matrices might be the result of the different geographical distribution of the two racial groups. With any possible combination of values of $(P_{22})_m$ and $P'_{22})_m$, the opportunity statistic for southern whites is greatly in excess of that for southern Negroes. Similar, although less pronounced, results are obtained from examining the data pertaining to the non-southern states. The conclusion suggested by these data is that the differing geographical distribution of Negroes and whites does not account for the observed differences in the income opportunity statistics. Consequently, one is led to accept the observed differences in the income opportunity statistics as being indicative of discriminatory practices rather than reflecting any accident of geography.

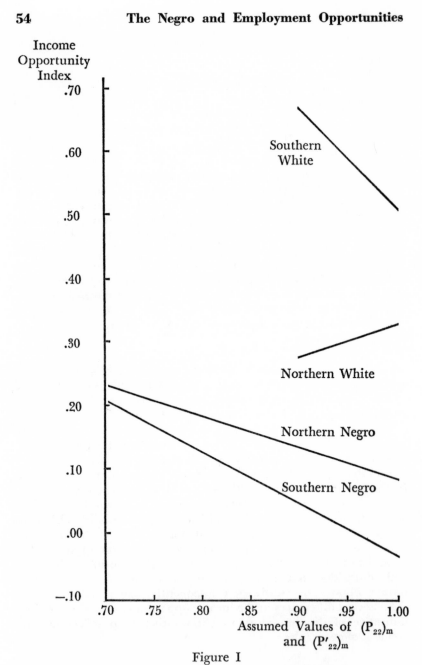

Figure I

Income Opportunity Indices, Various Assumed Values of $(P'_{22})_m$ and $(P'_{22})_m$, by Region, United States, 1955-1958

INCOME OPPORTUNITY BY AGE GROUP

While the aggregative estimates of Negro-white income opportunity are informative, even more interesting results can be obtained by subdividing the samples by age. The data are available by five-year intervals from age 20 through age 59 and for the group aged 60 and over. For determining age the reference year is 1959.[11] From these data income opportunity statistics of the weighted type were calculated for each age group by race. These are shown in Table II

TABLE II

INCOME OPPORTUNITY, 1955-58, 1959 MALE WAGE
WORKERS, BY AVERAGE AGE 1955-58, AND RACE

Average Age, 1955-58	White	Negro	Difference Between White and Negro
19.5	1.666	.484	+1.182
24.5	2.870	1.174	+1.696
29.5	3.063	.884	+2.179
34.5	2.377	.619	+1.758
39.5	2.337	.494	+1.843
44.5	2.045	.652	+1.393
49.5	1.786	.617	+1.169
54.5	2.071	.243	+1.828
59.5 and over[1].....	.830	.340	+ .490

[1]Age group 60 and over in 1959.
Source: Social Security Administration, 0.1 per cent Continuous Work
    History Sample.

and illustrated graphically in Figure II. The results of these calculations paint a rather clear picture of the process by which the relative impoverishment of the Negro takes place. His pattern of income opportunity shows that his maximum opportunities for increasing his level of income occur in the age group with an average age of 24.5 over the period 1955-58. Beyond this point, the income opportunity statistic for the Negro male generally declines. Yet, at this point of maximum opportunity for income advancement, the American Negro male's opportunities are less than 40 per cent (as measured by the opportunity statistic) as good as his white counterpart's. And the worst is yet to come! While the Negro male reaches the peak of his opportunity for income advancement at an average age of about 25, the white male's income opportunities are his greatest at an average age of about 30. This in part undoubtedly reflects the longer periods of schooling of white males and a later entry into the labor force but, whatever the cause, the effect is to further widen the gap between the income opportunity statistic for white males and that for Negro males: at an average age of about 30, the Negro's income opportunities are less than one-third as promising as a white's. Beyond this age, the relative position of the Negro improves but only because of a more rapid decline in the income opportunities of white males. All that this improvement accomplishes is some moderation of the decline in the relative income position of the Negro. Data from the decennial census of 1960 show that the nonwhite male's median income amounted to 64 per cent of white male median income in the age class 20-24. This is reduced to 58 per cent in the age interval 25-34, a decline of about 10 per cent in the relative income position of the nonwhite. Over the next 20 years there is a further decline to 53 per cent which is a loss of less than 10 per cent in the relative income position of the nonwhite. Thus, the decline in relative income position is greater between average ages of about 22 through 30 than it is between average ages of about 30 through 50.[12]

The truly discouraging aspect of the data shown here is the implication that, as a group, the American Negro's ultimate economic status is essentially determined at about an average age of 25, an age at which the Negro is at the greatest relative disadvantage in terms of possessing opportunities for income advancement. It is during these critical years before the age of 30 that so many Negroes are committed to an economic status that ensures that they will, in the future, appear among the low-income groups in numbers that are disproportionate to their relative numerical importance in the population.

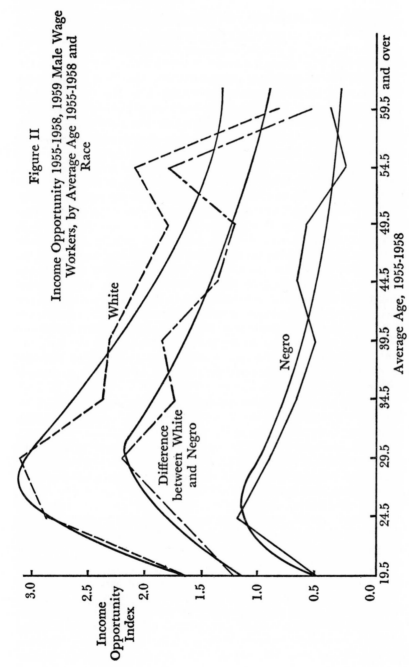

Figure II

Income Opportunity 1955-1958, 1959 Male Wage Workers, by Average Age 1955-1958 and Race

THE IMPACT OF WORK EXPERIENCE AND ECONOMIC CHANGE ON INCOME OPPORTUNITY

In order to complete our picture of the nature of the income opportunities available to whites and Negroes in the United States, some discussion of the impact of work experience and economic change upon such opportunity is needed. The data describing income opportunity for the group with an average age of about 20 suggest that at a very early stage in the working life of a Negro male he is at a marked disadvantage in terms of income opportunity. This initial disadvantage is probably the result of two factors: differences in levels of education and the "taste for discrimination" in American society. But, as we have noted, the Negro's disadvantage becomes greater as older age groups are considered. In part this is the result of an even greater disparity in educational levels of the two groups: 1960 census data show a definite increase in the differential between white and nonwhite educational levels as age increases over the range 20 through 34.[13] However, an additional aspect that needs to be considered is the impact of job experience and economic change upon income opportunities. It is conceivable that the acquisition of job experience by the Negro enables him to offset some of the initial advantage that whites possess by virtue of the differential in educational levels. Also, it is possible that the processes of economic growth will tend to offset some of his disadvantage.

In order to explore these possibilities, the probability of an individual's appearing in the lowest income class employed in this paper was estimated by age group for each of the years 1955 through 1958. By comparing these probabilities as we move through the period 1955-58, it is possible to obtain some idea of the impact of additional years of job experience and the pattern of economic growth upon the income opportunities of the two races. The results of these calculations are shown graphically in Figure III. The trend lines which are indicated for each age group have been estimated visually as there were too few observations to permit any systematic determination.

An examination of the data for the two youngest age groups shows that both Negroes and whites benefit substantially from the combination of job experience and economic change. With the youngest age group the probability of being in the lowest income class decreases from about 60 per cent for both whites and Negroes to values of slightly more than 20 per cent for whites and between 35 and 40 per cent for Negroes. Of course, part of this decline

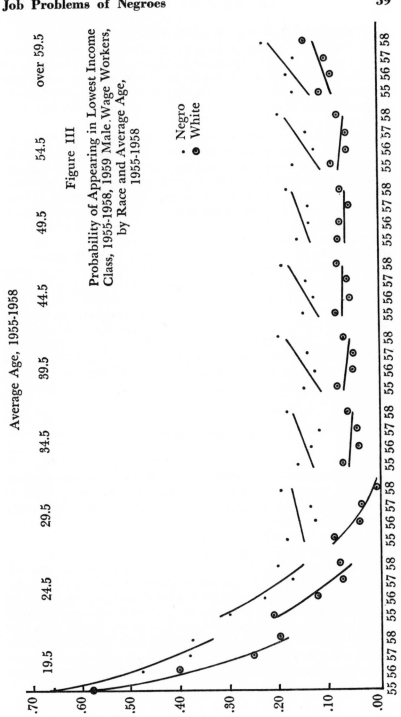

Figure III

Probability of Appearing in Lowest Income
Class, 1955-1958, 1959 Male.Wage Workers,
by Race and Average Age,
1955-1958

• Negro
◉ White

may simply be the result of individuals' shifting from partial labor-force activity to full activity as they complete their formal education. Whatever the combination of factors involved, the white male's probability of being in the lowest income class drops more substantially during these two earliest periods than does the Negro's. Thus, the Negro's initial disadvantage is compounded during these periods.

Once beyond these two youngest age groups, the white male continues to profit from the combination of work experience and change through the group with an average age of about 30, but the Negro male does not. In fact, for all the succeeding age groups the combination of experience and economic change during the period 1955-58 actually led to an increase in the probability of a Negro male's appearing in the lowest income class. On the other hand, white males showed either modest decreases or little change in their chances of appearing in this income class until the oldest age group was reached. An explanation of the Negro's worsened absolute position can be found in the economic downturn that characterized 1958; however, the Negro's worsened absolute position is not the important thing for our purposes. What is important is the obvious implication that the relative position of Negroes is not improved by the combination of additional years of job experience or the normal processes of economic change. Quite the contrary, there is every indication that the impact of these forces is a further worsening of his standing.[14]

CONCLUSIONS

In the reading of any research paper a point is reached at which a reader is prompted to ask, "What does this all mean? What is its significance?" Assuming that we have reached that juncture, let me indulge my artistic impulse and sketch in rather broad and symbolic strokes the portrait of Negro impoverishment that emerges from the more technical aspects of this paper.

Perhaps the appropriate art form for conveying the desired impression is the triptych. For the first scene, there is a representation of the young Negro entering a bazaar (symbolic of the labor market) carrying a sack in which are contained the best products of his skill. As he surveys the surroundings of the bazaar, he is surprised to discover that there are other merchants (fair-skinned ones) already ensconced in the choice positions and, more than that, he is shocked to find that many of these are attempting to sell a product which is admittedly superior to his. He begins to wonder whether the craftsman to whom he was apprenticed has taught him all that he should know in order to be able to vie with his fair-skinned competitors and, as he contemplates the unfavorable location from which he will have to merchandise his wares, he becomes actually aware of the possibility of economic failure.

In the second scene, picture this same Negro, now several years older, still selling the same product. However, several things have changed. His once unfavorable position in the market place is no longer his; rather, he now finds himself in an even more disadvantageous location. The product he sells has been substantially improved as he has acquired greater and greater skill. However, his competitors have also improved their merchandise, perhaps even more than he has been able to better his. And the "times": economic conditions are markedly improved over the previous scene, but the improvement seems to have helped his competitors more than him.

The third and final scene depicts our same Negro, again several years older. He has now been pushed further back among the stalls of the market place. There is no longer any question of his competing with his fair-skinned rivals; the product he sells is serviceable, but no more than that. His face now possesses the resigned look that accompanies acceptance of one's position in life. He has arrived at the economic level which was to a great extent preordained for him at the time he first set foot in the bazaar.

APPENDIX

Certain of the parameters used in disaggregating the observed income transition matrices into regional matrices require some further explanation as to their meaning and the sources of the values of these parameters which are used in the calculations. The parameters in question are defined as follows:

(a)
$$\alpha_{ik} = \frac{(N_i)_k}{\sum\limits_{k} (N_i)_k}$$

(b)
$$\lambda_{ik} = \frac{(N_i)_k}{\sum\limits_{i} \sum\limits_{k} (N_i)_k}$$

(c)
$$\rho_j = \frac{\sum\limits_{i} P_{ij}\overline{N}_{1j}}{\sum\limits_{i} \sum\limits_{j} P_{ij}\overline{N}_{1j}}$$

where N denotes the number of individuals in the ith income class of a region (denoted by k) at a given point in time, the subscript j denotes income class in a succeeding period, and $\overline{N}$ indicates the number of individuals in the ith income class in the aggregate at a given point in time.

Estimates of the values of α_{ik} and λ_{ik} were obtained from *United States Census of Population, 1960, United States Summary, Detailed Characteristics*, PC (1), 1D, Table 263. This table describes income in 1959 of persons by age, color, and sex for the regions. In calculating α_{ik} and λ_{ik}, income classes identical to those used in the text of the paper were employed.

The value of ρ_1 used in the calculations was obtained from the sample data used to calculate the various transition matrices.

FOOTNOTES

1. See, *inter alia*, Wilbur J. Cohen and Eugenia Sullivan, "Poverty in the United States," *Health, Education, and Welfare Indicators*, February, 1965; Michael Harrington, *The Other America: Poverty in the United States* (New York: Macmillan, 1963); and Robert J. Lampman, *The Low-Income Population and Economic Growth*, U. S. Congress, Joint Economic Committee, Study Paper No. 12, 86th Congress, 1st Session, December 1959.
2. The discussion to follow makes no pretense of theoretical elegance. For a highly sophisticated treatment of income distribution as a stochastic process, see D. G. Champernowne, "A Model of Income Distribution," *Economic Journal*, June, 1953, pp. 318-51.
3. *United States Census of Population, 1960, United States Summary, Detailed Characteristics*, PC (1), 1D, Table 219.
4. Gary Becker, *The Economics of Discrimination* (Chicago: University of Chicago Press, 1959).
5. The term "white" is used in the ensuing portions of the paper for convenience purposes despite its being technically somewhat inaccurate. The data employed are classified by all workers and Negro workers. Thus, the "white" category is derived as a residual. However, it includes nonwhites other than Negroes, although they are undoubtedly few in number.
6. Milton Friedman, *A Theory of the Consumption Function* (National Bureau of Economic Research [Princeton: Princeton University Press, 1957]). Some evidence relating to this phenomenon is presented in Ralph B. Bristol, Jr., "Factors Associated with Income Variability," *American Economic Review*, May, 1958, pp. 279-90.
7. See Appendix for detailed definition of α_{ik}.
8. It might appear that two additional constraints could be obtained from expression (5) by considering more than one region. However, these constraints are implied by (5) and thus are redundant.
9. Again, it might appear that additional constraints could be obtained by varying j. However, these are also redundant.
10. See Appendix for detailed definition of λ_{ik}.
11. With a 1959 reference date for age, the average age over the period 1955-58 of the groups being analyzed is approximately that of the lower limit of the classification; e.g., those who were aged 20-24 in 1959 had an average age of 19.5 over the period 1955-58. In order to avoid confusion, the age classes have been translated into approximate average ages in the text.
12. *United States Census of Population, loc. cit.*
13. *United States Census of Population, op. cit.*, Table 173. For the 14 to 24-year-old male group the median number of years of school completed by nonwhites is 9.6 years compared to 10.8 for whites, a difference of 1.2 years. For the 25-29 group the difference is 1.9 years (12.4 for whites and 10.5 for nonwhites), while in the 30-34-year-old group the

difference increases to 2.5 years (12.2 for whites and 9.7 for non-whites).

14. Admittedly, it may be questioned whether the time period for which the data are available represents a normal period of economic growth in that the recession year of 1958 is the concluding year. However, cyclical swings of the magnitude of the 1958 downturn are a reasonably normal part of our economic life, and what we have emphasized here is the worsening of the Negro's position relative to whites, not his position in absolute terms. Obviously, before any conclusion could be drawn about the impact of job experience and growth upon the absolute position of the two racial groups, data decribing the full course of a business cycle would be required. But, for purposes of assessing the impact of these factors on the relative position of Negroes, the data at hand are probably quite sufficient.

PART II

Political Approaches
Two Views of Equal Opportunity Legislation

3

EFFECTIVENESS OF EQUAL OPPORTUNITY LEGISLATION

George Schermer*

My first exposure to governmental policy on non-discrimination in employment occurred in the late 1930's. As an employee of the Chicago Housing Authority, I was assigned the task of reviewing and adapting to local conditions certain clauses having to do with social policy in the standard contracts supplied by the United States Housing Authority. My recollections are hazy concerning the precise language, but there was a clause requiring that contractors employ non-whites in proportion to their numbers in the population as established by the latest census. If that was not the language, that was the way it was interpreted.

The form contract specified that there was to be no discrimination in occupancy because of religion or national origin; race and color were not mentioned. There was a "gentleman's agreement" that the racial character of the neighborhood would not be changed. Thus, a project in a white neighborhood would be all white; one in a Negro neighborhood would be Negro; and one in a mixed neighborhood would be mixed.

In Chicago the definition of neighborhood was so finely drawn that, when the Jane Addams Houses were built on both sides of Taylor Street, units were rented to whites only north of Taylor and to whites and Negroes south of Taylor, because that had been the pattern before clearance.

This concept of neighborhood spilled over into the employment policy so that contractors building on the North Side of Chicago were required to employ fewer Negroes than those building on the West or South Sides of the city. The ratios were not broken down by sub-contract or skill. If the required ratio was 10 per cent and 10 per cent of the total man hours were performed by

---

*Consultant and former Chairman, Philadelphia Commission on Human Relations.

Negro common laborers, the equal opportunity requirements were met.

I do not recall that the Authority itself had to comply with any quota requirements. In any event, the Authority employed no more than two or three non-whites in its administrative staff until an all-Negro project was built, at which time Negroes only were employed for the project staff.

If we are inclined to look back upon those requirements with critical amusement, let us remind ourselves that those were beginnings and that probably no other government agency was doing more or as much.

THE MARCH ON WASHINGTON

One of the great political reversals of American history was the shift of the Negro voters from their traditional adherence to the party of the Great Emancipator to the Democratic Party of President Roosevelt. In 1932 Negroes were still voting Republican, almost unanimously. In 1936, in the urban areas outside the South, they were voting Democratic with almost equal fervor. By 1940, the switchover was nearly complete. A major factor contributing to the change was the fact that the welfare programs advanced by the Roosevelt New Deal were all that kept Negroes from starving to death in the large cities. Equally important, however, had been the personal concern of President and Mrs. Roosevelt. Never before had a president or his wife demonstrated a personal recognition for the Negroes' aspirations for dignity in a manner that carried conviction, such as Mrs. Roosevelt's resignation from the D.A.R. when that organization barred Marian Anderson from singing in Constitution Hall.

It seems paradoxical, therefore, that the most critical confrontation ever to occur between a president and Negro leadership was actually between Roosevelt and the then strong man of the emerging Negro civil rights movement, A. Philip Randolph. The confrontation had developed before the 1940 election, but the Negro community seemed unaware of it. It came to its climax in June of 1941.

The story has been chronicled by Herbert Garfinkel in his book, *When Negroes March*. I comment on it briefly here because it is pertinent to the general thesis of this paper: that government and law have come to the aid of Negroes only when they (Negroes) have confronted the nation (or a locality) with a challenge and have tended to be ineffective unless the challenge was present.

Enthusiastically loyal though they were to the New Deal, Negroes in the United States had not gained much in the eight years from 1932 to 1940. The New Deal and the posture of the presidency had provided hope and the WPA, but no significant gains in education, training, employment, or housing. The 1940 census, taken in April 1940 *after* the war had begun in Europe, but *before* its impact had registered significantly on the American economy, reported unemployment among Negroes at 22 per cent as compared to 15 per cent among whites. That figure was misleading because thousands of employable Negroes had simply dropped out of the labor market. In cities such as St. Louis, Chicago, and Cleveland, the percentage of Negroes on welfare was three to four times that for whites. Eighty-nine per cent of the employed Negroes were in service and unskilled occupations compared to 53 per cent among whites.

In 1940 the *Pittsburgh Courier,* sensing that the emerging defense effort would offer new and unusual opportunities for Negroes, sponsored the creation of a Negro Committee on National Defense with Rayford W. Logan of Howard University as chairman. This committee pursued the traditional forms of pressure on Washington — mainly polite representations to friendly congressmen and the White House. The results were nominal. A clause forbidding discrimination in the selection of trainees was inserted in the Selective Service Act, but it was almost completely negated by another clause that permitted the heads of the Army and Navy to reject those who were unacceptable.

Under the pressure of rising war clouds and the need for national unity, the posture of the White House shifted from one of concern for the aspirations of Negroes to compromise with the traditional prejudices and practices of both the armed forces and the nation's industrial apparatus.

A. Philip Randolph, President of the Brotherhood of Sleeping Car Porters, more than anyone else, recognized that this was the moment for Negroes to strike their own blow in the war for democracy. If there was to be victory it would have to come on two fronts, overseas and at home. If Negroes did not get themselves out of the back rows for this performance, they might never move forward.

On September 27, 1940, in the thick of the presidential campaign, Randolph, Walter White, National Secretary of the NAACP, and T. Arnold Hill of the National Urban League called upon President Roosevelt for a stronger policy against discrimination in the armed forces. Immediately after their departure, and thus with the implication of their consent, the White House released a statement that "the policy of the War Department is not to intermingle

colored and white enlisted personnel in the same regimental organizations."

This statement led to a serious breakdown in relationships between the Administration and the national Negro leadership. In
January 1941, the NAACP conducted protest meetings in 23 different
states calling for picketing of national defense plants. That same
month A. Philip Randolph called for 10,000 Negroes to march on
Washington. There was no immediate response to either the
NAACP's plea for pickets or Randolph's call to march. Negroes
in the United States had long been conditioned to defeat and were
content with pleas for small favors. A posture of marching and demanding was too unorthodox to be taken seriously. Nevertheless,
by May of 1941, March on Washington Committees had been organized in Washington, New York, and Chicago, and the Negro press
was enthusiastically endorsing the idea. By early June, the March
idea had caught fire among Negroes to such an extent that the Administration appealed directly to White and Randolph to call it
off. They refused. On June 25, 1941, President Roosevelt issued the
famous Executive Order 8802, and Randolph agreed to "postpone"
the march. The march was finally held on August 28, 1963.

Executive Orders 8802 and 9346

The first of the orders, issued in 1941, created a Fair Employment
Practices Committee within the War Manpower Commission headed
by Paul McNutt. When McNutt interfered with the committee's
plan to conduct public hearings on employment practices in the
railroad industry in 1943, several members resigned, and the committee fell apart. On May 29, 1943, President Roosevelt issued
Executive Order 9346 reconstituting the committee, giving it relatively independent status and extending its powers. The order
declared that it was "the policy of the United States that there shall
be no discrimination in employment of any person in war industries
or in government by reasons of race, creed, color or national origin;
and it is the duty of all employers, including the several federal
agencies and all labor organizations to eliminate discrimination in
regard to hire, tenure terms, or conditions of employment or union
membership." Contracting agencies were directed to include in all
contracts a provision obligating contractors not to discriminate. Implicit in the order was the power to rescind a contract in instances
of non-compliance with such a provision.

The first committee began with a budget of $80,000 and a profes-
sional staff of seven. In 1945 the second committee received an
appropriation of $500,000 and employed a professional staff of 56.

By 1945 the committee was receiving complaints at the rate of 4,000 per year. However, in the entire war period only 52 complaints were reported as satisfactorily adjusted. A total of 22 hearings were held involving 93 employers and 34 unions.

The committee had no subpoena powers, and its implied power to rescind contracts was probably never taken seriously. Unions in particular were impervious to the order since they were not contracting parties.

On the record, then, the wartime FEPC's achievements were puny indeed. More than 10,000 complaints were filed, and only 52 were reported as satisfactorily adjusted. However, during that same period, the nation witnessed by far the most impressive advance in the economic position of Negroes ever made. During that period the rise in incomes for the Negro population over the nation as a whole not only kept pace with that of whites but began to catch up. In 1939, the median income for Negroes in urban areas had been less than 40 per cent of that of whites. By 1949 it had risen to just under 60 per cent.

The greatest gains were made in what might be called the "middle occupations." In 1940, 57 per cent of employed Negro males outside the South were in unskilled labor and service occupations; 20 per cent were operatives; and 19 per cent were in the skilled, white collar, technical, and professional classes. By 1950 the ratio of employed in unskilled labor and service occupations had declined to 46 per cent; the ratio of operatives had increased to over 27 per cent; and the skilled, white collar, professional, and technical workers had increased to 24 per cent. These data become even more significant when one considers that the 1950 ratios include those additional hundreds of thousands of Negroes from the South and from the ranks of the unemployed who had moved into the labor force of northern and western cities.

Was this very substantial improvement the direct result of the Executive Orders and the Fair Practices Committees? No one familiar with the situation would agree. The greatest single factor, by far, was the wartime demand for manpower. The second most important was the impact of wartime psychology. Negroes by the hundreds of thousands believed the war represented opportunity and that the nation could not and would not refuse them a place in the war effort. They acted on their beliefs. Finally, even though there was tremendous resistance from many employers, unions, and white employees, there was a greater inclination among whites to accept partnership with blacks in the war effort.

Did FEPC have any impact at all? My guess is that it was very substantial. The filing and processing of individual complaints accomplished little, but the fact of the order and the presence of the committee must have constituted both encouragement to Negroes and sanctions for those who had to make the decisions.

In 1944 Senator Russell of Georgia obtained the passage of an amendment to an appropriation bill preventing the President from using appropriations to pay the expenses of any agency unless Congress specifically authorized that use. His target was the FEPC, and the Committee came to an end in 1945.

Efforts to pass a federal fair employment practices law were lost by Senate filibuster in 1946 and again in 1950. Presidents Truman and Eisenhower both continued the Executive Orders and committees for the administration of the orders. However, the postures of the committees were weak, public respect and confidence declined, and complaints dropped to as low as 150 per year.

The greatly strengthened Order 10925 issued by President Kennedy in 1961 is discussed later.

STATE AND LOCAL FEPC LAWS

In 1944 New York's Governor Thomas Dewey appointed a commission to study employment practices in that state. The commission, headed by Charles Evans Hughes, recommended that the state adopt a law prohibiting discrimination in employment and creating a commission for its administration. The proposed legislation was passed in 1945. While there have been many modifications, the New York law has been a model for similar legislation in twenty-one other states. In addition to these twenty-two, six other states have laws barring discrimination in employment but do not provide for a special administrative agency. Twenty cities, most of them in states which also have fair employment laws, have adopted fair employment ordinances and created agencies for their administration.

The primary differences among the various state laws are:

(a) Coverage — some states cover *all* employers, some exempt employers with fewer than 5, 8, or 12 employees, while Illinois and Missouri exempt employers with fewer than 50.

(b) Some have the power to subpoena witnesses and/or to initiate complaints, and some do not.

(c) Some provide for full-time salaried commissioners, some for paying commissioners per diem, and others for paying commissioners nothing.

(d) Procedures for the enforcement of commission orders and the nature and severity of the penalties vary widely.

City ordinances are not discussed since all but one of the cities are in states that also have fair employment laws. With the exceptions noted above and below, the state laws tend to conform to the New York model, which declares it to be an unlawful employment practice:

(a) For an employer to refuse to hire or employ, to discharge or to discriminate against an individual in compensation, conditions, or privileges of employment;

(b) For a labor organization to exclude or to expel from membership or to discriminate against any member, employer or employee of an employer;

(c) For any employer or employment agency to print, circulate or cause to be printed or circulated, any statement, advertisement or publication, or to use any form of application for employment which expresses directly any limitation, specification or discrimination,

if any of those acts, limitations, or statements are related to race, color, religion, or national origin. The law further declares it to be an unlawful practice:

(d) For an employer, labor organization or employment agency to discharge, expel or otherwise discriminate against any person because he has opposed practices prohibited by the act or because he has filed a complaint, testified or assisted in a proceeding under the act.

Michigan and Ohio laws, which were drafted much later, are more precise in their definitions of unlawful practices pertaining to employment agencies and joint apprenticeship committees.

Powers of Administrative Agencies

Seventeen states provide for relatively independent administrative commissions, while five have set up divisions within established departments. New York, Massachusetts, Ohio, and Rhode Island invest the primary power and responsibility for administration of the law in the commissioners. New York provides for seven full-time, highly-paid commissioners. The three others pay part-time salaries. All the other state laws provide that the primary responsibility for administration shall rest with a director and staff selected by the commission, with the commission acting as a policy board. However, it is almost universal that the power to conduct formal hearings and to issue findings and orders rests only with the commissioners. (Nearly all the states have provisions for paying commissioners a modest per diem rate.)

The commissions or divisions are empowered to:

1. Receive, investigate, and pass upon complaints alleging un-

lawful practices. (Ten of the state commissions are empowered to initiate complaints, and in six others the attorney general is so authorized.)

2. Endeavor to resolve the complaint and to eliminate the unlawful practice by conference and persuasion.

3. Hold hearings, subpoena witnesses (although not all have the subpoena power), compel attendance, administer oaths, take testimony, require the production of records. For enforcement of these powers, the agencies must go to court.

4. Issue orders requiring respondents to cease and desist from unlawful practices and to take affirmative action such as to remedy the specific practice complained of, to instate or reinstate the applicant or employee, and to reimburse for loss of income.

The laws also generally provide that the commissions shall or may:

(a) Promote and conduct educational programs to further the objectives of the law.

(b) Create and service advisory committees or agencies to further the objectives of the law.

(c) Conduct studies of discriminatory practices and to issue reports and findings.

While the power to conduct studies has been generally interpreted as meaning the power to study *patterns* of discriminatory practice and to seek to remedy such practices by persuasion, only the Ohio and Philadelphia Commissions are empowered to hold hearings, to compel the appearance of witnesses, and to issue formal findings.

About half of the state commissions are empowered also to administer laws prohibiting discrimination in either public accommodations or housing or both.

The Weight of Government Support

The strength and power of an administrative agency of government is likely to be measured more in terms of the *apparent* support it receives from the administration, the legislative body, and public opinion than in the statute itself. The most authoritative report of the operation of fair practice laws to date has been done by Paul H. Norgren and Samuel E. Hill in their *Toward Fair Employment,* published by Columbia University Press.

Norgren and Hill report that in 1960 the New York Commission received an appropriation of $950,000; California with two-thirds as large a Negro population plus an almost equally large Spanish minority population received $203,000; Ohio with six-tenths as many Negroes had a budget of $100,000; and Michigan with half as many Negroes had a budget of $148,000.

The comparison of state appropriations in relation to size of minority population is, of course, the crudest kind of measure. Conditions differ among the states; some of the commissions focus upon employment only, while several embrace complex programs including housing, public accommodations, education, and community relations. In some states such as Pennsylvania, there are strong commissions in the larger cities that share in the administration of the laws and may collectively have larger appropriations than the state commission.

Nevertheless, it seems that Norgren and Hill's basic thesis holds. They find that there is a fairly close correlation between the relative size of the appropriation and administrative staff and the effectiveness of the law. In their estimate, the only really effective operations were those of the New York State and City of Philadelphia Commissions, both of which received much the greater appropriations in relation to size of constituent population. There is no quarrel with Norgren and Hill's thesis as far as it goes, but it can be contended that there is more than a mechanical relationship among dollars appropriated, staff employed, and effectiveness. The size of the appropriations may be as much a symptom of success as a cause. It may be that the size, posture, and power of the minority public and the concomitant posture of the political powers have as much or a greater impact.

Complaint Procedure and Commission Strategy

The underlying assumptions upon which the New York act was drafted have permeated the operation of every fair employment commission. These were: (1) Negroes were barred from jobs by conscious, overt policies and practices of discrimination; (2) once such practices were outlawed, most employers, having respect for the law, would desist; (3) Negroes, waiting eagerly at the gates of opportunity, would pass through as soon as the bars were down; (4) the law would be more effective if it were clothed with education and persuasion; and (5) coercion would be exercised only as a last resort.

All of the commissions, with the exception of New York, were extraordinarily modest and apologetic in their initial requests for funds, and most of them never changed in that respect. Undoubtedly that posture was imposed by the governors, state fiscal authorities, and the general climate in the legislatures. This modest approach was in no way challenged by the Negro or any civil rights groups.

Once the law was on the books a victory had been won, and the concerned people went home to rest.

The commissions all started bravely enough with the publication of regulations and succinctly-drafted informational and educational pamphlets telling employers what to do and what not to do and telling the minority group public about its rights and how to file complaints. Sporadic educational conferences were conducted, mainly for the edification of the already informed and committed. Employer representatives attended the first few such conferences but were so persuaded by soporific assurances that they were not threatened with vigorous compliance activity that their attendance fell off almost completely.

The commissions went out of their way to assure both employers and prospective complainants that the law could function *only* if the complainant was fully qualified for the job. Since most Negroes already suffer from extreme lack of self-confidence, those that heard the message were persuaded that they ought not to apply or, if they were turned down, not to file complaints.

The complaint procedure is not discussed. It is not important. There are not enough complaints to make it worth the time. The major mistake in the entire enterprise was the reliance upon complaints.

The New York State Commission, which had by far the largest complaint load, reported a total of 3,262 complaints adjusted after 15 years of operation, roughly 200 a year. New Jersey averaged only 50 per year and Philadelphia slightly over 40. Space does not permit a detailed analysis. A notion of what even these small figures mean is gained if it is mentioned that only one-third of the New York cases involved findings of "probable cause," while the other two-thirds involved technical violations and findings of practices "not unlawful but discriminatory" that were adjusted. In Philadelphia a complaint of an unlawful entry in an application form was reported as "adjusted" when the form was corrected even though no person was found to have been refused a job.

Why so few complaints were filed or why so few of those filed proved to be valid has been the perennial subject of the annual meetings of the Conference of Commissions on Human Rights. The explanations ranged from the declaration that the minority community "didn't have the word," to the idea that Negroes just were not qualified or motivated, to the suspicion that the over-cautious posture of the commissions simply did not inspire public confidence.

As each explanation became popular, the commissions would alter the emphasis of their programs. For a time there were increased efforts to channel information to the minority public. Then there was renewed emphasis upon encouraging Negroes to undertake training to improve their competence. Eventually, a few commissions began the re-examination of the assumptions upon which the laws were based and which had tended to govern the strategy of the commissions.

Now, before further pursuing the effectiveness of the laws, we should bring ourselves up to date on the current Executive Orders and Title VII of the Civil Rights Act.

EXECUTIVE ORDERS 10925 AND 11114

Early in 1961 President Kennedy issued Executive Order 10925. The order differed from the earlier ones under Roosevelt, Truman, and Eisenhower in several respects:

(a) The Roosevelt Order had placed responsibility for administration and enforcement with the President's Committee. The committee was handicapped by lack of subpoena power and absence of explicit enforcement procedures. The only sanctions available were the implied threat of contract cancellation or penalties which could be exercised only by the contracting agencies which, in their alliance with industry, were not inclined to act. In the end, the Russell Amendment crippled the President's Committee.

(b) Under Truman and Eisenhower all responsibility for compliance rested with the contracting agencies. The President's Committee could only study and recommend. The pressures upon the contracting agencies were nominal and upon contractors almost non-existent.

(c) The Kennedy Order was explicit, whereas the earlier ones were only implicit in granting to the President's Committee or the contracting agencies the following compliance powers:

   1. Recommend to the Department of Justice that proceedings be brought against contractors to enforce the non-discrimination provisions or for falsification of information.

   2. Terminate all or portions of contracts, make continuance of contracts contingent upon adoption of programs of compliance, or disqualify firms from future contracts until the President's Committee is satisfied that the contract requirements are or will be met.

3. Collect and publish information and data to be supplied by each contractor concerning patterns of minority group distribution in the work force and all steps and procedures taken to remedy inequities.

(Executive Order 11114 clarifies and extends 10925, explicitly applying the order to all plants of a contractor, whether or not involved in the production under contract, to sub-contractors and to contractors on grant-in-aid work.)

In addition, the Committee and/or the contracting agencies are authorized to conduct public hearings, but do not have the power of subpoena. Since 1941 each of the succeeding Presidental Committees established a complaint procedure. In the absence of a statute delegating explicit enforcement powers and defining procedures, the processing of complaints has been cumbersome and indecisive.

The major innovations of the Kennedy-Johnson Committee have been the requirements for reporting (Form 40) and compliance reviews. The compliance reviews have been in the nature of compulsory self-surveys. Many contracting firms have resented the process, but most of them not only have gone through the motions, but appear to have taken it quite seriously, at least in the first two years.

A second innovation of the committee is the *Plans for Progress* program which has used the prestige of the President to persuade many of the nation's largest corporations to pledge themselves to voluntary plans to advance and equalize employment opportunities for minorities. While the President's Committee has issued positive reports on this effort, many objective observers have been cautious and often dubious about the tangible results.

TITLE VII OF THE CIVIL RIGHTS ACT OF 1964

The latest addition to the legal armament for equal employment opportunity is Title VII of the Civil Rights Act of 1964. With this title we now have a federal fair employment law that will reach into all of the states. Covered employment includes all employers, employment agencies, and labor unions engaged in industries affecting commerce. It goes into effect for employers of 100 or more employees in July 1965, for those of 75 or more in 1966, and eventually for those employing as few as 25. An Equal Employment Opportunities Commission is established to administer the law. Extensive provisions are made to assure that states having equal employment laws shall retain jurisdiction, providing the requirements of federal law are met. The procedures for receiving, investigating, and adjusting complaints by persuasion are similar to those employed by the states. However, the federal EEOC will have much less muscle, as an enforcement agency, than the typical state commission.

If efforts at conciliation fail, the complainant must be notified of the failure and of *his* right to file an action in a federal district court. The Commission does not bring the action. The Attorney General may intervene. If the court finds evidence of discriminatory practice, it may enjoin the respondent against the continuance of the practice. If the respondent fails to comply with the court's orders, the Commission may commence proceedings to compel compliance.

The act is heavily weighted with protections for the respondent. In the light of the history of complaint procedures before state commissions to date, not much is likely to come of complaints under Title VII.

One highly unusual provision in Title VII permits the Attorney General to file an action for an injunction where he has cause to believe that any person or group of persons is engaged in a "pattern or practice of resistance."

One other unusual provision prohibits discrimination because of sex. This may prove to be the most controversial and precedent-shattering aspect of the law, since much of the existing state and federal legislation regulating the employment of women may either be in conflict or may be interpreted as discriminating against men. Many union contracts may also be in conflict.

EFFECTIVENESS OF THE LAWS

There have been many pronouncements and claims by both the proponents of fair employment laws and the several administrative commissions concerning the effectiveness of the laws. The only really objective and definitive attempt at evaluation to date is Paul Norgren and Samuel E. Hill's *Toward Fair Employment.* Norgren and Hill admit that it is extremely difficult to isolate the law's impact from a whole series of other factors such as up and down trends in the economy, shifts in technology, the political and social climate, the temper and sophistication of the minority groups, education and training, and geography. They compare the rate of improvement in employment patterns in New York State, which had an

enforceable law throughout the decade of 1950 to 1960, with Indiana, Illinois, and Missouri which did not. The overall ratio of
nonwhites to whites in these three states is comparable to that in
New York State, and the total rate of increase in the several states is
also comparable.

The improvement rate was many times greater in New York than
in the tri-state area. Norgren and Hill developed an index which
registers the rate of gain or loss for Negroes in their advancement
into occupations of higher skill, status, and pay, allowing for relative
increase in the population. The gain in New York for managers and
officials was 164 compared to 6 for the tri-state area, in retail sales
work it was 41 to 15, for foremen it was 75 to 37, and for construction
craftsmen 46 to 8. If the gains in New York are solely attributable
to the fair employment law, then we have proof positive. The differences are not nearly so great, however, if other states such as
New Jersey, Pennsylvania and Michigan — also with fair employment laws — are used for comparison. Norgren and Hill did not apply their index to the other states, primarily because several of
them did not adopt the laws until the middle of the decade, and also
because other factors were less comparable.

Rarely, if ever, do the commissions report unsuccessful disposition
of valid complaints. On the average, from 70 to 80 per cent of all
complaints are dismissed on such grounds as "no probable cause,"
"no discrimination found," "lack of jurisdiction," "insufficient evidence," "withdrawn by complainant."

From 19 to 29 per cent are reported as "discrimination found and
satisfactorily adjusted." Less than one per cent have reached the
point of a formal finding of "unlawful discrimination" after a public
hearing. (Among those that *have* reached that stage, however, the
orders to cease and desist the practice and to provide affirmative
remedy to the complainant have been firm, and those appealed have
been generally sustained by the courts.)

In many of the "adjusted" complaints, the adjustment consisted
of a formal, binding agreement to cease and desist with remedies
to the aggrieved party. The "adjusted" complaints are not publicized
by name of complainant and respondent, although they are reported
statistically.

If a complaint cannot be adjusted by persuasion, the commissions
become very cautious about formal findings of discrimination after
public hearing. At this point they are moving toward litigation, and
they have demonstrated great reluctance to risk reversal in court.
Unless the facts will strongly sustain a finding of unlawful discrimination, the commission is likely to dismiss the complaint for insuf-

ficient evidence. This statement is based on personal experience and upon the statements of my colleagues in the field. Norgren and Hill do not make this point in their book.

The annual reports and public relations pamphlets of the commissions have, until the last two years, been replete with self-praise that few complaints have ever reached public hearing or litigation. This was the measure of success — that employers were not being harassed.

On the record it appears that the commissions were, indeed, very successful in gaining compliance on the *valid* complaints. The problem was that so few valid complaints were filed.

The paucity of complaints was especially apparent with respect to employment agencies and labor unions. "Probable cause" complaints against employment agencies averaged only six per cent of the total, and those against unions averaged under ten per cent. In Philadelphia, the ratios were four per cent and seven per cent, respectively. Norgren says, and I agree with him, that unions are overtly and legally responsible for only a small amount of the total practice of discrimination since they control hiring only in certain of the construction crafts, the railroads, the typographical crafts, and a few others. A few commissions, notably New York, Connecticut, and Massachusetts have won signal legal victories over discriminating unions, but the net change in employment patterns in the traditionally exclusive or segregated unions has been meager at best. Discriminating unions have been as obdurate and resistant as Southern school districts.

In summary, as to the effectiveness of the law, we can conclude:

1. The law *and* the administrative commissions have a high ratio of success in resolving, litigating, and obtaining compliance on those complaints that are well supported by the facts.

2. The valid complaints have been too few to have value in changing patterns.

3. Patterns of employment have improved much more rapidly in New York than in other states where there are large numbers of non-whites, and more rapidly in FEP states than in non-FEP states.

4. Until very recently, only New York and Philadelphia ventured beyond the complaint procedure in attempts to affect underlying patterns of discriminatory practice.

ELEMENTS FOR EFFECTIVENESS IN ADMINISTRATION OF EQUAL EMPLOYMENT LAWS

As indicated above, Norgren and Hill rate New York far ahead of any other state as to effectiveness of the law. They cite the city of Philadelphia as second, well ahead of other states and cities, but substantially behind New York.

There are three reasons, they say, why New York is ahead with Philadelphia having two of the three to its credit. The differences are these:

(1) The New York State and Philadelphia Commissions have gone far beyond the complaint procedure in bringing pressure upon employers for affirmative action.

(2) New York State and Philadelphia invest much more money and employ larger staffs (per capita) in administration.

(3) New York has the benefit of full-time, highly-paid commissioners.

Each of these three points merits much more discussion than can be permitted in this paper. The second (appropriations) can be disposed of by referring back to earlier comments on the weight of government support. Considering the size and complexity of the task, even the New York State and Philadelphia Commissions are grossly under-financed. The others, figuratively speaking, are being starved into ineffectiveness. Not only are the commissions unable to handle the work-load, but the public perceives that the governing powers are *making certain* of their ineffectiveness.

On the question of full-time, paid commissioners, there are arguments pro and con. I think that a very competent professional staff should be established, and commissioners should be paid generously on a per diem basis. It is unrealistic to expect commissioners to work without remuneration if the responsibility of adjudicating complaints rests with them.

Norgren and Hill's point about affirmative action is well taken. They may have given the New York and Philadelphia Commissions more credit in this respect than they deserve. Experience has revealed that few employers or their agents consciously adopt policies or procedures or consciously make decisions to discriminate. Few people will admit to themselves that they discriminate. Decisions that are, in fact, discriminatory are rationalized prejudicially by reasons that are considered proper and non-discriminatory. Even in those situations where an employer has taken all appropriate steps to prevent discrimination against qualified applicants for employment, little change will occur unless he takes affirmative measures to purposefully discover, encourage, recruit, train, and upgrade minority group employees.

A passive posture of neutral non-discrimination by an employer is only a little better than one of overt discrimination. A posture of neutral, umpire-like disinterest by a commission has been demonstrated as only slightly more effective than no commission at all. A commission must make its presence felt. It must use every opportunity to involve employers in affirmative procedures designed to bring the formerly-excluded minority group members into the employment structure.

A judicious application of compliance reviews, industry-wide investigations, public exposure, and coercion of recalcitrant employers, combined with industry advisory committees and demonstrated good will toward employers who have problems is necessary. Equally important are all of the actions and information programs required to capture the attention and participation of the minority public.

This paper does little more than mention "affirmative programs." Since space does not permit a lengthy discussion, it does not detail what such programs can or should be.

THE POSTURE OF THE MINORITY PUBLIC

We return now to the earlier thesis. The presidential orders and equal opportunity laws came into being in response to a posture of strength from Negro organizations, backed up by broadly-based, racially-inclusive civil rights, civic, and religious groups. Effective results have been obtained only when there was a happy combination of favorable circumstances and/or very strong support from the same groups that pushed for the legislative action.

Thus far we have seen little evidence that employers will act affirmatively even when there is a law on the books. There is equally little evidence that individual members of the minority groups will exercise the initiative under the laws which are there for their benefit. This means that reliance upon complaint procedures is unavailing.

We cannot, then, judge the effectiveness of the law in a vacuum. The law without active and aggressive civic action and support becomes neutral. On the other hand, if there is no law or no competent administrative agency, aggressive civic action can produce counter-actions, conflicts, and a stalemate. What is required is organized community pressure for constructive action, regulated by law.

ELEMENTS OF AN EFFECTIVE PROGRAM

The general conclusion, then, is as follows. The law itself and the administrative commissions are not the sole keys to an effective equal opportunity program. They are essential elements, and without them there would be no program. However, to have a successful program, all or most of the following conditions and elements must be present:

1. A local economy that is expanding; or, at least, one that is capable of offering job opportunities for a substantial part of the local population.
2. An alert, articulate, aggressive, and astutely-led civil rights or minority group movement.
3. Sufficient strength among the minority groups to impress the political powers and a concomitant political posture of support for strong and vigorous administration of the law.
4. A well-conceived, carefully-drafted fair employment law which grants to the administrative commission the powers to undertake affirmative compliance measures with employers, employment agencies, and labor unions.
5. A strong, independent administrative commission — adequately financed, well staffed and, above all, enjoying the support of the political powers.
6. A broadly-based community program involving employers, labor, educational, and civic institutions — vigorously committed to extending employment opportunity to all.
7. An educational system geared to meeting the needs of all the children, youth, and adults, particularly those whose cultural background is not equal to the demands of the modern economy.

Once more, in final summary, equal opportunity laws are essential elements of an effective equal opportunity program, but they are no more than elements of a much more comprehensive program.

4

EQUAL OPPORTUNITY AND EQUAL PAY*

Herbert R. Northrup**

During World War II, the shortage of labor, successful agitation for fair employment opportunities, and pressure from the government to open up jobs to all those who were being asked to risk their lives in war, combined to increase job opportunities for Negroes in areas which had hitherto been closed to them.[1] The booming demand for the products of industry which followed World War II helped to insure further gains for Negroes, as did the industrial expansion which resulted from the Korean War.

Nevertheless, even in these good times, Negroes suffered far more from unemployment than did white workers. The data in Table 1 show that Negro unemployment has always been substantially in excess of that for white workers; that male Negro unemployment has been twice that of whites since 1950; and that in every recession period since World War II—1949, 1954, and 1958—it has taken Negroes much longer to get back on the employment rolls than has been the case with white workers. Indeed, it can be stated that Negroes have not recovered from the 1958 recession. First fired and last rehired is still, therefore, an unhappy, but apt, description of the Negro worker's situation.

Other minorities—Puerto Ricans, Mexicans, American-Indians, and others—also often suffer discrimination in the labor market. Since the numbers of Negroes are so much greater, and their problems usually so much more severe, an analysis of equal opportunity laws in terms of Negro employment problems will provide a sound basis for understanding and evaluating the problems of minorities and the laws designed for their protection. A final

---

*This article appeared in the *Management of Personnel Quarterly*, Fall, 1964, vol. III, no. 3, pp. 17-26.

**Professor in and Chairman of the Department of Industry at The Wharton School of Finance and Commerce at the University of Pennsylvania.

section of the article discusses laws designed to prevent discrimination because of sex or age.

TABLE I

UNEMPLOYMENT RATES BY SEX AND COLOR

	MALE			FEMALE		
Year	White	Non-White	Ratio N—W/W	White	Non-White	Ratio N—W/W
1940*	15.5	19.3	1.3	13.5	16.8	1.2
1948	3.1	5.1	1.7	3.4	5.2	1.5
1949	5.2	8.8	1.7	5.2	7.2	1.4
1950	4.5	8.9	1.7	4.9	7.8	1.6
1951	2.4	4.4	1.8	3.7	5.4	1.5
1952	2.2	4.5	2.0	2.9	4.8	1.7
1953	2.2	4.4	2.0	2.6	3.7	1.4
1954	4.4	9.2	2.1	4.9	8.2	1.7
1955	3.4	8.2	2.4	3.9	7.5	1.9
1956	3.1	7.3	2.4	3.8	8.0	2.1
1957	3.7	8.4	2.3	4.3	7.4	1.7
1958	6.1	13.7	2.2	6.2	10.8	1.7
1959	4.6	11.5	2.5	5.3	9.5	1.8
1960	4.8	10.7	2.2	5.3	9.5	1.8
1961	5.7	12.9	2.3	6.5	11.9	1.8
1962	4.6	11.0	2.4	5.5	11.1	2.0
1963	4.7	10.6	2.3	5.8	11.3	1.9

*The 1940 figure is from the census of that year.
Source: Unpublished paper "The Case for Structural Unemployment" by Robert Evans, Jr., based on data from the *Manpower Report of the President*, 1964. Courtesy of Professor Evans.

The Declining Utilization of Unskilled Labor

The experiences of the 1958 recession and the five-year period thereafter deserve special analysis in any discussion of the problems of Negro workers, for it was in this period that the proportion of Negro unemployment exceeded 10 per cent (Table 1), and during which the income differential between the white and Negro population widened. Of special significance is that the demand for production workers in industry has been relatively constant since 1956, while the demand for unskilled labor in industry has remained absolutely constant since then. Meantime, the great employment expansions have occurred in white collar and professional jobs. But Negroes have been concentrated in the unskilled jobs and have been underrepresented in the white collar jobs.

Moreover, three trends which culminated during this period accentuated the Negro employment problem. The first was industry's rapid substitution of machinery for unskilled labor. Ever higher minimum wages, the rapid rise under union pressure of unskilled labor rates, and the competition from West European and Japanese industry (with the much lower labor rates paid in these countries) all spurred this labor-replacement program. Negroes laid off as a result of these developments and young Negroes who found that industry was no longer hiring the unskilled became significant proportions of the hard-core, long-term unemployed.[2]

Concentration in Cities

Combined with this trend toward the elimination of unskilled labor were the rapid mechanization of agriculture and its declining importance in our economy. By 1960 only 6 per cent of the work force were employed on the farms. Nearly 2.5 million farms disappeared between 1940 and 1959, and all the loss was recorded for farms smaller than 260 acres.[3]

Negro and white farmers have flocked to the big cities of the North and West, which are now the growing centers of Negro population. One-fifth of the Negro population now resides in six such cities—New York, Chicago, Philadelphia, Detroit, Washington, and Los Angeles. Southern cities also have had increased Negro concentrations resulting from rural outmigration.[4] Thousands of Negroes who under conditions existent prior to World War II would have been underemployed as marginal farm workers migrated to the cities. As an unskilled group, they found that the demand of industry for their services was slight, and therefore they frequently were unemployed and on relief.

Declining Industrial Role of the Cities

While Negroes were migrating to the cities, industry was dispersing its plants away from the older locations. High city taxes, inadequate automobile transportation and parking facilities, and high-cost, outmoded, multi-story buildings, combined with the movement of the population westward, encouraged industry to expand facilities in the newer areas, either in the South or Midwest, or in suburban rather than in city locations.[5] Thus as the Negroes migrated in, often industry migrated out, or at least expanded elsewhere than where the new concentrations of Negro workers were found.

Negro Protests of the Early 1960's

Along with the increasing difficulties which Negroes were having in the labor force was the problem of segregation in public accommodations in Southern and some border states. To the increasing number of educated Negroes, this was particularly unpleasant. In 1961, Negro college students in the South began a series of "sit-ins" in restaurants and other places of service which denied Negroes equal treatment. Boycotts of businesses, patterned after a most successful one initiated by followers of Dr. Martin Luther King against a Montgomery, Alabama bus company, were initiated to fight segregation. The use of these economic weapons resulted in substantial successes in the attack against segregated facilities.

The results achieved by this direct action, combined with the slow results in obtaining school desegregation a decade after the United States Supreme Court ruled against such segregation, led to more direct action. In the North, the use of the weapons of conflict —boycott and picketing, especially—was aimed at improving the job opportunities of Negroes. In Philadelphia, for example, *The Bulletin,* one of the three daily papers, the Sun Oil Company, and the A & P supermarket chain all were boycotted into increasing the number of Negro employees. Whereas the fight in the South was for equal accommodations, that in the North was for better jobs —undoubtedly a step that the South will be pushed for once the goal of equal accommodations has proceeded a pace.

As in all protest periods, the direct action of Negroes to assert rights in the early 1960's gave rise to abuses and violence, with riots and numerous serious clashes of pickets and marchers with counter-demonstrators and police, North and South. These outbursts contributed to the intervention of the Kennedy, and later Johnson, Administrations and the passage in 1964 of an equal rights law with the first national fair employment, or equal employment opportunity, legislation.

Background of 1964 Equal Opportunity Law

The 1964 equal employment opportunity law was not enacted without prior executive and legislative experience in the field. In the early New Deal period, it was found, for example, that Negroes were systematically shut out of employment on public works projects. Accordingly, a program requiring the use of Negro workers consistent with their representation in the area population was inaugurated as early as 1934 and achieved some success. Non-discriminatory provisions were also incorporated into bills for defense and wartime training.[6]

Presidential Committees

Then in order to avert a "march on Washington" by Negroes protesting continued job discrimination, President Franklin D. Roosevelt, by executive order, established a Fair Employment Practices Committee, which operated throughout the war period. Although the committee held hearings, dramatized the issue of Negro employment, and undoubtedly contributed to the increase in the utilization of Negro manpower, its lack of statutory authority prevented it from securing compliance with its orders when discriminating employers or unions balked. Thus it failed to make an appreciable change in the employment practices of the railroad or West Coast shipbuilding industries where employers' discrimination was buttressed by active support, if not leadership.[7]

The President's Committee on Fair Employment Practice ended its life in 1945 after being denied funds by Congress. It was followed by a succession of committees whose jurisdiction was limited to establishments doing business under contracts with the federal government. These committees were first set up by President Truman and then reorganized by each succeeding President. For the most part they relied on persuasion and publicity but until the Kennedy Committee on Fair Employment Problems, headed by then Vice-President Lyndon B. Johnson, was established in 1961, these committees did not exert much authority. Moreover, they lacked jurisdiction over unions, who are not party to government controls, but who, particularly in the construction industry, are often, as the suppliers of labor under closed shop contracts,[8] the focal point of discrimination.

The Kennedy Committee was the first to spell out sanctions and to give notice of attempting to enforce them. Such sanctions are ultimately the cancellation of the government contract. At least four contractors were blacklisted, at least temporarily, for non-compliance with fair employment, and threats of similar action were made to obtain results.[9] Such sanctions are often unworkable, because the cancellation of a key contract can endanger the country's defense program or otherwise interfere with the performance of a necessary governmental function.

Plans for Progress

Perhaps the most effective work inaugurated in this sphere was the "Plans for Progress," which were initiated by the then Vice-President Johnson early in the Kennedy Administration. Many of the country's large industrial employers were persuaded to review their employment practices, submit facts on employment by race and occupation, and report on programs designed to improve their employment of minorities. Although some companies have remained indifferent after signing pledges, a number have made vigorous and successful attempts to further Negro employment. In addition, others, which took the equal opportunity pledge lightly, changed their minds after Negro demonstrations began, and commenced pursuing a more vigorous policy toward fair employment.[10]

To overcome the weakness of its lack of jurisdiction over unions, another "Plan for Progress" was established by the Kennedy Committee. Most unions signed, pledging equal opportunity on jobs and in all aspects of union affairs, but a number of independent railroad and petroleum unions and seventeen AFL-CIO affiliates declined to participate. These unions were primarily in the industries where union discrimination has bulked large.[11]

State Fair Employment Practice Commissions

While the federal government was attempting to improve Negro job opportunities by extra-legal executive improvisations, twenty-five states enacted enforceable fair employment or equal opportunity laws.[12] (See Figure I). Beginning in 1945 with the enactment of the New York and New Jersey laws, those laws now cover most of the industrial states of the North and West plus the border states of Delaware and Missouri. In addition several cities, including Baltimore (the only border metropolis involved), Cleveland, Minneapolis, Philadelphia, Pittsburgh, St. Paul, and Toledo, enacted laws before the states in which they are located followed suit. Usually the state laws then permitted the municipal agencies to handle cases arising within their boundaries.[13]

Twenty-two of the state laws provide for a "fair employment," "equal opportunity," or "human rights" commission to administer the laws. These commissions may hear complaints, take testimony, hold hearings, issue orders, and apply to courts for enforcement. They are patterned to a large extent on the administrative model of the National Labor Relations Board or of state labor relations boards, except that in five states—Alaska, Delaware, Hawaii, New Jersey, and Oregon—the commissions are specially-created divisions of established state departments instead of independent agencies. Three states—Idaho, Iowa, and Vermont—make discrimination a misdemeanor punishable by fine or imprisonment. In such cases,

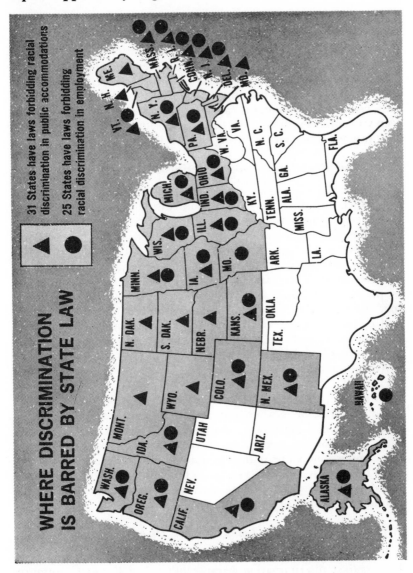

FIGURE I

Reprinted from *U.S. News & World Report,* published at
Washington. Copyright 1964 U.S. News & World Report, Inc.

the aggrieved individual must file his case with the appropriate law
enforcement agency, where it is handled like other misdemeanors.

Although state commissions against discrimination have the power to hold public hearings, most have utilized this power very sparingly. Following the lead of the pioneer New York agency, these agencies attempt first to accomplish their aims by conciliation. This is usually successful, because of the threat of bad publicity involved in a public hearing. Thus New York's agency ordered only twenty-nine complaint cases to public hearings in the first fifteen years of its existence, and two-thirds of these were settled before they reached this stage or during the hearing itself.[14]

State Law Prohibitions and Administration

Most of the state laws are modeled on the pioneer New York law which prohibits *employers* from discriminating in any way in the employment relationship—hire, promotion, discharge conditions, or wages—because of race, color, creed, or national origin; prohibits *unions* from excluding, expelling, or in any other way discriminating on such a basis; prohibits *employers* or *employment agencies* from advertising or causing to be circulated in any way or placed in an application for employment, any such discriminatory limitations or specifications; and prohibits *employers, unions,* and *employment agencies* from discriminating in any way against a person because of that person's opposition to the type of discrimination proscribed under the law.

All the commissions—state and local—are meagerly staffed except for those of New York State and Philadelphia. Only New York has well-compensated, full-time commission members. The remainder of the state or local commissioners are part-time functionaries, or governmental personnel, who are paid a modest salary or a per diem rate and are free to devote time to other pursuits. Where the commissioners are part-time state employees, there are usually some full-time staff members who do the basic work. But, as already noted, only New York State and Philadelphia have well-paid, abundantly staffed organizations.[15]

Effectiveness of State Laws Against Discrimination

It is difficult to assay directly the effect or effectiveness of state laws against discrimination because other factors have constantly acted and reacted upon employment opportunities of minority groups. It is obvious that many Negroes and members of other minority groups have obtained jobs because of the existence of these laws. For example, soon after the passage of the New York law, banks and department stores in New York City commenced utilizing Negro tellers and clerks to a degree heretofore not done.

It is also obvious that in all of the states which have enforceable fair employment laws, discrimination because of race has not ceased. One still finds companies with sparse minority group employment; a study conducted by the author for the 1938-1943 period found substantial discrimination by railroad and building trades unions applied with very few exceptions, and twenty years later the same was true both in states having fair employment laws and in those which have not.[16]

The careful study of state fair employment practice laws by Professors Norgren and Hill credited all state agencies with improving minority group employment status, but they found that the New York law and agency were by far the most effective. Norgren and Hill point out that the New York Commission has concluded agreements with several thousand firms, where it found discrimination, to alter past practices. The New York Commission follows up these agreements by periodic studies and as a result can point to a substantial altering of past practices, including those in areas where traditionally Negroes have not been employed: banking, insurance, other white collar occupations, and supervisory positions in manufacturing. Similar, but less comprehensive, progress was found by Norgren and Hill in New Jersey and Philadelphia.[17]

A specific reason for New York's superior progress is, according to this study, the manner in which the New York Commission, on its own initiative, utilizes its superior budgetary and personnel resources to study the racial patterns of an entire industry operating in the state and then makes recommendations (backed up by possible sanctions) to alter discriminatory practices. Where such an agency does not take the lead in altering employment patterns, there is no social organization to play the role which unions have in unfair labor practice cases. A worker who believes that he has been discriminated against because of race or color may secure some assistance from a race relations organization or a legal aid group, but no such organization exists which is primarily engaged in handling such matters before fair employment practice agencies. As a result, many complainants do not follow through even if they make complaints.[18]

Unions and State Fair Employment Laws

The state fair employment commissions seem to have had less success in dealing with unions, although all unions which barred Negroes by written constitutional provisions had deleted these rules by 1964 and although hundreds of workers are now union members who would have been excluded before the passage of state fair employment practice laws. Nevertheless, and in spite of the fact that union, and particularly AFL-CIO, support was often a decisive factor in gaining state legislative approval of fair employment laws, some of the most intransigent cases brought before state fair employment commissions, and usually the first cases to go to public hearings or the courts, have involved unions.[19]

Professor Ray Marshall's careful appraisal found that by the fall of 1963, state commissions had "not changed the basic employment patterns in most unionized industries." He found local unions relatively impervious to moral pressures and cited a number of cases where court action (including in one case, fining of the local by a Connecticut court in a contempt action) was necessary, or where it took mass demonstrations by Negroes to gain union membership. He concluded that "recalcitrant local unions will change their practices when their power sources are threatened by government regulation, retaliation from the Negro community, and alienation of public opinion." But to be effective, these sanctions have to be applied directly to the unions and not to the employer when the unions are at fault.[20] It was not, for example, until the New York agency took a Sheet Metal Workers' local to court that it abolished its rule limiting apprentice candidates to relations of the all-white local's members.

The Federal Law of 1964

Despite the relative success of the state commissions, Negro employment progress after 1958 was actually less than that of whites, so that by 1962 the income differential between whites and Negroes widened. Agitation over employment problems in the North and continued facility segregation in the South resulted in the national consensus which produced the Civil Rights Act of 1964. Title VII of this act deals with equal employment opportunity and is effective as of July 2, 1965, one year after the passage of the act.

Coverage and Content

The equal employment opportunity law applies to all employers who employed 25 or more persons at least 20 weeks the preceding year but excludes the federal government (which is nonetheless directed to insure non-discriminatory employment within its own ranks); state governments or subdivisions thereof; private membership clubs (except unions); religious organizations; or the employment of aliens outside their country. Additional exemptions were granted for one year to employers having fewer than 100 employees; for two years to those having fewer than 75 employees; and for three years to those having fewer than 50 employees. Other than explicit exemptions, the act applies to employers who are defined as such by the Landrum-Griffin Act, which contains the most comprehensive such description in federal law.

The equal opportunity law also applies to employment agencies, including the United States Employment Service, state and local employment services utilizing federal funds, anyone acting to procure employees for work, and unions which maintain hiring halls or procure employees for work. Finally, the law covers unions which have 100 members or more the first year, 75 or more the second year, 50 or more the third year, and 25 or more thereafter. Unions are thus covered in the same manner as employers. Moreover, unions are defined to include local, national, and intermediate bodies.

The basic proscriptions of the law are set forth in Figure II. The coverage of the law extends to joint labor-management committees and other organizations controlling apprenticeship—thus closing a loophole found in many state fair employment laws. It permits religion, sex,[21] or national origin to be utilized where valid occupational classification calls for such a distinction (e.g., a model, a Kosher butcher, or a teacher in a girls' school or in a religious seminary); it excludes from the coverage any protection to members of the Communist Party, or of any organization "required to register as a Communist action or Communist front organization by final order of the Subversive Activities Control Board pursuant to the Subversive Activities Control Act of 1950," and it also excludes persons from its protection who have failed to gain security clearance under any federal security program insofar as access to secret or confidential governmental work is concerned. In order to avert charges of discrimination involving such ordinary employment practices as regional wage differentials, benefits and seniority, the act permits an employer to apply such different standards to employees in different locations "provided that such differences are not the result of an intention to discriminate because of race, color, religion, sex or national origin." The law also permits employers on Indian reservations to continue to give employment preferences to Indians.

Administration

The act established an Equal Employment Opportunity Commission, a five-man independent agency appointed by the President with the consent of the Senate. Like other federal agencies, this

FIGURE II
Unlawful Employment Practices Under Title VII
CIVIL RIGHTS ACT OF 1964

DISCRIMINATION BECAUSE OF RACE, COLOR, RELIGION, SEX, OR NATIONAL ORIGIN

Sec. 703. (a) It shall be an unlawful employment practice for an employer—
(1) to fail or refuse to hire or to discharge any individual, or otherwise to discriminate against any individual with respect to his compensation, terms, conditions, or privileges of employment, because of such individual's race, color, religion, sex, or national origin; or
(2) to limit, segregate, or classify his employees in any way which would deprive or tend to deprive any individual of employment opportunities or otherwise adversely affect his status as an employee, because of such individual's race, color, religion, sex, or national origin.
(b) It shall be an unlawful employment practice for an employment agency to fail or refuse to refer for employment, or otherwise to discriminate against, any individual because of his race, color, religion, sex, or national origin, or to classify or refer for employment any individual on the basis of his race, color, religion, sex, or national origin.
(c) It shall be an unlawful employment practice for a labor organization—
(1) to exclude or to expel from its membership, or otherwise to discriminate against, any individual because of his race, color, religion, sex, or national origin;
(2) to limit, segregate, or classify its membership or to classify or fail to refuse to refer for employment any individual, in any way which would deprive or tend to deprive any individual of employment opportunities, or would limit such employment opportunities or otherwise adversely affect his status as an employee or as an applicant for employment, because of such individual's race, color, religion, sex, or national origin; or
(3) to cause or attempt to cause an employer to discriminate against an individual in violation of this section.
(d) It shall be an unlawful employment practice for any employer, labor organization, or joint labor-management committee controlling apprenticeship or other training or retraining, including on-the-job training programs to discriminate against any individual because of his race, color, religion, sex, or national origin in admission to, or employment in, any program established to provide apprenticeship or other training.

* * * * *

OTHER UNLAWFUL EMPLOYMENT PRACTICES

Sec. 704. (a) It shall be an unlawful employment practice for an employer to discriminate against any of his employees or applicants for employment, for an employment agency to discriminate against any individual, or for a labor organization to discriminate against any member thereof or applicant for membership, because he has opposed any practice made an unlawful employment practice by this title, or because he has made a charge, testified, assisted, or participated in any manner in an investigation, proceeding, or hearing under this title.
(b) It shall be an unlawful employment practice for an employer, labor organization, or employment agency to print or publish or cause to be printed or published any notice or advertisement relating to employment by such an employer or membership in or any classification or referral for employment by such a labor organization, or relating to any classification or referral for employment by such an employment agency, indicating any preference, limitation, specification, or discrimination, based on race, color, religion, sex, or national origin, except that such a notice or advertisement may indicate a preference, limitation, specification, or discrimination based on religion, sex, or national origin when religion, sex, or national origin is a bona fide occupational qualification for employment.

commission is empowered to establish regional offices and to appoint staff pursuant to civil service regulations, to subpoena records, and to prescribe rules and regulations for carrying out its duties.

Following the provisions of the New York and most other state laws, the commission is required to attempt first to settle complaints by conciliation. Moreover, where there is a state law or municipal ordinance proscribing discrimination or providing for a means of relief, no action may be taken by the Equal Employment Opportunity Commission until it has notified and given the state or local agency 90 days to act; or if the state or local agency is in its first year of existence, 180 days to act. The law specifically permits state laws to exist concurrently, provided that such laws do not require or permit the doing of any act which would be an unlawful employment practice under the federal law. Moreover, the commission is urged to enter into agreements with state agencies for the utilization of the latter's services to carry out the functions of the federal law. Records are required to be kept by employers, unions and employment agencies, but if such records must be kept for state agencies or by Presidential Executive Order 10925, pursuant to government contracts, and there is no question of compliance, no additional records need be kept.

Where an alleged violation of the law is not subject to a state or local law, or such state or local agencies have not acted, and where conciliation has not succeeded, the aggrieved may file a civil action in an appropriate United States District Court. The Court may appoint an attorney free of charge to the complainant and may permit the United States Attorney General to intervene. The Court may enjoin the practice and may order reinstatement, back pay, hiring, union membership for an employee, or other remedies, provided the unlawful practice was found to be *intentional* on the part of the respondent, and provided the discrimination was not for any other reason than what is unlawful under the act. Courts may also appoint masters to determine facts. Continued non-compliance after an order permits the commission to commence proceedings to compel compliance. (See Figure III for a diagram of the procedures).

An additional section (707) permits the Attorney General to bring a civil action where he believes that any person or group of persons is engaged in a pattern or practice of resistance to the full enjoyment of any of the rights guaranteed by Title VII of the act, requesting relief, including an injunction, to overcome such resistance. The Attorney General may request the appointment of a three-judge court to hear such a case, in which case appeal is directly to the Supreme Court, thus by-passing the Court of Appeals.

Before proceeding to court, the commission may hold a public hearing, examine witnesses, and make findings. Individuals subpoenaed or otherwise objecting to an investigation may appeal to the courts within twenty days after being served.

Analysis

How the equal opportunity law will work out in practice is of course dependent on many factors, but on the basis of the law

FIGURE III

Procedures, Title VII, Civil Rights Act of 1964

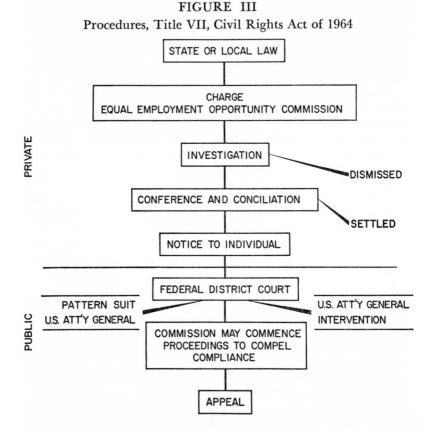

itself, and on the experience of the state laws already in effect, certain predictions may be made with reasonable safety.

In the first place, the major impact may be on the South. There are two basic reasons for this. First, by leaving authority in the hands of already existing state and municipal agencies, the federal law does not alter the situation in most Northern states, except insofar as these existing agencies may be spurred into more aggressive activity by the fear of losing their jurisdiction to the federal government; or insofar as the Negro community might take advantage in a more aggressive manner of the rights under the state laws, now that the federal government is also committed to furthering equal opportunity.

In the second place, before the federal law became effective nearly every major corporation in America had already reappraised its minority group employment policies, and many were moving to implement these appraisals with effective programs to employ Negro personnel both in greater depth and throughout their organizations. This was particularly true of companies which dealt directly with consumers, but by no means excluded others. Negro boycotts and demonstrations in 1963–1964, pressure from governmental contract provisions or "Plans for Progress," and a determination to avoid problems while there was still time all played a role. By June, 1964, Negro college graduates were among the most sought-after graduates in America.[22] Negro unemployment rates declined during early 1964 at a more rapid rate than did those of white workers, including a significant drop in unemployment among Negro teenagers and expansion of Negroes in the white collar and professional jobs.[23] Most of these gains occurred in Northern industrial centers, although national corporations in many Southern centers were increasingly moving toward fair employment.

For the North, therefore, compulsory fair employment practice will not be new; for the South, it will require considerable adjustment. One may expect Southern legislatures to pass fair employment laws in order to take jurisdiction of these questions, but the federal agency can and will intervene if these laws are merely dodges.

But in neither North nor South will the equal opportunity law solve the Negro unemployment problem. The law does not qualify a man for a job. He must be able to do it. Despite recent gains, Negro unemployment remains twice that of whites. Only through training and development can this problem be rectified. Now, however, there is hope for Negroes to take training—this is undoubtedly the main gain from the new law in addition to the jobs it will insure those already qualified, for real progress will require many years.

"Wagner Act" Stage in Fair Employment Legislation?

There are two other aspects to the equal opportunity law which deserve attention. In the real sense, it marks the "Wagner Act" stage of fair employment practice legislation. For the restrictions are entirely on those who might discriminate. But consider what can happen to an employer (or union or employment agency) who has a thoroughly fair employment policy by any objective standard. The law would apparently protect that employer from picketing or boycotts by groups aimed at subverting this policy. In addition, the Equal Opportunity Commission is authorized "upon the request of an employer, whose employees or some of them refuse or threaten to refuse to cooperate in effectuating [the law] . . . to assist in such effectuation by conciliation or such other remedial action is as provided by [this act]. . . .," which would seem to include a request by a court order.

On the other hand, there is nothing in the law to protect such an employer (or union or employment agency) from picketing, boycotts, or other economic action by minority groups that are not satisfied with the policies of such employer *even though the law is satisfied.* Thus an employer can be severely damaged even though he is in compliance with the law.

This is no remote possibility. There are several national and local organizations vying for support of the Negro community. In Philadelphia, the Congress of Racial Equality ordered a boycott of a building project after the unions and contractors had made a settlement on Negro employment agreed to by the National Association for the Advancement of Colored People. In California, CORE has picketed 20 of the Bank of America's 864 branches even though the bank was the first major employer in California to sign a formal statement of racial equality with the California Fair Employment Practice Commission. CORE justified this action because the bank declined to (1) waive its high school education requirements for Negroes which the bank insists upon for all new hires; and (2) supply CORE the elaborate statistics on employees which the bank had already supplied to the California Commission.[24]

Such occurrences have been sufficiently frequent to remind one of the period when the AFL and the CIO were struggling for power with the employer caught in the middle. Will the "Wagner Act"-type Civil Rights Act of 1964 be followed by a "Taft-Hartley Act"-type some years hence, containing restrictions on minority group activity as well as protecting minority group rights? And later, will there follow a "Landrum-Griffin Act"-type also protecting individuals within minority group organizations?

Relation to Other Laws

As we have noted, the equal opportunity law drafters were

very careful to consider the effect of the new law on similar state and local enactments. But there is no mention of Taft-Hartley, Landrum-Griffin, or other federal statutes. For example, a union may be charged with an unlawful employment practice by the Equal Opportunity Commission for discrimination against Negroes at the same time it is being certified as the bargaining agent for these same discriminated-against employees by the National Labor Relations Board. The equal opportunity law also sheds no light on whether picketing or boycotts by racial groups are "labor disputes" within the Norris-La Guardia Act, a decision which judges will have to make before deciding whether such demonstrations can be enjoined. Similarly no attempt was made to be certain that the new civil rights law conforms with the recently-enacted equal pay law, discussed later in this article with the prohibitions on sex discrimination. Thus, our federal labor legislation continues to grow without reference to its impact on existing federal law or to the complexities in which labor and management find themselves when caught in the cross-fire between two laws or agencies.

Effect on State Employment Services

All states maintain employment offices and related services which are heavily subsidized by the federal government. These offices, like private ones, make little attempt to alter the preferences of their "customers." Federal funds are allocated on the basis of number of placements. Hence state agencies are anxious to make placement, rather than to risk alienating an employer.

In the South, these state agencies are either directly segregated, or located by neighborhood and therefore "de facto" segregated. Over 90 per cent of their nonwhite placements are likely to be in service or unskilled work, whereas nearly that percentage of white placements are in higher categories.[25] It is obvious that the new Equal Opportunity Commission can commence its policing of employment agencies by starting with those which utilize federal funds.

DISCRIMINATION BECAUSE OF SEX

The year 1964 was a banner one for the feminists. In June, the "equal pay for equal work" law, enacted in 1963, became effective.[26] And then, just a few weeks later, Congress passed the equal opportunity law which forbade discrimination by sex, as well as by race, color, creed, or national origin. This law, as noted, is effective as of mid-1965.

Equal Pay for Equal Work

The equal pay law was enacted as an amendment to the Fair Labor Standards Act. Therefore its coverage is identical with that of the federal minimum wage law, and it is administered by the Wage-Hour and Public Contracts Division of the United States Department of Labor. For one year, the Division announced it would advise employers about compliance without penalties; thereafter enforcement will be the same as under minimum wage legislation.

The equal pay law in brief provides that it is illegal to pay women (or conversely, men) less than men (women) for doing the same work, and it is unlawful for a union or its agents to cause or attempt to cause an employer to discriminate in wages on the basis of sex. Furthermore, existing differentials can not be eliminated by a wage reduction. The act contains a general exception for differentials based on any factor other than sex. In addition, three specific exemptions—wage differentials based on merit, seniority, and piece-rates or incentives—are specifically permitted.

It may take years of litigation to determine what is or is not equal pay. For example, if the employment of women requires additional material-handling personnel in order to move heavy parts, obviously women are not doing the same work as men who could move the material as well as do the work being done by women. But there are many gray areas which are not so obvious. The best protection for both employers and union is to have a well thought-out formalized wage structure based on job evaluation so that rates are as objectively established as possible. The application of such a program can eliminate any vestiges of wage differentials, and, perhaps more important, preclude charges that they exist. The fringe areas may also cause trouble, but because this area is closely involved in discrimination because of sex, we shall discuss it in the section below which deals with that topic.

State Equal Pay Laws

In addition to the federal law, equal pay laws exist in twenty-four states.[27] The earliest laws were enacted by Michigan and Montana in 1919; the latest, by Missouri and Vermont in 1963. These laws vary in coverage and content and do not seem to have generated either much litigation or any substantial changes in industry's pay practices. Testimony of federal government and union officials maintained that this proved that a federal law was needed.[28] Little evidence was produced before congressional committees that wide wage discrimination against women actually exists, although there is no doubt that women are subject to job discrimination. It is for this reason that the equal opportunity law may have a far greater effect on the earnings of women than will the equal pay bill. For the latter is silent on job opportunities—it merely requires equal pay whenever women do equal work.

Impact of the Two Laws

The equal opportunity law's provision against discrimination because of sex could well have a major impact on industry, unions, and employment agencies. For example, must industry open up its secretarial jobs to men? Can an air line refuse automatically the application of a qualified aviatrix for a pilot's job? Will the help-wanted advertisements no longer be able to be divided into male and female? Will women be regularly students in executive-development seminars? One could go on, adding numerous other questions concerning the manner in which industry has developed a sex-occupational division of employment over the years and the potential for change therein as a result of the equal opportunity law.

To be sure, the role of women in the labor market has been fluid. But adherence to the patterns of the past will be no guarantee that illegal discrimination will not result. The so-called "Negro revolution" of the early 1960's could result also in a vast expansion of employment opportunities for women—and perhaps even the return of the male secretary, now almost extinct.

There are a whole host of practices in the fringe area and in state laws which raise some very serious questions of conflict with the new equal opportunity laws. For example, if retirement for women is required at 62 but of men at 65, is this sex discrimination? Frequently in health and welfare plans, dependent coverage is included for men but not for women. This would appear to be an obvious discrimination and also raises questions of equal pay for equal work. Some companies have rules that pregnant women must resign or that married women can no longer work. Is this discrimination? For example, must the air lines retain married stewardesses?

In the realm of state legislation there appear to be many conflicts with the new federal equal opportunity law. State laws which require that women cannot work beyond a certain time obviously discriminate against women. Minimum wage laws exclusively for women, maximum hours laws exclusively for women, and laws requiring the layoff of pregnant women at a certain time also discriminate against women. Are they in conflict with the new law and therefore unconstitutional under the preemption doctrine? These are just a few of the many questions which this law raises and which must be adjudicated.

DISCRIMINATION BECAUSE OF AGE

One more type of discrimination is forbidden by law—that because of age. Ten states[29] and Puerto Rico outlaw such discrimination in their fair employment practice legislation, and eight others[30] have separate laws dealing with this subject. Although these laws really represent a statement of public concern rather than much more, there have been cases arising under them. For example, in Wisconsin, a recent case found an employer guilty of age discrimination by reason of his forcing certain employees to retire before the regular retirement age. Some state laws, for example that of Pennsylvania, exempt actions made pursuant to provisions of pension plans approved by the U. S. Internal Revenue Service. But there is a fundamental conflict between the early retirement proponents and those opposing any discrimination because of age. The matter may arise at the federal level. For although the equal opportunity law now does not proscribe age discrimination, it provides for a study by the Secretary of Labor with a report to Congress by June 30, 1965. One may well expect the report to suggest outlawing such discrimination also.

CONCLUDING REMARKS

A great new area of federal regulation will commence when the equal opportunity section becomes effective in 1965. Unlike the analagous case of the Wagner Act in 1935, large employers are not fighting the law. Rather they are moving to comply with it before it becomes effective. Likewise employer organizations—the National Association of Manufacturers, the Chamber of Commerce of the United States, their affiliates and other employer groups—are offering constructive advice and seminars on the law, what it means and how it works, in fact and in spirit, within its confines and requirements.

Similarly, the leaders of labor unions are urging their members and affiliates to obey the law and to open up doors to Negroes and other minorities where equal treatment does not exist. One hears no rancor such as that which greeted both the Taft-Hartley and Landrum-Griffin Acts.

To be sure, there are those in industry and labor who are opposing fair employment in fact and/or in spirit. Some do so for fear of losing customers or electorates. But those are a small and probably dwindling minority.

In a real sense, therefore, the equal opportunity law is being received with more favor by those whom it would regulate than any other labor legislation in our history. How the law will work out will depend to a large extent upon those who administer it and upon those whom it would protect. Will the new bureaucracy which this law is bound to create attempt, like all its bureaucratic predecessors, constantly to expand the intent of Congress and therefore the scope of its work? Will minorities understand that equal opportunity means just that and no favored treatment or privilege without qualifications? How these two questions are answered will determine whether the favorable climate in which the law was inaugurated can endure.

FOOTNOTES

1. Problems of this period are discussed in Herbert R. Northrup, *Organized Labor and the Negro* (New York: Harper Bros., 1944) and Robert C. Weaver, *Negro Labor — A National Problem* (New York: Harcourt, Brace & Co., 1946).
2. For cases in point, see Richard C. Wilcock and Walter A. Franke, *Unwanted Workers* (New York: Free Press of Glencoe, Inc., 1963). Recent studies in South Bend, Indiana, following the 1963 closing of the Studebaker plant, again demonstrated the difficulties which Negroes have had in gaining employment.
3. *Manpower Report of the President*, 1964, p. 80.
4. *Ibid.*, p. 96.
5. See e.g., Daniel Creamer, *Changing Location of Manufacturing Employment, Part I: Changes by Type of Location, 1947-1961* (New York: National Industrial Conference Board, 1963), Studies in Business Economics, No. 83.
6. Weaver, *op. cit.*, Chapters II-IV.
7. Northrup, *op. cit.*, Chapters III and X.
8. The ban on closed shop, as written in the Taft-Hartley Act and as modified in the Landrum-Griffin Act, has never been effectively enforced in the construction industry.
9. See Paul H. Norgren and Samuel E. Hill, *Toward Fair Employment* (New York: Columbia University Press, 1964), p. 159.
10. Based on field interviews.
11. Norgren and Hill, *op. cit.*, pp. 171-175.
12. These states are in the chronological order of their enactment: New York and New Jersey (1945), Massachusetts (1946), Connecticut (1947), New Mexico, Oregon, Rhode Island, and Washington (1949), Alaska (1953), Michigan, Minnesota, and Pennsylvania (1955), Colorado and Wisconsin (1957), California and Ohio (1959), Delaware (1960), Idaho, Illinois, Kansas, and Missouri (1961), Indiana, Iowa, and Vermont (1963). However, Colorado, Wisconsin, Kansas, and Indiana had voluntary laws for several years before making them enforceable. In addition, Arizona, Nebraska, and Nevada enacted laws in 1961 prohibiting discrimination by firms supplying their state governments.
13. Norgren and Hill, *op. cit.*, p. 94, note 3.
14. *Ibid.*, pp. 106-107.
15. *Ibid.*, pp. 96-104.
16. Northrup, *op. cit.*, Chapters II and III.
17. Norgren and Hill, *loc. cit.*
18. Norgren and Hill buttress their arguments in favor of the New York state law by citing census data which show much greater improvement for Negroes in New York than in comparable states. But the validity of this is subject to limitations because of various industry mixes, migration, and other factors. Nevertheless their conclusion that New York has the most effective law seems correct.

19. This section is based upon the work of Professor Ray Marshall, whose recently published book, *The Negro and Organized Labor* (New York: John Wiley & Sons, Inc., 1965), is the most complete on the subject of Negro-union relations.

20. See the testimony of Dr. Marshall in *Nation's Manpower Revolution: Hearings before the Subcommittee on Employment and Manpower of the Committee on Labor and Public Welfare.* U. S. Senate, 84th Congress, 1st Session, 1963, Part 4, pp. 1192-1210.

21. The question of discrimination by sex is discussed later in this article.

22. See *New York Times,* June 7, 1964.

23. *Monthly Report on the Labor Force,* April, 1964, p. 7.

24. *Business Week,* June 13, 1964.

25. Norgren and Hill, *op. cit.,* pp. 35-39.

26. Labor agreements have up to an extra year to conform to the law.

27. Alaska, Arizona, Arkansas, California, Colorado, Connecticut, Hawaii, Illinois, Maine, Massachusetts, Michigan, Missouri, Montana, New Hampshire, New Jersey, New York, Ohio, Oregon, Pennsylvania, Rhode Island, Vermont, Washington, Wisconsin, and Wyoming.

28. See, e.g., U.S. Women's Bureau, *Economic Indicators Relating to Equal Pay,* pamphlet 9, 1963, for a summary of the evidence which does exist.

29. Connecticut, Delaware, Hawaii, Massachusetts, New Jersey, New York, Oregon, Pennsylvania, Washington, and Wisconsin; and Puerto Rico.

30. Alaska, California, Colorado, Louisiana, Massachusetts, Nebraska, Ohio, and Rhode Island.

PART III

Equal Opportunity at the Company Level

5

A VOLUNTARY APPROACH TO EQUAL OPPORTUNITY

Harry C. Baker*

Many of the problems of the underprivileged among minority groups are varied, frustratingly complex and, at least in appearance, insoluble: employment, housing, education, welfare, public accommodations — to name only a few. Because they are problems of people, their consideration and resolution are inhibited by the strong emotional climate which surrounds them.

A few general observations about the solution of these economic and social problems are made before some views on the topic "A Voluntary Approach to Equal Opportunity" are discussed. There appears to be general agreement that there is an inter-relationship between most of these socio-economic problems and, as a result, many of us are inclined to seek one common denominator — a sort of "pat answer" which, when properly implemented, will result in substantial improvement on all fronts simultaneously. We should resist the temptation to seek one solution for all of these problems for the best of all possible reasons: it does not work. After making that flat declaration, I will be the first to subscribe to such an easy approach and limit my remarks to equal employment opportunity in industry.

It is difficult for either the average layman or the professional practitioner in the field of personnel administration to study this question without interjecting personal views. But we can draw one conclusion, and it is an objective one: the established polls show that minority group leaders are almost unanimously maintaining that, out of the total area in which minority groups seek rights and opportunities, the least real progress has been made in the area of highest priority — employment and jobs.

---

*Manager, Employee Relations Department, International Harvester Company.

Where Negroes are turned down for jobs, how much is due to outright discrimination, and how much takes place because of a genuine lack of qualification? Of course, one would expect a wide variation of opinion on this among the so-called extremists on both sides and among the least informed groups. More significant, therefore, is the disparity of views of the more responsible company executives and Negro leaders.

According to a survey of a leading firm, only 7 per cent of company executives believed that Negroes were turned down for jobs because of prejudice. Twenty-four per cent thought the turndown was due to a combination of prejudice and lack of qualification. On the other hand, 54 per cent of the Negro leaders attributed the turndowns to prejudice alone and 43 per cent to a combination of prejudice and lack of qualification. In other words, 97 per cent of the Negro leaders, but only 31 per cent of the company executives, see prejudice as a significant factor in job opportunity. With such divergent views, there is small wonder that a solution to some of these problems is so long in coming.

In discussing this subject, there is an attractive temptation to chart the most neutral or popular course. This is true even though responsible management people believe in equal employment opportunity. If we in good conscience believe this, what are the issues or problems?

The real questions to be considered are:
1. How much unfair job discrimination exists against minority groups?
2. If inadequate education and training are restricting job opportunities for minority groups, what role, if any, should employers play in solving this problem?

A DIVERSITY OF VIEWS

Let us examine what some employers and others are saying toward these points.

One executive states: "It is just good citizenship and good business management for those of us in free enterprise to help furnish leadership in integration of minority groups into the employment rolls."

A second executive says: "We have hired several Negroes at the executive level — engineers, chemists, etc. But we refuse to be stampeded into mass hirings. We are eager and happy to have

Negroes on our staff, but we insist on maintaining our high standards in personnel."

A spokesman for another company says: "We're working on the problem very hard and are doing something about it. One thing we do not intend to do is to hire Negroes just to sit near the door so that they can be pointed out to visitors to show how liberal we are."

The president of another corporation believes that serious, prolonged civil rights tension as a part of the effort of the Negro to achieve his constitutional equality is unnecessary and threatens the economic welfare of this country.

A former secretary of labor once urged management to try to give jobs to Negroes who would not entirely qualify under present hiring standards. In this regard, he stated that it is not unthinkable that an employer should say: "If you have the aptitude but lack the skills, we'll train you."

It also has been suggested that it is important to avoid job discrimination because of color among the *lesser* qualified, on the basis that industry hires and upgrades many white people whose education and skills are marginal. The point is well-taken: equal treatment for the lesser-skilled Negroes is as much an obligation as for the semi-skilled or professional members.

It can be seen from these diverse opinions that the issue comes into its sharpest perspective. During the course of this paper, it is my intention to outline my views regarding some of the points raised in these observations.

EQUAL EMPLOYMENT OPPORTUNITY AT INTERNATIONAL HARVESTER COMPANY

Turning now to the things I know best in the realm of equal job opportunity, I would like to discuss non-discrimination and voluntary equal employment opportunity at the International Harvester Company. In doing so, it is certainly not my intention to try to glorify our way of doing things or to ennoble our treatment of these problems, but rather to limit my comments to those aspects of this subject with which I am most familiar.

One additional prefatory comment should be added relative to a voluntary approach to equal job opportunity. Except by degree and method, those things that we formerly did on a purely voluntary basis are substantially the same as we are required to do under the various laws, executive orders, and rulings. It may be that we are now spending a little more time assuring people outside the company that we are doing what we are doing. On the other hand, the very fact that we are called upon to furnish statistics and related information means that we, in turn, require more information from our operations; this may, therefore, suggest to them that we are now "policing" more closely their behavior in the area of non-discrimination. Thus, it may have the salutary effect of making them more conscious of their obligations.

First, a little about our early history in this area, and more importantly, about our current views, activities, and experiences under the several executive orders and our own pledges made as a Plans for Progress Company.

A Look At the Past

Our company has believed in voluntary non-discrimination and has worked toward that end for many years. Non-discrimination was formally enunciated by top executives as a fundamental policy more than forty years ago and was communicated to all managerial employees. More than twenty years ago the practice of publicizing this policy in writing came into general use. Since then it has been declared in union contracts, in employee handbooks, in advertising directed to communities where the company has established new factories, and in other media. In fact, it has been our historical practice to make a thorough investigation of the social mores of the business firms in cities where we are starting new operations, to discuss with community leaders our basic policy of equal employment opportunity, and to interview the appropriate business and civic leaders so that we can acquaint them with our policies and practices.

Since 1948 company policy has been stated as follows: "there shall be no discrimination against any person because of nationality, race, sex, political or religious affiliation, or membership in any labor or other lawful organization."

Although International Harvester was unquestionably among the early leaders in this area, its activities during the early years did not eliminate or, in some areas, even significantly reduce discriminatory employment practices. For example, it was not until a few years ago that the last vestiges of segregated facilities were removed from the last of several Southern facilities. Also there are a few operations where, while Negroes are employed in substantial numbers, yet, somewhat inexplicably, they are not employed in certain work areas or departments. More importantly, their absence cannot be easily explained away solely by something such as the obvious lack of qualified candidates.

Why do some of these practices continue to exist? For one thing, the company's policies are administered by people whose attitudes and emotions are pre-conditioned by environment, cultural background, and education. Also, the implementation of company policy in any area, certainly this one, is especially difficult where the communication of top policy must be disseminated to thousands of management people who represent us at the employee and community level. Has there been some discrimination at International Harvester under some of these policies? I am sure there has been — some due to pressures and influences of internal matters, some because of human failings, and others by external forces beyond our control. While we know that the overwhelming majority of our employees agree with the approach to this problem, there are always small pockets of resistance in any company concerning any program — particularly any change from the "status quo." Nevertheless, in the final analysis, the employer must provide the momentum for the elimination of discriminatory practices. It is a responsibility which cannot be delegated. Neither can it be conditioned upon its popular appeal.

Staff people charged with the administration of this policy will invariably find employees who will subscribe to the theory, admit the equity of the principle — but who then proceed to find one or more reasons why "here and now" in *their* operation, it cannot be put into practice. But if the initiative is taken, if the power of persuasion that is the tool of most corporate staff departments is discreetly exercised, it is amazing how easily the policy can be adhered to and the practice adopted — and without upsetting all the straw men that are supposed to tumble.

These temporary delays and obstacles should be looked upon as just that and nothing more. They should never be allowed to act as a justifiable excuse for failure to act. Even though company policy and its implementation did not eliminate all incidents of racial bias, fortunately, there have been some important successes — some under severe test conditions.

For example, several years ago at one of the company's major Southern plants a Negro was promoted to a welder's job in keeping with our policy of promoting the senior qualified employee. His promotion touched off a strike, involving approximately 200 employees. In the face of strong open resistance to this move by so-called white supremacy groups, the company's position was reviewed at the executive level at the commencement of the strike. An official public position was publicly stated by the president of the company that we would do no less than affirmatively support a policy which we had undertaken and supported for many years. Although the strike continued for four or five days, its strength was dissipated following the company's firm public stand and international union support. Since then similar promotions have occurred without important incidents.

A move to desegregate locker and rest room facilities at one of the Southern plants also created a temporary problem — a test of sincerity. With company approval, a group of Negro employees moved — collectively — into a locker room previously used by all-white skilled-trades employees. There were minor, temporary disturbances, and threats of more difficulty, but plant protection people were placed immediately in the area to enforce non-segregation in those areas. Closer supervision by operating foremen and industrial relations people also was arranged, and a letter that went to all employees' homes from the plant manager clearly spelled out company policy. After these steps were taken, the organized resistance disappeared.

Whether such actions constituted a violation of local law requiring separate facilities in "public places" was not tested, even though it was understood that a building permit would not have been issued for the construction of our facilities unless provisions were made for the separate facilities.

The Present Situation

We turn now to the more current activities and experiences of the last several years. No particular purpose would be served in treating separately those things that are done as a requirement under Executive Orders 10925 and 11114, as a Plans for Progress Company, and under the basic company policy of non-discrimination, because activities of the company with a policy of non-discrimination over the years and as a Plans for Progress Company encompass and frequently exceed obligations under these executive orders.

The company became a Plans for Progress Company on February 2, 1962, with the signing of a joint statement of undertakings by President Johnson, then Vice-President and executive head of the President's Committee on Equal Employment Opportunity, and the president of International Harvester Company.

The pledges undertaken by the company were reproduced in pamphlet form and were distributed along with other appropriate literature to all management employees immediately following the signing of the joint statement with the President's Committee.

Major Elements of the "Voluntary Program"

What does the "voluntary program" actually entail? Time will not permit a full account of all of its details, but a few excerpts will serve to illustrate its scope:

In the area of recruitment

In developing its sources of applicants, International Harvester is continuing to re-emphasize its non-discriminatory recruitment and hiring policy among state employment offices, college placement offices and the offices of principals and guidance counselors in secondary schools as well as among community-group representatives who are directly in a position to help the company continue achieving its objective of equality in employment opportunity.

In employment, placement and upgrading

The company is continuing to examine regularly its practices in connection with employment, promotions, layoffs, recalls, and terminations to assure that the non-discrimination policy is being applied and is regularly examining and refining its central personnel records to improve the guidance they may give in the avoidance of discrimination.

Of a More General Nature

The company is continuing to cooperate with agencies devoted to the improvement of intergroup relations within the communities where it operates and is continuing to participate in "Career Day" type programs in connection with any schools which serve as a company recruitment source.

Although policy affirmation at the executive level followed by appropriate communication of the policy to all employees is an important and necessary first step, some specific examples of how the company has attempted to implement it are presented below:

1. Implementing our policy to work with schools and agencies in any manner that will contribute toward improved skills of minority groups and to communicate job opportunities, some of our people have visited with classes of students at Negro high schools and colleges and have informed them of job opportunities in the company and the kinds of skills and training needed to prepare for such jobs.

2. In college recruiting efforts, special letters have been sent to all placement directors at the universities where we recruit, notifying them of the company's policies and that we do, in fact, solicit referrals of qualified minority students. Re-

cruiting has been expanded to eleven Negro colleges this
year. In addition, recruitment brochures and related material, including posters announcing recruiting dates, all
prominently display the "Equal Opportunity Employer"
statement.

3. We continue to carry on re-examination of our present employee inventory to audit previous evaluations of experience, skills, and potential.

4. We are currently re-emphasizing our program of placing
qualified employees in the general salaried area as well as
providing the opportunity for more minority employees
in our management organization including the entry into
management jobs.

5. We are encouraging company operations to examine more
carefully the manner in which employment receptionists
and interviewers fulfill their roles, recognizing that an overwhelming percentage of job applicants are seen solely by
these company people.

   While we have conducted training sessions with management
   groups including industrial relations managers, we have
   found that at times policy has not been communicated or
   explained fully to the employees assigned to these particularly key positions, who are the front line representatives of
   the company with the public. It is these people, rather than
   the industrial relations managers, who deal with 95 per cent
   of our job applicants and project its corporate image.

6. In support of the belief that the ultimate resolution of the
complex problems of minority groups will be solved, at least
in part, by the kind of relationships established between industry, the community, and responsible Negro leadership,
we have been placing greater emphasis within our management organization on the need for a vital, continuing
participation in a variety of community activities by responsible community organizations designed to further equal job
opportunity.

Unfortunately, it is not possible to describe all of the many activities carried on by the company to implement policy, but the foregoing indicates the general program.

The Underlying Philosophy

Some of the basic policies and practices regarding non-discrimination in hiring and promotion have been outlined, and a few of the
problems and accomplishments have been described. The com-

pany's interest in this subject can be viewed in fuller perspective after examining motives behind the program. What is the underlying philosophy in this program? Why, for example, does the company have the policy it professes, do the things described, as well as some other things it still hopes to do?

First, to dispel any possible preconceived notions anyone may have, it should be stated that we do not regard ourselves as "social crusaders"; nor do we consider ourselves as "liberal visionaries" in personnel management. The company believes in equal employment opportunity on the basis of merit, because it is convinced that this serves *our* best interest as well as that of the *country*. We are an economic entity, one thread in the vast American economic fabric. We believe that the country can prosper best when all members of society are permitted full participation; that is, the opportunity to make the best possible livelihood without regard to race, color, or creed. We believe this as a matter of conscience and moral principle. The American economic system cannot thrive and prosper unless all segments of the population have an opportunity to contribute their skills and talents.

That is, admittedly, a simple, economic motive. We say that we ought to have the greatest productive employment of the greatest possible number of Americans, because the contributions of all citizens to the economy are necessary if the company — and the country — are to prosper. This is a "self-interest" motive, of course, and we are not embarrassed to say so, but it is also a valid and compelling reason, one in harmony with the democratic principles of our country, as well as in the best Judaeo-Christian tradition.

There is another underlying factor which influences the company thinking in this field. Any corporation, once it has become successful and assumes a certain size, takes on a certain social character in the community. Because of the economic impact it makes, it cannot be operated solely in the interests of the stockholders, customers, and employees. Rather, its policies and actions — its behavior — influence the economic and social climate of the community in which it operates and upon which it depends for its prosperity. Thus, it ought to conduct itself in such a way as to deserve the respect and confidence of all the community's citizens.

Industry's success in promoting equal job opportunities, on a voluntary basis, with the consequent increased earning levels generated among minority groups, is one of the most important contributions that can be made toward the solution of many of the other economic, as well as social and cultural, challenges involving minority groups. Equal employment opportunity in its fullest sense (including hiring, upgrading, training, and promotion), indeed can be the catalyst that sparks the elimination of other problems, such as those in housing and education, that prevail among minority groups.

The company policy is one of *non*-discrimination, which is another way of saying that it is not one of favoritism — to any group. We would not, for example, hire or upgrade a Negro because he is a Negro any more than we would discriminate against him for the same reason. It would be a disservice to the company and to the economy to employ any "double-standard" in our hiring and promotion policy. To do so would be to short-change the company's stockholders who expect us to hire the most qualified persons.

Although we have no intention of extending preferential treatment in the employment office, we do make a special effort to recruit and otherwise search out qualified minority applicants. However, having made this special effort, at the point of hiring we will employ applicants on the basis of qualifications alone, without regard to race, creed, or color.

CONCLUDING REMARKS

Finally, attention is called to the fact that a program for non-discrimination in industry is the kind of subject which, by its very nature, taxes the initiative, the ingenuity, and — perhaps most of all — the patience of those who are most interested in making it work.

It is hampered with special problems because of the volatile emotions encountered on all sides. It is complicated by the sense of urgency it produces in the minds of some people *who believe they are being arbitrarily deprived of their right — or,* by the people who feel they are being pushed too hard and too fast. So it becomes increasingly more important that we do not lose sight of our objective, but press forward with continuing dedication, according to the moral and legal responsibilities as we see them, *without regard to the outside diverting influences going on around us.*

The competent and skilled personnel management man is a realist who knows how to distinguish fact from fiction when it comes to picking out human capabilities and observing human behavior. It is his heavy responsibility to know what factors are relevant to the quality of an employee's performance. It is not likely that he will regard the color of a person's skin as anything but irrelevant when he looks for those factors.

This is not a challenge facing only those specialists in personnel. It is an exciting one in which all management people can — and ought to — participate. No one in industry can insulate himself from this vexing problem; it is too urgent, too pervasive, and too far-reaching to leave to the personnel office. It is the kind of problem that calls for the sympathetic interest and the active participation of all management people if the American people are to have the kind of successful, progressive industrial management they have a right to expect.

6

EQUAL EMPLOYMENT OPPORTUNITY AT HONEYWELL, INC.

Gerry E. Morse*

Today industry is faced with a very serious challenge — the challenge of providing equal employment opportunity for all citizens regardless of race, color, creed, or national origin. If industry fails to meet this responsibility through voluntary planning and aggressive implementation, attempts at solutions which may not be sound either economically or socially may very well be forced upon us.

Civil rights is a problem that has plagued our country for generations — one for which there are no easy or quick solutions. It is a problem that has deep roots and touches all phases of our society — including industry. In fact, underlying all the action for more equality of opportunity in education, housing, and voting, is the desire to secure equality of opportunity in employment. The chance to make a good living is of paramount importance to any lasting correction for the disadvantaged. As business leaders we cannot turn away from our direct involvement in this problem. It is our responsibility to help find a solution because at the present it has, and in the future it will continue to have, a very real and direct impact upon our economy and upon the fortunes of our individual enterprises. This problem will not go away if we disregard it; in fact, if neglected, it will undoubtedly grow worse.

At Honeywell we are convinced that the United States must find sound ways to make full and effective use of the productive capability of each individual in the work force, no matter what his race, color, creed, or nationality. If an individual is qualified — and let me repeat, qualified — he must be assured an equal opportunity to obtain and hold a job commensurate with his performance. If he is not qualified, but has the potential to become qualified, he must be assured an equal opportunity to get the education or training that

---

*Vice-President, Employee Relations, Honeywell, Inc.

will permit him to qualify himself.'Our country cannot afford to waste its manpower talents and resources. In the world competition in which we are increasingly engaged, our very existence and that of our free enterprise system depend upon our ability to maintain economic progress and growth. Our chances for success are increased in proportion as we can locate, develop, and use the talents of all our people most effectively. Honeywell management believes free men, freely given the opportunity to develop and use their talents as they themselves think best, will out-do those working under any other system.

'Honeywell is the world's largest producer of automatic controls, with a very technical and diverse product line." It includes temperature controls for heating and air conditioning; high speed computers and electronic data processing equipment for business, scientific, and government use; guidance systems and components for missiles and space vehicles; indicating, recording and controlling instruments and systems for industry; and many others. Such highly technical products require large number of scientists, engineers, and other technically trained employees. At Honeywell about one out of every ten of almost 50,000 employees is a scientist or an engineer. A great amount of effort goes into research and advanced engineering development. The shortage of qualified employees for such work continues to be a problem for the company. Furthermore, the shortage of qualified minority group individuals — Negroes in particular — in these fields is even more serious. Not enough of them who have the potential for it have received technical educations. Worse still, for many of those who have, the level of education and training has been very inadequate. Certainly, many have been interviewed for whom the level has not been up to the standard provided by the major accredited engineering schools, and definitely not up to the level required for them to have any chance for success in the work we have to do.

On the other hand, the need for well-educated and capable employees to fill expanding work requirements over the years resulted long ago in a non-discriminatory employment practice at Honeywell and a willingness on the part of managers and supervisors to employ qualified applicants without discrimination because of race, color, creed, or nationality. Over the years the company felt that non-discriminatory employment practices did work and that it was providing Negroes and members of other minority groups with equal employment opportunity. However, the record has proven that the company was wrong.

A PLAN FOR PROGRESS AT HONEYWELL

Honeywell signed a Plan for Progress with the President's Committee on Equal Employment Opportunity on February 7, 1962. As a result of the incentive that that gave us to seek out qualified minority group applicants, the company has made more progress in finding, hiring, and promoting qualified minority group individuals after signing that plan two and one-half years ago than it had in all the previous period of seventy-five years, and under all the compulsions of the various city and state fair employment practice laws. Many of the 268 other companies — totalling over eight million employees — that have signed a Plan for Progress have had a similar awakening.

It should be emphasized that this progress was made without changing or lowering our employment requirements or standards and without establishing any ratios or quotas for determining how many minority group employees the company should have. In order to continue to succeed and to grow in the highly competitive electronics, instrumentation, and computer fields, the company cannot compromise on qualifications; it must continue to maintain high employment and promotional standards. Our Plan for Progress experience has shown that equal opportunities for all applicants and employees nevertheless can be provided.

To understand this, let us look more closely at the Plan for Progress. First, the program provides a voluntary approach to non-discriminatory employment. The chances for better understanding, cooperation, and a friendly, objective attitude towards overcoming the inevitable problems of the employment relationship are more likely in an atmosphere of voluntarism than in one of compulsion and reluctance. The results at Honeywell, as well as at other companies, indicate that there has in fact been considerable progress in minority employment and in minority employee relationships as a direct result of Plan for Progress commitments. Second, voluntary action seems to obtain better results than legislation or government compulsion. The Plan for Progress is a voluntary, yet firm, commitment by companies to take positive and aggressive steps to insure equal employment opportunity for members of minority groups. The key to its success seems to be change of emphasis. It changed Honeywell from a passive attitude toward non-discrimination, that is one which emphasized avoiding discrimination, to an active seeking out and hiring of qualified minority group applicants. It created a similar change in the evaluation of minority group employees for possible training, development, and advancement.

The company's attitude now is a positive one for equal opportunity. Even though the Civil Rights Bill is now law, it, like all such laws, emphasizes passive avoidance of discrimination, so the company is convinced that it can and will continue to make its best progress through a positive, active Plan for Progress approach.

Implementation of the Program

Now let us take a look at some of the specific actions that are being taken to implement the program at Honeywell. We have found that the success of this, as of most programs, depends first on the attitude and actions of the top corporate executives and the general manager at each Honeywell location. Positive attitudes openly expressed and positive actions taken by these executives and managers set the stage. Without this a program of passive nondiscrimination would have probably continued. With this the company created and is maintaining an active positive program of equal employment opportunity.

Next, specific commitments were made. The introduction to the Plan for Progress between Honeywell and the President's Committee on Equal Employment Opportunity, signed by then Vice-President Johnson and the author, reads as follows:

"It is in the interests of the United States and its business community that the talents of all persons be utilized to their fullest extent. Both the national welfare and sound business practice require this. It is, therefore, the national policy and the policy of Honeywell Inc. that all employees be recruited, hired, trained, assigned, and promoted without discrimination because of race, color, creed, or national origin."

It goes on to say:

"The Committee and the Company both recognize that full use of this equal employment opportunity by minority groups will not be achieved immediately. However, Honeywell will affirmatively carry out this Plan for Progress to reach this goal. It is also recognized that an increase in employment of minority groups can only be achieved where there exists properly trained and qualified applicants for those openings for employment available within the Company."

The Plan then sets forth a detailed plan for affirmative action. To the company these commitments are just as much a part of running a business as sales or production commitments.

As the next step, these commitments were communicated to all managers, supervisors, foremen, and employees. The initial announcement came directly from Honeywell's president. Each location was told of its own responsibility to live up to these commitments in its own employment activities, utilization of facilities, and application of all personnel policies and practices. The locations have responded well. Their approaches have been varied and tailored to suit each plant's individual problems. In order to implement the program, each location works with a variety of agencies, such as private employment agencies, state employment offices, the Urban League, the President's Committee on Equal Employment Opportunity, and special local community committees.

A few examples of local plant and office action may illustrate the interest and initiative that has been generated as a result of directly involving all units of the company.

— At one location the personnel department worked closely with the local Urban League to produce a booklet entitled "Plan and Prepare." This booklet presents a concise but complete review of opportunities available to Negroes in industry. It points out the importance of education. It emphasizes the importance of high school and vocational education as well as that of college. This booklet, published by the Urban League, has received nation-wide distribution.

— A location in the South was interested in making Negro educators more aware of the extreme demands of technical jobs. They did so by providing summer employment to members of the faculty of an all-Negro university. The experience provided them with a better first-hand understanding of requirements, and it is hoped that this will result in an improvement of their curriculum so that their graduates will be able to meet the increasing technical demands of industry.

— At another of our Southern plants, the personnel director is the career counselor at a Negro high school. In this capacity, he provides vocational counsel and guidance to seniors and graduates.

— A Midwest location with about 400 production employees had only one Negro employee. He was a professional accountant. The location had been doing little or no hiring. In fact, there had been a slow general reduction in the work force over a four-year period. When an upturn in business came about a year ago, Negro employees were added to the production work force for the first time. Today over 40 Negroes are employed out of a total of 450 production employees. The plant has been integrated without incident and production has not suffered in any way.

— A West Coast plant has had a similar experience integrating Orientals.

— At another of our Midwest plants, our employment manager is a Negro. And so it goes.

The final step taken to implement the program at Honeywell was to publicize that the company does not discriminate. This publicity has been especially directed to minority groups. It is most important that they know and understand the policy. That encourages them to qualify themselves and to seek the company out for employment. They have been informed of the kind of products the company produces and the types and kinds of job opportunities available at Honeywell. An effort is made to acquaint members of the community, educational institutions, and representatives of minority groups with the education, training, and experience required at Honeywell so those who apply are likely to be hired and those who are hired are likely to succeed and advance.

As part of the publicity, company representatives have actively participated in meetings and conferences throughout the country. For example, at a recent meeting jointly sponsored by the College Placement Council and the President's Committee on Equal Employment Opportunity, over 300 representatives of industry met with the presidents and placement directors of 70 predominantly Negro colleges to discuss a problem of mutual interest — how to better educate and utilize Negroes. A statement by Arthur A. Chapin, Assistant Secretary of Labor, at this conference summarized the problem and a positive course of action for solving it. He said:

"Isolation has too long hobbled and fettered the knowledge by faculty and students of the emerging technology in America. Growing up with automation is less painful than feeling its impact after leaving the campus. I further suggest that business encourage student and administration . . . visits to their industrial plants, computer centers, research establishments, and office headquarters, in order that graduates and teachers alike understand the realities of our industrial society . . . We cannot afford to waste our human resources."

Another example of publicity through meeting participation was the Career Day for minority group high school students in Minneapolis and St. Paul, sponsored by the Urban League. Playing an active role in this program provided an opportunity to communicate directly with the Negro community about the company — its products and its job requirements. As a result, the Negro students who attended the conference may well become interested in technical careers since they now know that opportunities exist and that they will be given equal consideration. Moreover, they now understand what is required of them in the way of education and training if they are to qualify for these positions. Let me re-emphasize this point. It is imperative that Negroes know that the employment doors are open to them. But what's equally important — they must know just what is required of them if they are to qualify themselves for these opportunities and to be successful in them. We do not solve the problem, we worsen it when through misguidance we raise false hopes.

Results of the Program

But the test of the whole approach is: how has it worked? We have made gains. Our last Plan for Progress report shows that in two and one-half years under the plan the total employment at Honeywell has increased by only 10 per cent, while minority employment has increased by 42 per cent. Let me repeat my earlier statement — we have continued to maintain our standards for employment and promotion. These standards are applied fairly and consistently to all applicants and employees. We judge the individual on his qualifications, ability, and performance — not on his race, color, creed, or nationality.

CONCLUDING REMARKS

The progress toward equality of opportunity in employment made to date has not been easy. We realize that the future may be even more difficult. Many companies, like Honeywell, have been making progress by hiring qualified minority group applicants who had prepared themselves in spite of the odds against their having a chance to use their talents. We have been upgrading and promoting these few in our plants and offices. Some of this small number of qualified minority group employees hold important positions in our company. The limited supply of qualified Negroes is probably close to full employment. The real challenge lies ahead. In the future, the problem may well be more to afford opportunity for education than for employment. Placing individuals in positions they are not trained or qualified to hold sets them up for failure and humiliation, harming the individual as well as the company. Therefore, it is imperative that attention be directed to assuring equal opportunity for sound education and training.

We in industry can help by visiting schools and colleges that serve minority group students and discussing with the school officials and faculty our employment needs and the types of training required to meet them. We can assist them in reviewing their curriculum in light of the changing industry needs. We should invite key minority group leaders and educators to visit our plants and facilities in order that they may better understand our employment needs. This will also provide them with a better basis for altering and improving their curriculum and for communicating to students and other members of their community what they need to do to take advantage of employment opportunities.

These activities have worked for Honeywell and have contributed to the progress it has made so far. But the job is far from done. The great bulk of the task is still ahead.

7

MINORITY GROUP EMPLOYMENT AT GENERAL MOTORS

Harold S. McFarland*

This article pertains to minority group employment in the General Motors Corporation. It will cover the General Motors policy and the way in which it has been disseminated, discuss the manner in which the work force has been integrated, outline some of the recruiting practices, and touch upon participation in activities which are related to minority groups.

HISTORICAL

General Motors had a well-established, published nondiscrimination-in-employment policy in effect for a number of years prior to the introduction of the Plans for Progress Program.[1] Originally, this policy stipulated that equal employment opportunity would be extended to all persons without regard to the individual's race, creed, color, or national origin. Subsequent developments at the state and national level required the company to amend the policy to add age and sex to the aforementioned factors of race, creed, color, or national origin. This was accomplished several years ago, and we are convinced that the provisions of the policy will meet the stipulations set forth in Title VII of the Civil Rights Act when it becomes effective in July of 1965.

Prior to the introduction of the Plans for Progress Program, the General Motors policy of nondiscrimination in employment was disseminated to management at the corporation and plant level through the means of executive conferences and policy letters. In recent years, emphasis has been placed upon disseminating the

---

*Director of Personnel Services, General Motors Corporation.

policy through special meetings which have been held with all members of supervision in plants and facilities. In addition, the policy has been brought to the attention of employees through bulletin board posters and by means of quotations in employee handbooks, plant newspapers, and other media. All sources for recruiting personnel, such as schools, colleges and employment agencies, have been notified in writing regarding the corporation policy.

The Collective Bargaining Agreement

The collective bargaining agreement with the UAW-AFL-CIO, covering upwards of 340,000 employees, contains this provision:

> It is the policy of General Motors and the UAW-AFL-CIO that the provisions of this Agreement shall be applied to all employees covered by this Agreement without regard to race, color, creed, or national origin. Any claims of violation of this policy may be taken up as a grievance, provided that any such claim must be supported by written evidence by the time it is presented by the Shop Committee at a meeting with Management.

Promotion and Advancement

Promotions and advancements in General Motors are made on the basis of ability and capacity, with due consideration to length of service and without regard to age, race, color, sex, creed, or national origin. Likewise, wages, salaries, and benefit plans are uniformly applicable to employees without regard to age, race, color, sex, creed, or national origin. None of the physical facilities are segregated or limited as to use or availability by reason of race or color.

PLANS FOR PROGRESS

When the President's Committee on Equal Employment Opportunity adopted its program in 1961, General Motors was among the first companies to subscribe to the Committee's Plans for Progress Program. Under the provisions of that program, the company submits an annual report showing the number of nonwhites employed in various categories. The data are obtained from a head count survey conducted by responsible members of supervision in our plants and facilities using the definitions provided by the President's Committee on Equal Employment Opportunity.

Employment, Training and Utilization of Manpower

(1) General Motors employs some 44,000 nonwhites in the United States.

(2) Nonwhites employed by General Motors represent 9.2 per cent of the company's total employment in the United States.

(3) General Motors' total employment in the United States during 1963 increased 4.1 per cent over 1962. Nonwhite employment during this same period increased 13.2 per cent, or more than three times the 4.1 per cent increase in total employment.

(4) Nonwhites are employed by General Motors as engineers, researchers, supervisors, draftsmen, analysts, accountants, librarians, foremen, plant protection supervisors and patrolmen, physicians and nurses, safety inspectors, suggestion plan investigators, labor relations representatives, skilled tradesmen, and general office workers, as well as in a wide variety of production and maintenance jobs. Of the more than 44,000 nonwhite employees working for General Motors, in excess of 37,000 (85 per cent) hold jobs or positions falling in the assembly, fabricating, processing, skilled trades, office, clerical technical, sales, professional, administrative, and supervisory categories. The remaining 15 per cent are employed as laborers or service workers.

At the same time, the percentage of nonwhites in better job classifications has been increasing, the percentage of nonwhites in laborer and service jobs has been decreasing, clearly indicating the availability of better jobs for qualified workers. In addition, the number of nonwhites in training (at General Motors expense) for skilled and supervisory positions has increased substantially since 1961.

Nonwhites are in apprentice training for skilled jobs such as tool and die making and other crafts. Nonwhites are also included in cooperative programs for high school and college students. One of the divisions recently set up the first cooperative program in engineering ever established at Tuskegee Institute, a Negro institution.

Nonwhites participate in General Motors "in-plant" training programs leading to skilled trades positions and production foremen on the basis of their qualifications.

Nonwhites are included among the engineering students at General Motors Institute, a fully accredited engineering college at Flint, Michigan, which is financed entirely by General Motors.

(5) The nonwhites employed in production and maintenance jobs receive average wages well in excess of $6,000 per year. This taken alone means that they are in the top one-third income group in the nation.

But this is not the whole story. They also share in the company benefit plans, which include group life insurance, sickness and accident pay, the pension plan, supplemental unemployment benefits, and other programs paid for by the company which are for the protection of the individual employee.

(6) Nonwhites employed in technical, professional, and supervisory positions have a higher level of income and also have comparable benefit programs for their protection.

The integration of the work force in General Motors has, in line with the corporation policy, been accomplished over a long period of time. Aside from a few problems which occurred when nonwhites were promoted to higher paying classifications in some Southern plants at the beginning of World War II, the implementation of the policy has been completely effective and no incidents of a serious nature have occurred.

Compliance with Fair Employment Measures

The policies and practices of General Motors in this field are subject to constant observation by a federal agency — the President's Committee on Equal Employment Opportunity. In connection with its broad activities, this official agency has made 109 compliance surveys in more than 70 company operations. Based on its findings, the agency has commended General Motors for the progress already, and continuing to be, made. Furthermore, any individual who feels that he has not been treated fairly has recourse to the President's Committee on Equal Employment Opportunity, or to any Fair Employment Practices or Civil Rights Commission which has been established in his state or community.

Operating as it does in all fifty states, General Motors has not been found in violation of any municipal, state, or other local unit of government's fair employment practice code or statute.

At the federal level, only 49 cases of alleged discrimination have been filed with the President's Committee on Equal Employment Opportunity since the inception of that committee in 1961; and of these, 39 cases were dismissed as being without merit, while the remaining ten have not been adjudicated.

Among the nonwhites now employed in skilled jobs and in supervisory, engineering, and other so-called white collar jobs, there are quite a number who have held such positions for many years. Others have been promoted as they acquired skills through training programs or qualified for better positions on the basis of self-improvement and spare-time study under such programs as the General Motors Tuition Refund Plan. In addition, the company actively recruits qualified nonwhite engineering and other college graduates in colleges and universities across the country including a number of institutions whose student population is predominantly nonwhite.

THE NEED FOR BETTER EDUCATION

It is generally recognized that the subject of nondiscriminatory employment and employment opportunities is one which is broader than the policies, practices, and experience of any one company. More must be done to increase the number of nonwhites who have the educational background and qualifications for the clerical, managerial, and professional positions which are open in industry. As an example, in its college graduate recruiting program, General Motors, by the nature of its business, is looking for engineering graduates who have an interest in the automotive field. There are some 36,000 engineering graduates each year, but very few of these are nonwhites. The situation has special significance insofar as predominantly Negro colleges are concerned. Very few of these colleges and universities have an engineering curriculum, and information supplied by the United States Department of Health, Education and Welfare discloses that fewer than 200 students in these predominantly Negro colleges annually receive B.S. degrees in engineering. There has been an increasing demand for accounting majors at General Motors in recent years, and our experience shows that nonwhites who are trained in accounting are in very short supply.

In order to increase the number of nonwhites who are qualified for the better positions, work must be done in the grade schools, the junior high schools, and the high schools, so that those who have the ability will complete the courses necessary to gain admission to the engineering schools and other programs of training which lead to careers in fields in which there is a need. To this end, the company has participated actively in, and provided financial support for, programs which have been set up for the purpose of providing information to high school principals, guidance counselors, and teachers, outlining in detail the requirements necessary for minority youths to qualify for entry jobs in the plants and facilities of the corporation.

General Motors has joined with agencies working on this problem at the community level. Our personnel directors have participated in panel discussions to bring to the attention of students and their parents information on the opportunities which are open to those who continue their education and prepare themselves. Representatives of General Motors serve on the Board of Directors of such local organizations as the Urban League, and the company provides financial support for it at both the local and national level.

General Motors is one of the largest contributors to the United Negro College Fund, and company executives have been active in its support.

General Motors has an extensive program of support for higher education which includes a scholarship program, first announced in 1955 and now providing educational opportunities for more than 1,600 students at some 220 colleges. The selection of students to receive these awards is made by the colleges, and since the inception of the program in 1955, nonwhite students have been included among the recipients.

CONCLUDING REMARKS

The areas of personnel policy and administration which are discussed herein have been matters of concern to General Motors for many years. We expect to continue our efforts, both in the implementation of policies within the company, and in broader cooperative efforts which will provide the basis for further progress in the future.

8

WESTERN ELECTRIC'S COMMITMENT TO FAIR EMPLOYMENT

R. G. Lawrence*

The concerted attention Western Electric has given to its equal employment opportunity policy has had a dual effect in the company. It has increased the number of Negroes in every job level from production worker to management. And it has generated among its management a heightened awareness of the company's relationship to society.

Western Electric, manufacturing and supply unit of the Bell System, has had a policy of recruiting, hiring, and assigning employees on the basis of merit alone at least since 1924, when it was spelled out in a document defining employment policies. But in July, 1961, it reaffirmed that policy — and pledged affirmative action to fulfill it — when it joined the first group of corporations which signed a "Plan for Progress" with the President's Committee on Equal Employment Opportunity.

The areas spelled out in the plan involved: 1) dissemination of information about it; 2) administration; and 3) employment, recruitment, and training.

DISSEMINATING INFORMATION

Within a day after the plan was signed, all Western Electric's management employees were informed through a special bulletin that the company had adopted the Plan for Progress. Supervisors in turn were expected to transmit this news to non-management employees. Subsequently all employees were sent letters, signed by a vice-president or the head of the location where they worked,

---

*Director, Personnel Administration, Western Electric Company.

explaining the Plan for Progress. Since these original messages were sent, the company has used WE Magazine, which is distributed to all its employees throughout the nation, the employee newspapers published at its various locations, and bulletin board displays to feature company activities — and to reflect the policy — stemming from the Plan for Progress. Newsletters for management personnel periodically have contained detailed interpretations of what the plan means to Western Electric, and of the progress achieved to date. In observance of the third anniversary of the signing of the plan, the company published a special report delineating the entire spectrum of activities conducted under the Plan for Progress.

But written communications alone could not convey the full weight of the company's commitment to the Plan for Progress. In order to emphasize its importance, compliance has been reviewed regularly at the President's Conference, a semi-annual meeting of the company's president, executive staff, and heads of major manufacturing and service locations. This subject frequently has been on the agenda of many other organizational conferences within the various divisions of the company.

Simultaneously the officers of the company undertook an effort to emphasize Western Electric's endorsement of the policy of equal employment opportunity in appearances before the general public and before company employees. For example, in the course of an address delivered at Little Rock, Arkansas, in November, 1961, the president of the company listed three reasons why Western Electric people should be interested in alleviating the plight of the Negro and of all the nation's disadvantaged minorities. "The good opinion of the world is only one of them," he said. "A more compelling one is that prejudice breeds waste, the most tragic kind of waste, the waste of human resources. But in the final analysis there is one reason above all others for giving our best management attention to making equal opportunity come true — and that is because it is right." Like all talks on this subject by company officials, this speech was reported prominently in company publications.

The company moved on other fronts as well to disseminate information about the policy embodied in the Plan for Progress. For many years the subject of the Negro in America has been discussed in various training programs offered to the different levels of Western Electric management. This phase of these training programs has been intensified. For example, this subject has been included in the curriculum of the six-month Management Training Program ever since its establishment in 1947. But now participants in this program, who are selected for their promise as potential executives, make an extensive study of the nature of prejudice. In addition to readings, they participate in two days of lectures and discussions conducted by leaders such as Dr. Harold Lett of the National Conference of Christians and Jews, Dr. Kenneth Clark, Professor of Psychology at City College of New York, and James Baldwin, the noted novelist and playwright.

To further underscore the company's commitment to the Plan for Progress, the heads of all Western Electric locations — from the largest plant to the smallest distribution center — were invited to a Plan for Progress conference on the premise that once they returned to their home locations they would be able to transmit the knowledge they gleaned to all their subordinates. In order to provide for face-to-face discussions and seminars, it was decided to have two conferences — one for location heads in the East, the other for those in the West.

The first of these conferences was held in November, 1963, the second in January, 1964. The format was basically the same. First the company's policy of equal employment opportunity was affirmed by H. G. Mehlhouse, Vice-President of Personnel and Public Relations. Then a brief history of the civil rights movement was presented, along with an analysis of the major organizations serving the Negro community. Next the conferees saw a videotape of a program featuring the Rev. Dr. Martin Luther King, James Baldwin, and Malcolm X. Dr. Clark then took over the podium to discuss the current aspirations of the American Negro. He also moderated a panel discussion in which the participants were James Farmer, executive director of the Congress of Racial Equality, James Foreman, executive director of the Student Nonviolent Coordinating Committee, Roy Wilkins, executive director of the National Association for the Advancement of Colored People, and Whitney Young, Jr., executive director of the National Urban League. So stimulating were the discussions initiated by this panel that they were continued by Western Electric's managers and the guest panelists late into the evening. P. A. Gorman, president of Western Electric, the dinner speaker, emphasized company policy and described the challenge ahead when he said, "We have a responsibility — both as a corporate citizen and as individual citizens — to do what we can to make the promise of America come true for all her people."

The second day was devoted to discussions of the company's experience in hiring as well as upgrading Negroes and members of other minorities and the manager's community relations responsibilities. In addition, each location head was presented with two items: an outline for a conference involving local Negro leaders that he could arrange at his own location and a discussion guide that provided the basis for a series of small group meetings with first and second level supervisors.

Among the materials sent out in advance of the conference was a checklist providing detailed guides for those responsible for implementing the company policy. Sample questions asked in the checklist were

— Do you maintain regular contacts with local groups concerned with racial problems?

— Are you a member of, or do you have a personal representative on, local community bi-racial committees?

— When you advertise for job openings, do you advertise in Negro newspapers?

— Are you recruiting applicants at high schools with predominantly nonwhite enrollments?

— Does your location cooperate with and support community vocational training programs?

Following the company-wide conferences, several locations have had meetings of their supervisory staffs to review the implications of the Plan for Progress. Others have had conferences in which their supervisory staffs and leaders of the local Negro community have participated. In still other cases, supervisors have met with Negro leaders to review areas of mutual interest in their home communities.

Thus, through written materials, lectures, company conferences and training programs, the broad scope of Western Electric's commitment to equal opportunities is being communicated on a continuing basis to all the company's employees.

ADMINISTERING THE PLAN FOR PROGRESS

The Plan for Progress assigns responsibility for supervising Western Electric's performance to the vice-president, Personnel and Public Relations. In discharging this responsibility, he periodically reviews the progress made in employment, and he recommends programs that will improve the company's performance. He also keeps informed of the activities of other Plans for Progress companies generally.

As another instrument for reviewing and improving compliance with the Plan, the company established an Interdivisional Coordinating Committee on Nondiscrimination. Composed of representatives of the various divisions of the company — manufacturing, service, personnel, legal, and so forth — it meets frequently to review matters of current interest in the area of equal employment opportunity policy and to recommend appropriate actions.

The coordinating committee reviews such subjects as recruiting among minorities, personnel advertising in the Negro press, and participation of nonwhites in out-of-hours activities — those sponsored by the company and those sponsored by employee organizations. On its initiative, the company's testing procedures are constantly reviewed to assure that they are fair to all applicants.

While the mission of the coordinating committee is wide, its primary responsibility — to maintain emphasis on equal employment opportunity for all qualified persons — is very specific.

Thus, by assigning responsibility for this program to one of its top officers and by creating a high-level committee to review results on a continuing basis through both formal and informal reporting procedures, Western Electric has taken steps to assure that its Plan for Progress is carried out in all company locations.

EMPLOYMENT, RECRUITING, AND TRAINING

Since Western Electric signed its Plan for Progress, employment of Negroes has increased in all job categories — in the ranks of managers and supervisors, of professional and technical employees, of clerks and stenographers, and of craftsmen as well as operatives.

This increase was achieved through a broad spectrum of company activities designed to assure members of the Negro community that they would be welcome as Western Electric employees and would have opportunity for advancement.

For example, while Negro personnel were encouraged to improve their qualifications, a special inventory of employee skills was made to assure that all recent educational achievements were being utilized by the company. It was found that a number of Negro employees had taken advantage of the company's college tuition refund plan to advance their own education. Among them was a man who, while assigned to handling materials in a shop, had completed college and law school on his own initiative. He since has been promoted to a supervisory rank.

Nonwhites were encouraged to take advantage of company-sponsored training programs to advance their skills.

The company also has undertaken a number of other activities in order to locate qualified Negro employees. For example, the company's manufacturing plant in North Andover, Massachusetts, organized a nine-week program of career seminars for selected marginal students in Andover and North Andover high schools. This program had four objectives: 1) to broaden the students' interests, 2) to familiarize them with job opportunities and requirements, 3) to point out the relationship between education and the kind of employment they could expect, and 4) to encourage them to continue their studies through high school and, if possible, beyond. This program involved a series of meetings between the students and a group of young Western Electric employees who informally discussed their own high school days — the courses they liked and disliked, their scholastic strengths and weaknesses, the role played by different courses in qualifying them for employment, their search for jobs, and similar subjects. So successful was this concept that it is now being introduced by school officials to industries in the nearby Lowell and Lawrence areas.

The company has donated the services of a number of specialists on its staff to the National Urban League's Skills Bank program, which is designed to locate vocationally and technically trained men and women, skilled craftsmen, and professional and semi-professional workers who currently are employed in jobs that do not fully utilize their talents or who are unemployed.

Along with a number of other employers, the company has helped support an eleven-week secretarial training program in New York City; this program emphasizes typing, shorthand, English, office practices, grooming, and deportment. Instruction for this course, which was organized by the National Urban League, is offered by New York University. It is designed for women who either have not had any actual work experience or whose skills are not up to standard. Graduates of this course are free to seek employment wherever they wish, and Western Electric succeeded in recruiting only a small number of them.

Western Electric's Hawthorne Works, located on the outskirts of Chicago, conducted a stenographic training program for women with sub-standard clerical skills. It was able to employ everyone who completed the course. The Hawthorne Works also has participated in an employment development fair held in the near North Side of Chicago, an area inhabited chiefly by Negroes and Puerto Ricans whose educational achievements are low and where the unemployment rate is about 17 per cent. The company's exhibit emphasized the importance of education. Company representatives were on hand to answer questions and to describe the procedures for obtaining employment.

The company's plant in Kearny, N. J., has worked with educators and representatives of other industries to effect a revision of the general high school curriculum offered to students neither bound for college nor vocational training. As revised, the curriculum includes practical physics, applied mathematics, and a general science course, all geared to the needs of industry today. The Kearny Works also is participating in a special program for dropouts under which they alternate classroom sessions and work experience.

As a matter of course, employment advertisements are placed in Negro publications. All such advertising, in whatever medium it appears, and all recruiting literature indicate that Western Electric is an equal opportunity employer.

The company also has extended its recruiting activities in Negro colleges. In 1962 it added four Negro colleges to the group of institutions at which Western Electric systematically recruits. Two years later recruiting was being conducted at twelve predominantly Negro campuses and plans are being made to increase this number still further. In the course of regular recruiting activities conducted on integrated campuses, Negroes are interviewed routinely and when found to be qualified their applications are processed. Furthermore, the company's various locations conduct their own recruiting activities at high schools, vocational schools, and colleges in their own vicinities, and consequently additional Negroes have been added to Western Electric's rolls.

Yet, despite this increased activity, Western Electric recruiters during their visits to Negro campuses became aware that the placement officers in some of these colleges were not familiar with the current needs of business or, because of past experience, hesitated to guide students toward careers in areas other than those traditionally open to nonwhites — teaching, civil service, medicine, and law. Consequently, after a series of exploratory conversations, Western Electric decided to co-sponsor a conference for placement personnel in Negro colleges. Devoted to the topic "New Demands on the Placement Officer," the conference was held in December, 1963, at Morgan State College in Baltimore, Maryland. It dealt with subjects such as "Opportunities in Business and Industry," "Pre-Recruiting Planning by the Placement Officer," "Employer Standards of Selection," and "Records, Forms and Transcripts." Speakers included placement officers from the University of Pennsylvania, Duke University, Lehigh University, and recruiting personnel from RCA as well as Western Electric.

It is expected that, as a result of this two-day conference, recruitment for business generally will be more successful than in the past on Negro campuses.

The cumulative effect of these programs has resulted in increasing numbers of Negro applicants. But the impact of what Western Electric is doing is best demonstrated by an event that took place in the summer of 1963. Three Negro professors were hired to work in the company on the theory that their job experiences would enrich their classroom programs. At the end of the summer, they met to review their experience. During this meeting, one professor admitted he had embarked on a teaching career without the conviction that his students ever would be able to apply fully what he taught them. However, he continued, after seeing what Western Electric is trying to do, his career suddenly had become a real challenge, since he now feels that if he teaches well his students will be able to use their knowledge constructively.

COMMUNITY LEADERSHIP

Western Electric's Plan for Progress specifies actions that the company and its employees will take to increase job opportunities for nonwhites. But the spirit it generated has led countless Western Electric people to work on their own time in their home communities to build a climate that will ease the tasks of eliminating discrimination and of promoting racial equality — the unfinished tasks of American democracy.

In doing so they were heeding the advice given by the president of Western Electric when he accepted the National Urban League's Equal Opportunity Day Award in November, 1963. At that time, he said, "the businessman's responsibility does not stop at the factory gate. No company is an island. Its fortunes are bound up with the community around it from which it draws its people. With the best will in the world, a company cannot make equal employment opportunity a reality if the community — through discrimination, deliberate or unwitting — deprives some of its citizens of the chance to qualify themselves for the more and more demanding tasks of industry. Equal employment opportunity and equal educational opportunity are inseparable."

Western Electric's president continued by suggesting that "the initiative businessmen apply to this urgent national problem ought not to be limited to providing jobs to demonstrably qualified people. What is needed is business leadership at the community level to join with other citizens in finding ways to level the barriers to opportunity — barriers which, if they deny the legitimate aspirations of some of the community's residents, will in the long run deny to all of them their fullest potential for growth and progress."

This injunction has been accepted by Western Electric people in a variety of ways. Some are members of civic groups or church organizations which are seeking solutions to the problems nonwhites face in their home communities. Thus, several engineers at the company's Indianapolis Works are participating in a community program to encourage youngsters to complete their high school education. These engineers function, in effect, as counselors for troubled high school pupils. They meet with youngsters identified by their teachers as potential dropouts and offer their support to help them overcome their immediate problems, meanwhile urging them to remain in school until they graduate. The youngsters can consult personally with their counselors and are invited to telephone them day or night whenever pressing problems develop.

While a machine operator in the Kearny Works is a member of the New Jersey Governor's Committee on Equal Employment Opportunity, a vice-president serves on a committee of the National Urban League. The Superintendent of Labor and Industrial Relations, Purchasing and Plant Services at the company's Allentown Works is a member of the Pennsylvania Commission on Human Rights and a member of the management staff of the distribution center in Nashville, Tennessee, serves on a metropolitan committee on human relations.

ENLARGED SENSE OF RESPONSIBILITIES

As was noted earlier, Western Electric's Plan for Progress is helping the Negro community. But equally important, though less tangible, it has enlarged the horizons of the company's management employees. They have become aware that each of them, whatever his level, has a personal responsibility for implementing company policy, and that progress of the company is no more than, and no less than the sum total of their individual efforts.

Finally, they are better acquainted with the problems of the society about them — problems of education, of urban blight, of housing, of health, of welfare. They realize that the company cannot isolate itself from the community in which it operates. This is a valuable lesson, because it reflects industry's growing awareness that the problems of society are its problems. Industry — and business in general — cannot function in isolation. In our free enterprise system, its responsibilities do not end at the plant gate.

As our people move creatively to resolve the problems of the society about us, and as they bring to their jobs the sensitivity and responsiveness they develop in coping with their community's problems, our company will benefit as will all citizens.

9

INTEGRATING THE WORK FORCE IN SOUTHERN INDUSTRY

E. G. Mattison*

In discussing the topic "Integrating the Work force in Southern Industry," I cannot speak for all southern industry. Emphasis is only on the Lockheed-Georgia Company, which is the largest industrial firm in the South. The purpose here is to relate some of the experiences, some of the concerns, and some of the hopes for the future at Lockheed-Georgia. This will in no way be a success story, simply because it is too early to write such a story.

HISTORICAL

The Lockheed Aircraft Corporation started and grew in California. Company policy there for many years was to give equal opportunity and treatment to all minority groups, and we were active in founding the Committee on Merit Employment in the Los Angeles area. In January of 1951, the Government asked Lockheed to reactivate Air Force Plant No. 6 in Marietta, Georgia, just seventeen miles from Atlanta, to handle two major national defense programs: modification of the B-29 and building of the B-47 jet bomber. To give an idea of the size of the Georgia operation, the main building is the largest factory under one roof in the free world, and the company is the largest private employer in the Southeast.

In establishing a new gigantic operation in Georgia, we were faced with a different climate in regard to integration than we had in California. We intended to implement the corporate policy of

---

*Director of Industrial Relations, Lockheed-Georgia Company, Marietta, Georgia.

147

non-discrimination, but this time, in an area with established customs and laws and strong emotions. We realized that if we were not careful in gaining community acceptance, we might have some unpleasant incidents and unfavorable publicity with which to contend. We went about it very quietly and slowly; not timidly, but wisely.

Picture with me those first few months of operation at Marietta. The plant had been built during World War II and was operated by Bell Aircraft in those days. The building was closed after V-J Day and used for storage of machine tools. In 1951, when Lockheed reopened the plant, the spider webs were cleaned out, new equipment was brought in, and a rapid increase of employment to 10,000 people began. By 1965 the company was to be 20,000 strong.

The Need For Skilled Employees

The company had a desperate need for skilled aircraft workers, tooling people, and engineers. Luckily, many experienced aircraft people were still around—former Bell Aircraft employees. Many migrated from other aircraft companies. We took all of the experienced people we could get, mostly white, but some Negro, when we could find them. The South, industrially, was then, and is now, young. Fourteen years ago there were limited opportunities for a man to become a skilled machinist, either through experience or through vocational education. There was no time to prepare or present extensive training programs at first. Underlying the whole problem was the urgency of the United States defense effort—to get the B-29's and B-47's out of the hangars and off to Korea.

From the very beginning the plan was to use Negroes in both skilled and semi-skilled jobs, as well as in managerial positions. It soon became evident, however, that there was a need for Negroes to upgrade their skills. Some were applying for jobs but they did not meet the standards. And, of course, the company could not lower standards. We could not allow a man to work on an aircraft who was not qualified to do so. Not only would this jeopardize the lives of that ship's crew, but it would endanger the very life of the company and its ability to offer employment to anyone—white or Negro.

Training and Apprenticeship Programs

We embarked on a major training effort for the entire work force. Some courses were required and given on company time. Others were voluntary and given on the employees' own time, at no expense to them. During these early days, we offered twenty-three different specialized courses in all phases of fabrication and assembly work. Evening training programs were very well received and hundreds of people registered for them. Many of these were Negro, but very few Negroes showed up for class. Those who did soon lost interest and dropped out. We found out later why this was so, and the reasons are discussed later. But it was very clear that a pattern was emerging: that minority group members lacked qualifications for hire and promotion, and they failed to respond to developmental opportunities when they were available.

In 1955 and 1956 the company solicited applications for Negroes to enter apprenticeship programs. There was a marked lack of Negro applicants. In 1959 announcements about the apprentice program were sent to high schools in the area, including twenty-two Negro high schools. The response: no Negro applicants. In more recent years, those who do apply make a poor showing on their screening tests. And still more recently, those who apply and are accepted do not perform well in their training classes. I am not pointing an accusing finger. I am simply reciting some facts that underlie our present approach to equal opportunity.

There are some other facts that gave us hope, however. More and more Negroes were being placed in a wider variety of job classifications. Professionally trained Negroes were hired as engineers, programmers, and mathematicians—all without incident. By 1955, seven of our supervisors were Negroes. In 1959, two Negro girls were hired as clerk-typists and placed into a previously all-white department—without incident.

A PLAN FOR PROGRESS

In May of 1961, the president of Lockheed Aircraft Corporation signed with then Vice-President Lyndon Johnson, a document entitled "Plan for Progress." This was a formal agreement between the company and the federal government to pursue a policy of non-discrimination—a policy we had actually had in effect for many years. Lockheed was the first company to sign such an agreement and over 250 other firms have since followed suit.

Recruiting Personnel

Continuing a policy of non-discrimination under the Plan for Progress, recruiters were sent to the campuses of Negro colleges, looking for qualified job applicants. It has been found that many

Negroes with college degrees are not as well-schooled as graduates from predominantly white schools. The standards of many Negro schools are not as high—and so the Negro graduate cannot compete on an equal basis. We, as industry, cannot close our eyes to this inequality. We feel we share a community responsibility to reduce this inequality—for the long-range good of our whole society. Our employment advertisements say that Lockheed is an Equal Opportunity Employer. To the Negro applicant who answers such an ad, shall we say, "Sorry, you're not qualified," and turn our backs?

I am thinking of a young Negro lad we hired into an apprentice program. He just barely met the minimum qualifications, but we were willing to give him a chance. Within a few weeks after Norman began the classroom part of his training, he failed his subjects. We could no longer keep him in the apprentice program and offered him a lower skilled job, which he accepted. As I reflect on this incident, I become very concerned and my concern is quite apart from the dollars we spent in testing, hiring, processing, and training this young man. I am concerned because I feel that we did Norm a disservice. We offered him a challenge that he could not meet. We made it possible for him to experience a failure, perhaps one of many for him in his struggle to better himself. This can be very damaging to a man's ego and ambition, and it is happening to Negroes and others every day. We should be very careful about opening doors for people who do not have a reasonable chance of succeeding.

This approach cannot stand by itself, however. We, as management, cannot say, "Do not come to us until you are skilled." We must couple our policy of avoiding failure with a responsibility—to do what we can to help Negro and other underprivileged citizens prepare themselves even before they enter our employment office. This is good business practice and will benefit the whole community.

Mention was made earlier of the fact that we had discovered why Negro employees were not responding to the opportunities offered for upgrading their skills. We realized that the Negro was coming to us from a world beyond the reaches of the plant, a world that had so often denied him the chance for improvement. Many of us, when we were younger, knew that some day we would choose an occupation and prepare ourselves for it. This has not been the case for a large segment of our population—Negroes included. They have not experienced the privilege of choice. They have not typically aspired to occupations materially different from those held by their parents. Expediency in earning a living today—not choice, and the longer road of preparation for the opportunities of the future—has prevailed in too many instances. The consequence of this has a great deal to do with the absence of Negro applicants for the "opportunity" job—and other frequent failures to compete, to persist on the job, and to achieve success—such as have been experienced in our Lockheed-Georgia plant.

Education and Community Projects

It seems there are things that happen to Negro citizens before they appear in the employment office—things that cannot be ignored if we are to follow the spirit, not just the letter of our Plan for Progress—hopelessness, improper counseling, poor motivational influences, and inadequate education. Lockheed has realized for some time now that these are the areas it must work in to assure true equal opportunity for all. We have gone into the community to do "grass roots" work that may not give us a job applicant next week or next month, but we hope a few years from now, through enrichment of the educational and motivational processes.

In this connection, here are some of the things the company is doing and attempting to do:

1. Colleges

The company has worked with Negro colleges and universities, trying to communicate to them what it looks for in their graduates —trying to tell them about company standards. Their staffs and faculties have been very eager for counsel. They, too, are aware of the inability of their graduates to compete in the professional labor market.

For instance, Negro college students by the busload have been brought in from Tuskegee Institute in Alabama to spend an entire day in the plant. They are permitted to observe professional and skilled people at work—at drawing boards, in chemical labs, metallurgical labs, and computer operations. The company tries to give them a feel not only for the available opportunities but also for the high degree of professional competence required.

Over the years, Negro professors from Tennessee Agricultural and Industrial College, North Carolina Agricultural and Technical College, and Tuskegee Institute have been hired for the summer. The main interest has been to have them carry back to their schools curriculum ideas to help them upgrade their standards.

The president of Morehouse College, a Negro school in Atlanta, called one day in 1959 to tell the company of his inability to find professors qualified to teach advanced mathematics and physics and to ask if we could help. As a result of his call, the company provided two top engineering specialists with doctoral degrees. Their work schedules were arranged so they could both teach and carry on their duties with Lockheed. This same situation occurred again in 1963.

We are working closely with the predominantly Negro colleges to help them upgrade their faculties, to assist and encourage curricular improvements, and to help them achieve an output of graduates with the preparation they need. In our case, this also means fewer sociology, biology, teaching, and physical education majors, and more emphasis on technical subjects.

2. *High Schools*

The company has also done a great deal of work with the high schools, trade, and vocational schools. As an example, a group of Negro high school counselors were brought into the plant for an all-day educational program, showing in detail the industrial application of high school math and other subjects to the apprenticeship program. This seemed to be particularly meaningful. Plant tours for Negro teachers, school administrators, placement officers, and students are held regularly to familiarize them with the variety of industrial jobs—technical and non-technical, skilled and semi-skilled, professional and managerial—all open to minority groups.

In speaking to high school and college counselors, teachers, and administrators, we always try to be as forthright and honest as we can. We do not paint a rosy picture for them or hold out glowing promises. We are realistic with them and hope they will be realistic with each other and with the students they teach and counsel. They like the approach: "You as educators have a responsibility to produce better qualified students. We in industry have a responsibility to help you."

3. *Community*

Aside from working with educational institutions, we are working actively with responsible community agencies. A member of the Training Department serves as the Chairman of Youth Incentives and Education Committee of the Atlanta Urban League. This committee deals with youth motivation, disseminating occupational and career information, stimulating guidance counseling in Negro high schools, sponsoring student visits to industries, helping to solve the school dropout problem, upgrading school standards, and promoting more enlightened views of competition in today's more technical world.

This committee is also a very fine vehicle for meeting with leading members of the Negro community, getting to understand the hurdles they are trying to clear, and discovering where we can help.

We feel deeply responsible in working with the community and its educational institutions because we realize that our policies will influence the practice of other businesses. We are not just operating within a climate. Because of our size and wide influence within the state, we help to create the climate. We are particularly fortunate in that we are in an area of the South where there has been relatively little racial strife. Schools, parks, and businesses have been integrated peacefully. This is making our job easier.

Recently, the Air Force made an audit at the Lockheed-Georgia Company of progress in providing equal opportunity. The audit report said that the plant was a "showplace" of smoothly carried-out integration and could be set down anywhere in the country as an example of what can be done. This makes us very proud and provides an additional incentive to continue grass roots work with the Negro community.

CONCLUDING REMARKS

But it is too soon to write the success story of the integration program at the Lockheed-Georgia Company—we have just begun. Perhaps, however, it is worth summarizing the crown points or distinguishing features which have brought the company where it is today.

First, the program evolved from a basic policy decision of non-discrimination—evidenced throughout the plant as a will and determination of management to provide equal opportunity for all.

Second, it has been based on careful, thoughtful planning.

Third, as we have gained ground, efforts have been accelerated within the limits prescribed by the climate existing at the time.

By 1961, we had come a long way, and the momentum of the program was well established.

When Executive Order 10925 appeared—when equal employment opportunity began to unfold—we knew that Lockheed was going to have a Plan for Progress.

We were ready to be the first Plan for Progress Company.

The Lockheed Plan contemplated and has resulted in renewed efforts in training, apprenticeship programs, recruiting, selection, re-examination of qualifications, communications, and cooperation —all designed for furtherance of, both in letter and spirit, the objectives of the President's Committee.

From this it can be seen that the company has a deep interest in the subject, manifest in our program of voluntary action over the years.

The real effort is to get employers to recognize that this is the country's problem. It is beyond the matter of law and compliance. The basic problem today is to help communities raise standards, help high schools, colleges, and universities to raise standards—to help motivate this country's youth to compete in a society whose very by-word is competition among the qualified.

This applies not only to all minorities, but to all underprivileged. The fallout of such an effort will be in the whole system of education in the United States. It does not involve quota hiring nor preferential hiring. That is not what we are seeking. Each individual is considered on his or her own merits.

This effort does, however, recognize that a sizable portion of our population is underprivileged and, therefore, it is a community problem.

If, as a nation, we are going to be successful in this effort, it will be through the voluntary action of employers, not necessarily exactly as we have done, but certainly with a forthright sense of responsibility for the basic precepts of equal opportunity for all and with a will and determination to do something about it.

10

PROGRESS IN EQUAL EMPLOYMENT OPPORTUNITY AT GENERAL ELECTRIC

Virgil B. Day*

Thirty years ago, Gerard Swope, then president of General Electric and a man of deep personal conviction on the subject of discrimination, included these words in a statement of company policy: "There shall be no discrimination by foremen, superintendents, or any executives of the Company against any employee because of race, or creed...."

This admonition does not seem remarkable today. But to the best of my knowledge, it was the first such declaration of non-discriminatory policy made by a large American manufacturing company. Whether it was first or second or sixth is not important; it was a pioneering statement. My associates and I, who are the inheritors of that pioneering spirit, feel a certain pride in it.

But as we look into the face of 1965, we cannot feel complacent.

A very few days ago we received a letter from a Negro man in California, commenting on a pamphlet we had prepared to encourage young Negroes to prepare themselves for careers in industry. He said in part:

"You tell these boys that they can get jobs, but they understand neither your words nor the assumptions beneath the words. I knew children in Chicago who were on the third generation of relief; they did not know adults normally work or look for work. They see nothing in their lives that shows education is useful. Many have no stable family structure; there is no continuity in their lives. Many Negroes, man and boy, live in almost a null-time; nothing much ever happens; if work is available, it seldom lasts long; no activity requires or regards their sustained attention. An appalling percentage of Negroes live lives not significantly different, yet they are told to become electronic engineers."

*Vice-President, Management Development and Employee Relations Services, General Electric Company.

No, we cannot feel complacent. We are still trying to make progress, and complacency is the enemy of progress. We recognize Mr. Swope's statement of 30 years ago for what it is: the formal starting point of one of two main thrusts of General Electric's equal opportunity effort.

EQUAL OPPORTUNITY EFFORT

The first thrust is the articulation and continued re-emphasis of a clear policy of non-discrimination. While this, in a sense, may imply a negative approach, its meaning is definitely positive for both society and for the company.

The second thrust is the creation of a corporate climate in which true equality of opportunity can flourish. It involves no less than applying the same kinds of initiative we apply in marketing, in production, in employee relations, in engineering to those aspects of civil rights which are the proper concern of a large manufacturing corporation.

We believe that these two approaches complement each other, and are, in fact, interdependent. The policy, to be truly effective, needs to be buttressed by affirmative action. And such affirmative action must be founded on the base of a clearly understood corporate decision. (In recent years, of course, it has also been founded upon various state laws, laws regarding defense contractors such as General Electric, upon Plans for Progress action, and now upon the Civil Rights Act of 1964. But as General Electric has made progress in the equal opportunities field, we have found it most helpful to be able to make clear to our own organization that our policy predates the law. We have not been dragged grudgingly into trying to do what is right, and our action was not dictated by government pressure or a desire to be well regarded.)

THE DEVELOPMENT OF THE PROGRAM

Let us look then at the development of these two paths over the years.

First, policy.

In this field, the basic policy must be reiterated periodically from the top if the men and women down the line are to understand that the company is in earnest.

Thus, Charles E. Wilson, who succeeded Mr. Swope as chief executive officer, reissued Mr. Swope's original statement over his own signature in a booklet distributed to employees throughout the country. In addition, Mr. Wilson served as Chairman of the President's Committee on Human Rights. Speaking for the committee, Mr. Wilson said, in part: "...the protection of Civil Rights is a national problem which affects everyone. We need to guarantee the same rights to every person regardless of who he is, where he lives, or what his racial religious, or national origins are." While this view was expressed as a part of the transmittal of the report to President Truman, it was also widely circulated throughout the company as a re-affirmation of Mr. Wilson's convictions on the equal opportunity question.

Ralph J. Cordiner, Mr. Wilson's successor, believed that discrimination is not only wrong in principle, but a handicap to the business. He stated: "We continue to feel that, as a matter of sound business we should offer both employment and advancement opportunities to the best qualified individuals available, without regard to their race, creed, or color."

A year ago, Fred J. Borch became president of the company, and immediately made it clear that the policy still applied, and that he expected complete compliance: "Our policy is clear, and each level of management must make sure it is well understood—and fully implemented at every location."

His words were underscored by those of the new chairman of the board, Gerald L. Phillippe: "Steady progress in providing equal opportunity will not only move our country closer to its high ideals, but also help to remove some serious obstacles to accelerated economic growth. General Electric's Equal Employment Opportunity Policy must continue to be implemented on a Company-wide front. This is what we all must do. *It is not an optional matter for any one of us.*"

These statements of position, each with different emphasis, but essentially statements of the same basic philosophy, have been widely circulated throughout the company. They have been buttressed with letters of instruction from our personnel practices component in New York to employee relations managers and personnel specialists in our various product businesses. They have been re-emphasized in national and regional conferences of employee relations personnel.

Implementation in a widespread, diversified, decentralized company of 250,000 people of an equal opportunity policy is infinitely more complex than taking a discriminatory sign off a door. Hiring decisions are made or influenced by literally thousands of General

Electric people, ranging from professional personnel specialists to the individual local sales manager who is trying to determine which of several qualified applicants he wants to serve as his secretary.

An unreceptive attitude on the part of an interviewer toward an individual applicant may, in effect, be just as discriminatory as "a sign on the door." Once the fundamental criteria of qualification have been established, employment decisions may tend to become more subjective than objective. And the factors affecting promotion are so diverse as to be almost infinite. General Electric has its own careful and detailed procedures for evaluating employee achievement. Has John Doe earned a pay increase? Is Mary Roe ready to move to a higher level job? Does Richard Coe qualify for special training to enable him to take on added responsibility?

Thus, we have become increasingly aware over the years that affirmative action, to complement the basic policy, is necessary, and we have worked hard at this. Some of the various kinds of affirmative action which are helping the company to achieve the kind of corporate climate it seeks are discussed below.

Union Relations: In 1938, Mr. Swope's statement of three years earlier was incorporated into the first agreement between the company and the United Electrical Workers. A similar non-discrimination clause was included in the first agreement between the company and the I.U.E. (CIO) in 1950. A similar statement now appears in agreements with more than one hundred other unions with which the company bargains.

Recruiting: Equal opportunity cannot simply be a matter of passive acceptance. In 1948, when Howard University in Washington became the first Negro school to earn accreditation by the Engineers Council on Professional Development, General Electric immediately sent its recruiters to the Howard campus—the first national firm to do so. Today, of course, we are but one of many national companies visiting Howard each year. In addition, our recruiters now visit eleven other predominately Negro colleges and the list grows each year. Furthermore, key General Electric personnel travel extensively to meet with Negro university leaders and participate constructively in their development programs.

Recruiting techniques, of course, can have a significant effect on the achievement of equal opportunity progress. To take a more current and popular example, a year ago the company was beginning to recruit about two hundred young men and women for good-paying assignments as guides and hostesses at our Progressland exhibit at the New York World's Fair. Consistent with company-wide practices, our Progressland managers rejected the idea of some arbitrary "ratio" of Negro participants. The establishment of some fixed ratio of Negro to white employees would conflict with the principle of hiring and advancement on the basis of qualification. Indeed, in some of our plants, the use of arbitrary ratios would probably inhibit the entry of qualified Negroes into industry. But simply to reject the idea of ratios is not enough. What was needed here (as in other locations in which we have had a relatively rapid build-up in employment) was affirmative action to make certain that numbers of qualified Negroes had the same opportunity to be considered as whites. The Progressland staff made the hiring procedures and qualifications known early to New York-area groups interested in equal job opportunity activities and to educational and civic leaders in predominantly Negro areas. As the result of this extra diligence we received applications from many qualified Negroes. Ultimately we were again accorded evidence that progress for General Electric means *human* progress no less than technical progress. One executive of the NAACP commented: "If we are able to encourage others to emulate your example, the World's Fair will truly be a peek into the future, a future full of more than just intangible dreams of equality."

And let me re-emphasize that this modest achievement was accomplished without resort to use of ratios or without compromising qualifications.

BEYOND OUR WALLS

Ultimately, even as we try conscientiously to assure fair and equal treatment for every job applicant and every employee, and as we try to assure that qualified Negroes are made aware of opportunities with General Electric, we are faced with the knottiest problem in the equal employment opportunity field: a disproportionately high number of Negro applicants simply do not measure up to the opportunities available. Most have not had what Lincoln called an "unfettered start." Those who do qualify often do so only after having overcome special, unusual barriers—economic, educational, psychological, social.

We know that an equal employment opportunity program cannot truly flourish while too many of the minority applicants are sorely disadvantaged, particularly in terms of education and training. We do, of course, have training courses for apprentices and dozens of courses aimed at encouraging all employees to upgrade their skills. Last year, for instance, about one in every eight employees participated in one of General Electric's educational programs. But such programs meet the need only within our walls.

We have had several well-meaning suggestions that we relax the qualifications a little for minority applicants. We do not believe that this is a useful solution. We would not be keeping faith with our customers, with our shareowners, or with our employees, white and Negro, each of whose jobs is dependent on the successful performance of all.

Once again, however, the alternative is to do something constructive. There are many examples:

Beginning in 1954 the company and the General Electric Foundation began support of the United Negro College Fund, representing thirty-two private Negro colleges and universities. Currently, for the period of 1964-67, a grant of $100,000 has been arranged in support of the Fund's special drive to broaden existing educational programs, reinforce teaching strengths, provide more student aid, and upgrade laboratories and other facilities.

Meanwhile at the high school level, General Electric is working in many cities with local educators to encourage careers in various skills required by the electrical industry and to combat the "dropout" problem.

For example, at the Benjamin Franklin High School in Philadelphia, where these is a substantial Negro enrollment, school officials have credited the work of people from the General Electric Missile and Space Division (many of them being Negroes) with a dramatic rise in numbers of student graduates and a correspondingly sharp decline in dropouts. Over a two-year period, Negro and white employee teams from the division—assemblers, engineers, secretaries, draftsmen—have spoken to more than 10,000 students in school assemblies and 15,000 more in individual career conferences in Philadelphia, in a public school system in which Negro enrollment is about 50 per cent.

In another plant-city, General Electric found that some teachers in the local public school system were encouraging Negro girls to concentrate on bookkeeping courses instead of stenography because they believed that secretarial jobs were closed to them. Later, when the girls did apply for secretarial tests, they often failed. General Electric, of course, tried to set the record straight not only on secretarial opportunities but on the other kinds of jobs for which we could foresee a demand.

Upgrading teaching skills is also important. Since 1945, General Electric and the General Electric Foundation have sponsored advanced, all-expense-paid courses for high school and college educators in cooperation with several leading colleges and universities.

Negro teachers have participated from the beginning. In 1963, for instance, eighteen of sixty high school teachers attending a six-week course at the University of Kentucky were Negroes—probably the highest percentage of Negroes ever enrolled in a given course in that institution.

Men and women who have left school often find they do not have skills for industry. A single company can properly help here, too. In Philadelphia, for instance, the Opportunities Industrialization Center, started less than two years ago by a local Negro minister, Rev. Leon Sullivan, has already attracted national attention for its success in training and placing unemployed or underemployed Negroes (and some whites). Local General Electric management was pleased to contribute financial and equipment support, along with others, and assistance in planning the curriculum.

Similarly, the Urban League across the country has been developing "skills banks" for the development and placement of Negroes. At the national level, Dr. G. Roy Fugal of General Electric, one of industry's most knowledgeable authorities in the equal employment opportunities field, has been working closely with such organizations as the League's Commerce and Industry Council. At the local level, the skills bank programs are receiving support of General Electric men in many of the communities in which the company has major facilities.

In New York City, General Electric joined with six other large employers and the National Urban League in sponsoring a secretarial training course, designed as a spring-board for minority group women seeking jobs with national corporations in the metropolitan area. This pilot course has been most successful and has encouraged similar approaches in other localities.

One of the problems which has come up again and again in discussions with educators whose student bodies include large numbers of Negroes is the lack of recognition of the real opportunities which are open in industry—not just General Electric, but industry as a whole—for qualified Negro applicants.

In the lower grades, this lack of recognition seems to be one of the factors which can breed apathy toward academic achievement. In college, it can predispose many competent young people to shy away from courses which would lead to careers in industry.

"It isn't enough for us to *tell* them about good job opportunities in industry," one of our recruiters was told last summer. "You have to *show* them."

As a result, we prepared an illustrated booklet, "At Work in Industry Today," covering case histories of 50 General Electric employees, all Negroes, who are building careers for themselves in a wide variety of jobs. Some are long-established employees with substantial records of advancement, others are apprentices or trainees. Some are managers, some are secretaries, some are factory workers, skilled and semi-skilled. They are working in engineering, in sales, in employee relations, in manufacturing, in finance. Some are high school and college graduates, others are school dropouts who have had to work extra-hard to overcome a lack of formal education.

We have distributed copies of the booklet to some sixty thousand guidance teachers and career counselors in schools throughout the country, and have made it available for use by various urban training centers and by other organizations, public and private, who are interested in upgrading the skills of Negroes. We hope it will help; it has already had some effects which we consider salutary. Two state governments have told us that they are seriously considering developing similar booklets on their own, with examples from their own states, and a number of other companies have expressed interest in preparing booklets drawing on examples peculiar to their own industries.

We have been considering here primarily the question of jobs: equal opportunity in employment, and in advancement, and beyond this the necessity to encourage the development of the skills and knowledge which make progress possible.

CONCLUDING REMARKS

The employment area is the one in which the American corporation has primary interest, if for no other reason than that American business needs all the skills it can obtain in these years of massive technological change and economic growth. We know that achievement of justice for each citizen does not rest solely on getting a good job, nor even on good education which will qualify him for a good job. None of us is simply an economic animal—much as the Marxists would have us believe it. Ours is a nation of the spirit, and our American economic system is meant to serve that quality. Many of our communities across the nation have problems which inhibit various minority groups from making the most of their American heritage. These problems warrant the attention of each of us as citizens.

Recently, Fred Borch made his first talk as president of General Electric to the administrative committee of a nationwide society of top-level General Electric managers and professional personnel.

He spoke as follows: "Most of you have heard that President Johnson recently appointed me a member of the National Citizens' Committee for Community Relations.

"One of the key roles which each member of the Committee has been asked to perform is: 'to emphasize the necessity of mobilizing all those forces available at the community level, which might be drawn on to create a climate for compliance....' Certainly, this is something constructive each of us can do within the communities in which we live—and I sincerely urge your participation as General Electric men and as citizens.

"The Civil Rights law is the law of the land, and we as good citizens should certainly do our full share in seeing that it becomes successful as an instrument for promoting social justice and equal opportunities for all Americans regardless of race, creed, or color.

"Don't underestimate the effect, good or bad, which each of you can create by the examples you set—or by the very things you say about these fundamental rights of others. In your service organizations and clubs in your hometown, in your boards of education, and in your town meetings, don't be afraid to stand up and be counted for the things that are positive and right. It doesn't take much courage or intelligence to be negative.

"All of us, working together, can make this a better America by helping to assure the legitimate rights of others. If, therefore, [you are] looking for ways to encourage [your associates] to render a real service to the country, you might want to raise the question as to whether [you] should consider some appropriate activities or projects on a voluntary basis. If we make contributions to human progress a primary criterion of every undertaking—in the investment of our own money and time on an individual basis, and in each business venture in General Electric—we will continue to broaden and strengthen our opportunities for growth and profit and service in the future through the good we do," said Mr. Borch. Knowing as I do the capabilities of the managers to whom this message was delivered and the numbers of communities in which they function, I cannot help but feel that their personal, individual efforts can have real impact.

These, then, are ways which one company has been trying to follow in the quest for true equal employment opportunity: the continued re-emphasis and implementation of our formal policy, and the effort both inside and outside the company to create a climate in which the words can become reality. We are going to have to continue to work on both fronts, with vigilance on the first and creativity on the second. We have no reason to be smug; even now, most probably, there are corners in our large decentralized company in which the cobwebs of old antagonisms still linger. But we are convinced that American industry can turn equal employment opportunity from a goal into an affirmative achievement—and that each individual company can help significantly by its own direct efforts.

PART IV

Union Policies and Programs for Equal Opportunity

11

UNION RACIAL PRACTICES*
Ray Marshall**

In discussing union racial practices, we shall emphasize racial exclusion from unions by formal and informal means, segregated local unions, discrimination in the building trades, and the ways unions influence economic opportunities of Negroes. Our discussion of union racial patterns will be followed by an analysis of some of the major factors changing those patterns.

Formal Exclusion

The number of national unions with formal racial restrictions has declined significantly in the last thirty years. In 1930, at least twenty-two unions formally barred Negroes from equal membership.[1] By 1943, mergers and changing racial practices had reduced the number of restrictive unions to about thirteen, seven of which were AFL affiliates (SNA, BRSC, IAM, MMP, RMA, WWPA, and the ORT).[2] In 1949 there were at least nine unions with formal race bars, two of which were members of the AFL (WWPA and ORT). The ORT removed its race bar in 1952, and the WWPA merged with the United Papermakers & Paperworkers. After the AFL-CIO merger in 1955 there would have been no major national affiliates with race bars if the BRT and the BLF had not been admitted to the merged federation. The BRT removed its race bar in 1960, leaving only the ORC, the BLE, and the BLF with formal restrictions. The BLF, the only one of these unions affiliated with the AFL-CIO,[3] removed its race bar in 1963.

The following forces caused unions to abandon exclusion by formal means or to adopt more subtle forms: expansion of Negro employment into jurisdictions covered by these unions, especially

---

*Hearings before the Senate Subcommittee on Employment and Manpower of the Committee on Labor and Public Welfare, September 10, 1963, *Nation's Manpower Revolution*, pp. 1192-1202.

**Professor of Economics, University of Texas.

during World War II; competition between unions for Negro votes in representation elections after the passage of the Railway Labor Act; the embarrassment of exclusionist union leaders at conventions and in the press by criticism from Negro and white union leaders; action by such governmental agencies as the wartime and state FEP committees, especially the creation of the New York State Commission Against Discrimination in 1946; and fear of the loss of exclusive bargaining rights, union shop provisions, or other legal privileges under the Railway Labor Act or the Taft-Hartley Act.[4]

Informal Exclusion

The decline in formal exclusion by international unions does not mean, however, that discrimination declined by the same degree because of local variations from official policies. Unions with formal race bars frequently have accepted Negro members, and the locals of some international unions with no formal bars, particularly in the building trades and on the railroads, have excluded Negroes by such informal means as agreements not to sponsor Negroes for membership; refusal to admit Negroes into apprenticeship programs; refusal to accept applicants from Negroes or simply ignoring their applications; general "understandings" to vote against Negroes if they were proposed (for example, three members of a BRT or BRSC lodge may bar an applicant for membership); using examinations to refuse Negro journeymen status which either were not given to whites or were rigged so that Negroes could not pass them; and by exerting political pressure on governmental licensing agencies to see to it that Negroes failed the tests. An examination of union racial practices in various building trades unions throws more light on this problem.

Building Trades

The pattern of racial exclusion in the building trades has been second only to the railroad industry in its rigidity.[5] The craft locals of the International Brotherhood of Electrical Workers (IBEW) and the Plumbers & Pipe Fitters (UA) have had an almost consistent pattern of discrimination throughout the United States, but the following other building trades unions are also prominent in the list of unions regularly charged with racial discrimination: Granite Workers, Flint Glass Workers, Structural Iron Workers, and Asbestos Workers. In addition, locals of the following organizations less frequently have been charged with discrimination by various civil rights organizations: Bricklayers, Masons & Plasterers (BMP); Plasterers & Cement Masons (PCM); United Brotherhood of Carpenters & Joiners (BCJ); International Union of Operating Engineers (IUOE); Lathers International Union; Painters, Decorators & Paperhangers (PDP); International Association of Sheet Metal Workers; and Elevator Constructors. Some of these latter unions, like the BMP, the PCM, and the Roofers are in occupations with relatively large Negro memberships, and the Bricklayers International Union seems consistently to have sought to abolish discriminatory practices — except segregated locals — whenever these have been brought to its attention. The unions in the so-called trowel trades and the Roofers have many Negro members in integrated or virtually all-Negro locals in the South, but there have been charges of segregation in the South and other forms of discrimination in many places in the non-South. Other organizations like the IUOE and the Teamsters have had reputations for barring Negroes in some places and accepting them in others.

International Unions

We should note the distinction between the policies of international unions and their locals. Both the Plumbers and the IBEW internationals have become concerned about the adverse publicity they are receiving, which has caused their actions to be carefully scrutinized by civil rights and government agencies and which threatens to jeopardize their control of the trades. The Plumbers established a committee in 1959 to study charges of racial discrimination against their locals throughout the United States, and in 1962 the international union included a nondiscrimination clause in its national agreement covering large contractors, which could be significant for some federal contractors. Similarly, the 1958 IBEW Convention adopted a resolution on civil rights, which resolved that it was the "enduring goal of our brotherhood to assure to all workers their full share in the benefits of union organization without regard to race, creed, color, or national origin."[6] In 1963, eighteen building trades internationals agreed to take more vigorous action to eliminate discrimination, and the powerful Brotherhood of Carpenters & Joiners adopted a nondiscrimination program, including the elimination of segregated locals. Moreover, building trades unions throughout the United States have recently responded to the widespread charges of discrimination against them by admitting some Negroes to membership. It remains to be seen, however, whether these equalitarian measures will produce significant changes in racial employment patterns.

Conclusions on Unions with Informal Exclusion

The evidence seems to support the following conclusions concerning unions that bar Negroes from membership by informal means:

1. Racial exclusion by informal means is not restricted to any particular geographic area. Though restriction is undoubtedly more rigid in the South, unions in the following trades probably have more Negro members in the South than some other places: the trowel trades, longshoremen, teamsters, roofers, hod carriers and common laborers, and hotel and restaurant employees. These trades have been practiced by Negroes in the South because they have been regarded as "Negro work" and because Negroes have sufficient supplies of labor to protect their interest and to protect their employers, who might be boycotted by whites. These occupations also are relatively old and have stable techniques, making it difficult for unions to exclude Negroes by monopolizing the latest technology.

2. While some craft unions have had egalitarian racial policies and some industrial union locals have refused to admit Negroes to membership, as a general rule the unions which practice exclusion are craft organizations. The members of craft locals have the ability to exclude Negroes from membership and from the trade if they can control the labor supply. Industrial unions, on the other hand, are forced to organize workers hired by the employer, while the craft unions determine in many cases whom he hires. In addition, craft unions at the local level consider it to their advantage to exclude workers, while industrial unions consider it to their advantage to organize extensively.

3. The foregoing factors are not, however, sufficient to identify the general character of excluding unions. Some other factors include the following: because of the egalitarian trend in race relations, those unions which are older, other things being equal, seem more likely to exclude than newer unions; in many cases the employer determines the hiring policy; whites are likely to attempt to exclude Negroes from certain status jobs like those of airline pilots, stock wranglers, locomotive engineers, white collar and supervisory jobs; and, in some cases, exclusion is directed against all except a particular nationality group. (It has been common practice in the building trades, for instance, for locals to be made up entirely of a particular nationality.)

Auxiliary and Segregated Locals

A number of international unions which did not bar Negroes from membership restricted them to auxiliary locals controlled entirely by whites; about the only thing Negro members of these locals were allowed to do was to pay dues.[7] Auxiliary locals were weakened by attacks from the wartime FEPC, court decisions which prohibited the closed shop where auxiliaries existed, NLRB decisions that the auxiliary could not be coupled with the checkoff of union dues, state FEP laws, the Taft-Hartley and Railway Labor Act amendments making the union shop unenforceable if all workers are not admitted on equal terms, and the Landrum-Griffin Act of 1959 which makes it possible for Negro employees to bring action to abolish auxiliary locals. A few auxiliary locals remained in 1959 but had become relatively unimportant by that date.

Segregated locals are theoretically different from auxiliary locals in that the Negro and white locals are equal and have separate charters.[8] This distinction sometimes is more theoretical than real, however, because the white local might in fact represent the Negro local in dealings with employers. We must note, though, that there are actually relatively few truly segregated locals in the sense of separate unions for Negroes and whites in the same plant or craft. A few unions almost invariably have had segregated locals in the South — the Carpenters, Longshoremen, the Paper Makers, the Pulp Sulphite Workers, the Brotherhood of Railway Clerks, the Tobacco Workers, and the Musicians — but industrial unions have very few — in 1959, the Textile Workers had about three and the OCAW, two (of 152 locals in the South). Even unions like the Tobacco Workers, with predominately Southern memberships have adopted a policy since 1946 of not forming segregated locals. Other unions, like the Bricklayers, have a relatively small number of segregated locals in the South; in 1959, 25 of that union's 168 Southern locals were segregated.

While it is extremely difficult to generalize about segregated locals, the writer's experiences suggest several broad conclusions:

1. Negroes in the South frequently favor a continuation of segregation because they would usually be in the minority and know that whites might discriminate against them;[9] Negroes have their own buildings and other property, as well as their own officers and representatives, and thus have a vested interest in perpetuating segregation;[10] some Negroes believe they can engage in nonunion matters of interest to Negroes better if they have their own locals.[11]

2. Whether or not Negroes oppose integregation depends partly upon the effects of segregation on their economic opportunities. Some unions, like the Bricklayers, Musicians, Longshoremen, Barbers, and others feel that their economic opportunities would not be improved if they integrated because they have protected territories.

In other cases, however, Negro workers are extremely unhappy with segregation because they are denied equal job opportunities. Almost everywhere, for instance, Negro Carpenters' locals in the South have virtually atrophied because they cannot get adequate job opportunities. The Painters have a number of segregated locals in the South and have had experience similar to the Carpenters. As noted above, however, the Carpenters adopted a policy in 1963 to merge these locals.

3. The ideological and philosophical positions of Negroes will also influence their attitude toward segregated locals. Some Negro leaders are opposed to segregation on principle and feel that the AFL-CIO should deliver an ultimatum to its segregated locals to integrate or be expelled. On the other hand, a majority of the Negro leaders in segregated unions in the South probably oppose integration. Younger Negro workers are more likely to insist on integration, but older leaders fear Negroes will suffer short-run losses from integration.

4. The proportions of Negroes in unions will influence the ability to merge segregated locals. If there are very few Negroes, whites will agree to merge, but if the Negroes are in the majority the whites will frequently oppose integration.

5. Negro resistance to integration has been reduced by special arrangements to make it possible for them to continue to have some control over their affairs when they integrate.

Finally, we may note the following developments concerning segregated unions in recent years:

(a) The practice of establishing segregated locals has been almost completely discontinued. Observers also detect tendencies for Negroes and whites to segregate themselves in union meetings less than they did twenty years ago. There are, moreover, increasing examples of integrated union social affairs in the South.

(b) A number of international unions have agreed to establish no more segregated unions (Painters; Tobacco Workers; Pulp, Sulphite, and Paper Mill Workers), and other organizations have taken measures to integrate segregated locals (International Ladies' Garment Workers, the National Association of Letter Carriers, the International Association of Machinists, the International Brotherhood of Teamsters, the American Federation of Musicians, the Carpenters, and the American Federation of Teachers). Most of the organizations with segregated locals in the South, however, have refused to integrate locals on the grounds of local autonomy, especially opposition by the colored members (Bricklayers, Longshoremen, Molders, Paper Makers, Railroad Clerks, Maintenance of Way Employees, Railway Carmen, Railway Trainmen).

(c) The AFL-CIO has taken a formal position against segregated locals but has refused to invoke sanctions or to establish a time by which segregated locals must integrate.

We should note, however, that to say a local is "integrated" might not mean very much. It could mean that one or two Negroes belong to the organization but never participate other than by paying dues. "Integration" might also mean that Negroes are members of the industrial union, but if they attend meetings they segregate themselves or are segregated by whites.

Control of Job Opportunities

Craft unions influence job opportunities for Negroes by controlling entry into the labor market through closed-union, closed-shop conditions, job referral systems, apprenticeship programs, and pressure on employers to hire or not to hire Negroes. Industrial unions affect job opportunities through control of hiring, transfer, promotion, and layoffs. Many employers are convinced that if they transfer Negroes into previously "white" occupations, the white workers will strike, and there is sufficient historical precedent to validate this belief, though it is rarely possible for a group of rank-and-filers to block the employment or upgrading of Negroes without the aid of either the employer or the international.

Finally, unions have positively influenced employment opportunities of minorities by promoting civil rights legislation, including nondiscrimination clauses in contracts and adoption of company-wide seniority agreements to make it possible for Negroes to break out of "Negro" jobs.

While our attention has been focused on problems of racial discrimination within unions, we have noted that unions also have contributed to the improvement of the Negro workers' position. In spite of these positive measures, however, racial discrimination is still a serious problem within the labor movement and probably cannot be solved by the unions themselves. This conclusion is based on the belief that those unions and leaders who want to change union racial practices do not have sufficient power to do so.[12]

SOME FACTORS INFLUENCING UNION RACIAL PRACTICES

Labor Market Factors

Technological change has an important effect on the employ-

ment opportunities of minorities, who are concentrated dispropor-
tionally in those jobs most likely to be replaced by innovations.
Sometimes the job is abolished by the introduction of new machinery
and at other times it is made more attractive; Negroes have been
replaced in both cases.

Racial trouble has frequently started when unemployment rises
and whites start moving into jobs held by Negroes or senior Negroes
are laid off while junior whites are retained. Unionism, while not
causing Negroes to have equal treatment, might make it possible
for them to get the same treatment in layoffs as whites who have the
same seniority because seniority clauses in union agreements give
Negroes legal rights they would not have in the absence of unions.

Economic conditions also affect the pace at which Negroes can
move up the economic ladder. If the labor market is slack and
there are few opportunities for advancement, the results of changing
the racial practices of unions and employers will be less significant.
For instance, the effort exerted over a long period to change racial
practices in the oil industry produced limited results because non-
technical employment in most companies declined after 1953, and
few new employees have been hired or promoted. Though separate
lines of progression were broken down in the major companies in
this industry, only a few Negroes have moved into better jobs.

Negroes also have found that tight labor markets — such as exist
during wars — make it easier for them to move into jobs from which
they were previously excluded. It is true that Negroes generally
have been the last to be committed to industrial employment during
these times and have been more vulnerable than whites to retrench-
ment during recessions, but it is nevertheless significant that Negroes were able to enter some jobs for the first time during wars.
Once in these jobs, Negroes were in a position to fight from within
unions and companies to improve their positions. While many
factors influence the employment opportunities of minorities, there
is little doubt that antidiscrimination measures would be much
more effective in a full employment atmosphere.

The ease or difficulty with which a trade may be learned and
practiced is a significant consideration in changing union racial
practices. If the trade is relatively easy to learn or Negroes can
learn it in trade schools, the Armed Forces, or by picking it up, the
union will have difficulty excluding Negroes or will be forced to
lower its economic conditions. In the plumbing and electrical industries where apprenticeships are important, it is relatively difficult
for Negroes to learn the trade because there are few colored craftsmen, and whites will rarely take Negro apprentices or trainees if the
admission of Negroes is opposed by the union. Trades where Ne-

groes have difficulty becoming journeymen because of union exclusion or governmental licensing arrangements will therefore not
have many Negro trainees. One of the reasons Negro bricklayers,
cement finishers, and plasterers have been able to perpetuate themselves in the South is that there are a sizable number of Negroes
who will teach the trade to others. Moreover, the techniques used
in these trades are relatively stable, so that new methods cannot
be monopolized by whites to exclude Negroes. Negroes were also
allowed to retain some jobs which were difficult to perform or had
other undesirable features.

Another labor market factor perpetuating racial job patterns is
the employer's preference for white or Negro labor. This preference
is influenced by stereotypes as to whether or not Negroes can do
certain kinds of work, have higher rates of turnover, are subject
to more wage garnishments, and the like. Negroes have been preferred by white contractors in the South for certain jobs which
colored workers have traditionally held — like those of longshoremen, hodcarriers, and cement finishers. Employers sometimes preferred Negroes for the same jobs held by whites because Negroes
would work for lower wages. In the past, Negroes moved into some
jobs during strikes because employers thought colored workers
would not join unions, a degree of preference which was intensified
by Negro leaders who felt that the colored worker's economic salva-
tion lay in an alliance with employers against unions. Today, many
of the strongest Negro community institutions favor unions and
exert their influence to prevent Negroes from being used as strike-
breakers. Employers no longer feel that they can count on Negroes
to be non-union, and the general extension of unionism has made
this attribute less important to the companies. Moreover, the virtual
abolition of racial wage differentials for the same jobs has eliminated
another reason why employers preferred Negroes.

Employers' preferences will also be affected by uncertainties as
to the reaction of white workers and the supply of Negroes who
possess the necessary skills if they are boycotted by white craftsmen.
Whether or not whites boycott an employer depends upon the availability of jobs and general market conditions. Boycotts will rarely
be initiated by whites in relatively stable industrial jobs; in construction work, on the other hand, it is a simple matter for workers
to boycott a particular employer. In longshoring, Negroes can
furnish enough workers to replace whites if the latter refuse to work
with them, but there are not enough Negro electricians or plumbers
to make this possible.

Supply of labor is related to the status of the job. In many cases,
employers prefer Negroes because they are more easily controlled

in low-status occupations. Since a sufficiently large supply of whites cannot be found for some of these jobs, employers prefer Negroes who are forced by occupational limitations into these lines.

The scope of collective bargaining is a factor influencing the union's ability to discriminate against minorities. Organizations which have purely local bargaining arrangements are more likely to discriminate than those that use national bargains, because the national union is usually more conspicuous, making it relatively easy to bring moral pressure to bear on it. There have been some widely publicized cases of racial discrimination by local unions, but as a rule locals are too insignificant to attract national attention. The widely publicized cases attract attention precisely because the locals are impervious to moral pressures, and there is usually no agency that can readily focus sufficient economic, physical, or political power on them to produce a change in their policies.

National bargains give the parent organization more power to deal with the local. Since nationals are more vulnerable to moral power, and since the prevailing moral sentiment in the United States is against discrimination, unions with national bargains will be more likely to cause their locals to conform with equalitarian racial policies.

The level of union wages in a plant covered by the national bargain influences the control that a national union can exert over its local affiliates. If union wages and conditions are much higher than prevailing wages in the local area, the international has more control over the local. In Memphis, for example, local white union members vigorously protested the United Automobile Workers' equalitarian policies, but segregationist elements did not secede from the international, partly because of national contracts and good wages and conditions. Some white members of the Memphis local considered pulling out of the international but were deterred by the realization that the international, not the local, was the certified bargaining agent.

Other factors which influence the international's ability to require its locals to observe equalitarian racial policies include the following: the effect of enforcement on the international's objectives as interpreted by its leaders and as it influences their official positions; whether the international has some reason to appeal to the Negro community, e.g., organizing a bloc of unorganized Negroes or Negro-labor political considerations; the available alternatives for the local, especially whether there is a rival union to which it can secede; the employers' attitude — the employer will be willing to cooperate with the international if he has some reason (government contracts, fear of boycotts) to oppose discrimination by the

local; the size and political significance of the local involved; the
dues structure and financial strength of the international and the
constitutional provisions relating to the ownership of the local's
property if it secedes; and the ease with which trusteeships can be
imposed upon the local.

The Courts

There has been considerable legal activity in the past twenty years
to define more clearly the duty of fair representation imposed on
unions as a result of the privilege of exclusive bargaining rights
granted by the Railway Labor and Wagner acts.[13] Under this duty,
unions were required to represent all workers fairly, even though
they were not required to admit them to membership. Some federal
courts have also held that employers are jointly liable with unions
for the duty of fair representation,[14] and aggrieved minorities
have brought suit against unions for damage resulting from violation of their legal rights.[15]

Negroes also sought to use the theory of the school desegregation
cases to eliminate discrimination by unions, but the Supreme
Court's refusal in 1959 to grant *certiorari* in the *Oliphant* case
would seem to perpetuate the doctrine that unions do not have
to grant membership to all members of the bargaining unit in order
to satisfy the duty of fair representation.[16] There is, however, a
minority of legal opinion, which seems to be growing, that unions
cannot represent workers fairly unless they admit all members of
the bargaining units.[17]

Negroes have not been able to change union racial practices very
much through the courts, however, because legal action is expensive, requires a great deal of time, is uncertain as to its outcome,
and has rarely resulted in damages to the plaintiffs. However, lawsuits are valuable to aggrieved minorities as a threat to discriminating unions, and injunctions have been used to prevent unions from
causing Negroes to lose their jobs.[18]

The NLRB

The disadvantages of court cases could be avoided if there were
effective administrative remedies, but the National Labor Relations
Board (NLRB) has been much more cautious than the courts in
interpreting and applying its power to prevent discrimination by
unions. Though the NLRB has entertained ". . . grave doubt
whether a union which discriminatorily denies membership to employees on the basis of race, may, nevertheless, bargain as the exclusive representative in an appropriate unit composed of members

of the excluded race,"[19] it repeatedly permitted unions which excluded Negroes to participate in elections covering bargaining units containing Negroes.[20] Indeed, the Board has ruled as follows:

"Neither exclusion from membership nor segregated membership per se represents evasion on the part of a labor organization of its statutory duty of 'equal representation.' But in each case where the issue is presented the Board will scrutinize the contract and conduct of a representative organization and withdraw certification if it finds the organization has discriminated against employees in the bargaining units through its membership restrictions or otherwise."[21]

Despite this threat, however, the NLRB has never actually revoked certification of a union for racial discrimination, though some unions have surrendered certification, apparently to avoid action by the Board.[22] It must be conceded, however, that the basic reason for the NLRB's past refusal to deal more directly with racial discrimination has been the repeated refusal of Congress to give the Board explicit authority to deal with racial matters.

While it is too early for an evaluation, the NLRB is showing belated signs of taking more direct action against discriminatory unions. The Board has not gone as far as the courts in enforcing the duty of fair representation, but there is some indication that it might respond to President Kennedy's increased interest in equal rights for Negroes by decertifying discriminating unions. In a recent case, for instance, a trial examiner recommended that the certification of an independent union in Houston be revoked because "where a union segregates members or excludes or denies full membership status to applicants, on racial grounds, it is violating its duty of fair representation to all members of the unit and should not be permitted to hold a certified status."[23] The Board has given some indication of the trend in its thinking by ruling that it will not permit an existing discriminatory contract to bar a representation election.[24]

It is, however, not clear whether decertification would have a significant impact on union racial practices. While unions appear to be greatly concerned about decertification, it is not necessary for a union to be certified in order to bargain with employers. Indeed, many craft unions have sufficient economic power to operate without certification. It is not clear whether these unions have the duty of equal representation if they are not certified. It could be, therefore, that in the absence of federal contracts or a state or federal fair employment practices (FEP) law, there are no legal remedies to prevent discrimination by strong craft unions, who are the ones most guilty of discrimination. Even where legal remedies exist, however, Negroes have not been satisfied with the extent to which they have been able to enter many craft unions and occupations. This is perhaps one of the reasons, as in the 1963 Philadelphia and New York examples, that civil rights organizations have resorted to mass demonstrations to get Negroes hired and to focus attention on the discriminating unions. Most of these demonstrations have been in states with FEP laws.

Government Contract Committees

While the various contract committees set up by the federal government since President Roosevelt appointed the wartime Fair Employment Practices Committee have not dealt directly with unions, they have had indirect effects on their racial practices. In the petroleum, pulp and paper, aircraft, and other industries in the South, for example, Negroes have changed union practices by threatening employers with the loss of federal contracts. In these industries, there has been some desegregation of seniority rosters controlled jointly by the unions and employers, especially since 1953. As a general rule, however, President Eisenhower's Committee on Government Contracts (PCGC) had a very limited impact on unions because it adopted the policy that unions were not parties to government contracts and were therefore beyond its control. Moreover, the PCGC's power was limited by the executive order which established it. In spite of these limitations, however, the PCGC was used by groups like the NAACP to promote equal job opportunities for Negroes.

President Kennedy's Committee on Equal Employment Opportunity (PCEEO), not only has more power than the PCGC, but also is directed to "cause any labor union . . . who is or may be engaged in work under Government contracts to cooperate with and to comply in the implementation of, the purposes of the order." Moreover, unions covering 90 per cent of the AFL-CIO's membership have signed voluntary pledges to comply with the provisions of the executive order. As a result of the PCEEO's activity, a number of unions have integrated their locals in the South and some jobs have been integrated, particularly at the important Lockheed aircraft plant in Marietta, Ga., where the International Association of Machinists has bargaining rights. In June, 1963, President Kennedy met with a group of labor leaders and got them to pledge their support to eliminate discrimination in their ranks as well as in the larger community. It remains to be seen, of course, whether the unions can implement these pledges.

State FEP Committees

Some of the most intransigent cases brought before the state FEP commissions, and usually the first cases to go to public hearing or the courts, have involved unions. It is not entirely paradoxical, of course, that unions have been the chief supporters of FEP legislation and have been among the most intransigent respondents before the commissions established by these laws, because there are many different kinds of unions and union members. Moreover, unions sometimes find it easier to support general civil rights legislation than to solve their own racial problems. In fact, George Meany, president of the AFL-CIO, advocates a federal FEP law partly on the grounds that such legislation is needed to help overcome union discrimination.

The FEP commissions have succeeded in changing the formal racial practices of a number of unions, particularly on the railroads, and have succeeded in directly obtaining the admission of hundreds of workers who were formerly excluded from membership in labor organizations. Moreover, the commissions have aided in the regularization of many job referral systems, making it more difficult for these to be used as vehicles for discrimination. Though it would be impossible to establish statistically, the commissions undoubtedly have also been indirectly responsible for gaining more equal opportunities for thousands of Negroes not directly involved in these cases. The FEP laws also have been used by some union leaders as justification for equalitarian changes that were not considered politically feasible before the laws were passed.

In spite of these positive accomplishments, however, the evidence suggests that the commissions have not changed the basic employment patterns in most unionized industries, and the 1963 racial demonstrations against unions in FEP cities and states suggest that Negro leaders are far from satisfied with the results of these laws. There are many reasons for the commissions' failures to achieve faster results, including the following: (*a*) The commissions use essentially the same tactics against unions as against employers; namely, conciliation, persuasion, and the threat of public hearing, though it is generally conceded that recalcitrant local unions are less responsive to these tactics than employers. (*b*) The commission's operations are complicated by such factors as internal union politics, nepotism, amicism, the natural intractability of employment patterns, declining economic opportunities in many industries where Negroes are concentrated or where they are attempting to get jobs, the natural slowness of the case method in proving racial discrimination, the fewness of verifiable complaints against unions in most states, the complicated hiring arrangements which make it difficult to prove discrimination in many casual occupations, and the autonomy of discriminating local unions.

Any effort to change union racial practices must be based on an understanding of union structures because power is transmitted to decisionmakers through these structures. Public policy must be sure that the right kind of power is applied to those parts of the labor movement responsible for discrimination. The real problem of racial discrimination is usually at the local level and whether or not locals will take corrective action depends upon the extent to which they may be compelled to do so by parent internationals or outside pressures. Generally, local unions seem to be relatively impervious to moral pressures but are more responsive to economic pressures. There are a number of cases (in Cleveland, Washington, D.C., Milwaukee, Hartford, San Francisco, Los Angeles, and other places) in which local unions have defied the most vigorous public and official denunciations of their practices but have yielded to economic pressures. The *Hartford* case, for example, involving an IBEW local, was resolved, after the local defied the state commission on civil rights, when the superior court found it guilty of contempt for refusing to admit Negroes to membership and fined it $2,000 and $500 for each week it remained in contempt.[25] Building trades unions in Philadelphia were impervious to vigorous public attacks on them but admitted five Negroes to membership after Negroes exerted direct pressures through mass demonstrations. IBEW Local 26 in Washington, D.C., resisted vigorous moral pressures to get Negroes in the union but finally relented in 1963 and accepted two Negro apprentices.

These and other experiences suggest that recalcitrant local unions will change their practices when their power sources are threatened by government regulation, retaliation from the Negro community, and alienation of public opinion. If the trends continue, these unions face the following possibilities: decertification by the NLRB; loss of control over state and municipal licensing provisions where these are used for racial discrimination; loss of control over hiring and referral systems; loss of control over appenticeship training; and being barred from federal, state, and municipal work.

Negro and Civil Rights Organizations

Another important factor influencing union racial practices has been the organization of Negro workers to promote equalitarian measures in unions. Indeed, changes in discriminatory union practices have rarely come about in the absence of organized pressures.

Within the labor movement, A. Philip Randolph, AFL-CIO vice-president and president of the Brotherhood of Sleeping Car Porters, has formed many organizations since the 1920's to fight for equal treatment of Negroes. The latest of these organizations is the Negro-American Labor Council, formed in 1960. Negroes have also organized caucuses within unions to promote their objectives. Outside civil rights organizations, especially the National Association for the Advancement of Colored People and the National Urban League, have been very important in helping Negro unionists organize, seeking the passage of legislation, financing court actions, and making public declarations. Other groups seeking to achieve equal treatment of Negroes within unions include such organizations as the civil rights committees formed in several unions and the AFL-CIO, the Jewish Labor Committee, and the Association of Catholic Trade Unionists.

CONCLUSIONS

We may conclude by noting some of the main changes in union racial practices in the last thirty years.

(1) The number of international unions with formal racial bars has declined from at least twenty-two in 1930 to two major unions today, and none of these is affiliated with the AFL-CIO. Moreover, informal exclusion has declined considerably, and recently some of the most intransigent craft locals have accepted Negro members for the first time.

(2) Negro union membership has increased from about 56,000 in 1930 to between 1.5 and 2 million today.

(3) The AFL-CIO has adopted a stronger equalitarian racial position than either the AFL or the CIO, though the federation really has little other than moral power to enforce its policies against offending locals. While implementation of the federation's racial policies has been impeded by difficulties within the federation and its civil rights committee and department, there is evidence that the AFL-CIO is moving with increasing vigor to abolish discrimination in its ranks; the external pressures being exerted on the labor movement by civil rights organizations have strengthened the federation in its dealings with its affiliates.

(4) Negroes occupy official positions within the labor movement. Two Negroes were elected to the AFL-CIO Executive Council, though one of these (Willard Townsend) died and was not replaced by a Negro. At least seventeen international unions have or have

had Negro vice-presidents or executive board members.[26] There are also many Negroes in positions of responsibility within local unions.

(5) The level of the debate over union racial policies has changed in the past thirty years. Thirty years ago discrimination was defined largely in terms of unions which would not admit Negroes to membership and the prevalence of racial wage differentials. Where Negroes were admitted, it was commonly to auxiliary locals. Today, the racial wage differential has almost disappeared in jobs covered by union contracts, and auxiliary locals are almost nonexistent. The main areas of conflict today involve the exclusion of Negroes from some craft locals, abolition of segregated seniority rosters, the election of Negroes to international executive boards, and overcoming Negro and white opposition to the desegregation of local unions. While many building trades and railroad locals continue to exclude Negroes from membership, and Negroes continue to be concentrated in the lowest job categories, segregated seniority rosters have been changed considerably in many industries. Moreover, while segregated locals exist in all sections of the country, it is rare to learn of the establishment of new segregated locals, and several international unions are taking measures to abolish Negro locals where they exist.

(6) Thirty years ago, Negro leaders frequently encouraged colored workers to act as strikebreakers. Today, in spite of the growing public split between the Negro community and the labor movement, many Negro organizations remain pro-union, and Negro strike-breakers are rarely heard of. Moreover, Negro-labor political alliances continue to be important forces in most industrial cities.

(7) A considerable body of law has been developed in union racial practices, and a number of organizations have evolved to which aggrieved workers can take charges of discrimination against unions. Indeed, one reason union racial practices have not been changed more than they have is the paucity of verifiable charges filed with these agencies.

There is ample evidence of discrimination against Negroes by unions, but it would be false to allege either that there has not been a significant lowering of racial barriers in unions in the past thirty years, or that the union movement has not made significant contributions to the Negro's welfare.

FOOTNOTES

1. The following unions are known to have had formal race bars in 1930: Brotherhood of Railway Carmen — AFL (BRC); Switchmen's Union of North America — AFL (SNA); Brotherhood of Railway & Steamship Clerks — AFL (BRSC); the Order of Sleeping Car Conductors — AFL; Masters, Mates & Pilots of North America — AFL (MMP); Railway Mail Association — AFL (RMA); Wire Weavers Protective Association — AFL (WWPA); Commercial Telegraphers — AFL; Boilermakers — AFL; International Association of Machinists — AFL (IAM); the Order of Railway Telegraphers — AFL (ORT); the Brotherhood of Dining Car Conductors; the American Federation of Railway Workers; Brotherhood of Railway Station Employees & Clerks (BRSEC); American Train Dispatchers Association; Railroad Yard Masters of North America; Neptune Association; Brotherhood of Locomotive Engineers (BLE); Brotherhood of Locomotive Firemen and Enginemen (BLF); Brotherhood of Railway Conductors; the Brotherhood of Railroad Trainmen (BRT); and the Railroad Yard Masters of America.

2. See *ibid.* for names of these unions.

3. BLE constitution of June-July, 1956 as amended in September, 1960. Sec. 28. BLF constitution, July-August, 1959 as amended Jan. 8, 1960.

4. See, for example, *James* v. *Marinship*, 25 California 2d 721 (1944).

5. See, for example, speech delivered by George Meany to the Sixth National Legislative Conference of the Building & Construction Trades Department of the AFL–CIO, Washington, D.C., March 14, 1960; New York State Commission Against Discrimination, "Apprentices, Skilled Craftsmen, and the Negro; An Analysis," 1960; Ben D. Segal, "The Practices of Craft Unions in Washington, D.C., With Respect to Minority Groups," in *Civil Rights in the Nation's Capital* (Washington: National Association of Intergroup Relations Officials, November, 1959), p. 35; Memo to the writer from David Sawyer, executive director of the Commissions' Council on Human Relations, Washington, D.C., June 3, 1959; Herman D. Bloch, "Craft Unions A Link in the Circle of Negro Discrimination," *Phylon*, Fourth Quarter, 1958; "Craft Unions and the Negro in Historical Perspective," *Journal of Negro History*, January, 1958; Herbert Northrup, *Organized Labor and the Negro* (New York: Harpers, 1943), Ch. II; National Planning Association, Committee on the South, *Negro Employment in the South* (New York, 1955), *passim;* Herbert Hill, "Organized Labor and the Negro Wage Earner," *New Politics*, Winter, 1962; *Idem*, "Labor Unions and the Negro," *Commentary*, December, 1959; National Urban League, "Negroes and the Building Trades Unions" (New York: National Urban League, Industrial Relations Department, mimeo, nd.).

6. National and local craft unions have different interests with respect to organizing; nationals gain power by expansion while locals gain power by exclusion and controlling the supply of labor.

7. This arrangement was usually adopted in lieu of outright exclusion by formal means and was sometimes the next stage adopted in a union's racial practices following the elimination of formal racial restrictions. Organizations which followed this practice included the Brotherhood of Railroad Carmen, the Blacksmiths, the Boilermakers, the Motion Picture Operators, the National Rural Letter Carriers, the National Federation of Rural Letter Carriers, the Maintenance of Way Employees, the Sheet Metal Workers Alliance, the Brotherhood of Railway Clerks, the American Federation of Railroad Workers, the Rural Letter Carriers Association, the International Association of Machinists, and the Seafarers International Union. All of these organizations except the American Federation of Railroad Workers and the Rural Letter Carriers Association were affiliated with the AFL.

8. The following international unions have or have had segregated locals: Brotherhood of Maintenance of Way Employees (BMWE); Brotherhood of Painters, Decorators, and Paperhangers of America (BPDP); Brotherhood of Railway Carmen of America (BRC); Brotherhood of Railway and Steamship Clerks, Freight Handlers, Express, and Station Employees (BRSC); International Brotherhood of Boilermakers, Iron Ship Builders, Blacksmiths, Forgers, and Helpers (IBBS); International Union of Pulp, Sulphite, and Paper Mill Workers (PPS); Sheet Metal Workers International Association (SMW); United Brotherhood of Carpenters and Joiners of America (UBCJ); United Brotherhood of Paper Makers and Paperworkers (UPP); the National Federation of Rural Letter Carriers (Independent); American Federation of Musicians (AFM); National Association of Letter Carriers (NALC); International Association of Machinists (IAM); Tobacco Workers International Union (TWIU); the Bricklayers, Masons, and Plasterers (BMP); the Journeyman Barbers International Union; the Oil, Chemical, and Atomic Workers (OCAW); the Textile Workers Union; the United Textile Workers; the International Longshoremen's Association; the Molders; the Glass and Ceramic Workers; the Amalgamated Clothing Workers; International Brotherhood of Teamsters; and International Ladies' Garment Workers Union.

9. For instance, in 1954, OWIU Locals 23 (white) and 254 (Negro) decided to merge after legal action to integrate seniority rosters. When the committees merged, the bargaining committee was elected by majority vote, and comprised entirely of whites, who then negotiated a discriminatory contract. The Negroes split with the whites again and brought legal action against the company and the white union.

10. This is a common problem encountered by the AFM, for instance, in its efforts to merge segregated locals throughout the United States. When this question was raised at the AFM's 1957 convention, there were 47 Negro locals with 7,620 members, only 14 of which were in the South. When a vote was taken on this matter, 40 of the Negro locals opposed the merger, five favored it, and two did not vote.

11. In New Orleans, for instance, ILA Local 1419 (Negro) owns several

business establishments and operates a political organization which conducts a school to teach Negroes how to register and vote. Negro leaders oppose integration with the white general longshore union because, they argue, it would be more difficult to continue these activities on behalf of their race.

12. See Ray Marshall, "Some Factors Influencing Union Racial Practices," *Industrial Relations Research Association Annual Proceedings,* 1961.

13. *Steele v. L. & N.R.R.,* 323 U.S. 192; Archibald Cox, "The Duty of Fair Representation," *Villanova Law Review,* January, 1957, p. 151; Benjamin Aaron, "Some Aspects of the Union's Duty of Fair Representation," *Ohio State Law Journal,* Winter, 1961, p. 39; *Wallace Corp. v. NLRB,* 323 U.S. 248.

14. *Central of Georgia Ry.* v. *Jones,* 229 F. 2d 648, cert. denied, 352 U.S. 848; *Richardson* v. *Texas & New Orleans Ry. Co.,* 242 F. 2d 230; 77 S. Ct. 230.

15. *Syres* v. *Oil Workers,* 257 F. 2d 479, 330 U.S. 892; *Rolax* v. *Atlantic Coast Line,* 186 F. 2d 473.

16. 262 F. 2d 349 (1948), cert. denied, 359 and 935 (1959).

17. See *Betts* v. *Easley,* 161 Kansas 459; Justice Murphy's concurring opinion in the *Steele* case, 65 S. Ct. 226; Judge Groner's concurrence in *Brotherhood* v. *United Transport Service Employees,* 136 F. 2d 817, 829 (CADC), reversed on other grounds, 320 U.S. 715, and Justice Fairchild's dissent in *Ross* v. *Ebert,* 275 Wes. 532, 82 N.W. 2d 315, 320.

18. See *Hunter* v. *Atcheson, Topeka and Santa Fe Ry.,* II Race Relations Law Reporter, 996.

19. *Bethlehem Alameda Shipyard Cases,* R—5963—94 (1943).

20. Carter Manufacturing Co., 50 NLRB 803.

21. NLRB, Tenth Annual Report, 1945, p. 18.

22. Larus & Bros., 62 NLRB 1085; also case No. 39—RC—854 (1955).

23. Independent Metal Workers Union and Hughes Tool Co., case No. 23—CB—429; United Steelworkers & Independent Metal Workers, case No. 23—RC—1748, Feb. 26, 1963, p. 12.

24. *Pioneer Bus Co.* v. *Transport Workers,* 51 LRRM 1546.

25. See 18 *Conn. Supplement,* 125-127; *Conn. Law Journal,* Oct. 7, 1952; p. 2; *IBEW Local 35* v. *Commission on Civil Rights,* Conn. Supreme Ct. of Errors, October term, 1953; and *IBEW* v. *Commission on Civil Rights,* Superior Ct., Hartford County, Conn. Mar. 26, 1954.

26. International Longshoremen's Association; Allied Industrial Workers; Hotel & Restaurant Employees; National Agricultural Workers; United Rubber Workers; Mine, Mill & Smelter Workers; United Packinghouse Workers; Tobacco Workers; Hod Carriers & Common Laborers; Oil, Chemical & Atomic Workers; National Maritime Union; Brotherhood of Sleeping Car Porters; United Transport Service Employees; the American Federation of Teachers; Retail, Wholesale & Department Store Union; the Amalgamated Meat Cutters & Butcher Workmen; and the United Automobile Workers.

12

HUMAN RIGHTS AND THE LABOR MOVEMENT

James H. Jones*

I am a firm believer that where labor and management alike, together or separately, state *clearly* and *positively* their positions on non-discrimination and equal opportunity and then plan, program, and effect a method of implementation so that all employees, union and non-union, will know in no uncertain terms that they mean what they say, this is the most important aspect of *Real Assumption of Responsibility*. This term, which I use frequently, is very high in priority of importance as it applies to organized labor. Labor has more than a legal responsibility to fight for equal opportunity and non-discrimination for all people regardless of race, creed, or color. Labor's foundation, its aspirations for a better way of life for all people, has a great moral responsibility it must assume if it is to be true to its own well-stated set of principles.

In my capacity as chairman of the Philadelphia Council, AFL-CIO's Human Rights Committee, I am at times one of labor's severest critics. This committee is a large one representing all segments of the labor movement who are truly dedicated people and who believe in what we are doing and trying to do in seeing to it that labor unions carry out national AFL-CIO policies.

THE PHILADELPHIA AFL-CIO HUMAN RIGHTS COMMITTEE

Some two years ago, it was labor's own human rights committee that issued a public exposé and denunciation of "certain building trades local unions," one of the "all-Negro local unions affili-

---

*Chairman, Human Rights Committee, Philadelphia AFL-CIO.

ated with Movie Operator and Theatrical Employees International Union," and one of the "all-Negro locals of the American Federation of Musicians."

This was done as a last resort because of our inability to get these particular building trades unions to open up their apprenticeship training programs to all qualified applicants irrespective of their race, creed, or color. It was also our finding that most of these unions had no Negro members and they could not, or would not, defend their policies nor would they meet with our committee so it could assist them in making whatever changes were necessary to comply with AFL-CIO policy.

The two all-Negro locals, for reasons only their leadership were aware of, and against the recommendation of their international union, refused to merge with their larger white counterparts. It was brought out by testimony at many hearings conducted by our committee that all job protection and seniority of the Negro members would be guaranteed. It was also found that the Movie Operators Local 307-A (Negro) was used by the movie house owners to cut rates of the industry, and it was admitted that they did take a movie away from the larger Local 307 (white) after an ultimatum by an owner to Local 307 (white) that "if you won't take what I'm offering I'll go to the Negro local," and he did. The Negro local's members are working for much lower hourly rates—some as much as $1.00 per hour lower—I am told.

We honestly believed these two mergers were in line with our policy to also eliminate segregation and the image of old-time all-colored and all-white—especially when the opposition to the merger was the Negro leadership. I have gone into more detail with these two local unions because of the importance the racial aspect could have on our overall program.

It should also be stated that there are other building trades locals that have exemplary records of equal opportunity; outstanding are the Carpenters locals, the Laborers locals, and others. Many outstanding improvements have been made by the building trades locals and they have established a human rights committee of their own which has agreed to work with our committee. The chairman of their committee is Joseph Burke of the Sheet Metal Workers, who is a highly respected labor leader. His local union has since eliminated the father and son requirement of the apprenticeship training program, and they now have their first Negro apprentice and more on the list.

I make these observations because *I am* one of labor's severest critics, and I make the following statement that I am also one of organized labor's greatest boosters, because no group in America has contributed more to the advancement of the principle of equality for all men, irrespective of race, creed, color, or national origin.

Yes, I am proud of the AFL-CIO and its reiteration of its policy and the expanding of the national AFL-CIO Civil Rights Committee under the directorship of Donald Slaiman. Don Slaiman is a truly dedicated person and no other action by President Meany could be more meaningful than the appointment of Don and giving more assistance to the committee to prove that the AFL-CIO means business.

SPECIFIC CASE STUDIES

I serve on the international union's civil rights committee and also on a four-man panel which includes the present Supreme Court Justice Arthur Goldberg, Roy Wilkins of the national NAACP, and Frank Shane, Executive Secretary of the Steelworkers' Civil Rights Committee. Its main job is to handle complaints from various NAACP local branches that cannot be resolved locally. While the specific case I would like to discuss does not involve this committee, it does involve specific action taken by me on behalf of my union, the United Steelworkers of America.

The Case of the Negro Brakeman

The case in point occurred at a basic steel plant owned by the United States Steel Corporation. It involved promotion of a Negro brakeman who had twenty-six years of seniority in his job and who had, over the years, trained a large number of engineers to run the engine. When the trainees (all white) were fully qualified under his instructions and guidance, he fell back to his job as brakeman. The case was finally decided by the company's finally giving in to the man's grievance, which was forcefully processed by the union, and the man in question filled a vacancy as an engineer in the all-white train crew.

I would like to make it clear that the company really wanted to make this move, which was long overdue, but it was afraid a strike would take place if it did. There is no condoning their lack of a positive position over the years and even when confronted with the union's strong and affirmative action and its own real and honest desire to do the right thing, they were still afraid of the consequences.

When the time came for the Negro employee to take out his first engine, the train crew (not all engineers—mostly engine repairmen) went on strike. These men were also members of the union. When this happened, to my surprise the company was willing to give up its sacred "company's prerogative" and called me to ask what they should do. Having negotiated many contracts with all companies insisting on their managerial rights to run their plant, and while agreeing with them (with minor reservations that we see to it that they ran it right, at this late date I was not going to assume any of their responsibilities, and told them so. In my role of seeing that they did run it right, I made a suggestion to the company—not very technical or statistical, but just a "wee bit" practical, and it was as follows: looking at the clock in the plant superintendent's office, I said, "If I were you I would tell them (the strikers) that if they are not back on the job in ten minutes, instead of one Negro engineer, all jobs would be filled by Negroes." I am proud to say that the company gave such an order, in such a manner indicating they meant business, and when eight minutes had passed, every one was back on the job, and production was resumed in full. That night, which was stormy (weatherwise also), the Negro engineer had brake trouble, and one of the leaders of the strike was the first to volunteer to help and did so. This proved that positive action on the part of both the union and the company made this plant one of the most integrated basic steel plants in its chain. The future plans and programs, jointly shared, worked so well, and the Negro workers, who were attending alternate day and night vocational and remedial schools, became so qualified that we had to slow the company down in certain jobs so as not to create a reverse problem.

The Case of the Printing Industries

Now I would like to explain another situation that involved the printing industries in Philadelphia, our AFL-CIO Human Rights Committee, and a representative of the Typographical Union.

Having seen the bad publicity and image given the building trades unions because of a few locals, there was a sincere desire on our part to see what could be done in the printing industries on a voluntary basis. There were some cases filed with the Philadelphia Human Relations Commission. The AFL-CIO Human Rights Committee and the commission had a signed formal agreement (the first of its kind in the country) to work cooperatively to resolve cases involving any AFL-CIO union, so we were actually in the process of handling these cases through the representatives of the industries.

All parties concerned had a desire to establish a broader participating committee which would also include some civil rights groups. An exploratory meeting was held with the following participating: the printing industries represented by the then Executive Director, John Seybold, and Personnel Manager, Malcolm Pritzger, representatives of the labor unions involved, our AFL-CIO Committee, the Urban League, Council for Equal Job Opportunity, an agency of the Philadelphia Fellowship Commission, the Philadelphia Human Relations Commission, and the Negro Trade Union Leadership Council of Philadelphia, on which I also serve as president. Many hard-working meetings followed in our efforts to draw up a real set of rules and regulations that would help to speed up integration in some areas and a beginning in others. Actual participation by many company personnel and managerial representatives gave us all the ingredients necessary for success if men of good will have honest desires to do so. I can honestly say that the agreement finally arrived at and the subsequent good results obtained therefrom are a real credit to everyone concerned and especially the representatives of the Printing Pressmen's Union, who were real solid men when the chips were down.

Our agreement with the printing industries and the organizations listed above has been hailed by the public press all over the country as a real breakthrough of great proportions. I am proud of our efforts, and it proves again that the voluntary approach can accomplish good results.

CONCLUDING REMARKS

In all of my speeches, no matter where or how large the audience, I am always compelled to speak proudly of two unions in particular, the International Ladies Garment Workers Joint Board and local unions, and the Amalgamated Clothing Workers Union Joint Board, all of the Philadelphia area. These unions have many minority group members, and they have their own directors of education, and with the weight of their joint board managers behind them they plan programs to effectively implement their policy of fair and equal treatment for all. They have classes that teach potential operators of the many machines and also classes in languages for the many foreign-born members. These continuous activities by the unions are in reality an expression of their desire to assume their responsibilities not only to their membership but also to the community as a whole.

13

INCREASING EMPLOYMENT OPPORTUNITY IN THE PRINTING AND ELECTRICAL TRADES

Theodore W. Kheel*

Few aspects of the Negro movement for equal rights and opportunities during the 1960's have won more notoriety in the press and other news media than alleged racial discrimination in the American union movement, particularly among the craft unions. This notoriety may seem to some appropriate and deserved when they read or hear such distressing statistics as these:

— Negroes comprise only 15 of every 1,000 electricians in the U.S. and 33 of every 1,000 plumbers and pipefitters.

— Of 5,658 skilled workers employed on major federal construction projects, a 1963 survey showed 300 were Negroes, a ratio of 1 in 19.

— Among 65 major industrial corporations under Plans for Progress, Negroes filled about 2½ per cent of the skilled craft jobs.

JOB OPPORTUNITIES AND THE CRAFT UNIONS

Under such circumstances — and there is a seemingly endless list of comparable figures available in the literature of the Negro protest — it is hardly surprising that national and local civil rights groups have selected craft unions, usually in the building trades, as prime recipients of demands for greater job opportunities for minorities. It is time, however, to view this issue in perspective, free of the emotionalism which has inspired furious verbal attacks and occasional violence between civil rights advocates and trade union-

---

*Mr. Kheel, as Director of the Office of Impartial Review of the New York City Electrical Industry and Impartial Arbitrator of the Joint Board of the New York City Printing Industry, has drawn primarily upon the New York City experience in preparing this paper.

ists, who are normally valuable allies in worthy social and political movements. We have delayed too long in evaluating the causes of some of these restrictive patterns. Upon analysis, it is fair to conclude that the exclusion of Negroes in certain trades, among them the electrical and printing trades, is not the sole or principal product of racial discrimination as such, by unions or by employers. In thus isolating the basis upon which denial of job opportunity has rested, we acquire a sense of direction in moving to enlarge it.

The Father-Son Tradition

One general practice among craft unions which has clearly served to restrict opportunities for Negroes and other minorities is the "father-son" tradition of perpetuating a particular skill among members of a family unit from one generation to the next. Obviously, a union which has no Negro members, and has never admitted Negro members, effectively blocks, by this practice, an aspiring Negro youth from access to the higher-paying jobs in its jurisdiction and its craft. This is undoubtedly legally indefensible under federal and state antidiscrimination laws. But we must not assume that such "favoritism," whether legally or even morally wrong, is necessarily discriminatory. Nor, for that matter, is it confined to craft unions. Thomas Watson and Henry Ford are able and successful executives. It does not in any way diminish their achievements to suggest that they were, at the least, aided by their kinship to their successful predecessors in the company. Not only does the tradition have its origins in the medieval guilds antedating the discovery of America, but similar nepotism goes unchallenged in the professions, in finance, industry, and politics. Patterns of exclusion have also resulted from a continuing clannishness among ethnic groups which migrated in the nineteenth century; there are union locals which for decades have selected their apprentices primarily from youth of Irish extraction, Polish locals which have excluded Italian-Americans, and so on.

The Economic Structure of the Industry

The economic structure of an industry also tends to affect the admission practices of its trade unions. The printing trades, particularly, are concerned with the introduction of automated devices, as we have seen and soon may see again, in the bargaining between Local 6 of the International Typographical Union and the New York City newspapers. The construction industry is subject, far more than others, to the boom-and-bust cycle in the long run, as well as to seasonal variations in employment. By the nature of the industry, the building trades unions tend to hold the advantage in the bargaining relationship and to control hiring. In their economic self interest — which, of course, is the motivation for the organization of a union in the first place — the printing and building trades locals tend to restrict membership both in periods of prosperity, since a shortage of skilled labor enhances their bargaining power, and in slack periods, since then they must divide the available jobs among their own.

"Discrimination by Default"

To the extent the Negro, the Puerto Rican, and the Mexican-American have been victimized by racial or ethnic discrimination in gaining employment opportunity in the building and printing trades, the blame for part of this discrimination rests with all of white America, not just with the union movement. We have effectively denied to the vast majority of these minority groups adequate educational opportunity to qualify, and the motivation to apply, for these highly skilled jobs. Since access to such jobs comes largely through the ancient apprentice system, the craft unions and their leadership are chargeable with "discrimination by default" — with the failure to seek out and recruit potential apprentices among the minority community, the failure to employ objective standards in the selection of apprentices, the failure to maintain adequate liaison with public vocational schools and state employment services, and the failure to publicize apprenticeship openings on a wide scale.

The fair employment title of the Civil Rights Act of 1964 offers one remedy for this form of discrimination. But it operates upon the basis of individual complaints, as do most state FEPC laws — which have not been notably effective in removing apprenticeship barriers. Certainly in the near future we must look to aggressive voluntary action by unions and employees in their joint apprenticeship committees for major breakthroughs in the electrical, printing, and other skilled trades. The experience of these two industries in New York City is particularly enlightening.

LOCAL 3, IBEW, APPRENTICESHIP PROGRAM

In 1962, New York City Local 3 of the International Brotherhood of Electrical Workers dramatically dispelled the myth that qualified Negro applicants for apprenticeship could not be found. As part of the agreement by which the union won a 25-hour work week, 1,000 additional apprenticeships were provided. The Joint

Industry Board dispatched 2,000 letters recruiting applicants for apprenticeships to the NAACP, the Urban League, the Negro American Labor Council, vocational high schools, the 450 employers with contracts with Local 3, the City Central Labor Council, the Puerto Rican Labor Office, the Committee on Inter-Group Relations, and nearly 120 other locals in the building trades. The board made it clear that it wanted qualified applicants for apprenticeships regardless of race, creed, or color. More than 1,500 applications were filed with a three-man screening committee consisting of Dean Harry Carman of Columbia University and two board representatives, one of them a Negro. The screening committee interviewed 1,100 applicants. Of the 1,020 apprentices chosen, 200 were Negro and Puerto Rican applicants. This result has repeatedly been singled out by commentators in the field — and hailed by the United States Commission on Civil Rights — as a major breakthrough in equal opportunity in apprenticeship training. Not every building trade local in every community can provide such a substantial number of new apprenticeships, and the employment picture in the New York electrical industry is perhaps unique: an existing construction boom and the precedent-making five-hour day enabled the industry to absorb a first-year apprentice class approximately equal in size to all the older classes combined. Obviously such a massive forward stride is not possible in every city, but it does underscore the direct connection between job availability and successful integration. Local 3 and the New York electrical contractors have also proved that vigorous affirmative action can produce substantial gains for minorities among apprenticeships when they do become available.

APPRENTICESHIP PROGRAMS IN THE PRINTING INDUSTRY

The Joint Printing Industry in New York City, which includes commercial printing establishments but not members of the Newspapers Publishers Association, faced a different problem in its apprenticeship selection procedure. The industry's 1963 contract with Local 6 of the ITU anticipated by several months enactment of a state law requiring objective standards in the selection of apprentices under any state-registered program. Prior to this contract, apprentice compositors were chosen on the basis of their seniority as "miscellaneous helpers" in the industry. This system, involving a delay of several years even in the right to apply for apprenticeship, had the effect of discouraging some of the outstanding younger workers from remaining in the printing trade. In order to remedy this situation, as well as to guarantee a fair selection process, the printing companies and the union agreed in the 1963 contract (1) that there would be no discrimination in the employment of apprentices, who would be "selected on the basis of qualifications and aptitudes in accordance with test procedures . . . and without regard to race, creed, color, sex, or national origin"; (2) that apprentice opportunities and selection procedures would be publicized; and (3) that annual examinations would be conducted beginning in October, 1964. The employers and the union agreed to a testing procedure to be carried out by impartial agencies and provided that any complaint of discrimination in apprentice selection be heard before an impartial arbitrator.

Among the 1,000 helpers eligible for the 1964 tests were approximately 300 Negro and Puerto Rican employees, so the problem was not one of inadequate representation of minority groups. Rather it was a question of assuring that the tests did not unfairly penalize minority youths, whose deficiencies in educational opportunity — whose "cultural lag" — might render them unduly vulnerable to standard testing procedure. Their basic aptitude and experience in the trade might well be ignored if the tests imposed reflected solely their educational background and achievement. No one seems yet to have devised a testing procedure that will absolutely compensate for this cultural lag, but the Joint Board of the Printing Industry — by leaving the actual testing to outside agencies and by suggesting a procedure giving maximum weight to the applicant's experience in the trade and his potential — has moved as far as now seems possible to secure an objective selection process.

The procedure devised was as follows:

All applicants were required to take the General Aptitude Test Battery for the printing trade devised by the United States Employment Service. Each applicant was also given an intensive interview with an employment service counselor to determine whether he might have a substantial potential in the trade regardless of his ability to meet the minimum standards in the test battery. Any applicant who either passed the test or was given a favorable recommendation by the counselor on the basis of the personal interview remained in the "pool" from which apprentices were to be chosen. The next hurdle for the remaining applicants was a test to measure their minimal verbal skills; applicants who passed the reading and either the grammar or spelling test remained in contention. The final series of tests covered their performance in arithmetical reasoning and trade knowledge, and the grades on these two tests, when combined with certain service and experience credits provided in the collective bargaining agreement, were used to determine the rank of the various applicants. Under the collective bargaining agreement, appointments as apprentices were to be made from among the highest scorers determined as outlined above.

CONCLUDING REMARKS

It is, of course, a truism of the issue of greater job opportunity for the Negro and other impoverished minorities that the problem cannot be analyzed and resolved except in the context of future employment trends. Continuing economic growth and an effective national response to automation and other technological changes are essential to any meaningful improvement in their economic status. As Secretary of Labor Wirtz has suggested, we do not want to pull down the "White Only Need Apply" signs and have them replaced by "No Help Wanted" posters. Nevertheless, the experience of the New York electrical and printing trades makes clear that, within the framework of the present economy, a determined program by management and organized labor can bring remarkable progress toward equal job opportunity without outside pressure, whether by governmental fiat or by picket lines and other demonstrations.

14

NEGRO EMPLOYMENT
IN THE CONSTRUCTION INDUSTRY

by

Joseph B. Meranze*

In order to understand the problem of Negro integration in the
construction industry, it is necessary to view it in its proper context.
Failure to do so makes the solution more difficult, and also engen-
ders a sense of frustration at the slowness of the process of resolution. There is no disagreement over the conclusion that the Negro
must be fully integrated in the construction industry. The only
question is when will it be accomplished.

The acceptance of certain basic facts will help place the situation in its proper perspective. These are (a) the complete integration of Negroes in the construction industry will still provide them
with relatively few jobs; (b) there are presently limited numbers of
Negroes, if any, who are qualified by training or experience to be
employed in certain crafts; and (c) there are only six crafts in Philadelphia out of thirty-seven that have been charged with racial discrimination.

HISTORICAL

The background of the crafts will also help explain some of the
difficulties experienced by Negroes in being admitted as members.
Philip Taft, in his recent book, *Organized Labor in American
History*, points out that the building crafts were among the first
and best organized labor groups in this country. They understood
the natural tendency of disintegration better than other labor
groups. This was because of the cohesiveness of their members.

---

*Partner, Meranze, Katz, Spear and Bielitsky, Philadelphia, Pennsylvania.

They were workers who had acquired special skills through long periods of apprenticeship training. Through this same process they had also acquired a fierce loyalty to their craft. They were zealous in preserving their group identity and resisting the admission of newcomers. They limited new members to sons and brothers, or others of the immediate family. This policy of selective admission led to the exclusion not only of Negroes, but all others not already represented in the group.

Despite this centralism, however, the national leaders of AFL, beginning with Samuel Gompers, its first president, were firmly against discrimination in the labor movement. They looked with disfavor upon trade unions having constitutional provisions excluding membership because of race or color. They fought to eliminate these restrictions. The issue was complicated, however, by the national scope of the labor movement. The Southern branches, with strong race prejudices, sought to prevent the eradication of these restrictions as the price for continued affiliation. The autonomy of internationals also presented an effective barrier to the federation's pressures for a non-discriminatory policy.

The influx of the Negro to the Northern industrial areas did not wholly help to resolve these difficulties and, indeed, created new problems. Coming from an agricultural background in the South, some carried with them the hostility of their Southern white neighbors towards labor unions. Because their financial resources were small, they were more easily intimidated by anti-union employers. The solidarity of organized labor in the North was threatened by the employment of large numbers of Negro strikebreakers.

The events called for greater efforts to organize the Negro. The leadership of A. Philip Randolph, first organizer and President of the Brotherhood of Sleeping Car Porters, added impetus to the drive by this minority against discrimination. Randolph became the leading trade spokesman for the Negro worker.

The formation of the CIO brought to the forefront of the movement a national labor organization which rejected from the start any kind of discrimination. It was made up of constituent internationals which had no racial problems. Its members were not skilled workers and accordingly long apprenticeships were not necessary. The membership consisted of mass-production workers, a large number of whom were Negroes and already employed. There were few locals in the CIO with the restrictive features characteristic of the crafts.

The forthright position of the CIO and the affirmative stand of the AFL leadership set the pattern against discrimination. The uniting of the AFL-CIO under the forceful leadership of George

Meany pointed up the determination of the labor movement to eliminate all racial discrimination. The National Negro American Labor Council and the Negro Trade Union Leadership Council in Philadelphia, labor groups organized and led by Negroes, were ultimately welcomed by the labor movement as allies in the goal for integration.

The elimination of restrictive membership requirements is not easy. Modifying practices of long duration will require perseverance and patient efforts. Those in the rank and file who continue to reflect environmental prejudices must be re-educated to a new way of life and thinking.

PRESSURES TO ELIMINATE RACIAL DISCRIMINATION

It can stand repetition to say that the Negroes' right to equal job opportunities in the crafts is unquestioned and long overdue. Historic steps to this end, in addition to those already mentioned, are in operation. It is these we now propose to discuss.

The Taft-Hartley Act and the NLRB

The *first* is that of the Taft-Hartley Act of 1947. The National Labor Relations Board, operating under the act, recently decided a significant case in the field of discrimination. This was the Hughes Tool Company decision involving an independent metal workers union in Texas. (147 NLRB No. 166, 56 LRRM 1289 (July 1, 1964)). In this case, the union maintained two locals. One was all white (Local No. 1) and the other all Negro (Local No. 2). The collective agreement with the employer covered the two locals and set up two levels of employment: one for only the white workers and the other for only the Negro members. Local No. 2 requested the elimination of this grouping of work force and an end of discrimination.. Local No. 1 refused. Three apprentice jobs became open but were made available to the white category only. A Negro bid for one of the jobs and was rejected because of his race. The grievance raised by the rejected worker was not acted upon by the union. An unfair labor practice charge was then filed with the Labor Board against the union and the employer.

The Labor Board found that the union had violated the act in discriminating against the Negro worker because of race and causing the employer to discriminate for the same reason. The Board's remedy included rescinding the representation certification issued by the union; directing the union to desist from discriminating against Negro members because of race, color, or union membership, to process the grievance of the Negro worker, and terminate the discriminatory provisions of its collective agreement with the employer based on race, color, or union membership.

The implications of this decision are significant. It makes it a statutory duty of a union to represent all employees in the bargaining unit without discrimination. A contract containing such discriminatory provisions will not only *not* be enforced but will not be considered a bar to an outside union asking for a representation election of the workers in the unit. The Board will refuse to certify a labor organization as the bargaining representative of workers when it is guilty of such discrimination.

Robert L. Carter, General Counsel for the NAACP, hailed this decision as an important breakthrough in labor law against racial discrimination. He felt that enforcement of racial equality through the Labor Board is easier, less costly, and more widely applicable than the fair employment provisions of the Civil Rights Act. He stated that three other cases of the Hughes Tool Company type are in process before the Board, and he plans to press more complaints of a similar nature in the future.

The Civil Rights Act of 1964

The *second* area of pressure to eliminate racial discrimination is the Civil Rights Act of 1964, signed by President Johnson on July 2, 1964. Title VII, "Equal Employment Opportunities," becomes effective July 2, 1965. It provides for the elimination of discrimination in employment because of race, color, religion, sex, or national origin in all industries affecting commerce. It is directed against employers, employment agencies, and labor organizations. It concerns itself with the terms, conditions, compensation, and privileges of employment. Particularly with respect to unions, the act prohibits discrimination in the admission of members. Title VII is enforced by a five-member Equal Employment Opportunity Commission. The commission interprets but may not sue against discriminatory practices. This is left to the individual grievant. The commission, however, may bring contempt proceedings to enforce a court's order. The Attorney General may bring injunctive action if he has cause to believe there is a pattern or practice of resistance to the law.

Where there is a state FEPC, the federal procedure yields to the state agency for 60 days, or 120 days if the state agency is in its

first year of operation. Federal agencies can make agreements with
state agencies for all or part of the enforcement functions. There
are twenty-five states that have FEPC laws.

To assist in the effective operation of the Civil Rights Act, the
AFL-CIO met on September 22, 1964, in Washington, D.C. It
approved the recommendation that all collective agreements have
non-discriminatory clauses. It agreed to provide educational material for the union members on the terms of the act. It urged the
government to provide adequate funds to enforce the law.

President George Meany outlined plans for union action to
bring about peaceful voluntary compliance with the Title VII by
labor organizations. He told the conference that showing the
unorganized workers of the unions' concern for their welfare "could
have a bearing on our organizing efforts."

The federation literature to be distributed will include "Civil
Rights—Fact or Fiction." It points out some of the fictions being
manufactured to defeat the operation of Title VII. One of these
fictions is the rumor that the law requires a fixed quota of Negroes
even if it means discharging incumbent whites.

The internationals are requested to appoint a staff man to
work with the AFL-CIO in developing community programs and to
assume responsibility for pushing civil rights programs among their
locals.

The State Agency

The *third* area of pressure is that of the state agency. In Pennsylvania there is the Pennsylvania Human Relations Act. (Act of
October 27, 1955, amended in 1961). The act prohibits discrimination in employment because of race, color, religion, ancestry, age, or
national origin. Like the Civil Rights Act, it is directed at employers,
employment agencies, and labor unions. The Pennsylvania act
prohibits printing any literature or applications indicating a preference in one of the above areas of discrimination. It prohibits interference where non-discrimination is in effect.

A Human Relations Commission consisting of eleven members is
established. Harry Boyer, President of the state AFL-CIO Federation, is chairman of the commission. It has power to investigate
and pass upon complaints. It can hold hearings to determine the
existence of discrimination and enforce its order through the
courts. Penalties are provided of contempt and fines.

The Building Trades Council of Philadelphia is working closely
with the Pennsylvania Human Relations Commission. The Building Trades Council has set up its own Civil Rights Committee,

chaired by Joseph Burke of the Sheet Metal Workers Local in Philadelphia. The Building Trades Committee on December 12, 1963, entered into an agreement with the state commission to effectuate integration in the crafts and apprentice programs without discrimination with respect to race, religion, or national origin. This affects the five-county area surrounding Philadelphia. The crafts agree to accept as applicants for admission to membership any qualified craftsmen or journeymen in the construction industry without discrimination. It will permit qualified and impartial observers selected by the commission to be present at examinations given by the crafts to determine qualifications. It was also agreed that there would be no denial of qualified applicants for apprentice programs because of race, etc. The commission reserves the right to refer applicants for enrollment. More than 50 per cent of the craft locals have executed the agreement to date.

Philadelphia Human Relations Commission

The *fourth* area of pressure is the Philadelphia Human Relations Commission. The commission was set up under the Philadelphia Home Rule Charter of 1951. The charter authorizes the commission to investigate, hold public hearings, and seek enforcement of its findings. The city also approved a fair practices ordinance on June 10, 1963. This prohibits discrimination in employment, housing, and public accommodations. With respect to employment, it covers the same area as does the state FEPC Act. It gives the Philadelphia Human Relations Commission authority to enforce it. The Philadelphia Human Relations Commission consists of nine members. Its chairwoman is Mrs. Sadie T. M. Alexander, a veteran fighter for racial equality.

In May, 1963, the commission cited six craft unions and four contractors in the construction industry for policies and practices which it charged led to the exclusion of non-whites from membership and employment opportunity. This pattern of exclusion resulted, it stated, from selection, training, and other factors incidental to job placement.

The commission, however, made some other significant findings. On the Municipal Service Administration Building, which was then being erected, there were 65 per cent nonwhites being employed among the laborers, carpenters, cement finishers, dock builders, and rod setters employed. There was no specific individual discrimination found. Moreover, after extensive efforts and announcements through the press, radio, television, and mail, and direct contacts with interested persons and agencies, only 300 applicants registered for employment in the construction industry. Of this number only 10 per cent were able to qualify either as journeymen or apprentices. It also pointed out, however, that there were 13,000 fewer jobs in the construction industry because of automation, prefabrication, and other labor savings devices in the past eight years; that because contractors have large permanent work forces which they shift from job to job, there are fewer job opportunities for new workers; and that the unemployment rate is high in several of the cited crafts.

The commission further reported in April, 1964 that the six cited craft locals have agreed to admit qualified non-whites to membership when members are being accepted; that they will administer objective tests for admission to apprentice training, and will refer qualified non-white workers to employers on a non-discriminatory basis where union hiring-hall contract provisions prevail. Three of these locals have now admitted Negroes to membership as journeymen, and four of them have accepted Negroes in their apprentice training programs. Two of these locals have not taken in nonwhite journeymen or apprentices because qualified Negroes are not available.

The Philadelphia AFL-CIO Council has appointed a human rights committee with James H. Jones of the Steelworkers Union as chairman. Mr. Jones is also president of the Philadelphia Negro Trade Union Leadership Council already mentioned. The human rights committee was instrumental in August, 1963, in bringing together the Graphic Arts Unions and the printing industries of Philadelphia in an agreement to eliminate discrimination in their trade. They set forth in their Memorandum of Understanding a program to achieve this objective. Implementing this agreement, in October, 1964, the Cuneo Eastern Press, Inc. signed with its craft unions to eliminate racial discrimination in its shop, and provision was made for the inclusion of Negroes in the apprentice program.

CONCLUDING REMARKS

It is evident from what has been said that active steps in many areas are being taken to achieve Negro integration in the construction industry. It is to be noted that agencies of the labor movement at every level are actively engaged to this end. The equal determination of labor and the Negro worker will bring the results both desire. It should not be forgotten that the just demands of the

Negro can be secured with greater ease through the labor movement. The Negro needs the labor movement to assure him a living wage. The labor movement needs the Negro worker because he is an integral part of the labor market. Neither can afford to ignore the other.

What should be done to further these efforts? There must be programs initiated to train the partially trained so they can qualify for apprentice and journeymen examinations. The Negro leadership must organize self-help programs such as the training project of the Reverend Leon Sullivan. It is receiving support from many sections of the Philadelphia community. Despite the short period of its existence, it is now considered a successful project.

The Philadelphia Public School System must increase its apprentice training programs to encourage more Negro applicants. The Board of Education in September, 1963, approved seven out of eight construction craft apprentice training programs as being nondiscriminatory. An eighth is being revised to meet this requirement.

The developing picture is an optimistic one. Numerous agencies, public and private, inside of labor and outside, are working to resolve a recognized problem. Through such united efforts, the common objective will be achieved.

PART V

Community Approaches to Equal Employment Opportunity

15

A SURVEY OF EMPLOYER ASSOCIATION ACTIVITIES IN THE CIVIL RIGHTS MOVEMENT

Richard L. Rowan*

The major emphasis of this symposium has been to highlight the approaches to the job problems of Negroes by business people, trade unions, the community, and the government. Outstanding examples have been presented to show the results of action-oriented programs initiated by various groups interested in providing equal employment opportunities for all citizens. Business people, as well as others, have spoken with great clarity about their individual and company efforts to eliminate discrimination in employment. In order to understand better how businessmen act collectively in regard to the problems discussed herein, a survey was conducted among Chamber of Commerce associations. On a random basis, several Chambers in the East, the South, and Midwest were contacted and asked to furnish any information that would reveal their respective work in the area of race relations and employment. The following presents the findings with some comparison and analysis of the various approaches that were discovered.

THE FINDINGS

The South

Atlanta, Georgia. The Atlanta Chamber of Commerce has not completed a study of segregation and economic development. "This organization has been active in the field of human relations since 1960. We have nothing resembling a finished study." As far as can be determined, the Atlanta Chamber does have an interest in the

---

*Assistant Professor of Industry, Wharton School of Finance and Commerce, University of Pennsylvania.

field, but no clear plan of action appears to have been developed. "We proceed from day to day, doing the best we know how, in good faith and in good conscience."[1]

Birmingham, Alabama. The Birmingham Chamber has not been very active in the area under consideration. "The Birmingham Chamber of Commerce has not made a study concerning community relations."[2]

Shortly before the passage of the Civil Rights Act of 1964, the Birmingham Chamber of Commerce sent a letter to members enclosing a memorandum pertaining to various aspects of the law. The memorandum advised that

> The clear choice of a policy of compliance or non-compliance belongs to each affected person or business. The clear danger . . . is in having no plan at all and to be confronted by one individual, or a crowd of undisciplined individuals determined to test compliance or non-compliance on their own or at radical instigation.
>
> Each person or business must assess or evaluate the effect of having no decisive plan, or the effect of a decision for compliance, or non-compliance upon his own custom or trade. Each must decide whether or not it may be useful to advise local law enforcement agencies of his decision, whatever it may be.
>
> • • •
>
> In Birmingham, if an establishment chooses to comply with the Act, it will be protected from disorder while it follows its own decision. The same rule will be applied in Birmingham when and if management declines to comply, subject to possible injunctive court action.[3]

In a Chamber "Preliminary Report of the Current Economic Conditions of Metropolitan Birmingham, Alabama," the following conclusion was reached:

> Apparently the massive assaults by civil rights opportunists during this year of 1963 have not materially affected Birmingham's sound economy.[4]

Charlotte, North Carolina. A rather active role has been assumed by the Charlotte Chamber in the city's efforts to remove racial barriers. In cooperation with the city, the Chamber "did encourage the operators of public facilities to integrate as soon as they could . . . and this has been done. . . . all of our public facilities — schools, parks, theatres, restaurants, cafeterias, hotels, motels — are integrated without regard to race, color, or creed." The Chamber has not concerned itself with the field of race relations except in the way described above. Employment has not been considered an appropriate area for their involvement. "The Charlotte Chamber of Commerce is not engaged in the field of Negro employment."[5]

Leadership in the mayor's office in Charlotte has contributed to the progress made in that city in race relations. Even though the central problem of employment has not been dealt with extensively, Charlotte has moved ahead in a quiet, orderly fashion to take down racial barriers.[6] The steps that have been taken can be traced in large measure to the excellent attitude and leadership of the present mayor. "I am most pleased to tell you . . . that Charlotte has moved voluntarily without duress or pressure to preserve racial harmony by correcting inequities of the past, dropping the bar of discrimination throughout our city, adopting merit employment in both government and private enterprises, and in other ways extending full citizenship rights and opportunities to all of our citizens."[7]

Columbia, South Carolina. The Chamber of Columbia has taken some measures in the past few years, and it appears that there is some understanding of the need for improved job opportunities in that community. "Our Chamber of Commerce, along with a committee of general citizens, has been studying the racial situation comprehensively for at least two years. We are making every effort to improve job opportunities, educational systems, and interrelationships between the races."[8]

The Chamber does not have a written report of its work in this area with the exception of official minutes of meetings.

Jackson, Mississippi. There has been no work done by the Jackson Chamber of Commerce in this field.[9]

Miami, Florida. The Miami-Dade County Chamber of Commerce has not made a study of segregation and economic development, but it has assisted in forming the Community Relations Board of Dade County, which has concentrated on three areas:

(1) "To organize itself formally into a functioning agency; (2) the handling of incidents of an emergency nature and a broader investigation of racial discrimination in the community; and (3) to measure the racial tensions which exist in this community."[10] The board is a relatively new organization, and the future will determine its effectiveness. Current attitudes seem to be indicative of progress. "The Community Relations Board of Dade County believes that racial discrimination in all its forms should be ended. If a public accommodations law is needed to end racial discrimination, such a law should be county-wide in its enforcement powers, instead of limited to a single community."[11] The experience in Miami has been a good one, and it is worthy of further study in order to show the effectiveness of a Chamber group in assisting in

the formation of bi-racial committees or community relations boards.[12]

Nashville, Tennessee. The experience of the Nashville Chamber of Commerce has been limited in this field, and it "has not conducted any studies pertaining to the general area of segregation and economic development in the South."[13]

The Mayor of Nashville appointed a Metropolitan Human Relations Committee in May, 1963. This group was created at the suggestion of the Nashville Chamber of Commerce and leaders in the Negro community. The committee was created "in furtherance of a public policy designed, a. to advance human rights, b. to anticipate and seek to eliminate problems in our community due to racial, religious, national, and cultural differences, c. thus achieving racial goodwill and friendly associations."[14]

The committee has had good results in its efforts to commit hotels and motels, restaurants, drugstores, hospitals, and public recreational facilities to a policy of non-discrimination. The committee reports that some progress has been made in the crucial area of employment. Employment "is an extremely broad field and presents diverse problems which vary with the size and type of the business involved, the number of employees, the skills required and many other factors. Therefore, conditions in this area are not readily subject to accurate generalizations. The Committee can report . . . that as of November 1, 1963, in addition to those large manufacturing concerns, utilities and some retail stores, which desegregated their employment practices some time ago, a similar policy is not in effect in the large insurance companies, the banks, and a great number of the downtown retail establishments. As regards the latter group it is significant to note that on October 16, 1963 the Board of Directors of the Nashville Retail Merchants Association formally approved a policy favoring impartial employment practices for all citizens regardless of race."[15]

New Orleans, Lousiana. The New Orleans Chamber of Commerce has not conducted "any studies relative to [the] area of interest."[16]

The East

Baltimore, Maryland. The Baltimore Association of Commerce does not have an active committee within its organization to work in the area of race relations, but it has been responsible indirectly and under the leadership of Herbert G. Bailey, Jr., Executive Vice-President of the association, for the establishment of a group outside its organization that has taken constructive action. The bi-racial group, known as the Voluntary Council on Equal Opportunity, Inc., consists of nineteen top Baltimore businessmen. Discussions are held on ways to improve job opportunities for Negroes. One council member said: "If a Negro doesn't have a job, if he doesn't have that ballast, all of the other things he wants are just candy puffs off in the distance."[17]

A monograph entitled *The Equal Opportunity Employer* was prepared by the council for distribution to business people and other interested groups. Its stated purpose was "to provide help to employers concerned about making job opportunities available for all, regardless of race, color or creed" and "to assure greater use of aptitude and skills among members of the Negro community, though some of the information is applicable in eliminating any form of employment discrimination." The monograph contains information relevant to the following: "Examination of Equal Employment Policies," "Establishment of Equal Opportunity Policies," "In-Plant Indoctrination," "Hiring Negro Employees," and "Understanding the Negro Community."[18]

Boston, Massachusetts. The Greater Boston Chamber of Commerce has been very active in the field of equal employment opportunity. The Ad-Hoc Committee on Racial Issues, consisting of five men, has been instrumental in developing programs in the employment area. This committee played a major role in formulating the Massachusetts Plan for Equal Employment Opportunity. In addition to this activity, the Chamber sent a staff member to Philadelphia to study its job training program. Also the Chamber's Personnel Managers Club devoted its November, 1963 meeting to the topic "The Negro in the Employment Market." The president of the Chamber has been appointed chairman of the Boston Committee on Youth Employment.

The Massachusetts Plan for Equal Employment Opportunity, mentioned above, has been supported by the Chamber. It is similar to the President's Plan for Progress, but it is administered and serviced by trade associations. The purpose of the plan is as follows:

> The Plan is designed to eliminate the historic economic gap between Negroes and whites through a voluntary, active program undertaken by a company to promote equal opportunities for qualified job applicants.[19]

Administration of the plan is carried out in several steps: (1) a company is contacted by the Chamber to see if it desires to participate; (2) if the company wishes to participate, it enters into a rigorous examination of employment and promotional policies and a policy statement is prepared on equal employment opportunity;

(3) the company is expected to develop a program of implementation of the policy set forth; (4) upon completion of the company's application, it is sent to the Chamber Advisory Committee on Equal Employment Opportunity, and, if approved as read, it is forwarded to the Governor's Committee on Industry, Finance and Commerce; and (5) when the Governor's Committee approves the application, the company is notified by letter by the Governor, who extends congratulations and explains the nature of the obligations involved.

At the present time, over twenty-five companies participate in the plan with ten of them coming through the Chamber's efforts. The Chamber stands firmly behind the plan — "Equal opportunity is good business; it is also right."[20]

New York. The New York Chamber of Commerce has not published any detailed studies relevant to the job problems of Negroes and community relations, although committees have studied the problems during the past two years. One of the studies made during the summer of 1963 by the Committee on Law Reform presents a review of racial tensions in New York State, with reference to New York civil rights legislation. Several observations made in the report highlight the need for emphasis on employment problems and the establishment of bi-racial committees to seek solutions. The report states:

> Negro leaders almost certainly realize the effective limits and diminishing returns of governmental action in New York State. It is for this reason that Negro demands in New York have been addressed not to the legislature but to community associations, labor unions and business organizations throughout the state. It is for this reason that the business community, whether it wills it or not, must bear a large share of the burden of Negro demands in New York. It is best able to take the responsibility for improving job opportunities at both lower and higher management levels. It can best organize and administer job training programs designed to qualify Negroes for better jobs. The business community can set the tone and style of a new acceptance of the Negro on all levels of life.[21]

On the subject of bi-racial committees, the report finds that they "should be non-political in character and essentially representative of the whole business community. Pending the completion by the Chamber of further studies already undertaken, we doubt the wisdom of the Chamber initiating the creation of such a committee. We strongly recommend, however, that if such a committee is formed the Chamber give active support to its work."[22]

Rochester, New York. The Rochester Chamber has not undertaken any particular studies, but it is presently planning to perform activities "in the area of employment of all groups in our area."[23]

Wilmington, Delaware. The Wilmington State Chamber of Commerce has not "conducted or initiated any studies in the general areas of civil rights and Negro employment."[24]

The Midwest

Chicago, Illinois. Activity in the area of equal employment opportunity at the Chicago Association of Commerce and Industry has been conducted by a committee known as the Committee for Full Employment. The committee, consisting of approximately 150 members, is broken down into six sub-committees charged with varying responsibilities: Survey Sub-Committee (design, distribution, tabulation, and summary of the Survey of Chicago Area Employers); Study and Analysis Sub-Committee (publication of a placement manual designed to aid employers); Publications Sub-Committee (wrote, edited, designed, and published the *Merit Employment Manual*); Placement Sub-Committee (designed and circulated among the members of the Chicago Association of Commerce and Industry a flyer asking them to designate one or more of nine different agencies training or placing people for jobs and in jobs with which they would ccoperate); New Enterprises Sub-committee (in close cooperation with the area's leading department stores, housing and shopping center developers, this sub-committee is in the process of actually forming a new enterprise: money has been subscribed for the operation of a contractual household cleaning service); and Training and Education Sub-Committee (attempts to obtain and provide information in order that a better utilization of manpower can be made).

Even though the various sub-committees have been in operation for only a little over one year, they have made important accomplishments such as publishing a merit employment manual; establishing a "clean home" service that employs relief recipients as workers; conducting a survey of employers; and publishing a directory of training and placement agencies in the Chicago area. At the present time, the association is setting up several individual industry meetings in order to provide a look at future job opportunities in the Chicago area.[25]

Cincinnati, Ohio. Ohio has a fair employment practice statute, and there are official and unofficial groups in Cincinnati that are working in the field of Negro employment. For these reasons, the Cincinnati Chamber "has not instituted a program in this field." It does "not wish to overlap the efforts of those already under way."[26]

Cleveland, Ohio. The Cleveland Chamber of Commerce has given support to groups outside the Chamber that have met to discuss problems in the areas of education, employment, and housing. Conferences have been held under the general direction of the chairman of the Chamber, but participating members have been drawn partly from outside the organization. Emphasis has been placed on keeping the meetings unpublicized with the feeling that this contributes to the success of the operation.[27]

Indianapolis, Indiana. The Indianapolis Chamber of Commerce has had an informal program wherein "group meetings of employers as well as much personal work" have been carried out. In addition to this activity, the Chamber has encouraged Indianapolis employers to provide employment and promotion on a merit basis without regard to race. This work has been supplemented by participating in work supported by the United Fund agencies known as Merit Employment and Flanner House.[28]

St. Louis, Missouri. The Chamber of Commerce of Metropolitan St. Louis has cooperated with the Mayor of St. Louis in establishing a commission on equal employment opportunities. This commission consists of a number of business and labor leaders in the City and its detailed program is administered by the St. Louis Council on Human Relations.

A "9 Point Program" has been developed by the Commission and fully endorsed and supported by the Chamber. It includes the following provisions:

THE EMPLOYER AGREES TO

1. Communicate to all levels of management a written statement of policy on equal employment opportunity.
2. Publicize its non-discriminatory policy so that all persons, regardless of race, creed, color, or religion, will know that they will receive equal consideration for employment on the basis of merit and qualifications.
3. Review for top management the employment records of present employees to determine if anyone is working below his level or has been denied a promotion or transfer because of race, and take affirmative action to insure that no person is discriminated against in hiring, placement, transfer, promotion or upgrading, or in the selection of apprentices.
4. Keep top management advised of the results of procedures and practices undertaken to implement the non-discrimination policy.
5. Operate all facilities such as cafeterias, rest rooms, recreational areas, clubs, etc., on a strictly non-discriminatory basis.

6. Inform all of its recruitment sources, both public and private, including the Urban League of St. Louis, of this employment policy.
7. Inform secondary schools and colleges where Negroes are enrolled of the company policy to employ on the basis of merit and qualification.
8. Display, where practical, the Cooperating with the St. Louis Commission on Equal Employment Opportunity seal in advertising for workers.
9. Keep the St. Louis Commission on Equal Employment Opportunity advised of progress toward equal employment opportunity, and also of lack of progress, including any lack of qualified applicants, so that the Commission can cooperate in establishing training programs in areas of skilled shortages.[29]

A COMPARISON OF THE VARIOUS APPROACHES

The following chart summarizes briefly the various types of action taken by the associations:

The South	*The Midwest*	*The East*
1. No studies	1. No active work in the past but some thoughts being given to problems at present	1. No active work
2. Advice on the Civil Rights Act of 1964		2. Committees
		3. Encouragement to groups outside the Chamber
3. Encouragement of integration of public facilities	2. Committees	4. Encouragement to employers to provide employment on merit basis
4. Committee meetings	3. Symposia sponsored by the Chamber	
5. Aid in establishing community relations boards and human relations boards	4. Encouragement to groups outside the Chamber to work in the area on a voluntary basis	5. Aid in establishing commissions such as a human relations commission

Some Comparisons

In comparing the activities of the various Chambers in the three parts of the country studied, some interesting points may be noted. *The Passive Attitude.* In at least one city in all areas, there is a "hands off" policy in effect by the respective group. The reasons for such a policy are perhaps quite different. Among others, Jackson, Mississippi; Cincinnati, Ohio; Birmingham, Alabama; and Rochester, New York, all report little or no activity in the area under consideration. Racial strife that has swept through Jackson and Rochester in recent times may produce a different outlook in those two places in the future. The Cincinnati Chamber has not taken action since it does not wish to "overlap" work already under way by other groups, and the feeling is that the Ohio FEPC law remedies cases of discrimination in employment. In Birmingham, an altogether different outlook has been taken. Not only have Chamber studies been prepared to show the lack of damage done to the economy through racial strife (a most amazing conclusion!), but members have been notified by communications from the Chamber that they would be protected by local law enforcement in case they decide *not* to comply with the Civil Rights Act.

On the whole, it may be pointed out that in those areas where there has been inactivity on the part of groups such as the Chamber of Commerce, race relations have been poor if not very strained. A cause and effect relationship cannot be firmly established, but it is obvious that if an organization such as the Chamber takes no action in this vital field, surprise should not be registered when unfavorable disruptions occur that can be damaging to the business climate.

Committee Action. Formal and informal committees within the Chamber have been formed in all areas studied, with the most active ones in Chicago, Boston, and Columbia, South Carolina. Constructive committee action has been taken by various Chambers since they understand that the issues involved are more than moral, legalistic problems. It is simply good business to provide equal employment opportunities to all qualified members of the work force.

The Chicago Full Employment Committee, reported on herein, represents the most comprehensive plan of any surveyed. It has a definite purpose and plan of action with superior organization to make it an effective instrument in dealing with equal employment opportunity. The Boston Ad-Hoc Committee on Racial Issues also has been very successful in developing programs in the employment area, cooperating and assisting in the administration of the Massachusetts Plan for Equal Employment Opportunity. The Columbia, South Carolina Chamber has sponsored some informal committees of local citizens who have come together to discuss racial problems with some reference to job opportunities.

The decision as to whether or not to form a committee to work in this area has been arrived at in varying ways. In Chicago, considerable support was given to the idea since it was felt that maximum effectiveness could be achieved by many people with special knowledge concentrating on the various aspects of the problem. Interestingly enough, and by contrast, the New York Chamber Committee on Law Reform came to the conclusion in 1963 that a bi-racial committee "could be a visible sign that New York does not intend to perpetuate inequitable practices and customs," but "we doubt the wisdom of the Chamber's initiating the creation of such a committee" even though "if such a committee is formed the Chamber should give its active support to its work."

There is nothing inherent in committee work that means successful operation. It can fail as well as succeed. The Chicago and Boston experiences give excellent examples of successful ventures, and they are worthy of attention by other groups in large urban areas.

"Moral Suasion." What might be termed "moral suasion" has been used by several Chamber groups in all parts of the country studied. In Charlotte, North Carolina, the Chamber has used its influence in attempting to encourage the peaceful integration of all public facilities — hotels, restaurants, theaters, parks, etc. (even before the Civil Rights Act of 1964) — and the results have been gratifying. In Baltimore, Maryland; Cleveland, Ohio; and Indianapolis, Indiana, the respective Chambers have encouraged the formation of committees or other groups to work in the area of equal employment opportunity, education, and housing. This approach has been predicated on the notion that voluntary compliance is the key to successful race relations programs.

The interesting thing to note in making a comparison here is the differences in focus of the various groups. Before the passage of the Civil Rights Act, the major goal to be achieved in the South by civil rights workers was in the area of public services and education, and there was not great emphasis on equal job opportunity. The Charlotte Chamber, for example, felt it could make a contribution by encouraging peaceful integration in the public service area while emphasizing that it was not primarily concerned with Negro employment. In other parts of the country, for example Indianapolis, the focus of the Chamber has been in encouraging employers to provide employment on a merit basis without regard to race. Problems in the public service area already have been met or avoided by integration for some time. In the future, it may be expected that the efforts in the South, East, and Midwest will be more nearly alike in respect to civil rights. As the South removes its barriers to public service areas — both voluntarily and under the Civil Rights

Act — it will begin to concentrate on what is probably the most crucial problem to be faced — unemployment.

FOOTNOTES

1. Letter, November 15, 1963.
2. Letter, November 15, 1963.
3. Birmingham Chamber of Commerce, "An Information Memorandum with Regard to the Civil Rights Act of 1964," June 23, 1964, p. 2.
4. Birmingham Chamber of Commerce, *Birmingham, Alabama: Preliminary Report of the Current Economic Conditions of Metropolitan Birmingham, Alabama,* December 18, 1963, p. 4.
5. Letter, November 15, 1963.
6. "A Different Way: Charlotte Has Built Its Own Integration Road," *Charlotte Observer,* Sunday, July 14, 1963.
7. Letter, December 16, 1963.
8. Letter, November 18, 1963.
9. Letter, November 25, 1963.
10. Undated letter, Metropolitan Dade County, Florida.
11. Letter, August 3, 1963.
12. Letter, November 21, 1963.
13. Letter, November 29, 1963.
14. Letter, December 5, 1963.
15. Report to the Mayor of Nashville by the Metropolitan Human Relations Committee, November 14, 1963.
16. Letter, November 22, 1963.
17. John C. Schmidt, "Negro Unemployment — What City Business Men Are Doing About It," *The Sunday Sun,* Baltimore, September 27, 1964.
18. Baltimore, Maryland, Voluntary Council on Equal Opportunity, Inc., *The Equal Opportunity Employer,* pp. 1-47.
19. Thomas M. Hennessey, "Equal Rights" in *The New Boston Report,* Boston, Greater Boston Chamber of Commerce, May 22, 1964, p. 1.
20. *Ibid.,* p. 4.
21. New York Chamber of Commerce, Committee on Law Reform, *Racial Tensions in New York State* (New York, 1963), pp. 36-37.
22. *Ibid.,* p. 37.
23. Letter, December 2, 1964.
24. Letter, October 29, 1964.
25. Committee for Full Employment, *Merit Employment Manual,* Chicago Association of Commerce and Industry, 1964.
26. Letter, October 30, 1964.
27. Letter, November 9, 1964.
28. Letter, October 30, 1964.
29. St. Louis Commission on Equal Employment Opportunity, *9 Point Program,* 1964.

16

EQUAL OPPORTUNITY AND EMPLOYMENT IN ILLINOIS

Frank H. Cassell*

Seldom, if ever, should one be invited to comment on his own work. Self-interest is too likely to cast a shadow over the objectivity of the commentary. Furthermore, people too closely involved with a project may not have the necessary perspective to place their work into proper relationship with other events. In spite of these handicaps, I shall discuss herein some of the work of the Governor's Committee on Unemployment of the State of Illinois, on which I had the honor to serve as chairman. Because of the limitations on objectivity from which any writer must suffer, I shall confine my paper to a firsthand account of the thinking and recommendations of the committee.

The Governor's Committee on Unemployment was made up of forty people who worked very hard and conscientiously to grasp the dimensions of one of the very complex problems of our time— the causes and cures of unemployment. It was a group of people who had courage to recommend plans, programs, and reforms which they felt were needed to reduce unemployment and increase the number of jobs in the state.

The main objectives of the committee were to establish a climate in which these problems could be faced in a rational manner and to provide to the people of the state the information necessary for their rational consideration.

In this commentary, I shall try to accomplish four things: To give some background on the organization and purposes of the committee; to summarize the data that the committee developed and used; to present its key recommendations and what has happened in Illinois since its report was delivered to the Governor on January 1, 1963.

---

*Assistant to the Vice-President, Administration, Inland Steel Company.

When the Governor of the state of Illinois, Otto Kerner, took office on January 1, 1961, 297,000 people in the state of Illinois or 6.9 per cent of the labor force were unemployed.[1] Unemployment costs in that year amounted to $181,000,000. Another $169,000,000 was spent on various forms of relief and welfare for some 334,000 people each month. Two-thirds of these people were receiving welfare benefits because of the direct or indirect impact of unemployment. These expenditures were 20 per cent of the total budget and were occurring at a time when money could not be found to improve the educational system.

But more important were the human costs. Two quotations from the introduction to the report illustrate the committee's concern for the individual:

> In a society where the common belief is that men who work are useful and those who do not work are not useful, unemployment becomes more than a problem of economics; it becomes one with deep moral and personal undertones. A job not only provides income, it provides standing in the community and self-respect. A job, and not just the income from it, is as much a necessity for the average American as is his daily bread, the clothing he wears and the shelter over his head.[2]

Again, the committee said:

> It is the effect of unemployment on the individual that causes the added concern, the unfortunate results on family life, the corroding effects upon standards of public and private behavior. Unemployment probably more than any other ailment afflicting modern man, operates to cut the person affected off from society around him.[3]

Unemployment moreover has been an exacerbating element in the relationship between the races. It has effectively limited the job opportunities of minority groups and increased resistance to their employment. It has prevented the most effective use of America's full manpower potential. It has raised questions throughout the world as to the capacity of the American private enterprise system to solve all these problems. These are some of the feelings and beliefs which governed the mood of the committee and influenced its work.

The composition of the committee was in itself interesting. It included representatives from industry, labor, and education together with elected and appointed government officials from both political parties. Its membership included an executive vice-president of a public utility, the dean of a graduate school of business, the president of an international union, state senators and representatives, the heads of both the state and local departments of public aid, and leaders of state and local educational institutions.

The backgrounds of the members guaranteed differences of viewpoint. But they were agreed upon one thing: the need for strenuous efforts to relieve unemployment in Illinois. How this group came to agree could be the subject of another paper, but suffice it to say that after eighteen months of discussion, study, and vigorous debate, all members of the committee were able to agree, and their report was published without dissent from any of its major recommendations.

FINDINGS

The committee began its work in relative ignorance. Little if any information was available to it about the characteristics of the unemployed. Practically no information was available as to why people were unemployed. Because of this lack of information, the committee, as its first major project, undertook in cooperation with the State Department of Labor a statewide survey to learn about the unemployed. The survey covered one hundred fifty thousand unemployed citizens of Illinois. Although it was not a representative probability sample, it was large enough to show important trends. Among them were these:[4]

1. The ranks of the unemployed included a smaller proportion of people with high skill than existed among employed workers; they also included a larger proportion of people with low skill or no skill at all.
2. The unemployed had fewer years of education on the average than the employed.
3. Of the unemployed, 45 per cent had been out of work five months or longer. Length of unemployment increased with the increase in age level.[5]
4. Primary wage earners, heads of families, constituted almost half of the total of long-term unemployed.
5. Forty-five per cent of the sample of unemployed were in the prime working age group of twenty-five to forty-five years of age.
6. The largest number of them (41 per cent) came from manufacturing, but manufacturing accounts for only 30 per cent of the total work force in the state.[6]
7. Thirty per cent of the unemployed, as against 10 per cent of the state's population, were nonwhite.
8. Negro unemployment exceeded white unemployment at

every occupational level; its greatest concentration was in the unskilled and semi-skilled occupations.

9. Unemployment among young people was three times higher than for the whole labor force.

Even at this early stage of the committee's work, the connection between education and unemployment began to emerge.[7] Further studies were undertaken, some by the committee itself and some by others encouraged by the committee. These began to fill in the picture a little more completely:

1. As bad as the urban situation was, unemployment rates in rural communities were very much worse. They ran up to 20 per cent in some areas.

2. Rural unemployment rates continued high despite a vast migration of young farm people to the cities. The farm population dropped from 20 per cent of the population of the state in 1910 to 8 per cent in 1950 to 5.6 per cent in 1960.[8] Eighty-one per cent of the people of Illinois now live in urban areas. Automation on the farm has reduced farm jobs and driven farm workers to the cities to find work.

3. But these people are ill-equipped to work in the cities. They were educated to meet the needs of 1900. For example: 114,000 students enrolled in state vocational education programs; the largest number, 60,000, were studying homemaking—a necessary skill, but one which hardly adds to employability. Thirty thousand boys were studying agriculture at a time when less than 5 per cent of the job openings were in agriculture. Schools which offered vocational training in expanding industries were rare indeed.

4. The quality of education of rural Illinois people and of people who migrated from the South was well below that needed to survive in an industrial society. One study which measured the educational competence of the unemployed in-migrant to Chicago showed that three out of five of those who said they had completed eight grades were functionally illiterate. They could not read well enough to learn a job which requires elementary reading and writing. Many could not fill out an employment application.[9]

5. Population and work force projections showed that in Illinois 75,000 new jobs needed to be created each year to stay even with the current rate of unemployment, but only 38,000 jobs a year were being created, or about half the number needed. This situation resulted because the rate of economic growth of the state was not fast enough to cope with the combined effects of a rapid growth of the labor

force and a substantial increase in productivity. The result was that unemployment remained disturbingly high until nearly thirty-six months of recovery had occurred.

6. The studies showed that during the sixties the work force of the Chicago area would increase 18 per cent. The fastest growth would be among women (27 per cent), nonwhites (43 per cent), and young people aged 20 to 24 (62 per cent). On the other hand there would be a loss of 2 per cent in the number of workers in the prime working age group of 35 to 44. The number of workers from 45 to 54 would increase 17 per cent. The total number of white employees would rise only 14 per cent; the total number of male employees, 13 per cent.

7. Unemployment in the inner rings of Chicago, other studies showed, ranges as high as 50 per cent in some areas. High school dropout rates go up to 80 per cent. Low family income, high relief rates, broken families, low educational attainment, and the Negro race are found together.

8. In areas where the educational level of Negroes equalled or exceeded that of whites, Negro unemployment was twice that of the white while the income level of Negroes was substantially lower than the white.

Thus, we see that not only had education emerged as one of the most important factors in unemployment, so had race and age. These, then, were the findings of the committee as to the supply of labor in the state in the coming years.

What would be the demand? The committee's projections added up about as follows: Jobs for the uneducated and the untrained were declining rapidly on the farms and in the cities, while the demand for high-talent, well-trained manpower was increasing at a rapid rate.

Demand for workers was increasingly concentrated in industry in the outer ring of the city, in the suburbs, and in rural locations —in areas remote from the high unemployment areas of the central city.

It was obvious that the skills of the people who would be available for work did not match the skills required in the available jobs. It was equally obvious that housing segregation kept workers apart from jobs. These situations existed at the time the committee was doing its research; they are more true today, nearly two years later, and they are likely to continue into the future.

The committee persisted in its efforts to find out exactly what jobs were opening up and what jobs were declining. At the time the committee began its work, and even today, most information is derived by inference. There is no way of reporting systematically the job openings occurring in the economy as they develop. We know about the manpower troubles long after they have occurred. We have no way to discover these trends early; consequently, our training programs, especially vocational education, lag far behind the actual requirements of the society.

Nevertheless, on very scanty data, some predictions were made. Our projections showed that the future, a bright future, was for those with good ability, and knowledge, and skill; these were the requirements of the emerging jobs and job patterns. For those of undeveloped ability, those lacking skills, those whose specialized skills were outdated, the future was bleak. And when one realizes that a high percentage of the Negro work force is characterized by these limitations and combines this with the virtual explosion of the Negro into the urban work force, one can begin to see the nature of the problem faced by the big cities.[10]

In-migrants, many of whom are illiterate, natural population growth in the ghettoes equal to the highest in the world, school conditions to match the ghettoes, segregated housing, unemployment three to four times as high as that of the whites, massive dependence upon relief for survival, disintegrated families, loss of the father as the family leader—these are the conditions under which new citizens are being produced. And across the board in industry, the requirement is high school graduation equipped hopefully with white middle class values, and in many cases, if they can help it, no Negroes, even if they have the education and the values. The educational requirements of business and industry are rising faster than the rising Negro educational level. The Negro schools in the cities and even the United Negro Colleges continue to lag badly, and the number of grades completed is often quite misleading.

Placing this Chicago and Illinois picture against a national backdrop, we can see the following: there are eight million functional illiterates in the United States; one-third of our young men if they were examined would be rejected for military service. One-half of these rejections would be due to failure on the mental test.[11] Illiteracy rates are four times as high among Negroes as among whites.[12] Daniel Bell has pointed out that what is different from the past is that education today — and tomorrow — is the chief means of social mobility, and that by charting the school dropout rates and matching them against future skill requirements, a rough picture of a class society can be sketched thirty years from now. It will be a class society and predominately a color society. Given the political tensions within this country, and the changed relations of the United States with a world which is dominated numerically, and perhaps politically, by Africa and Asia, one need not spell the consequences of the possibility that by losing out in the educational race the Negro will come to be the predominant and permanent member of the society of the disadvantaged. Even with the new Civil Rights Act, equal opportunity cannot be guaranteed unless the nation is prepared to spend money and effort in a massive catch-up program, which frankly places the immediate effort where the immediate need is the greatest.

With this broad picture of unemployment and the concomitant social problems in mind, the committee next turned to some of the questions of automation and what to do about them. The committee's orientation was, however, broader than merely automation. Rather, its major thrust was toward the questions of economic growth, industrial change, demographic changes, and the question of change in the society itself.

No one doubts that many of the difficulties besetting us stem from the fact that we are living in the middle of an enormous revolution which is characterized by technological change. Harrison Brown describes the closest parallel to this as being that which occurred 7,000 years ago when our primitive food-gathering ancestors learned that they could cultivate edible plants and domesticate animals. With the emergence of these new techniques, more than 500 persons could be supported in areas where previously only one could be supported. A small but important part of the population was liberated from the necessity of producing food.[13] In like manner, we have continued to liberate more people from the tasks of producing food, this time through advanced machine and chemical technology, and we are now liberating significant numbers of people through automation and machine technology from the production of goods. We are moving rapidly toward the liberation of people from the production of paper work and services.

As a matter of fact, we are liberating man from the work which machines can do and freeing him to do the work only men can do. Unfortunately, many men are better prepared to do the work of machines than they are to do the work of men, for the work of men is mostly the work of the mind, and the work of machines is work of the back and the finger. These considerations led the committee to focus heavily upon how to effect change, not oppose it; how to alleviate the stresses and hardships of adjusting to change; and how to create new forms of work.

It was not, therefore, accidental that the first analysis in the report concerned the question of economic growth. It began with these observations:

> Economic growth requires change, change in the types of goods and services produced, in methods of production, in the location of economic activity, and the skills required of the labor force. . . . The rising per capita incomes we have enjoyed in Illinois have emerged from a process of change, a process that will surely continue into the future. . . . Reduction of employment in an industry may in fact be proof of economic progress; it may point to increasing productivity in that industry with a consequent release of manpower for other productive work. If, for example, employment in agriculture had remained at the same proportion of the labor force that it was in 1890, the fifty-four million persons engaged today in such non-agricultural production as manufacturing, mining, construction, services, trade, transportation, and governmental work would be reduced to twenty-five million and our standard of living would drop accordingly.

In other words, the committee did not consider manufacturing as the sole model for creating work. Rather it saw the whole society, the whole domestic and world economic system, as its model for creating work and jobs. It recognized the inevitability of the automatic factory based upon continuous flow, feedback adjustment, and electronic computers to guide the entire operation, but it did not fear or oppose this development. Instead, the committee asked: How can this development be made to better serve mankind? How can people be prepared to operate this system? How can those displaced be trained and placed in other jobs and in other industries? How can people become more adaptable and more mobile?

In searching for answers, the committee decided that it should make recommendations in two areas: the creation of jobs and the preparation and adjustment of people for change. In the second area, it uncovered what it felt to be a number of powerful barriers or deterrents to change and adjustment.

The first barrier is the natural reluctance of people to change their ways. This reluctance is compounded by the fact that an individual is often not conscious of change and its significance to him. This blindness is not confined to the individual directly affected. It is also characteristic of business, labor, and governmental institutions.

People often oppose change because they mistakenly believe that opposition will prevent change and preserve a vested interest.

Another barrier is that of mobility, or rather immobility. We are a highly mobile nation, yet there are vast numbers of us who cannot make the necessary moves to take advantage of emerging job opportunities in other areas. The committee, in its report, said:

> Mobility of labor is a first condition to the achievement of full employment; if workers are not free or do not feel themselves free, to move to new jobs or to new areas, developing job opportunities cannot be used to offset declining job opportunities . . . . in an industrial society operated by private enterprise, jobs do not generally go to workers, workers must go to jobs.

Among the strongest barriers to mobility are age, race, seniority, pension and insurance arrangements, and a simple lack of information.

The committee's on-the-spot observations were that the older one is, the more reluctant he is to move away from home. He is attached to his community and to his investment in his home. In most cases that home represents his major savings, and in a declining area, he can seldom sell it without taking a substantial loss.

A committee study of unemployed workers showed that skilled workers were more willing to move than unskilled workers and that farm workers were especially willing to move.

The committee's feeling was that willingness to move depended more on the availability of jobs than upon an inherent reluctance to move stemming from sentimental attachment to the old job. Coal miners, however, often saw factory jobs as having lower status and were reluctant to change.

A number of barriers exist because of organizational rules. Certain forms of seniority, for example, have been a deterrent both because the worker is reluctant to leave the area and lose the advantages of the seniority he has built up, and because he fears that in any new job the seniority rules might make him the first to be laid off. Then there are his rights in pension and health insurance plans. Older workers, especially, need these protections. And, finally, workers are often completely ignorant of job opportunities in other labor market areas. This ignorance is not confined to the low-skilled or unskilled worker.

Race poses barriers to employment in special ways. In former years Negro workers, turned down at one hiring gate, would find other opportunities open to them; there were large numbers of unskilled jobs that needed filling. In addition, agriculture provided many jobs for Southern Negroes. Neither of these conditions is true today. The market for the unskilled is steadily shrinking. Even the qualified city-dwelling Negro is hampered in finding a job by the suburbanization of industry which, together with the elimination of public transportation facilities, removes the job effectively from him. In fact, the committee staff encountered employers who suburbanized specifically in order to assure themselves of a white work force.

An even more subtle barrier, and one affecting the college-trained Negro, is the fact that, because he has long been precluded from employment by business and industry, he is concentrated in the non-business fields — largely in the social and behavioral sciences and in medicine, teaching, law, and the ministry. Employers who want engineers, scientists, and graduates of the business schools, such as the Wharton School of the University of Pennsylvania, do not look to the older, more traditional professions, in which Negroes are trained, in their search for management talent.

A final set of considerations was the need for developing in Illinois a pool of high-talent scientific and non-scientific manpower to provide leaders for every aspect of human endeavor, including strengthening the economic base of the state and solving the problems of unemployment.

The committee recognized that leadership for today and for the future must draw from all our racial, ethnic, and religious groups. The committee called upon the people of the state to commit themselves fully to equality of opportunity in education, in employment, in housing, so that every racial and religious group would be free to produce the leaders needed by the state; leaders to create jobs, leaders to educate the future generations, leaders to solve our complex human relations problems, and leaders to fill the myriad of jobs which can make the difference between a leading or a lagging state.

RECOMMENDATIONS

These are only some of the problems and some of the considerations. What can be done about them? The committee's recommendations were in six areas:

1. Accelerating the state's economic growth;
2. Improvement of education and training in the state;
3. Strengthening community planning;
4. Improving the job-finding process;
5. Income for the unemployed; and
6. Special work programs for special groups of the unemployed.

First, as to economic growth — national economic policy as we all realize determines in large part what can be accomplished at the state and local level. Without a national effort to insure a rate of economic activity great enough to absorb most of the unemployed, state efforts will be futile. The $11 billion tax cut is part of such a national economic policy.

Since 1961, unemployment in the state has dropped from 6.9 per cent to 2.9 per cent. High economic activity has not only helped reduce unemployment, but it has provided the basis for equal job opportunity for many more people than would have been the case had the unemployment rate remained high.

In order to promote the state's economic growth, the committee recommended the establishment of a State Advisory Council on Economic Affairs, a State Department of Commerce and Science, and the encouragement of similar local groups. It recommended the strengthening of the economic infra-structure of the state by development of water resources and industrial parks and expanded urban renewal efforts. And it recommended stimulation of scientific research activities and increased attention to the special problems of chronically depressed areas. Finally, it recommended that the state undertake to expand its foreign trade and to improve the functioning of the job market through development of a means for gathering information on job vacancies.

Second, with respect to education and training — the committee recommended a concentrated anti-dropout campaign to be conducted by schools and communities. It recommended improvement of vocational education, the widespread development of technical institutes, extension of the compulsory education age to 17 or high school graduation, more post-high-school facilities, and a variety of other measures all intended to modernize the state's educational institutions. The committee emphasized the importance of competent and adequate guidance and counseling, both for young people and for present members of the labor force.

With respect to improving the job-finding process — the committee recommended strengthening the Illinois State Employment Service by a variety of measures including the establishment of a Board of Advisors, strengthening of cooperative placement efforts between the schools and the Employment Service, and by emphasis on upgrading and training the agency's staff.

Supplying income for the unemployed — the committee recommended the extension of work relief programs to provide both income and training, establishment of public works programs, expansion of sheltered work and rehabilitation programs, and establishment at the national level of a Youth Conservation Corps.

All of the committee's recommendations have not been covered by any means. Some of them have been accomplished, some of them have been started, and some of them are still only hopes.

The committee's major accomplishments were three:

First, it helped the people of the state to focus on the problem of unemployment. It made them aware and concerned.

Second, it served as a kind of blueprint for the many actions and studies which have been undertaken since. It was of interest to find that the platform planks of both Governor Kerner, who originated the study, and his opponent, Charles F. Percy, included many of the recommendations of the report. In fact much of the debate revolved about who could best reduce unemployment and make the state grow economically. And third, the study demonstrated the feasibility and value of state-level planning even as limited as was this effort.

More specifically, the report helped the Governor give impetus and direction to his efforts to solve the unemployment problem. It stimulated the establishment of a powerful and effective Foreign Trade Committee, headed by the president of the Caterpillar Tractor Company; it gave strong support to numerous state and local efforts to accelerate the state's economic growth. Programs for the widening and deepening of waterways and the development of recreational facilities were accelerated. Illinois, and Chicago in particular, has led the states in utilization of the Manpower Development and Training Act. In this connection, pre-apprentice toolmaker programs using MDTA money have eased entrance into the craft for many young people who would otherwise have been precluded from entering it.

In probably the largest tutoring program in the nation, over 3,000 volunteers from 17 Illinois college campuses, women's organizations, and business groups are working with some 7,000 children and teenagers. About 4,500 of these young people are receiving tutoring on a one-to-one or two-to-one basis. One study of the Northwestern University tutoring project showed that the schoolwork of those being tutored improved in 50 per cent of the cases. This effort grew out of the awareness of widespread illiteracy which kept people from jobs and from further schooling.

A massive effort (the JOBS program) to train 1,000 currently unemployable youth, many of whom are functionally illiterate, has met substantial success in developing attitudes necessary for employment, in teaching job skills, and in providing some job experience, so that participants can finally hold full-time jobs. (This program has been renewed for another year.) This is an example of a committee recommendation of a special program for special people. It is also expensive, as is most rehabilitation work, double the cost of educating a child in the Chicago Public Schools.

The Full Employment Committee of the Chicago Association of Commerce and Industry was a direct outgrowth of the committee's report. Its membership, which includes representation from every segment of the community, took as its first task that of breaking down the racial discrimination barrier among its 6,000 members. It issued an equal opportunity brochure and held seminars to provide the encouragement and know-how to employers, both large and small. It has supported the development of grassroots job opportunity fairs held in the areas where the people know little, if anything, about the realities of the world of work and about what it takes to get and hold a job. Employers of the Chicago area, the State Department of Personnel, and the Illinois State Employment Service have provided interviewers and counselors. Some 9,000 young people, their parents, and their teachers have participated in these fairs. Hundreds have been employed by the participating companies.

More sophisticated methods for providing labor market information are being developed by a Governor's Committee on Job Vacancies, headed by Professor Albert Rees of the University of Chicago. A sample study began in October of this year under the direction of the U. S. Bureau of Employment Security.

The extensive recommendations on education are limited by the availability of funds. In this connection, nowhere is there a clearer demonstration of how local inattention or absence of concern or false economy creates the pressures to go to the federal government for help. The Chicago school system is embroiled over the question of integrating the schools and is short of money to provide needed mass saturation programs. Many of the educational programs designed to relieve unemployment are being carried on outside the school system. The effort to raise money locally for the schools is held up by the alienation of a rural-controlled legislature from the urban people and the fear of the white ethnic groups of the Negro's invading their neighborhoods.

Finally, a number of the committee's recommendations have found their way into President Johnson's anti-poverty program. These include extension of work relief programs to more welfare recipients to provide useful work as well as income and to increase skills. They include the establishment of a Youth Conservation Corps, which was incorporated into the poverty program as the Job Corps, to provide work and training to disadvantaged young people. Since the number of young people in the labor force will grow 60 per cent in the next ten years, this program and related programs should be of great value.

These examples of action on the problems of unemployment and poverty are in some small part due to the atmosphere created by the publication of our report. A spirit of adventure and experiment has developed in the state, to which I feel the committee and the report contributed, and things are happening. The authors of the report could not have hoped for more.

FOOTNOTES

1. *Report of the Governor's Committee on Unemployment*, p. 31. As of October, 1964, unemployment had dropped to 131,000 persons or 2.9 per cent.
2. *Report*, Introduction, p. 11.
3. *Report*, p. 1.
4. These findings are given in detail in Chapter VI of the *Report*.
5. "Of the 4 million unemployed on the average in 1962, some 1.1 million were classified as long-term unemployed, i.e., unemployed for 15 weeks or more. . . . The size of hard-core groups, while also moving with the (business) cycle, has been distinctly higher as a proportion of total unemployment during the last five or six years than at any time since 1946." Adolph Sturmthal, *Current Manpower Problems* (Urbana, Illinois: University of Illinois, Institute of Labor and Industrial Relations, 1964), p. 5.
6. What is happening to employment in manufacturing is well described in the following comment by William Janovich: "The semi-skilled were those replaced by single-purpose machines, both men and women who are performing the tasks which can be performed by machines (and better) are most easily replaced by a machine. Machines are conceptually unindividual; no machine was ever created to perform a single operation just once. Men 'lost' control over their movements — natural rhythms — as individuals with the invention of mechanical clocks, an event that took place before the industrial society got into high gear." *Saturday Review of Literature*, July 18, 1964, p. 16.
7. The relationships between education and employment are explored in detail in Chapter IV of the *Report*.
8. A comparison of the average age in thirty-six distressed downstate counties: the average age of people in 1950 was thirty-two years, seven-tenths younger than the average person in the state. By 1960 it was thirty-four and two-tenths, or older than the state average by three years. Average age in other rural counties declined as did the average for the state. *Report*, p. 27.
8. Cook County Department of Public Welfare, *The Blackboard Curtain*, A Study to Determine the Literacy Level of Able-Bodied Persons Receiving Public Assistance (Chicago: Science Research Associates, 1963), p. 70.
10. *Report*, Chapter III.
11. *One-Third of a Nation*. Report on Young Men Found Unqualified for Military Service. U. S. President's Task Force on Manpower Conservation, 1964.

12. *Ibid.*
13. Harrison Brown, "Solve Social, Political Broils and Technology Offers Eden," *Business and Society*, Autumn, 1963, p. 4.

17

NEGRO EMPLOYMENT IN LANCASTER, PENNSYLVANIA*

Walter J. Gershenfeld**

Richard L. Rowan***

This study had its genesis in a number of conversations among members of the Lancaster Chamber of Commerce on the subject of minority group employment problems. Casual talks led to planned meetings. The individuals involved in these meetings were organized into a committee of the Chamber of Commerce, which was identified as the Employment Opportunity Committee.

The outward manifestations of the problem had been relatively minor in Lancaster in comparison with the rest of the nation. Nevertheless, it became clear to the committee that this troubled area of American life required an accurate appraisal of the local facts and a program for action based on those facts. The committee invited Dr. Herbert R. Northrup, Chairman of the Department of Industry, Wharton School of Finance and Commerce, University of Pennsylvania to prepare a proposal for the study of minority group employment in Lancaster. The proposal was accepted by the Chamber of Commerce, and the study was authorized as an official Chamber project as of February 1, 1964. The study was led by Dr. Northrup, whose staff included Dr. Richard L. Rowan of the University of Pennsylvania and Dr. Walter J. Gershenfeld of Temple University.

---

*This report was prepared for the Chamber of Commerce of Lancaster, Pennsylvania under the direction of Professor Herbert R. Northrup, Chairman, Department of Industry, Wharton School of Finance and Commerce, University of Pennsylvania.

**Assistant Professor of Management, Temple University.

***Assistant Professor of Industry, Wharton School of Finance and Commerce, University of Pennsylvania.

In authorizing the study, the Chamber agreed that we were engaged in an attempt to understand

A. The nature of the non-white population in terms of its skills, abilities, background, attitudes, and aspirations.
B. The nature of the jobs available in Lancaster generally.
C. The experience of minority groups in this labor market setting.

Almost immediately, it was realized that the Negro population was the only sizable minority group for whom a study of sufficient size could be made to warrant valid conclusions.

In designing and planning the field work for the project, opinions and experiences were solicited from the members of the Chamber Committee, the executive staff of the Chamber, community leaders, Negro leaders, and other interested persons. The final field work design was a three-part operation.

First, a broad-gauged analysis of the demand for labor in Lancaster was made. The questionnaire to employers asked them to identify by job title the number of people hired in 1963 as well as the number already hired in 1964 and that they planned to hire during the year. No attempt was made to identify the number of positions filled by Negroes. Rather, we wanted to know the "profile" of the hiring pattern for all people in Lancaster. It was felt that this was the significant fact, namely, the type of job opportunity in Lancaster without regard to color or any other factor.

Second, in the Negro community, we decided that a similar "profile" of the wage-earning community was needed. Here a questionnaire was drawn up with the assistance of Dr. Robert Kleiner of Temple University. This questionnaire was field-tested and then administered by Negro interviewers on a random-sampling basis to every third home in the heavily Negro-populated parts of the Seventh Ward in Lancaster. The administration of this part of the program was greatly facilitated by a carefully drawn map of the Negro community showing numbers of dwelling units and concentrations of Negro population.

Third, the survey information was supplemented by directly interviewing most of the key employers in the area. An attempt was made to interview virtually every employer of over 500 people in Lancaster and its immediate surrounding area. A pledge of individual anonymity was made to all companies participating in interviews, and this pledge has been honored. However, it is possible to present a general summary of the interview findings.

Prior to examining the results of the field research, it is in order to note briefly some pertinent facets of the Lancaster setting.

THE SETTING FOR THE STUDY

The Industrial Setting

Lancaster was destined to become a leading food-producing county from its very beginning. Earliest German settlers deliberately chose the area because it showed a heavy growth of forest trees nurtured in limestone soil. Careful handling of this soil for more than two centuries finds it more fertile than when it was first cleared. In fact, scores of farms are being operated by descendants of original settlers operating under land grants from William Penn. Tobacco and cattle were the leading agricultural products. This, in turn, led to tobacco conversion's becoming a major industry. It is interesting to note that the tobacco industry is now a minor one in the county.

Lancaster's industrial history includes such proud names as the Conestoga wagon and the Pennsylvania rifle. Industries of prominence were the tobacco industry; textiles, including silk, umbrellas, and clothing; watches; wood products; foundries and heavy machinery.

Industrially, changes have come thick and fast in the period since World War II. Many of the old names are gone. Some of the remaining old-line major firms are growing but achieving greater productivity with relatively fewer people. However, the most important developments have revolved around two factors: (1) the growing recognition of Lancaster, by diverse, major American firms, as an extremely desirable place to work and to live, and (2) the start of arterial belt highways ideally designed for industrial growth among their paths.

Probably the most interesting aspect of the post-war growth is the change of industrial emphasis. Lancaster has been uniquely successful in having had losses in some old-line Lancaster industries countered by gains in light industry. Communities the country over have vied for clean, light industry, such as electronics and small machine products. Lancaster has found precisely this type of company wanting to come in or to expand an existing facility. It should also be noted that some impressive gains have occurred in primary metals. The historic balance between agriculture and industry has continued, but with much better diversity in each of these groups.

The significance of the above lies in the fact that while substantial decreases were taking place in the Lancaster industrial picture, these were being counterbalanced by even more substantial increases in industries generally considered desirable. The Chamber of Commerce has found interest in a Lancaster location continuing apace on the part of many leading American firms. Virtually all of the companies which have entered Lancaster since World War II are still there and, even more significantly, have chosen to expand their Lancaster facilities in considerable measure.

The Race-Relations Setting

Lancaster has had a Negro population from its very beginning. Indeed, one of the earliest references to a Negro in the county occurred in 1736 and concerned a skilled tradesman, a blacksmith. In his book *The Susquehanna*, Carl Cramer noted that during a Maryland-Pennsylvania border dispute in November, 1736, the Sheriff of Lancaster County captured one Thomas Cresap, leader of a Maryland surveying party:

> In order to make doubly sure that their captive would not elude them, the possee immediately marched him to Lancaster and there employed a Negro blacksmith to fit him with iron handcuffs. . . .

Negro slavery existed in Pennsylvania throughout the entire Colonial period. It never found widespread acceptance as an institution, however, and as early as 1754 the Quakers officially condemned slavery and in the next year banned from meeting those who practiced it. In 1780 the commonwealth passed an act for the gradual abolition of slavery within its bounds. No child thereafter should be born a slave in Pennsylvania. The Quakers, who took the lead, enjoyed the quiet but effective backing of the Pennsylvania Dutch.[1]

The historic race-relations setting must include a note on the underground railroad. A number of the routes of the escape system for Southern slaves ran through Lancaster County. Lancaster and Columbia were both prominent way stations on the underground railroad. In fact, Columbia was generally conceded to be the capital of the railroad. The very name, "underground railroad," originated during a visit to Lancaster County by a disgruntled slave holder, who announced, "There must be an underground railroad out of here."

Thus, Lancaster has historically taken a liberal position when tested on the issue of race relations. A review of the past year, however, in Lancaster shows such newspaper headlines as:

NAACP Leads Protest Against Hiring Practices
Minorities Ask Say in Planning
NAACP Takes Survey on Jobs
NAACP Lists Job Progress

Clearly, ferment is present. The purpose of the remainder of this study will be to introduce the facts on the labor market situation in Lancaster as they affect Negroes and to present them so as to provide a basis for analysis of the situation.

The Employment Setting

Lancaster is considered—with considerable envy by her neighbors —to be a full-employment economy. Although this is not precisely the case, it comes reasonably close to the truth to be descriptive.

In the Lancaster labor market, defined by the Bureau of Employment Security of the Pennsylvania Department of Labor and Industry as being coextensive with Lancaster County, the average employment for 1963 by month was approximately 120,000 employees. Unemployment ranged between 3,000 in October and 5,300 in February, averaging 4,000 for the year. (See Table 1.) On a percentage basis, the average monthly unemployment for the year 1963 was 3.2 per cent. Further, unemployment was 3 per cent or less in the months of April, May, July, August, September, and October.

TABLE 1

EMPLOYMENT AND UNEMPLOYMENT, LANCASTER, PENNSYLVANIA, 1963

	Total Employment	Non-Farm Employment	Total Unemployment	Per Cent Unemployment
January	115,900	106,600	5,100	4.2
February	116,200	106,800	5,300	4.4
March	116,900	107,500	4,800	3.9
April	118,000	108,400	3,600	3.0
May	119,600	109,000	3,300	2.7
June	122,200	109,700	4,200	3.3
July	122,800	109,700	3,800	3.0
August	124,400	110,900	3,600	2.8
September	123,500	111,200	3,300	2.6
October	121,600	110,700	3,000	2.4
November	120,400	110,400	3,800	3.1
December	119,400	110,100	4,400	3.6

Source: Bureau of Employment Security, Lancaster, Pa. (Revised Series)

Unemployment rose sharply to 4.6 per cent in January, 1964.

However, this was attributed to the snow and bad weather which blanketed the county during that month. The rate thereafter fell quickly to 2.5 per cent by May and by October had declined to the almost incredible figure of 1.8 per cent.

TABLE 2

EMPLOYMENT AND UNEMPLOYMENT, LANCASTER, PENNSYLVANIA

January–October 1964			
	Total Employment	Non-Farm Employment	Total Unemployment	Per Cent Unemployment
January	116,600	107,400	5,600	4.6
February	117,700	108,400	5,100	4.2
March	118,300	108,900	4,300	3.5
April	119,100	109,700	3,400	2.8
May	125,300	113,000	3,800	2.5
June	124,700	112,400	3,800	2.9
July	125,400	112,300	3,300	2.6
August	125,600	112,400	3,100	2.4
September	124,600	112,600	2,500	2.0
October	123,100	112,400	2,300	1.8

Source: Bureau of Employment Security, Lancaster, Pa. (Revised Series)

Farm employment has continued to decline as a source of employment and now represents perhaps 8 to 9 per cent of the employment total. In the summer months this figure rises to approximately 11 per cent. The remainder of employment is almost evenly divided between manufacturing and nonmanufacturing industries.

There is nothing on the horizon to indicate that these trends of increased employment with low levels of unemployment are in any jeopardy in the foreseeable future.

THE DEMAND FOR LABOR IN LANCASTER

Methodology

A "profile" of the over-all demand for labor in Lancaster was desired. In effect, this meant that we were interested in *all* jobs which were being filled by Lancaster employers. There was no attempt to limit the analysis to those positions with which the

Negro is frequently associated. Instead, the deliberate decision was made to determine exactly what type of hiring was taking place in Lancaster without regard to such diverse factors as level of the job or color of the applicant.

Accordingly, two questionnaires were created. The first of these asked employers to list by job title the number of employees hired in 1963. The second asked employers to repeat this effort for 1964, but with the further proviso that they indicate their hiring plans for 1964 by calendar quarter. Since the questionnaires were mailed in the second quarter of 1964, respondents were quoting their actual experience for the first quarter and part of the second quarter and extrapolating for the remainder of the year.

The questionnaire was sent to seventeen employers of more than 500 employees in approximately a seven-mile radius from Lancaster. (It became quite clear that the effective labor market for the Negro community of Lancaster lay within that radius, if indeed it reached that far.) In addition, a sample of 169 smaller employers was constructed as follows from employer lists available to the Chamber:

1. All employers in the Lancaster urbanized area with over 100 employees were included.

2. The questionnaire was sent to approximately every sixth organization employing more than ten individuals. An attempt was made to include at least one company in each classification in a detailed breakdown of the firms by standard industrial classification code.

(The figures to follow are without benefit of replies from the construction industry. We were informed that the reason was largely the volatile and seasonal nature of contract construction. In 1963 the contract-construction industry ranged from a low of 4400 employees in February to a high of 6500 employees in October.)

Previous governmental surveys in other communities on the subject of manpower needs had provided their respondents with a long list of job titles for them to report against. The conclusion of many observers was that this approach tended either to frighten respondents about the magnitude of the task or to force a respondent to slot his openings exclusively into the listed categories. The decision was made to use an open-end questionnaire, permitting the employer to list his job categories in the manner in which he normally described them.

The Results — 1963

Forty-six usable questionnaires covering 1963 employment were received. The questionnaires represented employers with a total work force of 18,254 employees at the time of the survey. The labor force for the Lancaster labor market as a whole at the time of the survey was approximately 120,000 employees. Although there is no analysis available of the size of the labor market in a seven-mile radius of Lancaster, a reasonably informed view is that the respondent sample covered approximately one-quarter of the appropriate labor force.

It should be emphasized that the county results are not necessarily synonymous with these figures. There are two principal reasons for this. The employment mix in the seven-mile radius and in the remainder of Lancaster County is not the same. Further, responding firms tend to be heavily weighted by expanding firms.

Table 3 presents a summary of the data for 1963.

The first noteworthy fact is that these employers hired a total of 2,120 individuals during the year. This represents net new hires and does not include recalls or part-time employees. The high number does not mean necessarily that these companies were experiencing rather high turnover and were unable to retain their employees. Rather, it would seem to be more a function of corporate expansion and growth during 1963. We cannot tell how much of this employment went to already employed individuals. Nevertheless, the fact remains that the employment sign was out in Lancaster for a total of 2,120 positions, which were available to qualified job applicants.

Second, 40.6 per cent of the openings were for unskilled labor. According to U. S. Department of Labor figures, laborers and operative and kindred workers amounted to a total of 23.4 per cent of the labor force nationally in 1963. This would seem to imply that a relatively full employment economy such as Lancaster's may use a greater percentage of unskilled labor.

There are few surprises in the data for professional and managerial, clerical and kindred, and sales personnel. The 8.1 per cent figure for semiskilled personnel is noteworthy, however. It exists despite the strongly expressed preference or necessity for hiring employees in entrance jobs and upgrading them with on-the-job training. Although there are difficulties in categorizing machine operators as unskilled or semiskilled, approximately 8 per cent of employment did go directly to individuals in the semiskilled category.

The Results — 1964

The 1964 results were interestingly more complete than the 1963 results in coverage. Fifty employers, representing 22,627 employees, responded to this survey questionnaire.

TABLE 3

EMPLOYEES HIRED IN 1963

Type of Occupation	Number	Per Cent
Professional and Managerial	171	8.1
Clerical and Kindred		
General Clerical	284	13.4
Clerk-Typist	46	2.2
Stenographer, Secretary	46	2.2
Data Processing	11	0.5
Sales		
Sales Representative	20	0.9
Route Salesman	53	2.5
Sales Clerk	90	4.2
Service		
Building Service (including janitor, elevator operator)	97	4.6
Protective Service (including guard, watchman)	11	0.5
Personal Service (including waitress, bus boy, food handler, beauty operator)	26	1.2
Medical Service (including practical nurse, attendant, aide)	104	4.9
Skilled (excluding construction industry)		
General	66	3.1
Apprentice	21	1.0
Semiskilled		
General (including technician, mechanic other than 1st class, inspector, paint sprayer, bench hand, laboratory aide, seamstress)	171	8.1
Truck Driver	12	0.6
Fork-Truck Driver	30	1.4
Unskilled		
General Labor (including material handler, assembler)	423	20.0
Machine Operator	96	4.5
Heavy Labor	342	16.1
TOTAL	2120	100.00

The results for 1964 are compared with the 1963 results in Table 4 below:

TABLE 4

PERCENTAGE DISTRIBUTION OF EMPLOYMENT

Type of Occupation	1963	1964
Professional & Managerial	8.1	13.1
Clerical and Kindred		
General Clerical	13.4	10.3
Clerk-Typist	2.2	1.9
Stenography, Secretary	2.2	1.6
Data Processing	0.5	0.4
Sales		
Sales Representative	0.9	2.1
Route Salesman	2.5	2.8
Sales Clerk	4.2	3.5
Service		
Building Service	4.6	3.6
Protective Service	0.5	1.1
Personal Service	1.2	1.9
Medical Service	4.9	2.8
Skilled		
General	3.1	5.5
Apprentice	1.0	4.0
Semi-Skilled		
General	8.1	9.6
Truck Driver	0.6	0.7
Fork-Truck Driver	1.4	0.7
Unskilled		
General Labor	20.0	12.1
Machine Operator	4.5	6.1
Heavy Labor	16.1	16.5
Total	100.0	100.0

Basically, the data for 1964 are distributed much as they were in 1963. Nevertheless, a number of classifications showed significant increases or decreases. The categories covering employees classified as professional and managerial, sales representative, skilled craftsman, and apprentice contained most of the increases. These categories are noteworthy for being at the upper end of the employment scale in terms of background requirements and status. On the other hand, the most sizable decreases occurred in general clerical, medical service, and general labor categories. The decline in general labor from 20.0 per cent of new hires to 12.1 per cent of new hires was itself the single greatest change on an absolute percentage basis. Thus, the 1964 data report an emphasis in favor of higher-level positions on the economic scale when a comparison is made with the 1963 results.

One likely hypothesis is that major changes in a few large companies can account for the difference. For example, one large company added much more in the way of general labor in 1963 than it plans to do in 1964. On the other hand, another company has begun adding substantial numbers of employees in excess of its reported 1964 plans; it is our understanding that the increase includes many employees classified as general labor. Offsetting adjustments for such occurrences could well restore the 1963 relationship among the employment categories. Another possibility is a long-term, upward trend in skill requirements.

Whatever the reason, it must still be emphasized that employer reports for 1964 indicate that one out of every three openings will be in the unskilled-labor category. When unskilled service-trade positions are added to this total, at least 40 per cent of the openings will not require significant previous training and experience. Thus, it can be said that the 1963 result showing the prevalence of unskilled-labor openings still applies in 1964.

THE COMMUNITY QUESTIONNAIRE

Methodology

A twenty-four-question interview form was constructed to investigate the background, mobility, schooling, work experience, and aspirations of Negro wage earners in Lancaster. (See Appendix A-4).

The actual administration of the questionnaire was on a systematic sampling basis utilizing a carefully drawn map of the Negro community. The map showed the number of dwelling units in each block in the Negro community and indicated the Negro population concentration as heavy, moderate, or sparse. All blocks classified as heavily populated by Negroes and many of the moderately populated blocks were included in the same study. Together, these blocks constitute approximately 80-90 per cent of the Negro community.

Negro interviewers were used exclusively. Here it was felt that this would materially increase the reliability of the response. These interviewers were selected with the advice of leaders of the white and Negro communities. The purpose and content of the questionnaire was explained to the interviewers who then practiced a sample interview with members of the research committee. In addition, one interviewer field-tested the questionnaire over a one-week period.

The instructions to the interviewers revolved around the necessity of maintaining a proper sample. The interviewers were told to attempt to interview each member of the labor market in every third dwelling unit in their assigned territory. No substitutions of dwelling units were permitted. After an appropriate introduction, the interviewer asked for the number of individuals working or looking for work in the dwelling unit. In those few cases where no resident of the dwelling unit was in the labor market, the interviewer moved on to the next third dwelling unit. The interviewers maintained a control sheet log in which the number of every third dwelling unit in their assigned territory was listed. The interviewers were to return to any dwelling unit where they were unable to complete the interviews. In addition, they were asked to indicate the number of call-backs required to complete their interviews or the reason for failure to complete the interviews.

The interviews were to be conducted in the early evening after dinner or on week ends. These hours were used to permit the interviewers to find wage earners at home. Once the number of labor market participants in a given dwelling unit was properly ascertained, the interviewers were, of course, free to complete the interviews at any convenient time.

A total of 173 usable questionnaires were returned by the interviewers. These questionnaires were tabulated and constitute the basis for the information which follows on the characteristics of the Negro community in Lancaster. It should be noted that in some cases fewer than 173 responses have been tabulated. This may be accounted for by incomplete responses or responses otherwise difficult to tabulate.

GENERAL POPULATION CHARACTERISTICS

1. In what community (city, town, village) and state were you born?

As can be seen, approximately one-third of the Lancaster Negro population were born in Lancaster itself. If the remainder of Penn-

TABLE 5

PLACE OF BIRTH

Place	Number	Per Cent
Lancaster	55	31.8
Pennsylvania (other than Lancaster)	38	22.0
South (including Ala., Ga., Fla., N.C., S.C., Miss., Va.)	71	41.1
Washington, D.C.	2	1.1
Rest of United States	7	4.0

sylvania is included, fully half of the population are thus covered. However, almost all of the remaining half of the Lancaster Negro population were born in the South.

2. How many years have you lived in Lancaster?

TABLE 6

YEARS LIVED IN LANCASTER

Years	Number	Per Cent
Less than 1 year	7	4.2
1-5	15	8.9
6-10	17	10.1
More than 10	129	76.8

Over three-quarters of the Negro labor force in Lancaster have been there more than ten years. Apparently, a considerable portion of the Negro population of Lancaster has made Lancaster its home for a number of years. The hypothesis sometimes advanced to the research staff that large-scale Negro migration to Lancaster has been present in recent years does not stand up against this finding.

3. If you came to Lancaster as an adult, what brought you here?

TABLE 7

REASON FOR COMING TO LANCASTER AS AN ADULT

Reason	Number	Per Cent
Relatives	38	43.2
Friends	5	5.8
To seek employment	40	45.4
School	3	3.4
Military Service	1	1.1
Just roaming	1	1.1

The prime reasons advanced for coming to Lancaster, namely, relatives and employment opportunities, are fairly universal. Individuals tend to migrate toward family or employment.

4. Age.

TABLE 8

AGE

Age	Number	Per Cent
14-19	6	3.5
20-24	22	13.0
25-34	41	24.1
35-44	46	27.1
45 and over	55	32.3

The age distribution of the Lancaster Negro population in the labor force yields two conclusions of analytical import.

(a) Approximately one-third of the Lancaster Negro population in the labor force are over 45. This means that planning any employment program for Negro members of the Lancaster work force must be based on the notion that a substantial proportion of this labor force are mature.

(b) The small number of young people in the sample is a source of wonder. The hypothesis, here, is that the young Negro tends to leave Lancaster and strike out for his future in larger metropolitan areas. This happens despite the fact that few areas in the entire country can compete with the health of the Lancaster labor market. The reasons for this out-migration of young Negroes are undoubtedly complex and varied. Probably present is the age-old desire of the young to break off from the family and see what the rest of the world is like. Nevertheless, the extremely low unemployment rate in Lancaster would normally be considered enough to discourage a good part of this migration. The fact that it does occur may mean that the young Negro believes, or has found, that there is discrimination in employment or that he is unqualified for existing openings, but further information on this subject is needed.

5. Marital status.

The information on marital status bears out the notion that the Negro labor force in Lancaster is a stable one. Almost 70 per cent of the Negro labor force are married. The small number of divorced

TABLE 9

MARITAL STATUS

Status	Number	Per Cent
Married	117	69.5
Single	25	14.9
Widowed	13	7.8
Divorced	4	2.4
Separated	9	5.4

and separated individuals is a correlative indication that the Lancaster Negro labor force has well-established roots. (It should be noted that these figures do not, of course, include those households headed by a female whose primary source of income is a public welfare grant.)

6. Sex.

TABLE 10

SEX

Sex	Number	Per Cent
Male	85	50.3
Female	84	49.7

The significant fact here is that there is virtually the same number of individuals of each sex in the Lancaster Negro labor force. This would be contrary to the general belief that the Negro male dominates the labor force. In point of fact, nationally, there are three employed Negro males for every two employed Negro females.[2]

EDUCATION

1. What was the highest grade that you completed in school?

TABLE 11

EDUCATION

Years Completed	Number	Per Cent
1	0	0.0
2	0	0.0
3	0	0.0
4	7	4.1
5	8	4.7
6	7	4.1
7	10	5.9
8	21	12.4
9	20	11.7
10	19	11.2
11	22	12.9
12	43	25.3
College		
1	5	2.9
2	2	1.2
3	2	1.2
4	2	1.2
5	2	1.2

The data show that approximately one-third of the Negro work force have a high school education or better. The median number of years of education is ten.

2. What was your major high school course?

TABLE 12

MAJOR COURSES — HIGH SCHOOL

Course	Number	Per Cent
General	54	69.2
Academic	6	7.7
Commercial	12	15.4
Vocational	4	5.1
Home Economics	2	2.6

This table shows that more than two-thirds of the Negro work force with at least some high school education studied the General course. This finding is important in view of the conclusions found in the study entitled "School Survey of Lancaster Negro and White Students." This study, dated December 18, 1963, was the product of a joint effort by the Board of Education of the School District of Lancaster and the staff of the Pennsylvania Human Relations Commission. The study published the following two relevant conclusions:

> For a much larger proportion of Negro students than white students, high school is the end of their formal schooling. However, a larger percentage of the Negro graduates than white graduates have been competing for employment without having completed the Commercial, Vocational or Distributive Education programs.
>
> In relation to the large number of Lancaster graduates who do secure employment in secretarial, retailing and industrial positions, very few Negro students have taken the relevant training. The majority of those who did take pre-college and vocational education were successful in securing placement appropriate to their training.

The Human Relations Commission study found that during a four-year period, as of three to six months after graduation, 42 per cent of *all* graduates went on to college or some kind of technical or career school, while the corresponding figure for Negro graduates was 8 per cent. The need for counseling toward a commercial or vocational curriculum seems evident.

3. What was your major college course?

TABLE 13

MAJOR COURSE — COLLEGE

Course	Number
Social Studies	3
Pre-Ministerial	1
Education	1
Music	1
Physical Education	2
Languages	1
Mathematics	1
Home Economics	1

This table summarizes the fields of college study represented by Negroes in the Lancaster work force. Unfortunately, the number of individuals covered is too small to permit any valid generalizations to be drawn.

4. What type of specialized training have you had in the armed forces, trade school, business school, or otherwise?

TABLE 14

SPECIALIZED TRAINING

Type Training	Number
Armed Forces	
Radio	2
Languages	1
Molding	1
Heavy Equip. Operation	8
Truck Driving	1
Music	1
Clerical	3
Cryptography	1
Special Svcs.	1
Airplane Mechanic	1
Trade School	
Barber School	1
Shoe Repair	1
Industrial Arts	1
Glass Blowing	1
Engineering	1
Auto Mechanic	3
Electronic Repair	1
Brick Layer	1
Plumber	1
Carpenter	1
Mechanic School	2
Business School	
Clerical — General	5
Accounting	1
Secretarial	2
Other	
Practical Nursing	7
Beauty Culture	2
Deck Hand Training	1
Registered Nursing	1
Dental Technician	1
Theological Seminary	1
Art School	1
Home Economics	1
Tailoring	1

This table shows a wide variety of experiences educationally. Most of the categories involve only one individual's being exposed to the specific type of training listed. However, there are three categories worthy of note. Eight individuals report training in heavy equipment operations. A total of eleven individuals have been exposed to clerical training in one form or another in either the armed forces or at a business school, and seven individuals have taken training as practical nurses.

WORK EXPERIENCE

1. What type of work have you done most of your life?

TABLE 15

RANGE OF OCCUPATIONS

Type of Occupation	Number of Individuals	Per Cent
Professional and Managerial	7	3.5
General Clerical	12	6.1
Sales Clerk	2	1.0
Building Service	12	6.1
Protective Service	2	1.0
Personal Service	29	14.7
Domestics	30	15.2
Medical Service	8	4.0
General Skilled Trades	5	2.5
Semi-skilled	8	4.0
Truck Driver	7	3.5
Heavy Labor	21	10.6
General Labor	45	22.7
Machine Operator	10	5.1

There are four categories here with more than twenty responses each: Personal Service, Domestics, Heavy Labor, and General Labor. These four categories cover unskilled labor basically and represent approximately two-thirds of the Negro labor force.

2. Are you currently employed?

TABLE 16

EMPLOYMENT AND UNEMPLOYMENT

	Number of Individuals	Per Cent
Employed	146	87.6
Unemployed	21	12.4

Unemployment in Lancaster generally, during the period of time the community questionnaire was being administered, was under 3 per cent of the labor force. The figure of 12.4 per cent for unemployment in the Negro community is thus quite high. Nationally, it is common for Negro unemployment to be approximately twice as great as the figure for the economy as a whole.[3]
3. What is your current occupation?

TABLE 17

TYPE OF WORK DONE CURRENTLY

Type of Occupation	Number of Individuals	Per Cent
Professional and Managerial	9	6.3
General Clerical	7	4.9
Route Salesman	2	1.4
Sales Clerk	3	2.1
Building Service	10	7.1
Protective Service	1	0.7
Personal Service	21	14.8
Domestic	24	16.9
Medical Service	7	4.9
General Skilled Trades	2	1.4
Semi-skilled	5	3.5
Truck Driver	3	2.1
Heavy Labor	11	7.8
General Labor	22	16.9
Machine Operator	13	9.2

As might be expected, the figures show essentially the same pattern as was found in the replies to the question on what type of work the individual has done most of his life. The smaller number of responses here is due to the fact that some individuals reported two occupations as most frequently performed in reply to Question

1. In addition, the replies to this question included only those currently employed. The basic finding that two-thirds of the positions filled by members of the Negro work force are unskilled remains unchanged.

4. How long have you been on your present job?

TABLE 18

NUMBER OF YEARS ON PRESENT JOB

Length of Time	Number of Individuals	Per Cent
Less than 1 year	27	22.0
1-3 years	21	17.1
4-5 years	11	8.9
Over 5 years	64	52.0

Once again, the research data bear out the hypothesis that the Negro labor force in Lancaster is highly stable. Over one-half of the individuals who replied to this question have been associated with their present employer for a period of more than five years.

5. Do you have any part-time job (s) or second full-time job in addition to your regular job?

TABLE 19

EMPLOYEES HOLDING SECOND JOB

	Number of Individuals	Per Cent
Yes	16	10
No	144	90

The extent of reported moonlighting does not seem to present any significant problems in terms of its effect on the labor force.

ASPIRATIONS

A series of questions were asked in an attempt to ascertain some of the job-oriented goals and aspirations of the individuals being surveyed. The investigation covered such areas as type of work desired, interest in training programs, and career goals for their children.

1. What kind of occupation would you most like to have?

TABLE 20

TYPE OF WORK DESIRED

Type of Work	Number of Individuals
Machine operator	22
General clerical	12
Practical nurse	10
Sewing	8
Any suitable	8
Automobile mechanic	5
Secretary	4
Social work	4
Teaching	3
Construction work	3
Switchboard operator	3
Fireman	3
Electronics and TV Repair	3
Inspection	2
Cook	2
Truck driver	2
Accountant	2
Molder	1
Funeral director	1
Maintenance work	1
Policeman	1
Registered nurse	1
Domestic	1
Electrician	1
Architect	1
Painter	1
Janitor	1
Laundry worker	1
Carpenter	1
Beautician	1
Relocation officer	1
Machinist trainee	1
Art illustrator	1
Computer operator	1
Retail merchant	1
Engineering aide	1
Gas company worker	1

There are two striking facts here. First, we notice the tremendous variety of positions in which individuals are interested. The second major finding is that the job goals and aspirations of the Negro labor force are generally moderate. Of the five categories most frequently mentioned (machine operator, practical nurse, general clerk, sewing machine operator, and "any suitable"), only the practical nurse requires any type of extended training.

One further fact worth highlighting is that approximately one-third of the respondents voluntarily advanced the information that they were satisfied with the type of work they were doing.

2. What possible reasons could you give that would prevent you from getting this type of occupation?

A list of possible responses was given to the individuals and they were asked to select as many replies as were appropriate for themselves. These results are presented in Table 21 below:

TABLE 21

BARRIERS TO OCCUPATIONAL GOALS

Barrier	Number of Individuals	Per Cent
Lack of ability	1	0.6
Lack of training and education	63	35.2
Lack of opportunities; not getting right breaks in life	12	6.7
Lack of any clear and positive aim in life	1	0.6
Family background	1	0.6
Class I am in	0	0.0
Race I am part of	17	9.4
My religion	0	0.0
Illness	1	0.6
Lack of financial support	20	11.1
None	58	32.4
Other	5	2.8

Replies to this type of question might be expected to revolve around such factors as race, religion, or perhaps even social class. It turns out the respondents put the emphasis on training and education.

The fact that the second largest group of respondents saw no barriers in the way of attainment of their goals is quite noteworthy.

This would seem to be related to the moderate aspirations reported by many of the individuals replying to the previous question.

3. Please tell me what you are doing or have done to help you get this occupation?

TABLE 22

ACTIVITIES TO ACHIEVE OCCUPATIONAL GOALS

Type of Activity	No. of Individuals
Made application to industry	17
Made application to employment service	2
Attended school	2
Now in training	5
Applied for training	4
Hard work on present job	1

The important fact here is the small number of replies. There is a gap between desire and effort.

4. Are you interested in participating in a job training program?

TABLE 23

INTEREST IN PARTICIPATING IN JOB
TRAINING PROGRAM

Response	Number of Individuals	Percentage of Replies
Yes	103	62.0
Possibly	4	2.5
No	59	35.5

There is recognition of a need for training and a verbalized interest in participating in such programs by almost two-thirds of the individuals in the study.

5. If you had a son (or daughter) in school, what kind of occupation would you like him to have when he gets out of school?

TABLE 24

GOALS FOR CHILDREN

Career Goal	Number of Individuals
Child's choice	52
Nurse	15
Doctor	13
Undecided	9
Teacher	8
Lawyer	7
Secretary	5
White collar	3
Radio and TV repair	3
Armed services	3
Auto mechanic	3
Electronics	2
Engineer	2
X-ray technician	2
Accountant	2
Seamstress	1
Architect	1
Musician	1
Professional	1
Bookkeeper	1
Sports	1
Funeral director	1
Clerical	1
Medical secretary	1
Home economics	1

Although by far the greatest number of individuals responded by indicating that they felt this should be a matter of choice for the child, those respondents who specified occupations tended to list occupations with prestige. Among specific occupations listed, doctor, lawyer, teacher, and nurse were the ones most frequently mentioned. This is certainly in line with the American Dream and the universally expressed desire to have children reach beyond parents in attainment. The result is considered of consequence here from two points of view. First, individuals who replied by indicating modest goals for themselves definitely have higher-level ambitions for their children. Second, it is doubtful that many years ago

Negroes would have entertained these ambitions realistically for their children. There were simply too many barriers. Prejudice, finances, and schooling bars all made such goals unrealistic. The belief is that these goals are now being considered as meaningful by the Negro community because of the improved conditions for their attainment. Obviously, disappointment in this area will create a host of social problems.

    6. What possible reasons could you give that would prevent him from getting this type of occupation?

TABLE 25

BARRIERS TO OCCUPATIONAL GOALS

Barrier	Number of Individuals	Per Cent of Replies
Lack of ability	0	0.0
Lack of training and education	28	16.4
Lack of opportunities; not getting right breaks in life	7	4.1
Lack of any clear and positive aim in life	0	0.0
Family background	0	0.0
Class I am in	1	0.6
Race I am part of	11	6.4
My religion	4	2.3
Illness	0	0.0
Lack of financial support	30	17.5
None	89	52.1
Other	1	0.6

Here the same table used in asking respondents about barriers to their own accomplishment was presented in connection with their aspirations for their children. The preponderance of replies in the "None" column is substantiation of the notion advanced above, namely, that Negro parents are quite serious in holding high expectations for accomplishment by their children. Again, this is a level of accomplishment to which they do not aspire for themselves.

EMPLOYER INTERVIEWS

Methodology

    As indicated previously, a decision was made to interview the seventeen employers of approximately 500 employees each in the Lancaster urbanized area. The discussion which follows is based upon twelve interviews with respondent companies. Two companies declined to participate in the interviews, and time limitations made it impossible to conduct the remaining interviews.

The employers consenting to be interviewed participated freely and frankly. The interviewers were discussing a sensitive area and probing the subject of Negro employment in depth in many cases. Nevertheless, the companies generally gave every indication of wanting to place all facts on the table without any reservations.

The pattern of the interviews was highly informal, and no attempt was made to follow a structured interview under controlled conditions. For this reason, as well as the content of much of the questioning, the information here must be considered as highly subjective data. Nevertheless, the research group became convinced that many important observations were to be found in these interviews. Since the promise of anonymity can be maintained, the findings of these interviews are summarized below:

Findings

1. *Applicants.* In questioning the presence or absence of Negro applicants, transportation loomed large. The Lancaster Negro simply does not go very far to look for his work. Here, the automobile seems to be tremendously important. Lancaster plants not easily accessible other than by car generally report fewer Negro applicants. Employers outside a radius of approximately seven miles reported Negro applicants to be rare.

Employers noted that a successful Negro applicant for employment generally tends to produce an immediate response from the Negro community of additional Negro applicants. This apparently happens as word spreads through the Negro community that an individual has been placed with a given company.

Interestingly, in a number of cases where the charge of discrimination has been leveled, it has been against those employers with the best record in terms of hiring Negroes. There was some employer complaint that "pioneering" carried a high price, as Negroes were attracted to a company with a reputation for good hiring practices. Inevitably, a certain number of unqualified Negroes would become disaffected upon rejection.

Employers also report that it is difficult to find a satisfactory way to notify the Negro community of openings. Generally, it is felt that Negroes should be notified through the same media as the white community. However, in those instances where employers deliberately wanted to contact Negro applicants, they felt word of mouth or other referral techniques to be weak.

2. *Type of Jobs Available.* As seen previously, a high proportion of the jobs to be filled are at the bottom of the employment scale. In good part, this is due to the fact that skill needs require Lancaster employers to hire at the bottom and then upgrade their work force. In some cases, this is due to the pressure of a union contract calling for plantwide posting of openings. In-plant employees have an opportunity to bid for open positions before the employer hires anyone from the outside.

3. *Employment Standards.* Employers report, as above, that they maintain high standards for positions which, in and of themselves, do not require such high standards. Frequently the entry wage is considerably higher than the wage which needs to be paid to hire applicants competent to handle the entry position. Employers report that these high wage rates for relatively low-level positions make it imperative that they hire competent people. Failing this, the pipeline for upgrading would dry up, and the entry jobs would become dead-end barrier jobs. Employers note that insistence upon a high-school education and/or administration of a battery of aptitude tests have best enabled them to maintain these standards.

Employers also report that testing has enabled them to offer objective evidence to explain rejection of an inadequately qualified Negro applicant who charges discrimination. Employers report that this situation has been rare.

In terms of meeting standards, disappointment is voiced at the lack of preparation of Negro applicants.

4. *Negroes as Employees.* A number of industrial organizations report similar findings. Negroes, particularly those with a *minimum* of previous industrial experience, tend to be poor to fair employment risks. Work attitudes and absenteeism are the principal problems. However, the same concerns report that, given time — and here employers talk in terms of time periods in excess of normal probationary periods — these employees blend into the work force with work records not significantly distinguishable from those of analagous white employees.

Few experiences can be cited with Negroes in professional or managerial positions. When such situations were reported, the employers would indicate that the problem of a Negro with professional background lies largely in the housing area. Some highly qualified Negroes had come and gone from Lancaster because of an inability to find housing outside the Seventh Ward Negro ghetto area.

5. *The Attitude of White Employees toward Negro Employees.* Unanimously, employers find that white employees easily accept Negro employees. Although few Negro professionals are covered in the study, they were reported as being completely accepted in the work setting. Many organizations, particularly those pioneering in placing Negroes in positions heretofore not held by Negroes in their organizations, felt real trepidation before hiring Negroes. They were later delighted and gratified to find that the problem of attitudes on the job was largely a straw one.

6. *Negroes with Clerical Skills.* One fascinating result of the interviews was the discovery that many employers were simultaneously looking for Negro typists and stenographers. In many cases a decision was made to find qualified Negro clerical applicants. Such decisions were being made independently but concurrently by a number of different concerns. Unfortunately, the number of Negro girls with the appropriate skills was pathetically small. Some employers ranged far and wide in their search. Few were able to resolve it successfully. There is apparently a time lag between realization of the existence of this demand and the overt guidance and direction given Negro girls to prepare themselves for stenographic work.

7. *Discrimination in Favor of Negroes.* A very sensitive question was explored with a number of employers. In essence, the question asked was whether they felt that Negroes should be treated on the basis of complete equality with all other applicants or whether they should be given some preferential treatment in recognition of the fact that there had been discrimination against them nationally in many ways. Most employers feel that Negroes deserve full and equal treatment but that anything further represents a form of discrimination in reverse, which is completely unfair to the white applicant with a more appropriate background who might be rejected in favor of a Negro.

A minority position exists which says, in effect, that although we are not going to hire unqualified Negroes, we recognize that there is a circle of interaction of schooling, housing, and employment standards which makes it difficult for the Negro to obtain employment. Accordingly, we recognize a *range* of qualifications which is acceptable for positions. As long as Negroes meet the qualification range, we will consider hiring them. In other words, this group would consider hiring a Negro with lesser skills than a white applicant, provided the Negro possessed at least minimal qualifications for the job, and Negro employees were scarce in the organization.

SUMMARY

The Negro Labor Force in Lancaster

Stability. The Negro labor force in Lancaster is highly stable. It is dominated by individuals either born in Lancaster or resident there for ten years or more. This is not a group of recent migrants who are unfamiliar with Lancaster. These are people oriented toward Lancaster. On frequent occasion, respondents indicated that they considered Lancaster their permanent home and further that they liked life in Lancaster. Additional evidence of stability is the high percentage of married individuals in the Negro labor force.

Age and Sex. The survey group showed a surprising proportion of females in the labor force — approximately one-half. The age distribution showed both a small number of young Negroes in the labor force and a sizable proportion of individuals over 45 (approximately one-third of the group).

Education and Training. The median number of years of school for the group was ten. In addition, a number of individuals reported further training in trade, service, and other schools. In approximately 70 per cent of the cases, members of the Negro work force reported studying the high-school general curriculum. Only 5 per cent reported majoring in a vocational field — this despite the clear record that high school or a portion thereof was the terminal formal educational experience for a majority of the group.

Type of Work Performed. Although Negroes can be found in virtually all types of jobs and professions, there is little question that the group in Lancaster is dominated by individuals holding unskilled positions. Approximately two-thirds of the individuals surveyed are in positions of this type. One interesting survey result was the corollary finding and its relationship to education: One-third of the Negro work force in Lancaster are holding positions above the unskilled level, and this is precisely the percentage of individuals in the Negro labor force who are at least high-school graduates.

Unemployment Rate. Precise figures on the incidence of Negro unemployment in Lancaster have been unavailable up to now. This study with its broad-based sample, however, has revealed a strikingly high unemployment rate of 12.4 per cent. This is a figure which is four times the rate for unemployment in Lancaster generally.

Aspirations and Interest in Training. It was interesting to find that goals expressed by members of the Negro work force were moderate for themselves. Conversely, goals for their children were high. They generally felt that race was of less importance as a barrier to employment than the lack of training and education. There was a natural correlation here in that almost two-thirds of the Negro labor force proceeded to express interest in training programs which would permit them to either obtain other employment or upgrade themselves somewhat in their present employment.

Employer Hiring

Type of Hiring. One of the most remarkable findings in the survey of employer hiring patterns was the large number of individuals hired for essentially unskilled openings. Although the percentage of unskilled openings fell from approximately 50 per cent of all new hires to some 40 per cent of new hires between 1963 and 1964 (including projections for the second half of 1964), the fact remains that Lancaster is continuing to find a large number of unskilled positions open. It is the single most important fact about hiring in Lancaster.

Number of Openings. The employers in the sample covered approximately one-fourth of all employment in the labor market in a seven-mile radius from Lancaster. These employers reported a total of some 2,120 openings in 1963. The Lancaster labor market is, from all indications, generally healthy and active. Coupled with the relatively low turnover rates reported by county employers, this indicates that the bulk of job openings was probably attributable to economic growth.

Communication with the Negro Community. Employers consistently report that it is difficult to contact the Negro community on employment problems affecting Negroes. Although a majority of employers feel that direct contact for purposes of preferential hiring is undesirable, they almost all would like a professional source of aid within the Negro community which might be consulted on employment problems affecting Negroes.

Hiring Standards. Lancaster employers consistently report high hiring standards, even for entry positions. In many cases the standards are a product of special considerations such as the shortage of skilled personnel requiring internal upgrading of the unskilled. In other cases, entry wage scales dictated by contractual terms have been set so high that employers strive to obtain well-qualified individuals for the high rates. This means, essentially, that employees may accept work below their skill levels because the rates paid are satisfactory. Employers use such overqualified individuals in entry jobs as a source of talent for promotion-from-within policies. The fact that there is a logical basis for the situation does not alter the fact that it does operate to bar a substantial number of Negroes from positions which they are qualified to perform but whose formal qualifications they cannot meet. Full understanding of this problem was found among some employers who were reluctant to change the situation for practical reasons. They reported that if entry jobs were given to individuals qualified to perform the specific jobs, but lacking qualifications to go beyond, their promotion-from-within policies would have to be altered substantially or discarded.

Negroes as Employees. Employers reported that Negroes found little in the way of barriers to acceptance in the work force. A number of employers who had hired Negroes either for the first time or in positions new to Negroes for their companies reported that many of the anticipated problems turned out to be of apparently little consequence. More serious, they felt, was the reaction of the Negro employees themselves. They reported that a number of Negro employees adopted bad habits in terms of absenteeism and work standards. Employers who declined to accept any such form of behavior promptly discharged the Negroes involved. Employers who chose to persevere with some of these marginal employment situations reported real progress, but time periods in excess of normal probationary period standards were required. They felt strongly that a greater amount of self-discipline and self-policing was necessary for some members of the Negro work force.

The Clerical Situation. There was a finding here which warrants special consideration. Employer after employer indicated interest in hiring Negro secretaries, stenographers, and typists. In some cases this interest was limited to a hope that qualified Negroes in these categories would turn up. More often, however, the employer made a number of efforts to find such individuals. Inevitably, the efforts were doomed to failure simply because of the small number of Negro girls possessing the necessary skills. The question of communicating employer interest in these skills to the Negro school community and translating it into effective counseling is clearly important.

A Final Word

In our examination of the small but growing Negro labor market in Lancaster, Pennsylvania, a number of salient facts have been uncovered and reported above. It is noteworthy that many of the findings resulted in overturning what might be termed "conventional wisdom." It is precisely in offering facts rather than social myth that a baseline for useful and viable programs can be constructed.

The methodology employed in this study utilized a three-pronged approach, i.e., simultaneously studying characteristics of the Negro labor force, the demand for labor generally, and employer experience with minority groups. It seems clear that similar comparative studies in other labor markets can offer considerable insight into some of the pressing problems of the Negro labor force.

FOOTNOTES

1. P. A. Wallace, *Pennsylvania* (New York: Harper and Row, 1962), pp. 180-181.
2. *Manpower Report of the President* (Washington, D.C.: Government Printing Office, March, 1964), p. 101.
3. *Ibid.*

APPENDIX TABLES

Appendix A-1

OCCUPATION OF EMPLOYED NEGROES, BY SEX
1960, UNITED STATES

Major Occupation Group	Male Number (in thousands)	Per Cent	Female Number (in thousands)	Per Cent
Total employed	3,643.9	100.0	2,455.1	100.0
Professional, technical, and kindred workers	112.7	3.1	175.3	7.1
Farmers and farm managers	154.2	4.2	14.5	0.6
Managers, officials, and proprietors, except farm	63.2	1.7	24.8	1.0
Clerical and kindred workers	178.9	4.9	181.7	7.4
Sales workers	46.7	1.3	36.1	1.5
Craftsmen, foremen, and kindred workers	356.6	9.8	15.9	0.6
Operatives and kindred workers	887.4	24.4	310.2	12.6
Private household workers	27.3	0.7	888.2	36.2
Service workers, except private household	507.9	13.9	519.8	21.2
Farm laborers and foremen	256.7	7.0	69.5	2.8
Laborers, except farm and mine	745.0	20.4	23.6	1.0
Occupation not reported	307.3	8.4	195.5	8.0

Note: Detail may not add to totals because of rounding.
Source: U. S. Department of Commerce.

Appendix A-2

UNEMPLOYMENT RATES, BY COLOR, SEX, AND AGE
1963, UNITED STATES

Sex and Age	White	Nonwhite
Male		
All Age Groups	4.7	10.6
14 to 19 years	14.2	25.4
20 to 24 years	7.8	15.6
25 to 34 years	3.9	9.5
35 to 44 years	2.9	8.0
45 to 54 years	3.3	7.1
55 years and over	4.1	8.0
Female		
All Age Groups	5.8	11.3
14 to 19 years	13.6	33.1
20 to 24 years	7.4	18.8
25 to 34 years	5.8	11.7
35 to 44 years	4.6	8.2
45 to 54 years	3.9	6.1
55 years and over	3.4	4.6

Appendix A-3

UNEMPLOYMENT RATES OF EXPERIENCED WORKERS[1]
BY COLOR AND OCCUPATION, 1963, UNITED STATES

Major Occupation Group	White	Nonwhite
All occupation groups[2]	4.4	9.3
Clerical and sales workers	3.9	7.4
Craftsmen and foremen	4.6	8.2
Operatives	6.9	11.1
Private household workers	3.1	7.7
Other service workers	5.3	10.0
Farm laborers and foremen	5.0	7.1
Laborers, except farm and mine	11.0	15.2

[1]The base for the unemployment rate includes the employed, classified according to their current jobs, and the unemployed, classified according to their latest civilian job, if any; excludes unemployed persons who never held a full-time civilian job.

[2]Includes the following groups not shown separately: Professional and technical workers; managers, officials, and proprietors; and farmers and farm managers.

Appendix A-4

THE COMMUNITY QUESTIONNAIRE

1. In what community (city, town, village) and state were you born?

_____   _____
(Community, city or town)   (State)

2. How many years have you lived in Lancaster?
3. If you came to Lancaster as an adult, what brought you here?
4. When were you born?

_____   _____   _____
(Month)   (Day)   (Year)

5. At the present time, are you . . .
    1. Married
    2. Single
    3. Widowed
    4. Divorced
    5. Permanently Separated
6. Sex: Male   Female
7. What was the highest grade that you completed in school?
    None   0
    Grade School   1 2 3 4 5 6 7 8
    High School   1 2 3 4
    College or University 1 2 3 4 5 or more
8a. Are you going to school now?   1. Yes   2. No
8b. If yes, what are you studying?
9. What kind of work have you done most of your life? Please give me the title and a full description of the job.
10. Are you currently employed?   1. Yes   2. No
    If yes, skip to question 14. If no, ask — are you looking for work?   1. Yes   2. No.
    If yes, continue the interview. If no, discontinue the interview.
11. Did you work at all the past twelve months?   1. Yes   2. No
    If yes, skip to question 13.
12. How come you didn't work at all during the past twelve months?
    1. Sick
    2. Unemployed
    3. Armed Services
    4. Other (specify)
If Armed Services, change question 10 to yes and skip to question 14 and record Armed Services.   Go to 17.

13. What was the last full-time occupation you had? Please give me the title and a full description of the job. Go to 17.

14. What is your current occupation? Please give me the title and a full description of the job. How long have you worked at this job?

15. Have you had any part-time job or second full-time job in addition to your regular job last year? 1. Yes   2. No

16. What kind of work was this?

17. What kind of occupation would you most *like* to have? Consider your present, full-time or past-time occupation, or any other work you have held of would like to hold.

18. What possible reasons could you give that would prevent you from getting this kind of occupation?

  1. Lack of ability
  2. Lack of training and education
  3. Lack of opportunities; not getting right breaks in life
  4. Lack of any clear and positive aim in life
  5. Family background
  6. Class I am in
  7. Race I am part of
  8. My religion
  9. Own ambitions and high goals I have set for myself
 10. Illness
 11. Lack of financial support
 12. None
 13. Other (Specify)

19. Please tell me what you are doing or have done to help you get this occupation.

20. Are you interested in participating in a job training program? 1. Yes   2. Possibly   3. No
If yes, or possibly, answer questions 21 and 22.

21. What type of job training program would interest you?

22. How many months would you be willing to spend in such a program? ––––––––––––––––––––

23. If you had a son, of at least normal intelligence, what kind of occupation would you *like* him to have when he gets out of school?

24. In your opinion, what could prevent him from obtaining this occupation?

  1. Lack of ability
  2. Lack of training and education
  3. Lack of opportunities; not getting right breaks in life
  4. Lack of any clear and positive aim in life
  5. Family background
  6. Class I am in
  7. Race I am part of
  8. My religion
  9. Own ambitions and high goals I have set for myself
 10. Illness
 11. Lack of financial support
 12. None
 13. Other (Specify)

18

LANCASTER STUDY IMPLICATIONS
Walter J. Gershenfeld*

The central facts of analytical import in the Negro labor market in Lancaster, Pennsylvania are (1) the high level of unemployment among Negroes and (2) the existence of a substantial demand for unskilled labor. To understand these seeming anomalies, we will first examine the structure of unemployment and employment in Lancaster. Following, the Lancaster supply of labor will be investigated to determine significant trends, particularly with regard to demographic factors. Finally, the pieces will be assembled to look at the problem of the Negro in a prosperous community. Emphasis will be placed on the composition of labor demand in a healthy economic setting such as Lancaster and on the competitive effect of the nature of the labor supply on the Negro's job opportunities.

THE STRUCTURE OF UNEMPLOYMENT

Unemployment can be said to have a structure. That is, it is capable of being analyzed by geographic region, by industry, by sex, by age group, by color, and in many other ways. Analysis today takes place against a backdrop of persistent, relatively high unemployment nationally in the last decade.[1] Causes of this high unemployment include, *inter alia*, a structural component which has been defined by Albert Rees as follows:

> By structural unemployment, I shall mean persistent unemployment caused by automation and other forms of technological change, by shifts in the composition of demand, and by the competition of imports with domestic production. I shall also include in structural unemployment any persistent unemployment due to changes in the structure of wages in relation to the pattern of labor demand.[2]

---

*Assistant Professor of Management, Temple University.

Rees's reference to "changes in the structure of wages in relation to the pattern of labor demand" was probably made with an eye toward legislated minimum wages. In Lancaster, another wage-structure phenomenon is operative: the prevalence among employers of high entry wages, which have resulted in relatively high job standards for entry positions. These standards, which frequently cannot be met by Negroes, may then be considered a cause of structural unemployment among Negroes in Lancaster.

It is instructive at this point to look at the composition of the unemployed in Lancaster as shown by the application files of the Lancaster State Employment office at the end of May, 1964. The structure of the unemployed in Lancaster, as shown in Table 1, both parallels and differs from national unemployment data and Negro unemployment data in Lancaster in some striking ways.

First, there are more women than men among the insured unemployed in Lancaster. The national figures generally show five unemployed males for every three unemployed females. It is recognized that female employment and consequently unemployment are functions of female labor force participation rates. These in turn may be related to both the vigor of the labor market and the composition of employment opportunities in the labor market. In the case of Lancaster, there is no question about the health of the economy, and the employment pattern found in Lancaster is not unlike that of our national economy. Accordingly, the high female unemployment rate is something of an anomaly. The Negro community survey also showed an exceptionally high female unemployment rate.

The author will refer, at a later point in this paper, to data concerning labor force participation rates in communities with generally low unemployment rates such as are found in Lancaster. In this connection, the Director of the Bureau of Employment Security Research for the Employment Security Commission of North Carolina reported the following:

> The current sex distribution of the labor force is not available; however an estimate was developed using approximately the same male-female distribution that existed in the 1960 Census. These distributions, based on 1960 data, may be slightly conservative since female participation in the labor force has been on the increase and this trend is expected to continue. Additional analysis of available information, that may provide further insight into the amount of labor force participation by sex, indicates that approximately 57 per cent of the total unemployment, as submitted on our official U. S. Department of Labor ES 219 report for Greensboro-High Point during 1963, were females. However, insured unemployment records indicate that nearly 62 per cent of the jobless filing claims in that area in 1963 were women.

Employmentwise, women made up only about 36 per cent of the non-agricultural workers during 1963, while according to the 1960 Census (based on an April enumeration) around 39 per cent of total employment was female.[3]

The Greensboro-High Point, North Carolina area is similar to Lancaster in both size and the vigor of its economy. It is interesting to find that women comprise about 35 per cent of the labor force yet represent about 60 per cent of the unemployed.

It must be recognized that the measurement of unemployment among nonwhite females is an extremely difficult task. Data for domestics (888,000 strong and representing 36.2 per cent of employed nonwhite females according to the 1960 Census), along with other self-employed persons, are estimated. The estimate is derived by using a formula based on the fact that a relative change in "wage and salary employment" is accompanied by a proportionate change in "all other employment."[4] Adjustments are made to the data for atypical situations.

As Ewan Clague, Commissioner of Labor Statistics for the U. S. Department of Labor, recently noted, "The labor force is a fluctuating, pulsating, variable body of workers."[5] In addition, the official definition of unemployment includes those who "believed no work was available in their line or in the community."[6] Unemployment, then, is not only a condition of being, but just as much an attitude or state of mind. Decisions on withdrawal from and entry into the labor market are at times subject to momentary impulse. Considering the tenuous attachment of many females to the labor force, data on their employment status are difficult to measure adequately.

Second, an analysis of the unemployed in Lancaster by type of background shows one-third of the unemployed to be unskilled. This is not a figure which is surprising and is, in fact, in line with national norms. The semiskilled figure, too, is not unusual. On the other hand, however, the fact that 20.6 per cent of male unemployment is skilled is somewhat novel. The explanation for this seems to be that almost one-half of the male skilled unemployment is composed of craftsmen over 65. It is quite probable that many of these individuals have been retired under the terms of collective-bargaining agreements.

Third, there are few young people among the Lancaster unemployed generally. This finding is analagous with the evidence showing few young Negroes in the labor force. Finding a low unemployment figure for the very young may reflect the fact that they have chosen to leave the community. In the case of the Negro, outmigration may occur because the young Negro believes, or has

TABLE 1

COMPOSITION OF THE UNEMPLOYED, LANCASTER, MAY, 1964

Primary Skills	Numerical Distribution			Percentage Distribution		
	Total	Male	Female	Total	Male	Female
Professional & Managerial	126	100	26	5.3	8.4	2.2
Clerical	304	81	223	12.7	6.8	18.6
Sales	114	47	67	4.8	3.9	5.6
Domestic	47	0	47	2.0	0.0	3.9
Other Service	248	139	109	10.4	11.6	9.1
Agricultural	36	34	2	1.5	2.9	0.2
Skilled	304	246	58	12.7	20.6	4.9
Semiskilled	477	199	278	19.9	16.7	23.2
Unskilled and Entry	735	348	387	30.7	29.1	32.3
Total, May 1964	2391	1194	1197	100.0	100.0	100.0
Total, March 1964	2858	1637	1221			
Total, May 1963	2326	1315	1011			

Age Distribution

Primary Skills	Males					Females				
	Total	Under 22	22-44	45-64	65 & Over	Total	Under 22	22-44	45-64	65 & Over
Prof. & Managerial	100	4	43	30	23	26	11	14	9	2
Clerical	81	12	39	12	18	223	30	131	37	25
Sales	47	4	11	17	15	67	10	21	28	8
Domestic	0	0	0	0	0	47	9	27	10	1
Other Service	139	16	31	45	47	109	14	52	30	13
Agricultural	34	5	20	9	0	2	2	0	0	0
Skilled	246	3	61	66	116	58	4	31	15	8
Semiskilled	199	21	96	48	34	278	28	145	79	26
Unskilled and Entry	348	110	135	59	44	387	69	222	75	21
Total	1194	175	436	286	297	1197	167	643	283	104
% Distribution	100.0	14.7	36.5	23.9	24.9	100.0	14.0	53.7	23.6	8.7

Age Distribution, Both Sexes

	Total	Under 22	22 to 44	45 to 64	65 and Over
Number	2391	342	1079	569	401
Per cent	100.0	14.3	45.1	23.8	16.8

Source: Lancaster Office of Pennsylvania State Employment Service.

TABLE 2

TOTAL CIVILIAN WORK FORCE, UNEMPLOYMENT AND
EMPLOYMENT BY INDUSTRY, LANCASTER COUNTY
1950 AND 1963 ANNUAL AVERAGES*

Employment Status and Industry	1950	1963	Net Change	Per cent Change
	(In thousands)			
Total Civilian Work Force	107.1	124.1	+1700	+15.9
Total Unemployment	3.6	4.0	+400	+11.1
% Civilian Work Force	3.4%	3.2%	—	—
Total Employment	103.5	120.1	+16,600	+16.0
Farm Employment	13.1	10.8	−2300	−17.6
Nonfarm Employment	90.4	109.3	+18,900	+20.9
Self-employed, Unpaid Family and Domestic Workers	10.5	11.4	+900	+8.6
Nonfarm Wage and Salary Employment	79.9	97.9	+18,000	+22.5
All Manufacturing Industries, Total	42.1	48.0	+5900	+14.0
Durable Goods Industries, Total	22.5	28.1	+5600	+24.9
Stone, clay, and glass products	1.7	2.0	+300	+17.6
Primary metals	0.8	2.1	+1300	+162.5
Fabricated metal products	3.8	5.0	+1200	+31.6
Machinery and transportation equipment	6.4	10.0	+3600	+56.3

Other durable goods	9.8	9.0	−800	−8.2
Nondurable Goods Industries, Total	19.6	19.9	+300	+1.5
Food products	3.9	4.4	+500	+12.8
Tobacco products	1.2	0.8	−400	−33.3
Textile products	3.8	1.9	−1900	−50.0
Apparel and related products	5.5	6.1	+600	+10.9
Printing and publishing	1.3	1.9	+600	+46.2
Leather products	3.0	3.1	+100	+3.3
Other nondurable goods	0.9	1.7	+800	+88.9
All Nonmanufacturing Industries, Total	37.8	49.9	+12,100	+32.0
Contract construction	4.4	4.8	+400	+9.1
Transportation and public utilities	4.9	4.8	−100	−2.0
Wholesale and retail trade	13.2	17.1	+3900	+29.5
Finance, insurance, and real estate	1.6	2.3	+700	+43.8
Service and miscellaneous	8.1	12.7	+4600	+56.8
Government	5.6	8.2	+2600	+46.4
Federal government	1.8	1.5	−300	−16.7
State and local government	3.8	6.7	+2900	+76.3

Source: Pennsylvania Department of Labor and Industry, Bureau of Employment Security, *Labor Market Letter, Lancaster Area*, Vol. XIV, No. 4, April, 1964, Table 4.
*Manufacturing industry averages are based on data for monthly periods. All other averages are based on bi-monthly estimates for 1950 and monthly estimates for 1963.

found, that there is discrimination in employment or that he is unqualified for existing openings. It is worth noting that among young males, unemployment is dominated by the unskilled and entry category.

THE STRUCTURE OF EMPLOYMENT

The National Picture

According to the United States Department of Labor,[7] major structural changes in the industrial and occupational distribution of employment are indicated in the manpower projections for the next decade. Agricultural employment, under the spur of rising productivity, is expected to decline by some 100,000 employees. Among nonfarm industries, those furnishing services are expected to rise more rapidly than the goods-producing industries.

It is expected that the fastest growing occupations during the next decade will be professional and technical, along with clerical and sales occupations. Among manual positions, it is only the most skilled occupations that will maintain a growth rate as large as that for total employment. Semiskilled opportunities will expand at a rate only two-thirds of that of total employment. However, much of the growth expected in semiskilled occupations will take place in the service industries, particularly the rendering of personal services. Unskilled workers will number about the same as today, resulting in a continued lowering of their proportional share of employment opportunities.

In manufacturing, where the growth is expected to be modest, the increase will be dominated by professional, administrative, clerical, and sales occupations.

In essence, both the industry and occupational trends now foreseeable point to a continuing shift in the demand for labor. Increasingly, employers are expected to be demanding workers possessing more education and greater skill.

The Lancaster Picture

The picture shown by Table 2 coincides with the national picture of changing employment opportunities by industrial classification.

These data clearly show the decline in farm employment both absolutely and relatively in Lancaster. The growth in manufacturing has been moderate and is, in fact, slightly less than the growth of the labor force in Lancaster. The increase in manufacturing has been largely concentrated within the durable-goods categories with emphasis on machinery and transportation equipment, primary metals and fabricated metal products.

The increase in nonmanufacturing industries has been substantial. Indeed, in the thirteen-year period in question, percentage-wise it has doubled the increase in the labor force. The increase is almost entirely due to growth in wholesale and retail trade, services per se and the expansion of state and local government as a factor in the labor market.

Thus, from the point of view of the recent past, Lancaster exhibits labor-market growth patterns by industry which are substantially in accord with the Labor Department predictions for the decade ahead.

In analyzing the occupations of the employed, the only data available are from the 1960 Census. These data show the following:

TABLE 3

OCCUPATIONS OF THE EMPLOYED
LANCASTER COUNTY, 1960

Type of Occupation	Number	Per Cent
Professional, Technical, and Kindred Workers	10,214	9.0
Farmers and Farm Managers	5,733	5.1
Managers, Officials, and Proprietors (excluding farm)	7,240	6.4
Clerical and Kindred	12,642	11.2
Sales Workers	8,041	7.1
Craftsmen, Foremen, and Kindred	16,848	14.9
Operatives and Kindred	28,766	25.4
Private Household Workers	2,311	2.1
Service Workers (excluding private household workers)	8,170	7.1
Farm Laborers and Foremen	3,397	3.0
Laborers (excluding farm and mine)	5,335	4.7
Occupations not Reported	4,543	4.0
Total	113,240	100.0

Source: U. S. Bureau of the Census, *U. S. Censuses of Population and Housing: 1960, Census Tracts, Lancaster, Pa.* (Washington: Government Printing Office, 1962).

Probably the most noteworthy figure is the entry for operatives and kindred. Although this is the largest single group among the

Lancaster employed, it is precisely the group most likely to decline in number should Lancaster continue to follow national labor-market trends. This is likely in view of the fact that some of the largest manufacturers in Lancaster report considerably greater production today with fewer employees than were present in their plants a decade ago.

Thus, a review of the Lancaster employment situation shows a balanced economy, which by industry is following national trends rather closely. By occupation, however, there are some problems in that the unskilled and semiskilled operative and kindred group, now so numerous, may be expected to be a declining force. To be sure, although the category as a whole may be reduced, there will always be specific occupations which resist the trend and represent growth opportunities. The above represent reasonable hypotheses, barring the unexpected. In this connection, the lack of migration to such a healthy area stands out as a source of wonder. It may be questioned whether the low migration pattern will continue into the future as Lancaster's healthy industrial climate becomes increasingly well known.

Demographic Factors

The single most important fact about the age composition of the Lancaster Negro population emerging from the 1960 Census is the fact that 26.4 per cent of all Negroes were under ten years of age. Today, this same group is aged 4 to 14, and some are getting close to labor-market entry. This is almost entirely a native-born population and, given Lancaster's continued prosperity and the general interest prevalent in nondiscriminatory hiring, is more likely to seek its fortune in Lancaster than elsewhere.

The influence of this group of young people on the median age in Lancaster is quite dramatic. For Lancaster generally, the median male age in the 1960 Census was 30.8 years of age, while the median female age was 34.8. The corresponding figures for the nonwhite population were 23.7 for males and 22.5 for females. These, of course, are low because of the Negro population explosion, which will reach the Lancaster labor market in the not-very-distant future. Underscored is the need for better counseling and training programs for Negro youth if the difficulties other communities have experienced with regard to fair-employment problems are to be avoided in Lancaster.

The problem of the Negro young is highlighted by the fact that Lancaster is somewhat unique in not facing a deluge of the young. Although there are increases of 0.6 per cent and 1.8 per cent in

TABLE 4

POPULATION BY AGE GROUPS, LANCASTER COUNTY
1960 AND MEDIUM PROJECTIONS TO 1970

Age Group	1960	Per Cent	1965	Per Cent	1970	Per Cent
Preschool (0-4)	31,338	11.2	34,280	11.4	38,704	11.8
School (5-19)	74,607	26.8	84,934	28.2	93,918	28.6
Younger Working Age (20-44)	89,075	32.0	92,292	30.6	98,342	29.9
Older Working Age (45-64)	55,220	19.9	59,414	19.7	64,083	19.5
Retired (65+)	28,119	10.1	30,455	10.1	33,486	10.2
Total	278,359	100.0	301,375	100.0	328,533	100.0

Source: Lancaster County Planning Commission, *The Past, Present, and Future Population of Lancaster County, Pennsylvania,* August, 1962.

the preschool and school categories, there is actually a decrease of 2.1 per cent expected in the younger working group. This, of course, is precisely the opposite of the pattern to be expected in the Negro community.

Lancaster, then, will in general face fewer special problems associated with young workers than the rest of the country. However, it will have an above-average problem ahead, at least in terms of numbers, with its young Negro population.

THE NEGRO IN A LOW-UNEMPLOYMENT COMMUNITY

One of the most puzzling aspects of this study to all participants has been the finding of high unemployment among Negroes in Lancaster. This is contrasted with the generally high level of economic activity in Lancaster and an unemployment rate ranking Lancaster among a select small group of labor markets averaging less than 3 per cent unemployment.

Typical sources of employment difficulty for Negroes can be found in the Lancaster labor market. The skill levels possessed by the Negro population are not high enough to qualify for the majority of open positions. Our subjective analysis of interviews with employers reveals that some open prejudice against Negroes exists. It is believed, however, that the amount of discrimination found is no greater than that which can be witnessed in other labor markets.

In addition, there is a narrow geographical area, a radius of approximately seven miles from the center of Lancaster, in which the Negro conducts his search for employment.

The sole source of data showing unemployment figures separately for both Lancaster City and Lancaster County is the 1960 Census. The following rather striking figures emerge:

TABLE 5

UNEMPLOYMENT AS PERCENTAGE OF CIVILIAN
LABOR FORCE

Location	Per cent
Total Lancaster County	2.6
Lancaster City	4.1
Balance of Lancaster County	2.1

In 1960, there was a substantial difference between unemployment rates in city and county areas. Although existing labor-market data do not permit us to ascertain whether this trend has continued, it does suggest an explanation of high Negro unemployment. With all of his other disadvantages, the Negro is competing in the worst part of a good labor market.

These reasons for Negro difficulty in Lancaster are important but appear insufficient to explain the high rate of Negro unemployment in Lancaster. Similar barriers exist around the country. Why then should Negro unemployment be high in this area of otherwise low unemployment?

Two principal reasons will be advanced below: the first, from the point of view of demand; the second, from the point of view of supply. The first revolves around continual prosperity in Lancaster having the effect of forcing employers to accept unskilled labor when they would prefer greater skills. Therefore, they maintain high general entry standards to improve the prospects of internal upgrading of the work force. The second reason is a competitive hypothesis, which notes that the increased labor force participation rate in Lancaster calls forth additional entrants to the labor force who are better equipped than the Negro in the job search.

The Nature of the Demand for Labor in Lancaster

Undoubtedly, the most important single fact about the demand for labor in Lancaster is the prevalence of unskilled positions among employment openings in both 1963 and 1964. Unskilled workers filled 40.6 per cent of openings in 1963, while 34.7 per cent of 1964 openings went to the unskilled. These figures are subject to upward revision when an additional 5 to 10 per cent unskilled are added from the service occupations.

At the time of the study, this finding was greeted with considerable surprise. We have become indoctrinated to the demise of unskilled labor in our economy. Labor Department estimates for the decade ahead predict that unskilled labor and farm labor are the only major employment categories which are not expected to show an absolute rise in numbers. Considering the rapid growth of the population, this means that unskilled labor may be expected to lose considerable relative ground to such categories as professional, technical, and clerical.

Here we have the possibility that a high-employment economy such as Lancaster's may find it necessary to use greater numbers of the unskilled than other labor markets. It has been only recently that support for this notion has developed nationally. It is related to the fact that we are currently nearing an almost unparalleled fourth full year of uninterrupted recovery. The *Wall Street Journal* conducted an informal survey with the following results:

> The long U. S. business boom finally is creating more job openings for some groups that have had a prolonged high level of idleness — the unskilled, the less educated, women, teen-agers, and Negroes.
> That's the most striking finding of a survey of the hiring plans of 66 companies, big and small, from coast to coast.
> . . . hiring demand is no longer confined to skilled workers, such as welders and machinists — or even to adult men with high school diplomas and experience in the industries seeking them. Companies still fight each other fiercely to hire all such men that they can find. But they can't find many, and their sales are rising fast enough to require more workers in a hurry.[8]

And Philadelphia recently reported a decline in unemployment to a 4.8 per cent level, the lowest in amost eight years. Further:

> "The whole employment trend in manufacturing had been downward," said Morris Doren, BES research director here. "We had almost

come to the conclusion that in period after period the area would show declines in factory jobs."

Doren said the area's economy has shown considerable strength in the past several months, indicating that the business recovery, now in its 43d month nationally, is having a notable impact here.

Employers, Doren said, are beginning to have difficulty in finding semiskilled workers and are stepping up their recruiting efforts.[9]

As the rest of the nation reaches toward the level of prosperity found in Lancaster, it may produce some of the employment patterns found in Lancaster. For example, there is the alteration of the most desirable hiring mix and the consequent utilization of greater numbers of unskilled employees than desired. In part, this acts as an explanation of high hiring standards in Lancaster, which act as an indirect bar to Negro employment. Such standards may be enforced to improve the raw material for upgrading purposes, not as a *desideratum* but as a necessity.

It should be noted that these conclusions do not vitiate the finding that greater or different skills will be needed in the long run. In fact, there is little doubt that employers would prefer to hire employees with greater skill presently. *The key fact seems to be that employers can successfully restructure operations to accommodate greater numbers of unskilled employees if market conditions make it necessary for them do so.*

The need for increased skills in the hands of the Negro labor force is still present. However, a rise in the demand for the services of the Negro and other economically disadvantaged would permit us the socially desirable luxury of concentrating our efforts in meeting our new skill needs with the young, as opposed to a proliferation of efforts among all groups deeply affected by unemployment.

National data argue that a continued high level of prosperity is mandatory if we are to do anything about the problem of the economically disadvantaged, the unskilled, youth, older workers, and Negroes. The Lancaster experience indicates that this may be a necessary but is not a sufficient condition for large-scale employment of Negroes.

The Nature of the Supply of Labor in Lancaster

Labor force participation rates are demonstrably higher in Lancaster than in the rest of the nation for both male and female workers. We have generally accustomed ourselves to thinking of an increase in labor force participation as representing the introduction of marginal employees. In this connotation, the term "marginal" has raised the image of scraping the bottom of the barrel.

The notion advanced here is that we are witnessing individuals entering the labor market who are marginal only in the sense that they enter the labor market when job opportunities are plentiful. Further, the hypothesis is that they are not the least attractive employees, but individuals well qualified generally by educational standards to enter business and industry. Usually, their source of job knowledge is via closed circles of families and friends.[10] Their entry is facilitated by high wages and low-level entry duties. *In effect, we are saying that the Negro becomes disadvantaged in a healthy economy such as Lancaster's as though he were competing for scarce employment opportunities in a labor market marked by a high unemployment rate.*

Ideally, this hypothesis might be analyzed by identifying and isolating the marginal individuals who give Lancaster a higher labor force participation rate than the national average. Once these individuals have been identified, the task then becomes one of demonstrating that they represent superior competition as far as the Negro is concerned in the eyes of the employer. Obviously, the specific identification of these individuals is a rather difficult task. However, data can be presented which generally support the thesis.

Let us look at some of this evidence:

1. *Labor Force Partcipation Rates*[11]

Tables 6 and 7 which follow set forth labor force participation rates for the United States and for Lancaster at various times during the period 1960 to 1964.

It should be noted that in all categories—total civilian labor force, male civilian labor force and female civilian labor force—the labor force participation rate is greater in Lancaster than the national averages for the dates listed.[12]

It is interesting to note that there has been a decline nationally in nonwhite labor force participation rates. For example, Dr. Ray Marshall reports:

> The civilian labor force participation rates in 1962 were 60.0% for nonwhites and 56.1% for whites. Significantly, the nonwhite male participation rate (76.4%) was *lower* than the white male rate (78.6%), but the nonwhite female rate (45.6%) was much higher than the white female rate (36.6%). The participation rates for both nonwhite males and females were higher in 1948 (84.8% and 44.4%) than the rates for whites (84.2% and 30.6%). These rates tend to support the argument by some observers that much of the unrest in Negro communities is attributable to the deterioration in the economic opportunities of Negro males.[13]

The hypothesis was pursued further by identifying labor markets with an unemployment experience as good as that of Lancaster.

TABLE 6

LABOR FORCE PARTICIPATION RATES
UNITED STATES, 1960-1964
(IN THOUSANDS)

Category	1960	1963	January 1964	March 1964	May 1964	July 1964
A. Civilian Labor Force	70,612	72,975	71,793	72,810	74,742	76,218
B. Noninstitutional Population Aged 14 and Over	125,368	132,124	133,200	133,519	133,866	134,216
A. As Percentage of B.	56.3	55.2	53.9	54.5	55.8	56.7
C. Male Civilian Labor Force	47,025	47,867	47,041	47,411	48,577	50,347
D. Male Noninstitutional Population Aged 14 and Over	61,000	64,163	64,639	64,781	64,938	65,097
C. As Percentage of D.	77.1	74.6	72.8	73.2	74.8	77.3
E. Female Civilian Labor Force	23,587	25,109	24,752	25,399	26,165	25,871
F. Female Noninstitutional Population Aged 14 and Over	64,368	67,962	68,560	68,738	68,928	69,119
E. As Percentage of F.	36.6	37.0	36.1	37.0	38.0	37.3

Sources: *Manpower Report of the President* (Washington: Government Printing Office, March, 1964); *Employment and Earnings*, issued monthly by U. S. Department of Labor, Bureau of Labor Statistics.

TABLE 7

WORK FORCE PARTICIPATION RATES
LANCASTER, PENNSYLVANIA, 1960-1964

Category	1960*	1963	January 1964	March 1964	May 1964	July 1964
A. Civilian Work Force	116,679	123,900	122,300	122,600	124,500	128,700
B. Noninstitutional Population Aged 14 and Over	195,152	205,100	206,100	206,500	206,900	207,400
A. As Percentage of B.	59.8	60.4	59.3	59.4	60.2	62.1
C. Male Civilian Labor Force	76,550	81,300	79,950	80,300	82,000	85,200
D. Male Noninstitutional Population Aged 14 and Over	92,803	101,100	101,350	101,500	101,750	102,000
C. As Percentage of D.	82.4	80.4	78.9	79.1	80.6	83.5
E. Female Civilian Work Force	40,129	42,600	42,350	42,300	42,500	43,500
F. Female Noninstitutional Population Aged 14 and Over	102,350	104,000	104,750	104,950	105,150	105,400
E. As Percentage of F.	39.2	40.9	40.4	40.3	40.4	40.3

Sources: Data provided by Lancaster office of Pennsylvania State Employment Service; U. S. Census, 1960.
*Data for 1960 cover labor force: see footnote #11.

TABLE 8

UNEMPLOYMENT RATES IN SELECTED LABOR MARKETS
1960 AND 1963

Labor Market	1960	1963
Lancaster, Pa.	4.0	3.2
Cedar Rapids, Iowa	2.7	1.8
Des Moines, Iowa	3.0	2.4
Greensboro-High Point, N.C.	3.9	2.9
Kenosha, Wis.	3.9	3.2
Little Rock-North Little Rock, Ark.	3.9	2.9
Madison, Wis.	2.8	2.7
Newport News-Hampton, Va.	4.0	2.7
Richmond, Va.	3.0	2.3
Rochester, N. Y.	3.7	3.0
Washington, D. C.*	2.6	2.4

Source: *Manpower Report of the President* (Washington: Government
     Printing Office, March 1964), pp. 237-239.

*The analysis which follows excludes Washington, D. C. It is believed
that the special nature of the labor market in the nation's capital warrants this exclusion.

Table 8 lists the labor markets (among the largest 150 labor
markets in the United States) which had at least as good an unemployment rate as Lancaster in *both* 1960 and 1963. An attempt was
made to procure current labor force participation rates, as well as
data for 1960 and 1963, from four of these labor markets. The replies offered 1960 Census data and generally indicated that all later
data involved considerable estimation or simply were not available.
Thus, Table 9 shows labor force participation rates in these communities for 1960 only, largely based on Census data.

There are some interpretative difficulties in connection with the
data. These will be made clearer by an analysis of Table 10 showing
the relationship between the selected local labor market rates and
national rates.

The data for Lancaster show higher labor force participation
rates than the national average, as do the data for Cedar Rapids,
Iowa, and Des Moines, Iowa. The data for Greensboro-High Point,
North Carolina are substantially above national averages. The low
civilian male participation rates for Newport News, Virginia, and
Little Rock, Arkansas, are attributable to the presence of military
posts. The relatively low male participation rate in Madison,

TABLE 9

SELECTED LABOR FORCE PARTICIPATION RATES, 1960*

Category	Cedar Rapids, Iowa	Des Moines, Iowa	Greensboro-High Point, N.C.	Kenosha, Wis.	Little Rock-N.Little Rock, Ark.	Madison, Wis.	Newport News-Hampton, Va.	Richmond, Va.	Rochester, N.Y.
A. Civilian Labor Force	57,051	110,725	107,344	39,729	91,911	89,376	74,231	171,802	242,327
B. Noninstitutional Population Aged 14 and Over	94,834	185,872	171,002	69,078	159,745	152,864	146,257	288,167	413,648
A. As Percentage of B.	60.1	59.6	62.7	57.4	57.5	58.7	50.8	59.6	58.5
C. Male Civilian Labor Force	37,178	70,595	65,123	28,392	56,457	56,875	49,287	106,098	155,556
D. Male Noninstitutional Population Aged 14 and Over	45,291	86,661	79,976	34,736	77,585	74,715	72,564	132,065	194,841
C. As Percentage of D.	82.2	81.5	81.4	81.3	72.8	77.1	67.9	80.3	79.8
E. Female Civilian Labor Force	19,873	40,128	42,221	11,334	35,454	32,501	24,944	65,704	86,771
F. Female Noninstitutional Population Aged 14 and Over	49,643	99,211	91,026	34,342	82,160	78,149	73,693	156,102	218,807
E. As Percentage of F.	40.1	41.5	46.3	33.0	43.1	41.5	33.7	42.1	39.7

Source: U. S. Census, 1960.

*Data are based on Standard Metropolitan Statistical Areas.

TABLE 10

LOCAL LABOR FORCE PARTICIPATION RATES

AS PERCENTAGES OF NATIONAL RATES, 1960

Category	Lancaster, Pa.	Cedar Rapids, Iowa	Des Moines, Iowa	Greensboro-High Point, N.C.	Kenosha, Wis.	Little Rock-N. Little Rock, Ark.	Madison, Wis.	Newport News-Hampton, Va.	Richmond, Va.	Rochester, N.Y.
Total Civilian Labor Force	106.2	106.7	105.9	111.4	102.0	102.1	104.3	90.2	106.0	104.0
Male Civilian Labor Force	106.9	105.8	105.7	105.6	105.4	94.4	100.0	88.1	104.2	103.5
Female Civilian Labor Force	107.1	109.3	113.4	126.5	90.2	117.7	113.4	92.3	115.0	108.5

Source: Previous tables.

Wisconsin, is probably attributable to the influence of the University of Wisconsin and the large number of male students there. (Perhaps the high female labor force participation rate in Madison can be attributed to wives helping to put their husbands through college.) In the case of Kenosha, Wisconsin, there is no apparent reason for the low female labor force participation rate.

In general, though, the data lend support to the notion that low-unemployment communities tend to have higher-than-average labor force participation rates. They are far from conclusive, however, and offer us only a guide in understanding the plight of the Negro in a busy economy. Certainly, his situation, as well as a community's labor force participation rate, is affected by his share of the population. In the case of Madison, Wisconsin, the Negro population is barely over 1 per cent of the population. In the case of Richmond, Virginia, the figure is more like 40 per cent.

We conclude that the data have their principal relevance in the Lancaster setting. Here there seems to be definite evidence that a high level of prosperity in the community has induced a higher-than-average labor force participation rate.

It is appropriate at this juncture to examine the Lancaster data in greater detail.

2. *Lancaster Census Tract Data*

There are two census tracts among the fifteen in Lancaster which have a large concentration of Negroes. In neither tract do Negroes represent a majority of the population; nevertheless, the Negro population is sufficiently large to have a substantial effect on these census tracts. Population data for the two tracts in question are:

TABLE 11

LANCASTER POPULATION IN 1960 U. S. CENSUS

	Tract 9	Tract 14
White Population	3,625	3,230
Negro Population	1,566	845

If the hypothesis is correct that the Negro in an economically healthy community such as Lancaster suffers from increased labor force participation by individuals with educational (and presumably skill) levels superior to those of the Negro labor force, then census data by tracts should reflect some of this difference.

It may be seen from Table 12 below that virtually all other tracts have higher educational attainment rates than those tracts in which Negroes dwell. In a sense, this finding is predictable in that it is known that the population as a whole has a higher median educational attainment than the Negro population. Thus, the finding that tracts with above-average labor force participation rates have higher educational attainment than the Negro population may be expected. Nevertheless, the demonstration of higher labor force participation rates among those with greater educational attainment than the Negro is evidence in favor of the competitive hypothesis. No claim is made of a correlation between labor force participation rate and schooling. In fact, the existence of census tracts with high labor force participation rates may be products of many factors. However, whatever the source, their very existence introduces a note of strong competition for the Negro in that the individuals from these tracts possess superior educational qualifications than Negroes and thus are presumably more attractive to employers.

Conclusion

In our analysis of the Negro in Lancaster, a number of nonstandard reasons for high Negro unemployment have been explored.

The limited geographical area in which the Lancaster Negro seeks employment was noted. Data from the 1960 Census offer evidence that the Negro is thus limiting himself to competing in the less active portion of a busy labor market.

The first major conclusion is related to the presence of a large number of unskilled positions in Lancaster. National and Philadelphia data present the view that employers are increasingly turning to the use of unskilled personnel as prosperity continues and manufacturing activity expands. In many cases this undoubtedly results in a restructuring of productive activity, considered less than optimum by the employer. The hypothesis advanced is that the employer in such a situation seeks to minimize the dislocation by hiring employees with as high a level of general education as possible and then training them on the job for the skills needed by the company. While the hiring of the unskilled undoubtedly serves to improve the Negro's opportunities absolutely, he may still lose relative ground because of his weaker general education.

Second, the thesis has been explored that a busy economy tends to call forth a higher-than-average labor force participation rate and that the nature of the marginal worker is such that he represents difficult employment competition for the Negro. The

TABLE 12

LABOR FORCE PARTICIPATION RATES AND SCHOOLING
BY CENSUS TRACTS IN LANCASTER CITY, 1960

| Location | Labor Force Participation Rate | | Median Years of Schooling |
	Male	Female	
Lancaster City	77.7	43.8	9.6
Tract 9	77.8	48.6	8.3
14	79.4	41.4	8.8

Other Tracts with Above Average Labor Force Participation Rates:

Tract 1	79.2	51.6	9.1
2	83.4	40.3	10.8
3	77.9	46.7	9.8
8	84.1	43.1	10.9
10	79.7	43.8	8.8
11	80.9	41.4	10.0
12	90.9	38.3	12.0
13	81.6	40.3	8.8
15	84.2	31.5	9.6

Other Tracts with Below Average Labor Force Participation Rates:

Tract 4	77.3	45.1	9.0
5	42.5[1]	33.3	13.0
6	71.5	47.0	11.5
7	75.3	44.4	9.2

Source: U. S. Bureau of the Census, *U. S. Censuses of Population and Housing: 1960, Census Tracts, Lancaster, Pa.* (Washington: Government Printing Office, 1962).
[1]Tract in which Franklin and Marshall College is located.

data with regard to Lancaster consistently show a pattern of higher-than-average labor force participation over the past four years. Data for other labor markets with low unemployment rates tend to support this thesis but are far from conclusive. An analysis of census-tract data in Lancaster shows higher educational attainment in those tracts with higher labor force participation rates.

Thus, the Negro's position in a generally prosperous community such as Lancaster can be seen to be independent, in good measure, of both prosperity and low unemployment. The same prosperity which may be presumed to aid his search for employment may well call forth a countervailing competitive force which serves actually to decrease his employment opportunities and raise his unemployment rate. This marginal work force may, in practice, be precisely large enough to provide the difference between a "tolerable" level of unemployment for the Negro and a rate which is unconscionably high.

In effect, an increase in the demand for labor does many things in addition to opening jobs. It may require employer restructuring of the work force. It may step up internal company training. Further, it may call forth into the labor force individuals whose background results in significant alteration of the composition of the labor force. Finally, an increase in the demand for labor generally may have a quite disproportionate effect on minority labor. The demand curve may shift to the right insofar as the community is concerned, while it remains stationary for the Negro. The point at which an increase in employment carries with it a proportional or favorably disproportional effect on Negro employment is a matter of conjecture.

FOOTNOTES

1. *Manpower Report of the President* (Washington: Government Printing Office, March, 1964), pp. 24-33.
2. American Bankers Association, *Proceedings of a Symposium on Employment*, Washington, D. C., February 24, 1964, p. 26.
3. Letter from Hugh M. Raper, Director, to Walter J. Gershenfeld, October 23, 1964.
4. U. S. Department of Labor, Bureau of Employment Security, *Handbook on Estimating Area Employment of Self-Employed, Unpaid Family, and Private Household Workers — Nonagricultural Total* (Washington: Government Printing Office, August, 1963), p. 1.
5. E. Clague, "The Anatomy of Unemployment," address before the Conference of Business Economists, New York, New York, May 8, 1964 (Washington: Government Printing Office, processed), p. 6.
6. U. S. Department of Labor, Bureau of Labor Statistics, and U. S. Department of Commerce, Bureau of Census, *Concepts and Methods Used in Household Statistics on Employment and Unemployment from the Current Population Survey* (Washington: Government Printing Office, June, 1964), p. 2.
7. *Manpower Report of the President, op. cit.*
8. "Job Outlook," *Wall Street Journal*, October 2, 1964, p. 1.
9. D. Bedell, "Jobless Total at 8-Year Low in Philadelphia Area," *Evening Bulletin* (Philadelphia), October 22, 1964, pp. 1, 15.
10. See Ray Marshall, in "The Job Problems of Negroes," above, p. 8: "Since Negroes usually live in segregated neighborhoods, they rarely learn about jobs with few or no Negroes in them, and they apply for the kind of jobs they know they can get. Since aspirations are conditioned by one's associates, few Negroes are motivated to apply for jobs from which they have been excluded."
11. Definitionally, labor force is based on place of residence while work force is based on place of work. In using national data, this distinction raises no significant problems. In the use of local labor market data, however, the question of resident and non-resident labor force can become significant. In the tables which follow, national data and local labor market data derived from the 1960 Census are in terms of *labor* force figures. Lancaster data for all except the 1960 Census data are in terms of *work* force figures. This is the manner in which Lancaster and other local labor-market data are customarily reported. In this case, the Lancaster office of the Pennsylvania State Employment Service estimates a net work force loss by outmigration to work of approximately 1,000 individuals. This results in a conservative statement of Lancaster labor force participation rates. It is not considered significant, however, inasmuch as 1,000 individuals amount to only three-fourths of 1 per cent of the Lancaster labor force.
12. The possibility that the higher labor force participation rate in Lancaster is a function of the age distribution was explored. This was ac-

complished by applying 1960 national labor force participation rates by age grouping to the actual age grouping found in Lancaster according to the 1960 Census. For both male and female categories, this age standardization yielded a lower labor force participation rate than was shown by the actual data. Thus, the higher labor force participation rate in Lancaster cannot be considered a product of the age distribution.

13. Marshall, *op. cit.*

19

A COMMUNITY PROJECT WITH AN OPEN DOOR EMPLOYMENT POLICY: THE BUSINESS AND INDUSTRIAL COORDINATING COMMITTEE OF NEWARK, NEW JERSEY

Charles W. Garrison*

HISTORICAL

Newark is the 30th largest city in the country and largest in the state of New Jersey. Its population, 406,000 in 1960, is approximately 50 per cent nonwhite. Newark is an old city, which will celebrate its 300th anniversary in 1966. It is also a county seat and center of the nation's 13th largest metropolitan area. The economic and social problems of Newark are common to any community where racial discrimination has been practiced intentionally or otherwise. Community action in this highly urbanized metropolis became necessary to put into force "equal opportunities" for all regardless of race, color, creed, or national origin.

Under crisis conditions and almost by accident, the Business & Industrial Coordinating Committee (BICC) was formed in Newark in August, 1963 to partially address this problem. The BICC came into being on purely private initiative. It was nurtured along by Hugh J. Addonizio, Mayor of Newark, when civil rights demonstrations broke out on the construction site of the city's new five million dollar Barringer High School. This was the "hot" summer of 1963. The mood and temperament of the Negro community was sizzling. The unemployment rate among nonwhites was double that for whites.

Eight civil rights groups working together as the Newark Coordinating Council demonstrated against alleged discrimination by construction trade unions at Barringer. A meeting was later held

---

*Senior Vice-President, Bamberger's, a division of R. H. Macy & Co., Inc.

to involve downtown department stores to join the jobs dispute. The stores took no part in the Barringer controversy but agreed to develop more jobs for minority groups by greater integration within the total Newark-area labor market.

The department stores realized that the scope of the problem extended beyond the stores and into the fields of business, industry, labor, government, and social agencies.

While there had been no violence up to this point, there was a belief that the Negro community could erupt at any time. It became apparent that to maintain racial peace, the business community must examine its employment practices and proceed along the road of an open door policy of hiring nonwhites and that failure to do this would probably bring economic and social chaos to the city.

FORMATION OF THE COMMITTEE

The decision by the department stores to help organize this effort brought into being one of the most unusual non-official organizations dealing with civil rights problems.

The BICC is an unparalleled coalition of representatives from business, civil rights groups, government agencies, unions, and social welfare agencies who are trying to provide greater opportunities for employment, training, and upgrading of Negroes and Puerto Ricans in the Greater Newark area. It is an unofficial non-binding association held together by a set of by-laws. Its underlying strength is derived from the willingness of participants to administer a program aimed at the unemployment problems of minorities.

It has been a major vehicle that has helped dispel the anxiety existing in Newark during the past two summers when civil rights activities threatened to explode. Progress has not been as rapid as some civil rights groups would like, but there is a realization that many companies are now making a sincere effort to open their doors for the first time to the employment and upgrading of Negroes and Puerto Ricans.

The committee, when first formed, met weekly. Because of the mutual understanding and the respect achieved by this group, meetings are now held on a monthly basis with subcommittees working constantly toward the several objectives.

Composition of Membership

Company participation on the committee has grown from a

handful to over 150 with representatives from large and small employers in the fields of merchandising and retailing, banking, real estate, insurance, public utility, industry, and manufacturing.

Civil rights groups now total over twenty, and they include the Urban League, NAACP, and the Newark Coordinating Council.

Unions are represented by Negro unions, the Independent Unions of New Jersey, and the AFL-CIO. Little success has been achieved in getting representation from construction and building trade unions.

Government agencies are represented through the offices of the Mayor of Newark, the Newark Human Rights Commission, New Jersey State Employment Service, and various levels of the county, state, and federal government.

Churches are represented by clergymen from a number of Negro churches and white clergy from each of the three major faiths.

Social agency representation is largely the result of a central organization known as The Welfare Federation of Newark. Its main functioning body is the 132-member Council of Social Agencies of Newark, Irvington, Belleville, and West Hudson.

The Welfare Federation has been a prime mover in the formation of the continued operation of the BICC. Its Board of Trustees approved activity-coordination of the BICC as one of the responsibilities of its community relations director through a part-time coordinator. They have permitted the use of its headquarters building as a meeting place for the BICC and have assumed operating expenses. In addition, they conduct the annual United Appeals campaign.

Federal, state, and city agencies are cooperating to keep the committee aware of their services and how they can be of help to the BICC in the field of employment, education, and training.

Overall, about 300 representatives belong to the BICC.

Objectives

The highest priority is on expanding effort in the job placement area. This is essential, and it indicates to the civil rights groups and the Negro and Puerto Rican communities that BICC member companies are sincere in their open door policy of non-discrimination. It is also essential to the economic and social well-being of minority citizens who, in some instances, have been denied employment rights on an equal basis with others. Overall objectives are

1. To take positive action in a forum where open communications will be available at all times between business, in-

dustry, labor and civil rights organizations to openly discuss problems of mutual interest.

2. To place unemployed Negroes and Puerto Ricans in jobs based on their skills and ability.

3. To upgrade the placement of Negroes and Puerto Ricans working at jobs below their skill level.

4. To determine which areas of competence are lacking in job applicants and develop ways and means with community resources to develop programs which will give training in such areas.

How Does A Company Participate?

The BICC is continually approaching new companies for membership in its organization. This is done by letter or telephone at the executive level or through personal contact by members of the Jobs Available Committee.

Companies that join assign a representative to attend a monthly meeting or serve on a subcommittee. Company membership entails submitting to the BICC Jobs Available Committee a list of their job openings. This affords the BICC first "crack" at trying to fill a wide variety of jobs by its "job placement agency." This does not prevent a member company from filling the vacancies through other channels. Careful screening is done by the Urban League of Essex County (which serves as the BICC job placement agency), before referrals are made. Member companies of the BICC are not required to furnish statistics on their employment hiring practices. Subcommittee reports made at monthly meetings are summary reports and do not disclose the identity of individual companies. Companies are informed that the BICC has no authority to mediate disputes over employment. Under its by-laws the committee does not prevent civil rights demonstrations if conciliation is unsuccessful. There is no fixed membership fee. It has been only recently that the BICC solicited its business and industrial membership for a small contribution to defray expenses. In the main, major expenditures have been assumed by individual companies.

Why Would A Company Want to Join the BICC?

Businessmen in the city of Newark must be made aware of minority group problems. The economic, social, and moral issues affecting Negroes and Puerto Ricans are the concern of the entire community. The BICC affords an opportunity for all parties to gather around the conference table to discuss problems of mutual interest. Below are listed some of the reasons the BICC feels that a company should join its organization:

1. To take a more active part in employment problems that affect the entire community.
2. To take part in a conciliatory approach to working out grievances that might occur between employers and civil rights groups.
3. To demonstrate to the Negro and Puerto Rican community that business and industry are taking affirmative action in providing equal employment opportunities.
4. To obtain a greater number of qualified nonwhite workers.
5. To become better informed about methods of employing and upgrading qualified Negroes and Puerto Ricans.

Accomplishments

The BICC is happy to note its progress but is fully aware that its achievements fall somewhat short of solving the many problems of the minority groups in the city of Newark.

— It has provided the Greater Newark area with an organization that is an action-oriented vehicle composed of diverse groups concerned with unemployment and which is responsible for an attitudinal change on the part of the employers in the area.

— It has influenced many companies to take an unbiased inventory of their personnel for the first time. It has influenced area employers to look introspectively at policies of hiring, upgrading, and training as they pertain to ethnic makeup of employees. Affirmative action in recruiting minority group workers has been stepped up by the job placement agency of the BICC.

— In its first eleven months of existence, BICC member companies hired roughly 4,000 Negroes and Puerto Ricans — approximately 30 per cent of 13,000 new members employed. BICC cannot take direct credit for these totals but rightly assumes its influence was a major contributing factor in the high rise of nonwhite hiring.

— The BICC has co-sponsored with the Newark Board of Education a Work/Study program for 25 potential dropouts. The students spend a half-day in school and a half-day on the jobs furnished by member companies of the BICC.

— In its 16-months history, approximately half of the Urban League's total job placements were directly attributed to the BICC. The added load on the Urban League staff has prompted BICC member companies to provide competent personnel people to assist in an evening program of interviewing and screening hundreds of job applicants.

— The BICC has developed a proposal for on-the-job training and retraining and is now awaiting approval of its application under the federal Manpower Development and Training Act. The proposal is currently being reviewed by the Office of Manpower, Automation and Training (OMAT) of the United States Department of Labor. It has been hailed as a positive approach to the challenge of automation.

— An all-day conference for member and non-member companies on closing the gap between EMPLOYMENT AND THE MINORITY GROUP WORKER was sponsored by the BICC on October 15, 1964. Speakers included John H. Johnson, president of Johnson Publishing Company, Chicago, Illinois; Alan Zuckerman, U.S. Department of Labor, O.M.A.T., Washington, D.C.; and Raymond F. Male, New Jersey's Commissioner of Labor and Industry, Trenton. Prudential Insurance Company hosted the conference and provided facilities for workshops that were concerned with finding and placing qualified minority group employees and problems of testing nonwhites.

— The BICC has sponsored discussion meetings for private and government agencies who are involved in any kind of employment programs. The purpose was to acquaint organizations with overall employment efforts and to make some attempt to coordinate where duplications existed.

— The BICC has sponsored, with the Greater Newark Chamber of Commerce, a forum for companies within the business field to better understand the provisions for training under state and federal laws.

— Cooperative study sessions with schools, the Board of Education, personnel people, labor, professional management counsel, and many others have been conducted.

— The BICC's People Available Committee, in conjunction with the Urban League, is completing an in-depth study of 1,206 job applicants who were interviewed and screened during a two-month period. Applicants were grouped by age, sex, education, vocational skills, place of residence, marital status, number of job referrals, employed or not, and reasons for not being hired. The statistical data have been taken off the computer and collated. The study is slated for distribution before January 1, 1965.

— The Urban League of Essex County honored the BICC with its outstanding community service award at its Eighth Equal Opportunity Day Dinner, on November 19, 1964.

Activities in Progress

— We are attempting to expand BICC representation in the

Greater Newark area on the part of business, industry, and civil rights groups.

— The testing committee of the BICC is presently conducting a survey of testing techniques of several hundred area employers. An attempt is being made to produce information that might suggest more realistic criteria for the hiring of entry-level clerical workers that are selected by test means. Company identity is never disclosed but test operations, procedures, and most frequently used tests in the Newark labor market are what the testing committee seeks to learn about.

—The BICC is setting up an adjunct group to the training committee that will be conversant with funding for training, vocational-education, and retraining under the various assistance programs.

— BICC is attempting to establish a "crash" program for 50 high school graduates, who were BICC job seekers, referred to jobs, but who failed employer entry-level tests. These 50 have agreed to short-term training. They represent an exhaustive follow-up of 357 high school graduates who came seeking jobs, were referred, and failed employer hiring tests over a four-month period.

— Our public relations committee is working on the production of a public information program directed to every segment of our population utilizing all communication channels. This includes the production and distribution of literature and setting up a speakers bureau to reach every June high school graduate and assure him that equal employment opportunities exist in Greater Newark.

— We are working cooperatively with local programs and projects geared toward promotion of equal and full employment opportunities. Coordination of all programs for maximum effectiveness will be a major goal.

Officers

The officers of the BICC are two co-chairmen (who are elected), a secretary, and a treasurer. Their term of office is one year. The co-chairmen, one of whom represents business and industry, the other the civil rights groups, appoint the secretary and the treasurer and two co-chairmen of each operating committee; one chairman representing business and industry, the other representing the civil rights groups.

Executive Committee

This committee is made up of all officers and co-chairmen of the operating committees. It meets one week prior to the regular monthly meeting to discuss and review all committee reports and decide on matters to be placed on the agenda for the regular monthly meeting.

Coordinator

This position was created by the Welfare Federation with a view to its becoming a full-time salaried position if funds became available. The coordinator handles the day-to-day operations of the BICC and coordinates the assignment of committee functions. Presently, the Welfare Federation's general office pool and the secretary of the federation's director of community relations are handling the clerical functions.

Operating Committees

Finance — raises necessary operating funds and is in charge of finances.

Jobs Available — solicits and recruits membership in the BICC from business and industry within the Greater Newark area and actively works with business and industry to develop job openings for qualified Negro and Puerto Rican workers, and establishes procedural steps for job listings.

People Available — works with all civil rights groups to seek, attract, and refer qualified people for employment. It operates to insure that job-seekers are properly referred for testing, counseling, and training.

The Urban League of Essex County is the functional agency for this committee. They interview, screen, and refer qualified applicants to companies from which listings of job openings have been secured.

The Urban League uses the services of the New Jersey State Employment Office and keeps abreast of training programs under federal and state agencies.

Procedures — proposes and recommends to proper sources, solutions for problems coming before the BICC, and develops methods by which the BICC can be more effective.

Training — determines which areas of competence are lacking in job applicants and seeks to develop ways and means with community resources to develop programs which will give training in such areas.

The committee is divided into subcommittees, *Short range goals* and *Long range programs,* and is now in the process of setting up another subcommittee primarily concerned with getting financing for the training programs.

For short range planning, the committee has submitted a crash training program to equip applicants to pass pre-employment tests for beginning-level jobs. Funds for this have been requested under the Manpower Development and Training Act.

For long range planning, the committee is meeting with the Newark Board of Education to set up summer job training in business and industry for school guidance counselors and department heads with the ultimate goal of curriculum change better suited for business and industrial needs.

The current recommendations of the training committee are

1. An occupational program to be integrated within the comprehensive high school rather than the establishment of a separate facility.
2. An expansion of the dropout counselor program from four to eight schools.
3. An expansion of work study programs throughout senior high schools of Newark.
4. An expansion of the Central High School evening program to include pre-high-school and elementary subjects.
5. An adult school program (non-hobby) to offer upgrading skills and curricula more consistent with the world of work.

Public Relations — stimulates, publicizes, and promotes total program of the BICC. This committee is currently working on the formation of a speakers bureau and

— distributes leaflets to high school seniors,
— provides speakers for participation in high school career day programs in schools with a high enrollment of nonwhite students, and
— arranges for spot announcements for radio and comprehensive newspaper coverage in leading local and New York publications.

Upgrading — works with civil rights groups and business and industry to develop programs which will give training in such areas.

This committee is currently awaiting approval and funds under the Manpower Development and Training Act for a proposal it developed to retrain people now in positions that will be affected by automation and other job dislocation and obsolescent causes.

CONCLUDING REMARKS

In conclusion, it must be stated that continued efforts within the business and industrial field to gain more member companies must be made in order for the BICC to continue on a successful course.

The Negro and Puerto Rican communities are not fully aware of what the BICC is doing despite the distribution of 2,000 posters announcing that new job opportunities exist in Newark.

Communication within the community at grass root levels among more civil rights groups, clergymen, Negro churches, and the Spanish-speaking community must be greatly expanded.

PART VI

Dropouts, Training, and Other Urban Industrial
Problems

20

EMPLOYING NEGROES IN URBAN LABOR MARKETS

Walter H. Powell*

The integration of the Negro into industry has moved beyond the stage of theoretical discussion by management executives and has become a real operating problem for many firms. To many, it is a new meeting of an old challenge. The members of the business community have a very real and vital part in this challenge — it is they who provide equal opportunity employment, and, specifically, the hiring of Negroes is the central issue.

With the existing pressures, the implication is that industry does not wish to integrate and that it is painstakingly avoiding its responsibility. The moral responsibility has now become a legal requirement. Considerable controversy has surrounded the enactment of the recent civil rights legislation. Industry, in part, has reacted unfavorably toward this legislation. This is another manifestation of the struggle between self-interest and public policy in a free enterprise society.

While "Equal Opportunity Employment" is now enacted into law, rigid enforcement will probably not be tried for many years. It has been through voluntary action, government persuasion, and, when necessary, subtle government coercion that many business firms have become party to equal opportunity employment because of their defense contracts.

Many companies, by clear-cut, definitive declarations of policy have encouraged the employment of Negroes. The personnel officer has been given a mandate to embark upon a policy of equal employment and merit employment within the company. But even these mandates do not solve the problem, for the recruitment of eligible Negroes is extraordinarily difficult.

It is a paradox that in an urban community with a relatively

---

*Vice-President, International Resistance Corporation.

high rate of unemployment and with a large Negro population that the hiring of Negroes, even for semi-skilled jobs, should be such a difficult task.

THE LARGE URBAN LABOR MARKET

The entire Philadelphia community presents a real challenge in solving some of the present and future problems of Negro employment. It is a community with a changing labor force, high unemployment, and an increasing Negro population. The same problems which present themselves in Philadelphia undoubtedly will or already have presented themselves in other large urban labor markets, such as Chicago, Detroit, and Pittsburgh. These problems relate to recruiting, screening, and orienting successful applicants to the job situation. Each of these procedures is a normal step in bringing jobs and people together. The large urban community is a crude market place. Too often, the labor market is thought of as a place where the forces of supply and demand are so knowledgeable that the proper bargain will bring about the optimum hiring situation. This is far from the truth.

State Employment Agencies

One attempt to bring about a more efficiently functioning market place for potential employee and the potential employer is the establishment through the nation of a system of state employment agencies, operating under federal control. These agencies function in the administration of unemployment insurance and in the placing of people in open jobs. In the smaller communities, this works exceedingly well — the state employment office is usually the prime source for all employment. In the larger communities, more often than not, it serves only at the lower skill levels. Also, in the larger communities this government employment agency is often ignored by management. Only 15 per cent of all employment was done through this channel.

Imperfections in the Labor Market

In terms of employer efforts to recruit Negroes at any level of the skill ladder, employers generally know nothing about the Negro community and the Negro labor market. On the other side of the coin, the Negro community (whatever nebulous group that might be) neither knows about the availability of jobs nor how to advise its unemployed on the methods of a job search. There is presently no contact point nor effective channel through which to reach Negro applicants. When an employer continually states that a Negro has never applied to his company, it is not a prima facie case of discrimination. There are many companies which would welcome Negro applicants, but they do not know how to attract Negro candidates for employment. This is especially true of the smaller employer.

Even though the environment to encourage Negro employment has been growing ever since World War II, companies trying to comply with the fair employment acts of city, state, and federal government cannot yet find adequate numbers of eligible Negroes for their job openings. Companies with collective bargaining agreements that are obligated by contract to post all vacancies and promotional opportunities on bulletin boards are bewildered in that their own Negro employees do not take advantage of the opportunities for promotion or upgrading. Further, Negro employees, as a rule, do not recommend their friends or relatives for the job vacancies that are posted within their own companies.

In the case of our own company, we have a practice of posting nearly all salaried as well as the hourly jobs. The rationale is obvious. The referral of friends by our employees makes an excellent potential labor supply. In spite of this practice, for the past ten years and with a high Negro population within the company, the number of referrals has been so negligible as to be not even worth discussing.

As a company, we have continually advertised in the local newspapers with "open" advertisements, and even the inclusion of the statement that we are an "Equal Opportunity Employer" has not significantly increased gate applications. And this is in a community where we, as a company, have been identified with fair employment practices, where we are active members of the Urban League, and have maintained strong relationships with many interracial groups. How then does one penetrate the urban labor market? The urban labor market is imperfect. The communications are poor. Prejudices and fears are hampering the meeting of the forces of supply and demand. It is a job market in which the Negro has made very substantial numerical gains in employment but poor progress in merit employment. There are other factors that must be studied to determine whether or not the changes in the pattern of employment have been sufficient to warrant an optimistic attitude toward the Negroes' industrial future. In the 1940's, the outlook was none too rosy because discrimination was quite prevalent. During the 1950's, even though there was an erosion of prejudice, it would be naive to say it had disappeared. However, in the 1950's and

1960's, with the pressures of federal and state legislation, opportunities for Negro advancement in industry began to open up.

Merit employment was the driving theme of progressive and militant Negro organizations. This was a deviation from merely hiring Negroes for traditional jobs. As the 1940's matured into the 1950's and 1960's, stability and length of employment provided the Negro with sufficient seniority to withstand the variations in the business cycles. However, there has not been a tremendous amount of upgrading in industry among this group with comparatively low seniority. A comparison of this group with a similar grouping of white semi-skilled workers, employed about the same time, will not show that one group has advanced at the expense of the other.

The opportunities were for unskilled and semi-skilled jobs and not for skilled and managerial positions, and the persons filling those jobs did not have the attributes to be promoted.

In the latter part of the forties and though the fifties until today, the well-educated Negro trained in business skills has primarily sought employment in civil service. The protective nature of government employment against prejudice, and against the unknown, has provided a haven for competent Negroes. Thus, a heavy segment of the Negro population which is capable of being upgraded in industry is not within the ranks of industry. There are several explanations of this phenomenon. First, the jobs available during the war years were mainly unskilled and semi-skilled jobs. Second, the normal channels for securing white collar jobs have been closed to the Negro until recently. Third, the Negro has hesitated — and been reluctant — to take on responsibility in lower managerial jobs such as factory supervision. The reasons are sociological, economic, and psychological, and, while disturbing, they are not surprising. The Negro employee has not availed himself of the opportunities of apprentice training and upgrading guaranteed to him under most collective bargaining agreements.

Unfortunately, the heavy trend to civil service and government work for white collar jobs has meant under-employment for many capable people. Upgrading is possible, but the competition is probably more intense within the limited environmental factors of government than within the whole of industry. Efforts to dislodge this group from these cloistered jobs into the mainstream of industry have failed continually.

A NEED FOR LOCAL SOLUTIONS

The uncertainties of the labor market have to be solved locally.

The attempt by the National Urban League to establish a skills bank cannot succeed on a national basis. It must be carried out in every community. There are no Negro organizational agencies presently constituted to perform an employment agency function. Most Negro job candidates have not learned to use private employment agencies — either white or colored. The Urban League, the American Friends Service Committee, the NAACP are not capable of performing the functions of an employment agency. In Pennsylvania, as in some other states, special state employment offices have been created to service professional and technical job applicants and higher white collar jobs. Industry has not really been satisfied with these offices, and as a result these public agencies have not been a satisfactory source of supply for white collar jobs. The employment service has not been able to attract either the number of trained people or the skills required. A demand has existed for technical skills for the past few years that has increased the number of private employment agencies to satisfy these needs.

Thus, to provide the opportunity for equality in the job market and to provide the fullest potential in the way of job opportunities to all, a radical change will have to be made in the functioning of the labor market.

THE SEARCH FOR QUALIFIED EMPLOYEES

Within the past two months, our company went into the labor market twice to find male, semi-skilled employees. More specifically, the job specifications called for men who could read, write, and perform with training, jobs of janitor, warehouseman, material handler, and molder. Twenty work days are more than enough to train the average candidate for any of these positions.

The advertisements were placed in the two Philadelphia Sunday papers. We stated the name of the company, its address, and the fact that it is an "Equal Opportunity Employer." We stated that once an employee completes his initial qualification period, he is eligible to bid for any open job posted on the bulletin board. Thus, within the framework of the union-management agreement, we attempt to encourage free movement upward for all individuals. (Parenthetically, it is not surprising that we restrict lateral moves and downgrades and encourage promotions.)

As an initial condition for hiring employees, we think in terms of upgrading. It is not enough to hire a man as a sweeper in the lowest wage grade, because sooner or later he will want advancement, and it is to our advantage for him to be promoted. As part of our pre-employment procedure, we have established certain hiring agreements that are basic to all jobs.

The response to our advertising was exceptionally good. Over one hundred men appeared, but only seventy-six were processed. The others left without completing the application for employment. Almost 85 per cent of the applicants were colored. Out of the seventy-six men, we were only able to hire four immediately, and six are possible future call-ins.

Our recruiting and screening practice included giving a verbal or non-verbal intelligence test, seeking a minimum standard comparable to an eighth-grade education. We also gave four simple arithmetic questions calling for simple addition and subtraction skills. Two right was considered qualifying. A fourth- or fifth-grade student should be able to do all four correctly.

Eighteen of the seventy-five failed the test. Fifteen failed to complete all parts of the test. Twenty-seven could not get past the interviewer, either because of poor work history or attitude.

This pattern is not unusual; it has been repeated several times within our limited sphere of activity. Other companies in the Philadelphia community have had similar experiences that have taxed their facilities and their good intentions.

CONCLUDING REMARKS

Too often the concern has been with the demand side of the equation. The problem has become an increasingly serious evaluation of the supply side. Victories by militant groups to bring about equal opportunities melt into a handful of new jobs, because there are not enough competent applicants.

Harassment of industry is not going to solve the problems of merit employment. Insistent inspectors from over-zealous government agencies will foist impossible standards upon industry. In fact, too much token racial employment is already in existence. This token employment is obscuring the more serious problems which lie ahead.

These problems are basic to our society — they deal with dropouts, the inadequacies of our educational system, and the poorer-trained Negro who is seeking employment. Industry is faced on the one hand with the pressure to remain competitive through constant innovation, automation, and improvement of efficiencies of operation. On the other hand, the people available to help do this job are not in adequate numbers within our society. Prejudices and racial discrimination are contributing to this problem, and industry cannot continue to endure this pressure indefinitely.

It is a simple economic truism that increasing jobs, purchasing power, and opportunity for a significant portion of our population will in fact increase profits. Full employment is a common goal for every diverse segment of our economy.

Management has a responsibility in meeting the problems of merit employment — not mere technical compliance with the law, but an active participation in the affairs of the local community.

The future labor supply cannot be drawn from an inadequately educated population. By default the solution of these problems has been left to social workers, social agencies, and educators, well meaning in technique, and in their conscientious efforts, but absolutely ignorant of the industrial world around them. Industry must not only provide the environmental atmosphere within its plants but must take an active part in the community shaping the future of tomorrow's labor force.

Many of the frontiers of merit employment and integration have been established in the industrial world. Now the total environment for future citizens of all races and creeds must be firmly established and communicated to the innermost parts of the community so that it will offer the incentives for continuing education. Management knows that it cannot manage by default. Now it must learn that it must lead by example and with affirmative action in the world in which it lives.

21

TWO ISSUES OF NEGRO ADVANCEMENT

Arthur B. Shostak*

Especially striking in the matter of Negro advancement are two
unsettling problems we sometimes sense, but seldom discuss in
public.[1] For one, there is good reason to recognize that the cause
of Negro advancement is intimately related with that of urban
reform, and neither can progress without the other. Second is the
fact that for many businesses integration means the end of some,
but also the beginning of other, race-related problems.

NEGRO ADVANCE AND URBAN REFORM

For over one hundred years the nation has witnessed a steady and
large-scale migration of Negroes from backwoods and rural areas to
the nation's cities (where 72 per cent of all Negroes can now be
found), and the outmigration of whites from relatively integrated
cities to largely segregated suburbs.[2] In all states, but especially
Northern states, the nation's Negro population now concentrates in
key industrial cities (e.g., the Twin Cities have 85 per cent of Minnesota's Negro population; Milwaukee, 83 per cent of Wisconsin's
Negroes; Chicago, 81 per cent of Illinois' Negroes; New York City,
76 per cent of the Negroes in New York State; Philadelphia, 62 per
cent of Pennsylvania's Negro population; and St. Louis, 56 per cent
of the Negroes in Missouri).[3] Of equal significance is the white "exodus" to suburbia: Between 1950 and 1960 the twelve largest United
States cities lost over 2,000,000 whites at the same time that they
gained nearly 2,000,000 Negroes.[4]

The current civil rights drive and the campaign for equal opportunity operate in an environment more tenuous than is generally

---

*Assistant Professor of Sociology, Wharton School of Finance and Com-
merce, University of Pennsylvania.

321

realized. *The future of the Negro is inextricably related to the future of the city, and the future of the city is uncertain.*

American industry has a vested business interest in Negro advance *and* urban reform. For example, research and development can little afford the waste of talent inherent in an underdeveloped population of millions. Low purchasing power of underdeveloped groups has serious costs as does the continued strain of locating and competing for the services of the very few vocationally-prepared Negroes. Overall, companies can little afford the rundown and sometimes hazardous nature of the metropolis, especially as competition for scarce high-talent manpower, for example, often turns in part on the company's location. Executives-on-the-move are known to weigh heavily such non-work considerations as available schooling, climate of law and order, and general progressiveness of the community they are being asked to join.

It remains to be seen if cities can stay and alter certain ominous trends. Can the cities rehabilitate slum areas and integrate former slum dwellers? Can the cities meet the needs of their bi-modal Negro minority (very young and very old people), at the same time that the outflow of young and middlle-aged whites is slowed? Can industry be attracted back into the cities, or, alternatively, can city dwellers be helped with improved mass transportation to reach outlying industry?[5]

ROLE OF BUSINESS

What can be done? What is the role for American business in this two-part challenge of Negro advancement and urban reform?[6]

For one thing, the business community can bring its genius for fiscal matters to bear on questions of urban reform. Many city school systems, for example, rely on part-time sessions, over-crowding, substitute teachers, unlicensed instruction, non-resident staff members, and underpaid personnel because the system is starved for funds. How is the city to raise new revenue for welfare, schooling, and housing needs? What are the merits and shortcomings of such possible moves as increases in property or sales or income taxes, additional borrowing, or participation in a federal "share-the-tax" revenue plan? Businessmen who voluntarily engage in this particular dialogue with reformers and politicians can serve to warn against the unanticipated consequences of a simple tax-increase scheme, even as they point up possible savings in city fiscal reforms and call attention to important sources of revenue unfamiliar outside of business circles.

A second area of pertinent business competence is that of operations research and systems analysis. Many city reform efforts have failed because of duplication, waste, gaps, schedule misses, communication breakdowns, unrealistic commitments, and the sorry like. How can the city effectively coordinate its own reform efforts with those of foundation, parochial, suburban, state, regional, and federal groups? What kind of contribution can a PERT Network or some similar scheme make to the welfare efforts of public and private groups (from chapters of CORE through to Public Health and Welfare Councils). Businessmen who engage in this particular dialogue can introduce reformers and politicians to the latest advances in administrative science, even as they frankly encourage specific reforms of present organizational inadequacies.

A third area of business contribution concerns several sensitive community issues. How, for example, can the slum dweller be better protected against exploitation by unscrupulous real estate speculators, landlords, and retail dealers? Where can the self-help training programs of Negroes turn for proper guidance and material support? What can business do to stay the white exodus to suburbia? And how can the city attract new industry? Businessmen who would concern themselves, for example, with the regulatory issue might explore strengthening the local Better Business Bureau, putting teeth into industry association codes, and accommodating anti-trust regulations within vigorous self-policing efforts. Philadelphia offers a model for business involvement in Negro self-help efforts: The Chamber of Commerce in that city, along with 300 major companies, has given personal guidance and over $500,000 in machinery and supplies to the Eastern Seaboard's most significant self-help effort, Rev. Leon Sullivan's Opportunities Industrialization, Inc.[7] Philadelphia's business community has also pioneered in techniques to hold onto white citizens and profitable businesses; e.g., the construction of new downtown office buildings, the restoration of a large Colonial home area in center city, the creation of a central food distribution center to decongest old sections of the city and hold on to key food-handling firms, and the development of university non-credit courses in Philadelphia affairs for the Junior Chamber of Commerce.[8]

Finally, a fourth area of competence in which the business community can make a special contribution is that of public relations and education. Many city reform efforts have failed to accomplish much because of the unfamiliarity of citizens (urban *and* suburban) with the reform program. Several pressing questions remain: How do reformers reach into the councils of upper-income "influentials"? And where can reformers turn for feedback on public responses to reform efforts (and gaps)? Interested businessmen can make a contribution here by familiarizing themselves with reform plans and explaining these further to other "influentials" (urban *and* suburban). (How many of us, for example, now possess thorough understanding of "vest-pocket" housing, comprehensive social planning, networks of preventive mental health clinics, class-integrated housing projects, "halfway" houses, "enrichment" day-care centers, and residental high schools in slum areas.) Businessmen's tours of slum areas, such as that recently arranged by Philadelphia's Chamber of Commerce to enable business leaders to visit with welfare families, help round out an "education," as do also one-day "tours of duty" with caseworkers, school teachers, instructors in manpower retraining efforts, psychiatric social workers in mental health clinics, interns in welfare hospitals, and the like.

Overall, this point should not be forgotten: Negro advancement and urban reform will succeed or fail *together* — and the business community has much to say about this.

INDUSTRIAL INTEGRATION

This essay's second under-discussed problem concerns the situation that too often develops in the aftermath of industrial integration. The hiring of Negroes in business generally means an end to such problems as the threat or fact of boycotts, picketing, demonstrations, and other forms of outside pressure. It also opens up access to a vast manpower pool (19,000,000 Americans), facilitates gains inside of the $22 billion Negro purchasing market, and accommodates governmental and public pressures for concrete evidence of minority-group advancement. Integration (or hiring) is only the beginning, however, for the mixing of two races where there previously was only one gives rise to particular strains and tensions. Over and again the unusually frank businessman explains: "No one ever said it would be easy. But then again, we didn't really think it would be this hard."

Three kinds of present-day post-hiring problems demand attention: Negro employees are expected to behave in super-human fashion, and all are damned when some do not. Similarly, white employees are expected to behave in super-human fashion, and all are "understood" when some do not. Finally, mutual distrust is the order of the day, with status and image thought to be more valuable than justice and progress.

Especially in situations where Negroes are brought into previously all-white work places, but also in many up-grading situations, too much is expected of the Negro employee. Essentially, a Negro "pioneer" is expected to combine pride and humility, wisdom and receptiveness, strength and tolerance, soberness and humour, aggressiveness and patience, ambition and satisfaction, and all this simultaneously and in delicate balance. The job profile is unrealistic; the strain can prove too much for a mere mortal — regardless of his skin color.

When a "pioneer" momentarily "forgets" the expected balance and laughs too hard, too long, or not at all; or when a "pioneer" momentarily "forgets" and comes to work preoccupied with serious personal problems; or when, in short, a "pioneer" behaves at a point much like any other employee occasionally does, a confidential crisis develops. The whispering starts. In no time at all, the verdict is widespread: "That 'great' Negro the management brought in to satisfy the NAACP has shown his feet of clay." Or: "Sorry, but that Negro we all tried to help just has not worked out."

White co-workers often find themselves in much the same kind of situation. Too much is expected of them, not simply as employees in problem-fraught areas, but as individuals. Essentially, a white employee, and especially a supervisor, is expected in an integration situation to combine firmness with flexibility, impartiality with partiality, distance with closeness, objectivity with understanding — and all this simultaneously and in delicate balance. Again, the job profile is unrealistic; the strain can prove too much for a mere mortal — regardless of his skin color.

When a white employee momentarily "forgets" and anxiously seeks to curry favor with new Negro employees, or when a white supervisor "forgets" the expected balance and publically berates a Negro worker, fairly or unfairly, as he might any white; or when, in short, a white co-worker sometimes behaves like any man might, a confidential crisis develops. The whispering starts. In no time at all, several self-serving verdicts are adopted by different groups: "The whites are running scared" or "Good for him, he'll show 'em" or "The supervisor is a bigot" or "He will catch hell from the big-shots for upsetting things. He should know better than to look cross-eyed at a Negro nowadays."[9]

Finally, as is apparent from the above, in many situations mutual distrust is the order of the day. New Negro employees are often suspected of being "NAACP plants," "CORE agents," or "agitators for SNCC," with the standards of evidence generally reduced to the "fact" that they look suspicious, seem "uppity," speak too well, have too much education, or some other such thing. Previously accepting whites often regard upgraded Negroes as beneficiaries of favoritism, rank opportunists, and probably unworthy co-workers. And many white workers subject Negro colleagues to a scrutiny so exacting as to impart far-reaching significance to every act— no matter how insignificant it may be. Negro workers, for their part, sometimes suspect that routine job transfers, job engineering studies, transfer requests, or salary reviews are part of an insulting conspiracy aimed at their being downgraded, bypassed, or removed. And some Negro workers take refuge in false allegations of discrimination to rationalize instances of real personal failure.

Underlying all of this is management's failure to accompany its impressive program of Negro hiring with a sophisticated intergroup relations program of work force preparation and integration monitoring. Management often does not seem clear about what happens *after* the Negro employee is hired or upgraded, and it is bewildered by signs of trouble in morale, turnover, transfer, and productivity. It is time we publically recognized that in too many post-hiring situations, integration has not really taken place, and men are not interacting on relaxed and personal terms. Negroes and whites in these situations do not feel free to be themselves. Neither trusts in the company's objectivity, and both squander the rare opportunity available in integrated shops and offices to challenge the myths of prejudice with facts gained in human contacts.

THOUGHTS ON REFORM

The situation, albeit one with serious, inter-related problems, *is* amenable to reform. To paraphrase the weary complaint with which this section opened, "No one ever said it would be easy. But neither does it have to be so hard."

To begin with, we must squarely face the fact that the challenge is to integrate two groups of mortals, not super-men. While some early preparation is appropriate, Negro "pioneers" and those who follow after should be assured that adequate performance on the job, rather than Hollywood-style role-playing, is the paramount and overriding consideration. White colleagues should have the same point impressed on them, and, as soon as possible, the "solo spotlight" on the "pioneer" should be weakened for having to play over an increasing number of Negro recruits. Negroes should be fired as well as promoted, disciplined as well as commended, treated, in short, much like the men they are. The only thing that should remain "special" about the situation is the insignificance of the race factor.

White supervisors should receive assurances that good supervisory practice will be backed by the company, regardless of internal or external pressures from groups who innocently or deliberately allege discrimination. Attempts at extortion by Negro opportunists or white segregationists, however subtle, should be firmly dealt with — the company not shying from discharge where warranted. Attempts at race provocation, whether originating from white or Negro racists, should be similarly handled. Above all, employees should be helped to recognize a distinction between patient and reasonable support of the previously-deprived and unwarranted favoritism in overlooking errors, forgetting delinquencies, or allocating rewards.

SUMMARY

On closer-than-usual examination, two unsettling problems we sometimes sense, but seldom discuss in public, take on a new character. Racial integration in business appears more strained than company public relations officers would admit, even as it is more open to improvement than the compact of silence concerning it suggests. Negro advance and urban reform are both threatened by certain social trends, even as both can profit considerably from business recognition of their interdependence and expanded business involvement in remedial campaigns. The under-discussed problems reviewed in this essay *are* resolvable — if men involve themselves and act.

FOOTNOTES

1. I should like to thank a colleague, Dr. Everett Lee of the University's Department of Sociology; an associate, Mr. Paul Dandridge of the Philadelphia Commission on Human Relations; and a personal friend, Mrs. George Flemming of the Philadelphia Child Study Center for their assistance in reviewing this essay. The final version is entirely my own responsibility; only its strengths can be traced to the other parties named.
   Other sub-rosa items that demand a public airing include the sexual content of inter-group hostility, the inevitability of losers in a competitive order, the vast implications of de facto housing segregation, the minority position of whites in the world, and the like. My choice in this essay was dictated as much by the volume's focus and space limitations as by any emphatic personal ranking by "significance."

2. Sidney M. Willhelm and Edwin H. Powell, "Who Needs the Negro? From the Economics of Exploitation to the Economics of Uselessness," *Trans-Action*, September/October, 1964, p. 4. Note that the fertility of Negroes remaining in the South is such as to increase the absolute total of Negroes left in the region, even while the South loses through emigration Negroes in the most productive age bracket (18 to 34 years of age). The North has a rich resource in its influx of able-bodied, ambitious adults — if only both the North and the new arrivals can adjust to one another. For some disturbing thoughts in this connection, see Rose Stamler, "Acculturation and Negro Blue-Collar Workers," in *Blue-Collar World*, edited by A. Shostak and W. Gomberg (Englewood Cliffs, New Jersey: Prentice-Hall, 1964).

3. "Geography and the Negro Problem," *U.S. News and World Report*, August 26, 1963, pp. 50-51. In 1910, nearly 2.7 million Negroes lived in urban areas, with 7.1 million living on the land; in 1960, 13.8 million Negroes lived in cities, and only 5.1 million remained on the land. "The urbanization of the Negro . . . has served both to sharpen his own mood of rebellion and to dramatize his plight before the white world." William Brink and Louis Harris, *The Negro Revolution in America* (New York: Simon and Schuster, 1964), p. 39.

4. Willhelm and Powell, *op. cit.* "No basic change has taken place in the design reported in 1961 by the United States Commission on Human Rights." "There is an ever-increasing concentration of non-whites in racial ghettos, largely in the decaying centers of our cities — while a 'white noose' of new suburban housing grows up around them." Nat Hentoff, *The New Equality* (N.Y.: The Viking Press, 1964), p. 121.

5. See in this connection, Staughton Lynd, "Urban Renewal — For Whom?" in *New Perspectives on Poverty*, edited by A. Shostak and W. Gomberg (Englewood Cliffs, New Jersey: Prentice-Hall, 1965). See also Bernard Weissbourd, *Segregation, Subsidies, and Megalopolis* (Santa Barbara, California: Center for the Study of Democratic Institutions, 1964); Alvin L. Schorr, *Slums and Social Insecurity: An*

*Appraisal of the Effectiveness of Housing Policies in Helping to Elimi-
nate Poverty in the United States* (Washington, D.C.: U.S. Govern-
ment Printing Office, 1963); Robert Weaver, *The Urban Complex:
Human Values in Urban Life* (New York: Doubleday, 1964); Leonard
J. Duhl, ed., *The Urban Condition: People and Policy in the
Metropolis* (New York: Basic Books, 1963); Alexander L. Crosby,
Citizen Action for Housing and Renewal (Pittsburgh, Pa.: United
Steelworkers of America, 1964).

6. Note the important precedents for business involvement here available
   in the current contribution of business to manpower retraining efforts
   (OJT, manpower needs projections, etc.) and the Job Corps Program of the Office of Economic Opportunity (Philco, for example, is
   helping the University of Oregon set up a residential job training
   center for 1,250 male high-school dropouts; an I.T.T. subsidiary is
   helping Rutgers University; and Burroughs Corporation is assisting the
   University of Pennsylvania). Business has long cooperated in welfare
   endeavors through rehabilitation services to parolees, former alcoholics,
   ex-mental patients, and the physically handicapped, along with its
   tradition of philanthropic leadership.

7. An excellent discussion is available in Hannah Lees, "Self-Help in
   Philadelphia," *The Reporter,* December 17, 1964.

8. *Fortune* advises here: ". . . that flexible instrument, the U.S. industrial
   corporation, has a large part to play in eradicating 'the shame of the
   cities.' Indeed, the possibilities of redevelopment are endless. . . . As an
   extreme example, why not a project in Harlem that would combine
   slum clearance with corporate investment in fabricating plants, which
   would help provide jobs as well as roofs for those who need them? This
   kind of thing would be quite impossible for government alone to pull
   off, but is not impossible once corporations have been brought into
   the process." Hubert Kay, "The Third Force in Urban Renewal,"
   Fortune, October, 1964, p. 214.

9. A rare public discussion of the matter is available in the symposium
   in the April, 1964 issue of *Management Review,* "Equal Employment
   Opportunity: Company Policies and Experiences." Considerable word-
   weighing is obvious, and the reader is advised to "read between the
   lines." See also Arthur B. Shostak, "Human Problems in Improving
   Industrial Race Relations," *Personnel Administration,* March/April,
   1963; and *Wall Street Journal,* August 12, 1963; Eli Ginzberg, ed., *The
   Negro Challenge to the Business Community* (N.Y.: McGraw-Hill, 1964).

22

UTILIZING THE DROPOUT

C. Virgil Martin*

The high school dropout is most certainly a fit subject for this symposium. His job opportunities are definitely limited. His race or color may well handicap him further, but, no matter what his ethnic make-up, the dropout is in trouble when he seeks employment.

Let me say at the outset that I believe the question of equal opportunity, and the related problems of unemployment and dropouts, can and will be resolved within our free enterprise system. Resolved not only out of altruistic motives or a desire for social betterment, but also simply because it is good business.

We must stop thinking of the Negro, the dropout, the unemployed, and the unemployable as nameless statistics. They are potential wage earners, taxpayers, customers and a rich source of energy, innovation, and contribution to our communities. To write them off as "hopeless" or content ourselves with "paying them off" with welfare subsistence would be folly — it would be to cheat ourselves of their potential contributions.

I guarantee that, after Carson Pirie Scott's experience with utilizing the high school dropout, both Negro and white, from culturally deprived areas and affluent ones, we will continue to recruit dropouts as worthwhile productive members of our firm.

After three years of experience with our Double EE Program — EE standing for "Education and Employment" — interesting statistics about these youngsters have been amassed, and we have learned how they respond to counseling, to a meaningful combination of schooling and work experience, to a personal interest in their lives and futures.

The Chicago business community first became fully aware of the problem of our alarming dropout rate and its implications through the missionary efforts of Dr. Benjamin Willis, Chicago's school

---

*President, Carson Pirie Scott and Company, Chicago, Illinois.

superintendent. It did not take a special degree for certain of us to translate his alarming dropout figures into burgeoning relief rolls, lost income, and reduced purchasing power — particularly where there was an additional problem of equal opportunity. Dr. Willis pointed out that in some parts of the country the percentage of high school non-graduates is running as high as 40 per cent, and that in Chicago alone, some 10,000 drop out of high school every year.

Superintendent Willis asked Carson's if it would cooperate in an effort designed to provide employment for dropouts in a setting which would at the same time provide both the motivation and the opportunity to continue their schooling. We took it up with our personnel staff. Their reaction was not negative, but it was not all positive either. They were quick to point out the problems that would inevitably rise with employing considerable numbers of what were, in effect, society's "rejects." Without special work-related schooling, further development was doubtful; without guidance and counseling, they were quite apt to get swallowed up in Carson's nine floors and hundreds of employees; without additional social "orientation," we could hardly expect them to gain acceptance from customers or fellow-employees. Despite these problems, we decided to go ahead on a trial basis.

A PILOT PROGRAM

The final pilot program, which we hammered out in long sessions with school officials, covered all of these aspects. Carson's agreed to furnish classrooms, training facilities in the store, wages at a beginning scale, and a regular stipend for books and transportation. The Chicago School Board was to furnish, besides the dropouts themselves, teachers and guidance personnel under an initial special grant of $50,000, which Ben Willis and I were able to get from the Ford Foundation.

Our first class of 66 was screened and selected by school officials; Carson's only stipulation was that they be able to pass our regular physical examination. They ranged in age from 15 to 17, represented virtually every section of the city, and a little more than 50 per cent were Negro.

Together, we worked out a program whereby the youngsters would work three days a week and go to school two days, earning credit toward their high school degrees for the time spent in school. We are open six days; thus, two of them actually filled one job.

Each youngster was placed under one of our college graduate trainees as counselor. The counselor's job was to show a personal interest in his charge, help him with his problems and set a good example of behavior. This, we found, was one of the real keys to the success of the operation. Part of the reason that many of these children dropped out of school was the inadequacy of their parents to cope with life. The youngsters needed someone to talk to — to tell them how to dress, to behave, and to relate to others.

Most of this first group were placed, at least temporarily, in sales jobs. We soon found that we had to review arithmetic to enable them to write sales checks. But we also found that, for the first time in their lives, one of their studies had meaning — it related directly to something they were doing every day — and overall progress was excellent.

After the first five or six weeks, we allowed them to organize their own curriculum, and the first subject they requested was English! Remember that many of these youngsters had a fifth- or sixth-grade reading level, and most had shown very little interest in communicating. Yet, here they were, asking that English be a major part of their studies.

Why? My guess is that, in those few short weeks of dealing with people on a person-to-person basis in a practical situation, they felt a need to communicate — because they had found something to communicate about. Their lives had taken on a new meaning, and they wanted to express this and to become a part of the new world they had found.

We had given them a *reason* for going to school. For the first time they saw the relationship of the studies they had been pursuing — or not pursuing — to working and earning a living. As one of the more articulate members of this first group put it upon his "graduation" from the Double EE program, we "gave them back their lost incentive."

We were careful to keep these people on regular standards while they were on the job; we insisted that their performance measure up to that of their fellow-workers who had been hired off the street, and many of them actually excelled.

The lowest I.Q. we found in the whole group was a nice, but nondescript, little girl named Joan, who tested 80. Now, most of us would despair at an I.Q. this low and be willing to give it up as a bad job. But Joan's counselor discovered that she was interested in — of all things — leather goods. She was thrilled just to be around leather, and said that someday she hoped to own gloves and a handbag of her own.

Checking back to the high school, the counselor found that, sure enough, just about the only interest she had shown there had been in leather-tanning and manufacturing, anything to do with leather.

Here was a girl who had great difficulty in mastering the basic arithmetic needed to make out a sales slip, but we put her in the handbag department, and within six months she was writing more business per hour in her three-day week than any other girl on the floor. In fact, other people in the department had taken to consulting her on the qualities of various leathers. Her appearance improved remarkably, and today she is one of our most productive workers, even though the chances are she will never finish high school.

Of course, not all of them remained in sales. Some who did not do well meeting the public were transferred to stock or food service or central wrap — wherever there was a job they could fill which was better suited to their temperaments and abilities.

Much of their school work centered around retailing and, specifically, around the place of the individual within the store structure. Class sessions dealt with the role each one of them played in the broad spectrum of retailing, with the importance of their duties to the whole operation.

And beyond on-the-job training and work-related schooling, the youngsters were given an orientation to society and an insight into self-management.

Class sessions were held on the individual's rights and responsibilities under the law. The class was addressed by a judge and by lawyers; later the youngsters participated in mock trials in common kinds of cases in which they might become involved. They invited guest speakers from the Social Security administration and Internal Revenue office. After the first payday, it was apparent that they needed help in budgeting, and after that they kept careful accounts of their expenditures and earnings. Credit buying, interest rates, and financing plans were compared and explained.

All of the subjects they had rejected as a part of their formal high school experience — civics, mathematics, English, business and commercial subjects — suddenly became intensely interesting because they were no longer meaningless mumbo-jumbo, but had become an important part of their workaday life.

Every effort was made to involve the parents in the goals of the program and the progress of their youngsters in achieving them. We found that many of the parents, rather than deliberately neglectful, suffered personality defects and inadequacies themselves. They had lost contact with their children, and most of them were grateful for a chance to share something with them.

One year later, this pilot Double EE effort ended with well

over half still active, and these were asked to remain on the payroll. We had lost some to marriage, others to Uncle Sam, and some had returned to school full time, but out of the original 66, we had a lower turnover than we normally have in our general employment group. There are only a few of that first class still employed at Carson's, but I can assure you — and I think this is the most important thing we have learned — they are among the most productive and certainly the most loyal employees we have.

EXPERIENCES UNDER THE PROGRAM

So far, 186 boys and girls have received Double EE training at Carson Pirie Scott & Company. Many have succeeded, some have failed. But the record of this 186 is studded with success stories — stories which dramatize the kind of losses our society will suffer if we allow these youngsters to drift into jobless oblivion. Let me cite a few of these:

Susan, at 17, did not like school because she had no friends. Her poor record of achievement had made her the official "dunce" of her high school class, and the other students made fun of her inabilities. When her hostility expressed itself in petty theft, she left school by mutual agreement with officials. Enrolled in the Double EE program, she began to consult her fellow students on personal grooming; they took her under their wings, developed a protective attitude toward her, and her appearance improved. She gained, almost overnight, a confidence in herself that had always been missing or deeply buried. Later, she left Carson's and joined another Chicago retailer where she now has a stable and productive life.

Peter, whose only interest seemed to be stock car racing, became such a discipline problem in the Double EE school that he was suspended. But, through counseling by his "big brother" at Carson's, he was made to see the inter-relationship between his schooling and his job, and the importance of one to the other, and he began straightening out. His attitude changed almost overnight, with the result that the director of the program tutored him in trigonometry, and he was successful in his studies. When he left the program, he was accepted into the Army — and we must remember that 50 per cent of our youth are rejected from military service — and Peter now intends to finish high school. I recall that, when Peter came to Carson's, he sported what is known as a "duck-tail" haircut. As he progressed in the program, his hair was cut shorter and shorter, and the counselors actually started using it as an index of his sociability.

Sandra, at 16, was an unwed mother. Through her Double EE assignment in the billing department, she became a skilled biller and, upon completing her training, went to work full time and enrolled in night school. When a data processing change took her billing job, she was given another job in sales and continued typist training evenings. Though she was loud and brash at first, she greatly improved in attitude as she progressed. Now a full-time secretary, she has graduated from high school and is attending a junior college while her mother takes care of the baby.

Remarkable? Not at all. Joan and Susan and Peter and Sandra were not lacking in abilities or a desire to achieve. It is difficult to generalize, but I believe the thing they needed most was motivation: someone to take an interest in them, a role in a society which had lost meaning for them, recognition, encouragement, understanding.

These ingredients were supplied by the Double EE program, by parents and teachers and work supervisors and counselors working in concert and toward the common goal of the rehabilitation of one individual. And we must never forget the hours and hours of patient and unrewarded labor that have been invested in each one of these youngsters. Were the results worth it?

SOME RESULTS OF THE PROGRAM

Our Double EE people assure us that Carson's is dollars and cents ahead on our investment.

Ben Willis can boast that his brainchild has salvaged scores of youngsters from a lifetime of hopelessness and despair — youngsters who could not be reached through conventional educational methods.

We will have to leave it to social scientists to calculate the benefits society can expect from these youngsters as productive citizens rather than social problems, destined for a life on the welfare rolls — or worse.

But you can only learn the real answer to that question by watching these boys and girls in action — on the job or in the classroom —their faces eager, alert, and alive.

If you would like more evidence, I will cite a recent survey of 62 students who finished the program in May of 1963:

— 35 are employed full time, 23 by the company which hired them while they were students in the Double EE phase.

— 5 are in the armed forces.

— 4 have married and are housewives.

— 12 have returned to full-time schooling.

And, if one adds those figures up, the answer will come out close to the total of 62; in fact, all but one have had some kind of employment since their Double EE days.

Now, let us turn to the history of Double EE since those first tentative and exciting days of the pioneering effort.

The Idea Spreads

Needless to say, Dr. Willis has done a great deal of missionary work on behalf of the idea in the past three years. And since I saw the results with my own eyes, I have been known to stump around a bit myself. Carson's was only the first company that he managed to sell on the idea; at last count, more than 30 firms in the Chicago area alone have done their own experimenting with it, including such venerable names as A & P, National Tea, Sears Roebuck, the Fair Store, Prudential Insurance, Honeywell, and the Conrad Hilton.

At present, there are more than 100 present or past Double EE students at work in any number of jobs in Chicago and at many levels of responsibility and a total of some 300 in various phases of training across the country.

The program has drawn nationwide attention through the press and, particularly, through the granting to Carson's of a "Retailing Serves America" national award by the *Reader's Digest* and National Retail Merchants Association.

That is pretty dramatic progress for a program which three years ago was no more than an idea in a schoolmaster's head.

And the implications of "Employment plus Education" — or, if you prefer, "Utilizing the Dropout" — as one approach to the related problems of equal opportunity and youth employment go far beyond these relatively small numbers.

Lessons Are Learned

One of the most significant, I believe, is what we have learned about the Negro as a worker. Now, Carson's has followed a nondiscriminatory hiring policy for many years, and we have benefited greatly by it. The simple fact is that, where many doors are closed, those that remain open admit a wide selection. We have been able to choose from a number of very excellent people for any job opening.

The Double EE experience afforded us our first experience over a long period with the "other" Negroes — those who, because of youth and lack of education and training and cultural deprivation were hardly equipped to compete for *any* job. And the results have been outstanding.

While we have not kept many statistics on the matter, the non-whites in our program have done as well as or better than their peers. Given equal opportunity, they are quick to recognize it and take advantage of it.

And the great value of training like that given these youngsters is the fact that Double EE provides a mechanism to break the vicious cycle in many underprivileged families in which illiterate and often inadequate parents can provide neither example nor incentive for their offspring. In such cycles, poverty begets poverty.

Through efforts like the Double EE, business and industry can provide substitutes for inadequate home environment. Our counselors become, in effect, mother and father figures and thus help eliminate one of the major causes of high school dropouts — inadequate parents and inadequate homes. As part of their regular responsibilities as Carson's employees, these counselors are assigned "big brother" roles with individual Double EE students, but most of them gave much more than was expected in the line of duty. Many of them gave extra hours to tutoring and personal counseling, and it is my impression — I do not have actual figures to back this up — that our turnover rate among employees assigned this job has been much lower than normal.

Of course, business can't make up for deficiencies in the children themselves, but it can, through patient study and attention to the problem, find the right job for someone who would be unhappy and a failure in most other jobs. It can, through programs of employee relations, guide and nurture these youngsters and draw the very best out of them.

Business and industry also can work with education. By providing an objective and informed viewpoint, it can give boards of education the knowledge and stimulation that will help them to keep their curricula flexible, viable, and functional.

It may well be that modern-day educators feel they have resolved the conflict between those who stress the liberal arts and those who would teach every boy a trade. However, I do not believe this is true. I do not really believe that the problem will stay resolved. And certainly, there is no general agreement in all parts of the country on an ideal curriculum for high-schoolers.

As recently as 1961, James Conant, in *Slums and Suburbs,* offered the partial solution of

". . . developing meaningful courses for pupils with less than average abilities. To this end consideration should be given by every school and community to the expansion of work-study programs for slow students, and to the provision of at least an auto mechanics shop for boys in every high school in metropolitan areas."

Obviously, Conant's studies have shown that many areas — even large metropolitan areas — are still woefully inadequate in technical high school training facilities and programs.

VARIOUS APPROACHES FOR BUSINESS

Here is another way business can serve. Could not a dedicated committee from a cross-section of business and industry be helpful to the boards of education in answering questions like these:

1. Do our schools offer adequate training to the boy or girl who obviously is not college material, so that he or she can earn a living?

2. If technical courses *are* available, are teaching methods and equipment up to date with modern developments?

3. Are we developing skills for which there is no longer a need?

4. Are we overlooking — and I am very certain that we are — many areas in which the high school dropout or graduate could be happy earning a living?

Personnel directors in our industrial organizations could list, as an aid to educators, such untaught skills as, for example, the many specialties in the preparation of food, appliance servicing, and landscaping. But, industry need not confine itself to the educational system in its efforts to cut down unemployment.

In Chicago, the brilliant director of the Cook County Department of Welfare, Ray Hilliard, has given impetus to a dramatic movement to train welfare recipients to get jobs *with the help of industry*. It began with his conviction that there were enormous numbers of people who could not find jobs because they were illiterate — or almost so.

His research verified this belief. In Cook County in 1962, more than 50 per cent of the welfare recipients were so-called functional illiterates. This means that their reading level is 5th-grade or below and that most of them cannot find a job — let alone hold one. Of this group, almost 7 per cent were totally illiterate or Spanish-speaking, meaning they could not dial a telephone, read a want-ad or street sign, and would be afraid to ride a bus through unfamiliar territory.

By actually coercing these adults back into special schools, he has been able to train and find jobs for thousands as cab drivers, practical nurses, waiters, and in many other occupations.

The challenge to industry is simply this: are industrial leaders going to be able to see beyond the initial expense to the rewards to themselves and to the community at large of *this* kind of co-operation with educators and relief officials?

I think they are.

The stimulus is not always so remote as the higher taxes which industry must pay for welfare payments to the unemployed. There are other and more direct considerations.

Sometimes a company president finds himself in a situation which illustrates his company's involvement very directly with such problems. When Carson Pirie Scott & Company, for example, was staffing the Seven Continents restaurant and all of the other restaurants we operate at O'Hare International Airport in Chicago, we found a very serious shortage of master chefs, pastry chefs, salad chefs, even waiters and second cooks — and this at the same time that relief rolls were rising. Obviously, it is not strange for a company president under these circumstances to decide to do whatever he can to correct a ridiculous situation.

I might add that we at Carson's have taken some initial steps toward solving this particular problem and are training youngsters in food service both at the downtown store and at our airport restaurants.

And, in all honesty, the willingness with which we participated in the Double EE program grew out of many such experiences as this.

CONCLUDING REMARKS

The problem of providing equal opportunity does not lend itself to simple formulas. The barriers which must be faced by a teenage Negro in getting a living and just getting along must seem insurmountable. Not only must he contend with prejudice, but with a prejudicial heritage of inequalities which make it doubly difficult for him to master even the most basic tools of competition in a free enterprise system.

In this era of expanding technology and multiplying wealth, we are finally beginning to realize that it is possible to improve the lot of the poor without taking or taxing it from the rich. This myth — the redistribution of wealth — is fast disappearing. We have seen that increased production and aggressive marketing can generate an economy that will accommodate all Americans. For the first time in history, phrases like "War on Poverty" and "Full Employment" are being accepted as something more than impossible visionary dreams.

But we have also discovered that the vital missing ingredient in realizing an end to poverty and jobs for all is education. With a good education, the Negro can make his way in the face of the most violent prejudice; without a good education, the middle-class white will likely meet failure after failure in job experiences.

The importance of programs like the Double EE is that they make education more palatable, more meaningful, and in many cases, economically feasible.

Businessmen can no longer allow themselves the luxury of skimming the cream of high school and college graduates, competing intensively for the very best, and allowing the underprivileged and mediocre to find what work they can. Business must take immediate action to assure equal job opportunity, not because it is now the law, but because it is both morally right and good business to do so.

And the responsibility of business does not end with equitable employment practices. If, for reasons of prejudice or cultural deprivation or what we might call the "education-gap," many Americans are, indeed, *not* "equal," businessmen must do more. They must do all in their power — under the system of rights and responsibilities we call "free enterprise" — to give these "unequals" jobs, to train them, to educate them, to mold them, to work with them in removing these disparities and to make of them valuable employees and productive citizens.

23

A PROGRAM FOR HIGH SCHOOL DROPOUTS IN BAMBERGER'S, NEW JERSEY

Charles W. Garrison*

At a time when American business faces an imminent shortage of such skilled workers as trained machinists, tool and die makers, dental technicians, metal workers, electricians, nurses, auto mechanics, and dietitians — at such a time, one out of three students who enters high school fails to graduate. In New Jersey, for instance, there are 50,000 boys and girls currently out of school and out of work.

A Bureau of Labor Statistics Report states that 70 per cent of these students have normal or above-average I.Q.'s, and a surprising 10 per cent are of college ability. Without a proper education, however, they find job-getting a very difficult problem. High school dropouts usually are written off as academic, social, and economic liabilities. They therefore end by swelling the ranks of the unemployed and frequently becoming candidates for the relief rolls.

WHY STUDENTS DROP OUT OF SCHOOL

Why do these students drop out of school? School authorities point out that lack of motivation is the reason in many cases. If a student sees no hope of getting a decent job in a society where the new jobs being created by industry are getting further and further out of his reach, he sees no point in sweating out the long, hard grind of getting an education. One of the greatest contributions management can make to these troubled boys and girls, therefore, is to provide them with a sense of hope. In realizing this our per-

---

*Senior Vice-President, Bamberger's, a division of R. H. Macy and Company, Inc.

sonnel division decided in the latter part of 1962 to take a direct approach to the problem.

THE "D" SQUAD PROGRAM

The plan, which is called the Diploma or "D" Squad Program, seeks to accomplish the following:

1. To find some of New Jersey's dropouts and encourage them to finish high school by giving them adult responsibilities, earned cash, and a sense of being needed.

2. To aid in educating the public by calling attention to the economic and social implications of the present situation.

3. To open the door for other businesses and industries to frame similar solutions to the dropout problem.

4. To sponsor a work program that provides an incentive for the dropout to stay in school and that can be perpetuated without "creating" jobs.

5. To cultivate a new source of talent by providing a training ground for the development of future full-time personnel.

All of our eight stores make available evening employment as stock clerks or messengers, as vacancies occur, to qualified high school juniors or seniors who have dropped out or who are thinking of dropping out of school. Employment is given only on condition that the individual *return to* and *remain in* school; maintain satisfactory grades, attendance, conduct, and health; and perform his job satisfactorily. The agreement with the students and with their schools is that the company is permitted to fire them immediately if they do leave school. In addition, a career in retailing is possible for any member of the "D" Squad upon graduation from high school.

The stores operate on a two-shift schedule and can accommodate upward of 80 boys and girls in a year's time. At the outset, only those dropouts who were college material were recruited; but after an initial period of defining and redefining valid criteria for judging applicants, we decided to fill vacancies from among all those whose test scores and school records indicated they were capable of completing the work necessary for high school graduation and whom we felt we could salvage.

Initial referrals are made by vocational counselors in the schools of communities where our stores are located. The placement or guidance counselor is contacted by letter, and a form is provided by which the counselor can recommend a student. The counselor is asked to indicate whether test scores and school records indicate that the applicant is capable of completing the work necessary for high school graduation. It is made clear that the student must return to and continue in school in order to remain in Bamberger's employ. The reason why the student had left school is sought.

The referrals are interviewed by the personnel manager, who rates them with respect to appearance, personality, motivation, attitude, integrity, reliability, sense of responsibility, and financial need. The accompanying exhibit is a sample of the interview appraisal form used. They must also score satisfactorily on a Wonderlic Test and get approval and permission from their parents before they can be placed into positions in the stores. A letter is sent to the parents which explains the "D" Squad, and a form is enclosed which the parent must sign to indicate approval of the program and to give permission for the student to be employed. The parent agrees that the applicant must remain in school in order to continue working at Bamberger's.

The employment manager in each Bamberger store is responsible for the operation of the "D" Squad. He coordinates all correspondence among parents, counselors, school principals, and so on, utilizing appropriate "D" Squad forms. In his periodic checks with the school counselor, the employment manager asks him to rate the member of the "D" Squad on grades, attendance, conduct, and health, since eligibility to remain on the Squad depends on satisfactory attendance and grades at school. He also reviews the performance of all "D" Squad members monthly. In the review, he asks the member's supervisor to report on attendance, the quality and quantity of work, willingness to cooperate, initiative, appearance, effort, and any comments or recommendations which the member's department head sees fit to make.

PERFORMANCE UNDER THE PROGRAM

"D" Squad members have performed well in their duties. Among the first recruits were James Epp and Richard Dixon, both seniors at South Side High School in Newark. James was placed in the customer returns room and Richard in the addressograph department. Both subsequently graduated from South Side High School and are now in the U. S. Marine Corps.

We also have had failures, including a student who quit after misrepresenting the nature of his need for employment. Out-of-school training of the dropout is sometimes difficult because of his emotional block against formal learning. But the results to date have, on the whole, strengthened belief in the program and the feasibility of similar programs in other areas of industry.

The number of would-be dropouts saved by our stores may seem to be nothing, statistically, against a backdrop of 700,000 unemployed young people. The number is certainly nothing compared to the 1.5 million who will be idle if current trends persist. But we feel it is important to do whatever we can. Through programs such as this, the store helps accomplish the following: (1) it validates its responsible position in the community and also furthers enlightened self-interest; (2) students reclaimed through such activities add to the economic well-being of the country; and (3) they provide a source of stable, experienced personnel who can enrich themselves and the industry in retailing careers.

CONCLUDING REMARKS

Every firm, school, and parent in this country has an important contribution to make towards the solution of the problem. There is a crying need for more youth employment programs. Furthermore, a concerted effort to enlist the cooperation of every responsible segment of the community should be made, for to assist in the solution of this problem is to invest in the long-range economic health and stability of the communities in which we live and work.

APPENDIX
THE NEWARK DROPOUT PROGRAM*

In a pilot program, 100 unemployed high-school dropouts are being offered jobs in Newark by six major corporations — if the dropouts will enroll in a special high school being set up in downtown Newark. The program, which was suggested by the companies, is backed by the Board of Education of Newark, and the New Jersey Departments of Education and Labor. Participating companies are Standard Oil of New Jersey, Prudential, Bamberger's, Western Electric, Westinghouse, and New Jersey Bell Telephone.

The Board of Education is establishing a special high school in downtown Newark just for the dropouts, staffing it with experienced personnel, and providing it with a special curriculum. On the state level, Dr. Frederick M. Raubinger, Commissioner of Education, has recommended that the Department of Education grant money from its emergency fund to help support the project.

The Department of Labor's Youth Career Development Center is culling its list of 5,000 Newark dropouts for 300 candidates. These will be screened down by the Board of Education to the 100 who will participate in the pilot project. The youths selected will be boys or girls between the ages of 18 and 21, with a year or two of high school still to complete. They will be paired two to a job. One will work while the other is in school.

The subjects given in the special high school will be the same as those given in the regular Newark schools, but adapted to the needs of employed students. They will include English, mathematics, social studies, business education, and job orientation.

No employees will be replaced to make work for the dropouts, nor, when the dropouts earn their diplomas, will the companies be committed to offer them continued employment. Under the plan, each participating company will use its own salary schedules and conditions of employment applying to the jobs in which the students are placed. When a student leaves the program, or graduates from it, his place will be taken by another qualified candidate.

The head of the special school, with its enrollment of 100, will be Irving J. Goldberg, former administrative assistant at Weequahic High School. He will be assisted by four experienced Newark teachers of academic subjects plus three teachers specially trained as work-study coordinators and by two full-time guidance counselors and a social worker.

---

*The Industry Work-Study Group of Newark.

24

THE NEGRO WORKER IN PHILADELPHIA*

Leonard Rico**

The development and efficient utilization of manpower resources is a problem of increasing concern to the nation. This recently has been exemplified by the dilemma of finding suitable jobs for unemployed millions willing and able to work. One manifestation is the Negro's search for economic opportunity in the contemporary urban setting. The employment situation in large metropolitan areas challenges the ability of private and public institutions and leaders to come up with new ways to ease the social costs of economic change. Yet, it is precisely this dynamic quality of the economic environment which exacerbates the Negro, who often is unprepared or not permitted to enjoy areas of expanding job opportunities, while he is prepared or permitted to seek traditionally marginal jobs or non-traditional jobs with a declining demand.

Do equal employment opportunities exist for all citizens regardless of color? The answer to this question may be found by examining labor market data. Increasingly we have come to recognize that the quality of a nation's human resources is integral to its economic development and well-being. The American dream of the good life attained through self-improvement and equal opportunity supports the image of a purely competitive model of the labor market.

This paper, to a limited degree, questions whether or not a free market exists for the Negro worker in Philadelphia. The perfect labor market, in theory, assumes a homogeneous supply of labor

*The author acknowledges the research assistance of E. Barksdale Kizer, a Wharton School graduate student. The help and counsel of Paul Dandridge and Gordon Alexander, both of the Philadelphia Commission on Human Relations, are appreciated. This study was financed with the aid of a grant from the General Electric Foundation.

**Assistant Professor of Industry, Wharton School of Finance and Commerce, University of Pennsylvania.

to a firm or industry. In this system each hypothetical worker, seeking to maximize his wage, is perfectly mobile and willing to move whenever a higher differential wage is offered by another firm. All workers have perfect knowledge of alternative job opportunities and wage rates in the labor market. It is further assumed that each employer seeks the worker who will accept the lowest wage; the employer always is willing to replace his current workers for others who will work for lower wages. Also, the labor market is cleared by a single wage rate which no single employer can affect significantly, and no one willing and able to work remains unemployed. In addition, there are no labor unions or governmental regulations and controls to alter the operation of natural market forces in determining employment and wage decisions. Finally, there is no collusion, favoritism, or discrimination among the participants to the wage contract which gives any individual or group an economic advantage in the contractual wage agreement.

Of course, knowledgeable observers of labor market dynamics find it impossible to accept this abstraction of reality. There are, to be sure, but few examples to support the notion that labor markets exhibit, in full measure, the qualities mentioned above. Labor is not homogeneous, perfectly mobile and knowledgeable, motivated only by money, and unmindful of job security. The labor market is imperfect ("structured" or "institutional"), subject to union control (monopoly power), management control (monopsony power), and governmental restraints.

While the labor market is not perfect by any means, it is less imperfect for some workers than for others. Each individual faces different labor market barriers. Individual differences, motivation, and circumstances undoubtedly affect job-related achievements. Personality and cultural differences also influence employment decisions. However, employment discrimination, per se, already has been outlawed in many states and municipalities and will be outlawed in interstate commerce as well by July, 1965.

Nevertheless, labor market barriers based upon color have existed and will continue to exist in degree indefinitely. The major assumption of this paper is that differential patterns of employment, occupation, and income reflect and measure the degree of past and present systematic employment discrimination practiced against the Negro worker. Further, there is no inherent or innate physical or mental quality which justifies these differentials, or which precludes the Negro from full participation as an equal in every respect in the labor market.

Thus it is the purpose of this paper to explore the participation of the Negro as a member of the Philadelphia work force. To this end the paper documents the structure of the Negro's qualifications, status, and role as a worker in Philadelphia, with an eye toward providing a basis for greater understanding of Negro employment problems as well as a basis for policy alternatives to reduce racial barriers to equal employment opportunity. First, various labor market characteristics of resident white and non-white workers of Philadelphia are described and compared. These data are based primarily upon statistics from the United States Census. Then the data are summarized, and relevant conclusions are drawn.

LABOR MARKET CHARACTERISTICS OF PHILADELPHIA NEGROES

The characteristics treated here represent key variables affecting the quantity and quality of the Negro labor supply in Philadelphia, and relate, as well, to the pattern of its utilization. Data on Philadelphia Negroes are presented in the following categories: population and labor force participation; migration, mobility, and concentration; age-sex composition; education and vocational training; industrial and occupational patterns; individual and family income; unemployment and underemployment; and labor union membership.

Population and Labor Market Participation

Philadelphia's recent economic growth rate pattern is similar to that of other old, metropolitan areas of the Northeast. The average annual growth rate for Philadelphia is about half of the national rate, while suburban Philadelphia is growing at from four to five times as fast. The regional economy's growth rate closely parallels that of the national economy.[1] Social changes in Philadelphia reflect these underlying economic developments.

In Tables 1 and 2, population changes by race in Philadelphia from 1900 to 1960 are summarized. In 1960, the white population numbered 1,467,479; the nonwhite, 535,033.[2] The white population of Philadelphia has declined relatively in every decade since 1900 and absolutely in the 1930's and 1950's. Conversely, the nonwhite population has increased absolutely and relatively in every decade since 1900. Since 1900, the white population has increased by 137,803 (19 per cent); the nonwhite population by 471,009 (736 per cent). Other dramatic changes in Philadelphia's population are revealed by the most recent census data.

During the 1950's, Philadelphia's total population declined by 69,093 (−3.3 per cent) to 2,002,512. This overall decline resulted from a net loss of 225,158 whites (−13.3 per cent) and a net gain of 156,065 non-whites (41.2 per cent). These trends are consistent with those of other major metropolitan areas. If these trends continue in the same direction and to the same degree during the 1960's, by 1970 non-whites will number 755,467 (38.3 per cent) of a total Philadelphia population of 1,946,429. The assumption of a constant rate probably underestimates the prospective changes, but the magnitude of the population shift is impressive nonetheless.

TABLE 1

POPULATION BY RACE, PHILADELPHIA METROPOLITAN
AREA: 1900-1960

		White		Non-white	
Year	Total Number	Number	Per Cent	Number	Per Cent
1900	1,293,697	1,229,673	95.1	64,024	4.9
1910	1,549,008	1,464,549	94.5	84,459	5.5
1920	1,823,779	1,688,180	92.6	135,599	7.4
1930	1,950,961	1,728,457	88.6	222,504	11.4
1940	1,931,334	1,678,577	86.9	252,757	13.1
1950	2,071,605	1,692,637	81.7	378,968	18.3
1960	2,002,512	1,467,479	73.3	535,033	26.7

Source: "Philadelphia's Non-white Population, 1960." *Report Number 1, Demographic Data*. Philadelphia Commission on Human Relations, Nov., 1961, Table 1.

In 1960, Philadelphia's resident labor force numbered 851,000, a decline of 40,000 (4.6 per cent) within the past decade.[3] By 1962, the labor force had increased by 17,000. It is predicted that by 1970, the labor force will have increased to 914,500. In 1960, 218,923 (25.6 per cent) of the work force were nonwhite, while by 1970, it is forecast, 313,381 (34.3 per cent) of the work force will be nonwhite.[4]

Migration, Mobility, and Concentration

The nonwhite citizen of Philadelphia has experienced higher migration and mobility rates than the white. As indicated in Table 3, 5 per cent of Philadelphia's nonwhite population and 3 per cent

TABLE 2

POPULATION CHANGES BY RACE, PHILADELPHIA
FOR INTERCENSAL DECADES
1900 to 1960

Decade	Total Change		White Change		Non-white Change	
	Number	Per Cent	Number	Per Cent	Number	Per Cent
1900-1910	255,311	19.7	234,876	19.1	20,435	31.9
1910-1920	274,771	17.7	223,631	15.3	51,140	60.6
1920-1930	127,182	7.0	40,277	2.4	86,905	64.1
1930-1940	− 19,627	− 1.0	− 49,880	− 2.9	30,253	13.2
1940-1950	140,271	7.3	14,060	0.8	126,211	49.2
1950-1960	− 69,093	− 3.3	− 225,158	− 13.3	156,065	41.2

Source: "Philadelphia's Non-white Population, 1960." *Report Number 1,
Demographic Data.* Philadelphia Commission on Human Relations, Nov., 1961, Table 2.

of its white population had moved from another state between
1955 and 1960. The greatest migration, by far, was the influx of
Negroes (3.6 per cent) from the South.

During this five-year period, the nonwhite population was vastly
more mobile than the white. Negroes changed houses far more frequently, 45 per cent moving, compared to 28 per cent of whites
moving. The whites, however, were far more mobile as far as intra-
state movements were concerned. The mobility of the Negro probably is prompted largely by bad housing, a relatively low rate of
home ownership, and dislocations at urban renewal sites.

The census data indicate that the nonwhite population is un-
evenly distributed throughout the city. As shown in Table 4, the
greatest concentration of Negroes is in the north-central section
of the city (38.7 per cent in 1960). Between 1950 and 1960, the number of nonwhite households increased absolutely in every section
of the city except South Philadelphia. The Negro population grew
most rapidly, relatively, in the north and west, south of Market
sections of the city.

Age and Sex Composition

In 1960, the nonwhite population was more than eight years

TABLE 3

MIGRATION AND MOBILITY, BY RACE
PHILADELPHIA: 1955-1960

	White		Nonwhite	
	Number	Per Cent	Number	Per Cent
Population aged five and over, 1960	1,337,834	100.0	463,682	100.0
Lived in same house in 1960 as in 1955	851,502	63.6	210,940	45.5
Moved within city	376,033	28.1	208,963	45.1
Moved within state	29,129	2.2	3,681	0.8
Moved from other state:				
Northeast	22,086	1.7	4,435	1.0
North-Central	5,697	0.4	1,306	0.3
South	11,663	0.9	16,807	3.6
West	3,044	0.2	533	0.1
Live abroad in 1955*	14,301	1.1	1,644	0.4
Moved, no other information	24,379	1.8	15,373	3.3

*Includes territories.
Source: "Philadelphia's Non-white Population, 1960." *Report Number 3, Socioeconomic Data.* Philadelphia Commission on Human Relations, Dec., 1962, Table 11.

younger, on the average, than the white population; that is, the median age of nonwhites was 27.5 and that of whites, 35.9. Further, the median age in Philadelphia is increasing for whites and decreasing for Negroes. Among the nonwhite population, 38 per cent were under 18 years of age, while only 28 per cent of the white population were in that age bracket in 1960. Negroes made up 27 per cent of the population and 31 per cent of all persons under 40 years of age. These differences are related primarily to the exodus of young whites to the suburbs and the migration of young Negroes into Philadelphia. Second, the birth rate among Negroes is markedly higher.[5]

There were some important population changes during the 1950's. Between 1950 and 1960, the number of whites in all age groups except the 10-14 year-olds decreased. For example, during these years, in age group 25 to 44 there were 75,368 fewer white males and 85,340 fewer white females, decreases of 29.1 per cent and 30.9 per cent respectively.[6]

TABLE 4

DISTRIBUTION OF NONWHITE HOUSEHOLDS BY
SECTION OF CITY OF PHILADELPHIA: 1940, 1950, 1960

	1940		1950		1960	
Section	Num-ber	Per Cent	Num-ber	Per Cent	Num-ber	Per Cent*
South	1,944	29.7	23,528	23.4	22,831	15.3
North-Central	25,726	39.3	44,407	44.1	57,732	38.7
North	1,625	2.5	3,192	3.2	12,436	8.3
Kensington-Northeast	700	1.1	1,056	1.0	1,059	0.7
Germantown-Roxborough	2,445	3.7	2,991	3.0	7,823	5.2
West, North of Market	12,610	19.2	21,903	21.7	32,539	21.8
West, South of Market	2,942	4.5	3,608	3.6	14,680	9.8
Total	65,492	100.0	100,685	100.0	149,100	100.0

*Total of column deviates from 100.0 because of rounding.
Source: "Philadelphia's Non-white Population, 1960." *Report Number 3, Socioeconomic Data.* Philadelphia Commission on Human Relations, Dec., 1962, Table 5.

The existing and projected labor force in Philadelphia by race, sex, and age are presented in Tables 5 and 6. In 1960, about 64 per cent of the labor force were male; 74 per cent of the labor force were white. The forecasts made by John Culp, City Economist, indicate that by 1970 the labor force will be increasingly nonwhite (34 per cent) and female (40 per cent); the number of whites in age group 25-54 (both male and female) will continue to decline; the number of Negroes in age group 14-24 (both male and female) will double.

Education and Vocational Training

Education — The relative standing of the nonwhite population has improved with regard to the level of schooling, especially as indicated by the proportion who have graduated from high school. In 1960, the median number of school years completed by persons 25 years old and over was 9.8 for whites and 9.0 for nonwhites. These medians reflected a 0.5-year gain for whites and a 0.8-year gain for nonwhites over the preceding ten-year period.[7]

TABLE 5

EXISTING AND PROJECTED LABOR FORCE BY RACE,
SEX, AND AGE — CITY OF PHILADELPHIA

		Projected	
Labor Force	1960	1965	1970
Male	539,803	548,251	551,908
14-24 Years	75,743	94,384	108,405
White	57,008	63,241	65,142
Nonwhite	18,735	31,143	43,263
25-54 Years	352,919	341,948	332,457
White	264,448	241,463	223,557
Nonwhite	88,471	100,485	108,900
55 Years and Over	111,141	111,919	111,046
White	92,110	90,815	88,514
Nonwhite	19,031	21,104	22,532
Female	310,952	346,137	362,562
14-24 Years	59,235	75,629	82,192
White	44,393	51,766	51,455
Nonwhite	14,842	23,863	30,737
25-54 Years	194,028	203,518	206,936
White	128,509	124,371	117,637
Nonwhite	65,519	79,147	89,299
55 Years and Over	57,689	66,990	73,434
White	45,364	50,985	54,792
Nonwhite	12,325	16,005	18,642
Total	850,755	894,388	914,478
White	631,832	622,641	601,097
Nonwhite	218,923	271,747	313,381

Source: *Overall Economic Development Program, City of Philadelphia.*
Philadelphia Economic Development Committee, June 16, 1964,
Table 1-II.

TABLE 6

PERCENTAGE DISTRIBUTION OF EXISTING AND
PROJECTED LABOR FORCE BY RACE, SEX, AND AGE —
CITY OF PHILADELPHIA

		Projected			Projected	
	1960	1965	1970	1960	1965	1970
Male	63.5	61.3	60.4			
14-24 Years	8.9	10.6	11.9	100.0	100.0	100.0
White	6.7	7.1	7.1	75.3	67.0	60.0
Nonwhite	2.2	3.5	4.7	24.7	33.0	40.0
25-54 Years	41.5	38.2	36.4	100.0	100.0	100.0
White	31.1	27.0	24.4	74.9	70.6	67.2
Nonwhite	10.4	11.2	12.0	25.1	29.4	32.8
55 Years and Over	13.1	12.5	12.1	100.0	100.0	100.0
White	10.8	10.2	9.7	82.9	81.1	79.7
Nonwhite	2.3	2.4	2.4	17.1	18.9	20.3
Female	36.6	38.7	39.6			
14-24 Years	7.0	8.5	9.0	100.0	100.0	100.0
White	5.2	5.8	5.6	74.9	68.4	62.6
Nonwhite	1.8	2.7	3.4	25.1	31.6	37.4
25-54 Years	22.8	22.8	22.6	100.0	100.0	100.0
White	15.1	13.9	12.9	66.2	61.1	56.8
Nonwhite	7.7	8.9	9.7	33.8	38.9	43.2
55 Years and Over	6.8	7.5	8.0	100.0	100.0	100.0
White	5.3	5.7	6.0	78.6	76.1	74.6
Nonwhite	1.5	1.8	2.0	21.4	23.9	25.4
Total	100.0	100.0	100.0			
White	74.3	69.6	65.7			
Nonwhite	25.6	30.4	34.3			

Source: *Overall Economic Development Program, City of Philadelphia.*
Philadelphia Economic Development Committee, June 16, 1964,
Table 2-II.

TABLE 7

SCHOOLING COMPLETED BY PERSONS AGED 25 AND OVER, BY RACE
PHILADELPHIA: 1940, 1950, 1960

Amount of Education	White			Nonwhite*		
	1940	1950	1960	1940	1950	1960
Number finished college at least	42,361	56,105	54,144	1,740	4,180	7,943
Number finished high school at least	209,385	328,880	304,328	11,469	34,385	67,448
Number finished 7th grade at least	791,691	845,025	775,447	73,319	132,330	209,083
Total number**	1,022,970	1,044,400	925,778	143,866	209,360	285,719
Percentage finished college at least	4.1	5.4	5.8	1.2	2.0	2.8
Percentage finished high school at least	20.5	31.5	32.9	8.0	16.4	23.6
Percentage finished 7th grade at least	77.4	80.9	83.8	51.0	63.2	73.2

*1940 figures are for Negroes.
**Omitting cases not stated in 1940 and 1950.
Source: "Philadelphia's Non-white Population, 1960," Report Number 3, op. cit., Table 7.

Schooling completed, rather than the rate of change for the cited age group, is indicated in Table 7. In 1960, 30.7 per cent of the Philadelphia population aged 25 and over completed high school, 32.9 per cent of the whites and 23.6 per cent of the nonwhites. For the same age group and period, 5.8 per cent of the whites and 2.8 per cent of the nonwhites completed college. Further, from 1940 to 1960, the number of Negroes graduating from high school tripled; the number of Negroes completing college doubled. It is worth noting that the discussion so far has not distinguished between public and private (including parochial) schools. In 1960, over one-half of the white students aged 5-34 attended private schools in Philadelphia, while less than 10 per cent of nonwhites attended private schools. A report issued by the Philadelphia Board of Public Education documents the rapid racial changes taking place within the school system. As indicated in Table 8, by 1964, 53 per cent of the public school population were nonwhite. Such trends are expected to continue until 1980.

The quality of public education in Philadelphia is too complex a matter to discuss in detail in this paper. However, a few observations with regard to the quality of education for Negroes are in order.

The recent Board of Education report cited above reveals that, as of June, 1964, about 25 per cent of Philadelphia's elementary school students were *at least* one year behind in reading and arithmetic for their grade level. Moreover, about 30 per cent of all tenth graders were similarly behind in reading proficiency. Among individual schools there was considerable variation on the performance tests given. Thus, of sixth graders in schools with 70 per cent or more Negro students, only 30 per cent attained the overall

TABLE 8

PERCENTAGE OF NEGRO PUPILS

School Level	1957	1958	1959	1960	1963	1964
Elementary	45	47	49	51	56	57
Junior High	39	41	42	45	54	56
Senior High	30	30	31	32	36	38
Technical High	34	37	40	43	46	49
Overall	41	43	45	47	52	53

Source: *Report of the Special Committee on Nondiscrimination.* Philadelphia Board of Public Education, July 23, 1964, p. 2.

sixth-grade median reading score as contrasted with 92 per cent in schools with 30 per cent or fewer Negro pupils. In a similar survey, only 25 per cent attained the median arithmetic score in the predominantly Negro schools, while 93 per cent did so in the predominantly white schools.[8]

As of May, 1963, 52.5 per cent of all public school students were Negro, while at the high school level, 33.3 per cent were Negro. According to the Board of Public Education's report, there were 14,621 Negroes in high school. Of these, 3,177 were enrolled in "high content courses," 4,209 in "commercial B and C courses," 1,765 in "modified courses," and 1,982 in "trade preparatory courses," the latter two being referred to as "low content courses."[9]

These data are only suggestive of the causes of the disheartening picture of public education, especially for the Negro. The board made a comparison of predominantly white and predominantly Negro schools and found that, generally speaking, Negro schools were more overcrowded, almost a third being at least 10 per cent above capacity; ran more part-time classes; had a larger median class size, 36.8 pupils; had a greater number of classes with enrollments above 40 pupils, almost one-fourth; and had relatively the smallest number of classes with fewer than 30 pupils, roughly one-tenth.[10] Further, it is common knowledge that the predominantly Negro schools are older, have more teacher vacancies and fewer experienced teachers, and utilize a greater proportion of permanent "substitute" teachers. There are approximately 1,000 substitute teachers out of a total of about 9,000 teachers in the Philadelphia public school system.

In a recent National Education Association study it was reported that Philadelphia has the worst school dropout problem of any big city in the country. In fact, among 128 large and medium-sized school districts, Philadelphia ranked 127th in its ability to retain youngsters in the classroom! In 1963, only 53.4 per cent of the 1960 tenth graders graduated from high school. This compares to a 70.8 per cent completion rate for big city districts nationally.[11]

Vocational education. — Data on vocational training of Negroes in Philadelphia are scarce. We have seen that 49 per cent of technical high school students are Negroes, a 15 per cent increase from 1957 to 1964 (see Table 8). Out of a total of 8,668 Negro junior high school pupils (ninth graders), as of May, 1963, 6,914 or nearly 80 per cent were enrolled in a non-academic, i.e., job-oriented, program. Only 1,754 Negroes were enrolled in the academic program (college preparatory); the greatest number of Negroes in senior high schools were enrolled in commercial B and C, general, modified, and trade preparatory courses.[12]

For some years Pennsylvania has maintained a retraining program for the unemployed financed by state funds. Data are not kept to indicate the nature and degree of Negro participation in this program. However, the general impression obtained from local officials is that many of the participants, perhaps even a majority, are Negroes. In Philadelphia last year, 596 persons were enrolled for courses in five occupation categories. The majority of these trainees received instruction as practical nurses, sewing machine operators, and food supervisors, in that order. In the previous year, about 1,500 Philadelphians had been trained and placed by this state program.[13]

The problem of persistent unemployment prompted the federal government to enact the Manpower Development and Training Act (MDTA) in 1962. Its aim is to provide training and retraining for the unemployed. From 1962 through June, 1964, 41 course sections were completed in Philadelphia. It has been estimated that 80 to 90 per cent of the trainees were Negro. Some 480 persons completed training (51 per cent of those who had enrolled), while 320 trainees were placed on a job (34 per cent of those who had enrolled and 67 per cent of those who had completed training). Moreover, during this period, roughly 1,500 persons have undergone some degree of pre-vocational and semi-vocational training under a special MDTA project for the hard-core unemployed.[14]

Industrial and Occupational Patterns

Industrial patterns — The causes of the slackening demand for labor in Philadelphia in the face of increasing supply are vast and complex. The continuing decline in job opportunities confronts the Negro worker with additional difficulties in his attempts to achieve equal employment opportunity in all vocational fields.

Significant changes in the underlying structure of industry in Philadelphia explain the current and future structure of demand for manpower. The Office of the Development Coordinator in Philadelphia, using Pennsylvania Bureau of Employment security statistics, found that for the period 1952 to 1962 manufacturing employment declined by 63,300 (17.8 per cent), about equally, on a percentage basis, for durable and non-durable goods; and non-manufacturing employment fell by 89,200 (8.1 per cent). In manufacturing, the only increases in employment were to be found in the electrical machinery, printing and publishing, rubber and miscellaneous plastics, and chemicals and allied products industries. The major increased demand among non-manufacturing firms was in service and miscellaneous, finance, insurance, and real estate industries.[15]

The implications of these industrial trends are significant for the Philadelphia labor force and the Negro worker in particular. In 1960, the labor force was predominantly blue collar. About 43 per cent of the resident labor force were in semi-skilled or skilled occupations. Also about 44 per cent of the labor force were in white collar occupations. However, 80 per cent of Negro males were in blue collar occupations, nearly 20 per cent as laborers.[16]

There were significant differences among industry groups as far as employment of nonwhites was concerned. Census data reveal that 37 per cent of whites and 29 per cent of nonwhites worked in manufacturing in 1960; the differential was explained primarily by the fact that relatively fewer Negroes were employed in the durable goods sub-group. More whites (21 per cent) than Negroes (16 per cent) were employed in wholesale or retail trade. Similarly, 6 per cent of whites and 2 per cent of nonwhites worked in finance, insurance, and real estate. In contrast, more nonwhites held jobs in personal services — 17 per cent to 3 per cent, slightly more in public administration — 8 per cent to 6 per cent; and in construction the relevant ratio was 6 per cent as against 4 per cent. The proportions in professional and related groups were roughly comparable at about 11 per cent; the high Negro rate is explained by the inclusion of jobs in hospital and educational services under this industrial classification.[17] A more complete breakdown of occupations filled by Negroes follows.

Occupational patterns — Negro males, as indicated in Table 9, have made substantial progress in upgrading their skills relative to whites in Philadelphia. A comparison based upon census data for 1940 and 1960 reveals that Negro males held relatively more jobs as professional and technical personnel, as clerks and salesmen, as craftsmen, and as operatives. On the other hand, relatively fewer Negro men were employed as managers or officials, as domestic servants or in other services, or as laborers. In 1940, 5.9 per cent of all white workers were classified as laborers, compared to twice as many Negroes, or 29.7 per cent of the total Negro labor force. By 1960, while 4.2 per cent of the white labor force were classified as laborers, 18.9 per cent of the Negro labor force were laborers. This was an extremely significant decline in the largest occupation differential, i.e., laborers, between whites and nonwhites, but still a disconcerting fact of life for nearly 20 per cent of the Negro male labor force. Another sharp contrast is revealed in the 1960 breakdown of male occupations by race: 43 per cent of white males worked in white collar jobs as compared to 19 per cent of nonwhite males.

Projections of the future composition of the Philadelphia labor

TABLE 9

OCCUPATION OF EMPLOYED MALES BY RACE
PHILADELPHIA: 1940, 1960

Occupation	White				Non-white			
	1940		1960		1940		1960	
	Number	Per Cent	Number	Per Cent	Number	Per Cent	Number	Per Cent
Professional, Technical, and Kindred	29,211	6.7	41,140	11.2	1,205	2.8	3,908	3.9
Managers, Officials, Proprietors	49,602	11.3	38,036	10.4	1,361	3.2	2,527	2.5
Clerical and Sales	90,126	20.6	76,482	20.9	2,845	6.6	12,799	12.9
Craftsmen, Foremen	95,297	21.7	82,439	22.5	3,705	8.6	13,886	13.9
Operatives	108,906	24.8	84,096	22.9	8,972	20.8	30,348	30.4
Private Households	517	0.1	168	0.05	1,414	3.3	594	0.6
Other Service	38,025	8.7	28,187	7.7	10,737	24.9	16,544	16.6
Farmers and Farm Workers	711	0.2	378	0.1	50	0.1	224	0.2
Laborers	28,892	5.9	15,533	4.2	12,806	29.7	18,861	18.9
Total	438,287	100.0	366,459	100.0	43,095	100.0	99,961	100.0
Not Stated	3,380		20,236		324		11,631	
Grand Total	441,667		386,695		43,419		111,322	

Source: U. S. Bureau of the Census, *U. S. Census of Population, 1960, General Social and Economic Characteristics, Pennsylvania,* Final Report, PC (1)-40C, 1962, p. 431.

force are highlighted by changes which are of utmost importance to the Negro worker. The net demand for new jobs (including employer replacement needs) is expected to increase by 72.9 per cent for white collar workers and by 27.1 per cent for blue collar workers between 1960 and 1970. The greatest relative increase in net demand, by far, is to be for clerical and kindred workers (38.6 per cent); also, relatively strong increases are forecast in the net demand for service workers, excluding private household domestics (11.4 per cent), and operatives (10.1 per cent). An actual net decline in the demand for laborers (—2.6 per cent) is expected.[18]

Interesting statistics are available on the employment of Negro teachers in the Philadelphia public school system. Marked strides have been made in integrating school staffs since 1957. As of June, 1964, about 30 per cent of the teaching staff were Negro. By then, also, professional personnel in two-thirds of the elementary schools, in all but two junior high schools, and in all high schools were integrated. However, 7 of 131 elementary schools still had an entirely Negro teaching staff, while 68 elementary schools and 2 junior high schools had an entirely white teaching staff.[19]

As of 1963, the employment pattern for Negroes in administrative and supervisory positions in the Philadelphia schools was as follows: nineteen Negro elementary school principals had qualified by examination for the position, all of them supervising predominantly Negro-populated and staffed schools; one Negro high school principal had been appointed, supervising a predominantly Negro-populated school, with a well-integrated teaching staff; and there was one Negro district superintendent in an area where the student population was predominantly Negro.[20]

Several new provisional appointments of Negroes to administrative and supervisory positions were made: two new district superintendents, one assistant to an associate superintendent, and one principal on special appointment. Also, several Negroes were given permanent appointments: one assistant division head, one psychologist, four supervisors, one junior high school vice-principal, and one senior high school vice-principal. Finally, nine Negroes were appointed as elementary school principals.[21]

Individual and Family Income

The Negro worker in Philadelphia is disproportionately represented in the lowest and least desirable occupational categories, namely, laborers (53 per cent of the total) and domestic servants (86 per cent of the total). It is, then, not surprising to find that the median income of Negroes is considerably lower than that of whites who, on the whole, hold better jobs.

TABLE 10
INCOME OF INDIVIDUALS,* BY RACE
PHILADELPHIA: 1949 AND 1959

| | White | | | | Nonwhite | | | |
| | 1949 | | 1959 | | 1949 | | 1959 | |
Income	Number	Cum. Percentage	Number	Cum. Percentage	Number	Cum. Percentage	Number	Cum. Percentage
Under $1000	133,925	17.4	158,375	19.5	48,995	30.4	61,597	23.3
1000 – 1999	157,690	37.9	106,501	32.5	53,060	63.4	51,263	42.8
2000 – 2999	205,955	64.6	101,888	45.1	43,265	90.3	50,295	61.8
3000 – 3999	154,860	84.8	110,638	58.7	12,500	98.0	42,913	78.1
4000 – 4999	56,500	92.1	108,169	72.0	1,865	99.2	32,119	90.2
5000 – 5999	28,465	95.8	92,216	83.3	605	99.6	16,100	96.3
6000 – plus	32,260	100.0	136,020	100.0	700	100.0	9,664	100.0
Total	769,655		813,807		160,990		263,951	
Median income	$2,453**		$3,363		$1,594		$2,380**	

*Persons with income, aged 14 and over.
**Recalculated for above distribution: differs slightly from published census figure.
Source: "Philadelphia's Non-white Population, 1960." *Report Number 3, op. cit.,* Table 2.

Individual income — In 1949, the median income for nonwhites in Philadelphia was 65 per cent of the median income for whites; but in 1939, it was about 38 per cent of the average annual income of whites! By 1959, the median income of Negroes had risen to 71 per cent of that of whites in Philadelphia. However, since the relative median income of whites and nonwhites in suburban Philadelphia remained nearly constant, much of the relative improvement in median income of Negroes in Philadelphia may be attributed to the migration to the suburbs of many whites with high incomes.[22]

The individual white's median income in 1959 was $3,363 and the nonwhite's, $2,380, as indicated in Table 10. Further, in 1959 about 45 per cent of whites and 62 per cent of nonwhites earned *less* than $3,000 per year; about 17 per cent of whites and 4 per cent of nonwhites earned *more* than $6,000 per year.

Family income — Statistics on family income by race are shown in Table 11. It is found that in 1959, the white family's median income was $6,269, and the nonwhite family's median income was $4,248 (68 per cent of the white median family income). About 13 per cent of white families and nearly 31 per cent of nonwhite families had incomes lower than $3,000; about 53 per cent of white families and nearly 27 per cent of nonwhite families had incomes over $6,000. Setting the standard for "poverty" at a family income below $3,000 and for "middle class" at a family income of over $6,000, nearly one-third of all Negro families in Philadelphia were living in poverty in 1959, and over one-fourth were in the middle class or higher.

A more accurate picture of the Negro family's relative income standing may be reflected in the following comparison. The median family income for the Standard Metropolitan Statistical Area (or the eight-county area) in 1959 was $6,433. Among Negro families, 77 per cent fall below this median level compared to 52 per cent of white families.[23]

Unemployment and Underemployment

During the years 1957 through 1962, 76,000 to 107,000 of Philadelphia's workers were unemployed. This represented an unemployment rate of from about 9 to 12 per cent of the resident labor force. Moreover, many workers were underemployed (worked between 14 and 39 weeks per year). In 1959, of all male workers over 14 in the Philadelphia labor force, 13 per cent were underemployed. Among this number those particularly hard hit were the nonwhite and young workers. Hence Negroes, who constituted 26 per cent of

TABLE 11

FAMILY INCOME, BY RACE, PHILADELPHIA: 1959

Income	White			Nonwhite		
	Number	Per Cent	Cum. Per-centage	Number	Per Cent	Cum. Per-centage
Under $1000	11,257	3.0	3.0	9,085	7.6	7.6
1000 — 1999	16,599	4.4	7.3	12,624	10.6	18.3
2000 — 2999	21,133	5.5	12.8	14,981	12.6	30.8
3000 — 3999	29,475	7.7	20.6	18,302	15.4	46.2
4000 — 4999	44,405	11.6	32.2	18,054	15.2	61.4
5000 — 5999	55,074	14.4	46.6	14,402	12.1	73.5
6000 — 6999	47,729	12.5	59.1	9,987	8.4	81.9
7000 — 7999	38,684	10.1	69.3	6,995	5.9	87.8
8000 — 8999	30,500	8.0	77.3	4,915	4.1	91.9
9000 — 9999	21,741	5.7	83.0	3,389	2.8	94.8
10,000 plus	64,987	17.0	100.0	6,197	5.2	100.0
Total	381,584	100.0		118,931	100.0	
Median family income	$6,269			$4,248		

Source: "Philadelphia's Non-white Population, 1960." *Report Number 3,*
     op. cit., Table 3.

the labor force, accounted for 43 per cent of all unemployed in the city.[24]

Nonwhite unemployment has been much higher, in general, in Philadelphia. Census data indicate that in 1960 the total white unemployment rate was 5 per cent while the total nonwhite unemployment rate was 10.7 per cent. Among whites the unemployment rates for males and females are about equal. However, among Negroes the unemployment rate is significantly higher for males (11.1 per cent) than for females (10.2 per cent).[25]

The precise degree of unemployment among nonwhite youths in Philadelphia is not known. Data provided in a recent newspaper article, however, are indicative of the problem's sinister dimensions. Among Negro youths (between 14 and 19 years of age) in the labor force, 25 per cent are unemployed. This rate is twice as high as that for white youths. These percentages undoubtedly understate the rates of unemployment, since many youths out of school may not be actively seeking employment.[26]

Actually very little information is available on the characteristics of the Negro unemployed. For that reason, Table 12 is included here; it provides some data relevant to the discourse. The characteristics of MDTA trainees at the national, state, and city levels are detailed. Local administrators of the MDTA programs estimate that about 80 per cent of the unemployed trainees in Philadelphia are Negro and that, in specific courses, up to 90 per cent of the trainees are Negro.

It is particularly interesting to note that 55 per cent of the trainees referred for selected institutional training courses in Philadelphia had completed high school, and about 9 per cent had more than 12 years of schooling. Moreover, most of the people of this sample (about 70 per cent) were 22 to 44 years of age. Finally, nearly 68 per cent were among the long-term unemployed.

Labor Union Membership

Philadelphia has in its labor force 200,000 union members, of whom 25,000 are Negroes. While 12 per cent of all Philadelphia union members are nonwhite, 75 per cent of these Negroes are in industrial (old CIO) unions. Many Negro union members work in the construction industry, but not at the highly skilled jobs controlled by the AFL craft unions. It is estimated that the number of Negro laborers has increased by 50 per cent; yet, there is only token Negro membership in the twenty-odd building trade union locals in Philadelphia, except for the Hod Carriers and Common Laborers Union.[27]

In May, 1963, six building trade unions were cited by the Philadelphia Commission on Human Relations for discriminating against Negroes. The Plumbers, Steamfitters, Sheet Metal Workers, Composition Roofers, and Electricians locals were ordered to admit qualified nonwhites to membership, to administer objective admission tests, and to refer qualified nonwhites on a non-discriminatory basis in the two instances wherein exclusive hiring halls are permitted to exist.[28]

SUMMARY AND CONCLUSIONS

That the labor market is not perfect but "structured" is axiomatic. The meaningful question, then, is whether existing differential patterns of employment, occupation, and income for whites and non-whites are explainable solely by the factor of race. If so, the data, although not conclusive, at least indicate that the Negro worker in Philadelphia suffers from past and present systematic employment discrimination.

TABLE 12
CHARACTERISTICS OF MDTA TRAINEES

		National[1] Fiscal 1964[2]	Fiscal 1963	Penna.[3] Number	Per Cent
		Per Cent	Per Cent		
	Total			8041	
Sex	Male	56.5	63.5	6449	80.2
	Female	43.4	36.5	1592	19.8
Color	White	75.2	76.7	—	—
	Nonwhite	24.8	23.3	—	—
Age	Under 19	11.8	5.1	506	6.3
	19-21	23.1	19.1	1485	18.4
	22-44	54.6	64.9	5236	65.1
	45 and over	10.5	11.0	814	10.1
Educational Attainment	Less than 8th	2.1	3.1	359	4.5
	8th	5.6	7.6	725	9.0
	9th — 11th	27.9	30.1	3142	39.0
	12th	53.7	50.2	3550	44.1
	Over 12th	10.7	9.0	265	3.3
Duration of Unemploy.	Short-term Unemployed	54.7	50.7	3135	39.0
	Less than 5 wks.	30.6	24.3	1413	17.6
	5 - 14 wks.	24.1	26.4	1722	21.4
	Long-term Unemployed	45.2	49.3	4906	61.0
	15 - 26 wks.	12.3	17.4	1169	14.5
	27 - 52 wks.	12.5	12.9	1236	15.4
	Over 52 wks.	20.4	19.0	2501	31.1
Eligible for Reg. Allow.	Men	61.0	75.0	—	—
	Women	31.8	35.7	—	—
Head of Family	Men	61.7	75.9	4973	61.8
	Women	33.1	37.9	556	6.9

Source: [1]"Changing Characteristics of MDTA Trainees, Fiscal Year 1963-64." *Manpower Program Evaluation Report Number 6,* United States Department of Labor, Office of Manpower, Automation, and Training, Feb., 1964, pp. 2-6.
[2]The data are based on an analysis of the first five months of fiscal 1964.
[3]*Cumulative Summary of All MDTA Courses Through June 1964,* Pennsylvania Department of Labor and Industry, Bureau of Employment Security, July 20, 1964, p. 1.

TABLE 12 (continued)
CHARACTERISTICS OF MDTA TRAINEES

Characteristic		Referred to Institutional MDTA Courses, Philadelphia[4]			
		Mech. Drafts.		Stenog.	
		Number	Per Cent	Number	Per Cent
	Total	57		57	
Sex	Male	55	96.5	5	8.8
	Female	2	3.5	52	91.2
Color	White	—	—	—	—
	Nonwhite	—	—	—	—
Age	Under 19	1	1.8	7	12.3
	19-21	7	12.3	5	8.8
	22-44	44	77.2	36	63.2
	45 and over	5	8.8	9	15.8
Educational Attainment	Less than 8th	—	—	—	—
	8th	—	—	—	—
	9th — 11th	9	15.8	7	12.3
	12th	36	63.2	47	82.5
	Over 12th	12	21.0	3	5.3
Duration of Unemploy.	Short-term Unemployed	10	17.5	20	35.1
	Less than 5 wks.	—	—	8	14.0
	5 - 14 wks.	10	17.5	12	21.1
	Long-term Unemployed	47	82.5	37	64.9
	15 - 26 wks.	18	31.6	10	17.5
	27 - 52 wks.	16	28.1	10	17.5
	Over 52 wks.	13	22.8	17	29.8
Eligible for Reg. Allow.	Men	33	100.0	3	5.3
	Women	—	—	20	35.1
Head of Family	Men	38	100.0	3	5.3
	Women	—	—	21	36.8

[4]The data were obtained from internal administrative reports of the Commonwealth of Pennsylvania, Department of Labor and Industry, Bureau of Employment Security. The courses selected represented the five most heavily enrolled job classifications in each occupational group, e.g., professional and managerial, clerical and sales, service, skilled, and semi-skilled. Selection of the particular course section was random. Courses were started as early as Feb., 1962, and some were concluded in Feb., 1964.

TABLE 12 (continued)
CHARACTERISTICS OF MDTA TRAINEES

| | | Referred to Institutional MDTA Courses, Philadelphia[4] | | | |
| | | Waitress | | Welder | |
Characteristic		Number	Per Cent	Number	Per Cent
	Total	9		33	
Sex	Male	3	33.3	33	100.0
	Female	6	66.6	—	—
Color	White	—	—	—	—
	Nonwhite	—	—	—	—
Age	Under 19	—	—	—	—
	19-21	—	—	—	—
	22-44	8	89.9	24	72.7
	45 and over	1	11.1	9	27.3
Educational Attainment	Less than 8th	—	—	3	9.1
	8th	—	—	4	12.1
	9th — 11th	4	4.4	20	60.6
	12th	5	55.6	5	15.2
	Over 12th	—	—	1	3.0
Duration of Unemploy.	Short-term Unemployed	3	33.3	13	39.4
	Less than 5 wks.	—	—	3	9.1
	5 - 14 wks.	3	33.3	10	30.3
	Long-term Unemployed	6	66.6	20	60.6
	15 - 26 wks.	—	—	2	6.1
	27 - 52 wks.	2	22.2	9	27.3
	Over 52 wks.	4	44.4	9	27.3
Eligible for Reg. Allow.	Men	1	11.1	31	100.0
	Women	3	33.3	—	—
Head of Family	Men	1	11.1	33	100.0
	Women	3	33.3	—	—

[4]The data were obtained from internal administrative reports of the Commonwealth of Pennsylvania, Department of Labor and Industry, Bureau of Employment Security. The courses selected represented the five most heavily enrolled job classifications in each occupational group, e.g., professional and managerial, clerical and sales, service, skilled, and semi-skilled. Selection of the particular course section was random. Courses were started as early as Feb., 1962, and some were concluded in Feb., 1964.

TABLE 12 (continued)
CHARACTERISTICS OF MDTA TRAINEES

Characteristic		Referred to Institutional MDTA Courses, Philadelphia[4]			
		Auto Ser. Sta. Mech.		Total	
		Number	Per Cent	Number	Per Cent
	Total	29		185	
Sex	Male	29	100.0	125	67.6
	Female	—	—	60	32.4
Color	White	—	—	—	—
	Nonwhite	—	—	—	—
Age	Under 19	1	3.4	9	4.9
	19-21	7	24.1	19	10.3
	22-44	17	58.6	129	69.7
	45 and over	4	13.8	28	15.1
Educational Attainment	Less than 8th	1	3.4	4	2.2
	8th	—	—	4	2.2
	9th — 11th	18	62.1	58	31.4
	12th	9	31.0	102	55.1
	Over 12th	1	3.4	17	9.2
Duration of Unemploy.	Short-term Unemployed	14	48.3	60	32.4
	Less than 5 wks.	9	31.0	20	10.8
	5 - 14 wks.	5	17.2	40	21.6
	Long-term Unemployed	15	51.7	125	67.6
	15 - 26 wks.	3	10.3	33	17.8
	27 - 52 wks.	3	10.3	40	21.6
	Over 52 wks.	9	31.0	52	28.1
Eligible for Reg. Allow.	Men	19	100.0	87	47.0
	Women	—	—	23	12.4
Head of Family	Men	19	100.0	104	56.2
	Women	—	—	24	13.0

[4]The data were obtained from internal administrative reports of the Commonwealth of Pennsylvania, Department of Labor and Industry, Bureau of Employment Security. The courses selected represented the five most heavily enrolled job classifications in each occupational group, e.g., professional and managerial, clerical and sales, service, skilled, and semi-skilled. Selection of the particular course section was random. Courses were started as early as Feb., 1962, and some were concluded in Feb., 1964.

The population of Philadelphia is becoming increasingly non-white. During the previous decade there was a net decrease in the white population and a sizable increase in the nonwhite population. The forecasts are that these trends will continue. Further, the total labor force of Philadelphia also decreased during the 1950's, but currently is increasing and is becoming increasingly nonwhite. It is forecast that by 1970, 34 per cent of all workers in Philadelphia will be nonwhite.

The Negro worker in Philadelphia is far more migratory and mobile than the white worker. The migration rate for Negroes into Philadelphia, especially from the South, is higher than that for whites. The Negro also is far more mobile within the city limits than is the white. Whites are far more mobile in intra-state moves, e.g., the exodus to the suburbs. The fact that the Negro population is highly concentrated within specific neighborhoods is significant for obvious social and political reasons. The fact that nonwhites, especially youths, define the area of movement within the city to "safe" neighborhoods results in a labor market segmentation as yet unexplored.

The labor force in Philadelphia is becoming younger and increasingly female. The number of whites in the 25 to 44 age group has decreased. The nonwhite worker in Philadelphia is eight years younger, on the average, than the white worker.

The Negro has made impressive strides in improving his relative degree of educational attainment in Philadelphia. During the decade of the 1950's, the rate of Negro high-school completions tripled, and the rate of Negro college completions doubled. However, the quality of education in the public school system in Philadelphia mitigates, to a degree, the significance of these achievements. Many courses of instruction are so woefully thin in content that high school graduates cannot meet even minimum job specifications. The problem is particularly acute for Negroes, since their schools are generally inferior in every important respect.

Almost no data are available on the various programs to provide vocational training in Philadelphia. These programs, sponsored by all governmental levels, are under scrutiny, and officials loathe to discuss them. However, all sources apparently agree that the programs leave much to be desired. The technical high schools, state vocational education programs for the unemployed, and the MDTA efforts in Philadelphia are not noteworthy for success. These facts are particularly significant for the Negro worker, since he is more likely to seek vocational training as a youth or unemployed adult whose employability is severely limited.

Changes in the structure of demand for labor in Philadelphia hit the Negro worker especially hard. The city has experienced a general decline in manufacturing and non-manufacturing employment. Among Negro male workers, 80 per cent are in blue collar jobs and 20 per cent of these are laborers. The majority of Negro workers are employed in non-durable manufacturing, personal services, public administration, and construction.

The Negro male worker in Philadelphia has upgraded his work skills substantially, relative to whites, as reflected by a large decline in the differential of white and nonwhite laborers. Yet Negro white collar workers still are relatively few in number. As demand declines in blue collar occupations currently filled by Negroes and demand increases in occupations traditionally barred to them, an occupational shift of heroic proportions must take place.

The Negro's industrial occupational pattern is reflected in his level of remuneration. The Negro seems to have made vast strides in narrowing down median individual and family incomes relative to whites within the recent past. However, demographic changes, such as the outmigration of relatively high income whites to the suburbs, tend to distort the degree of Negro progress. Therefore, while the Negro male's median income was 71 per cent of the white male's, a substantial gain, more meaningful are the facts that almost two-thirds of all Negro males earned less than $3,000 and only 4 per cent earned more than $6,000 annually in 1960, well below percentages for whites.

Recently compiled statistics show that Negro workers comprise 26 per cent of the work force and 43 per cent of the unemployed. The unemployment rate for Negroes has run at the rate of about twice that of whites; the rate has been higher for Negro males than for Negro females. In addition, 13 per cent of all workers in Philadelphia have been classified as underemployed. Young workers, especially Negroes, are the hardest hit as regards unemployment and underemployment. Statistics on characteristics of unemployed workers referred to institutional MDTA courses reveal that 80 to 90 per cent were Negro.

Finally, the Negro has been excluded from membership in certain unions and thus has been precluded from employment in certain occupations. Most Negroes are in industrial, e.g., non-craft, unions; only a token number of Negroes have been admitted to certain skilled trades.

The conclusion derived from these data is that the Negro worker in Philadelphia does not enjoy equality of economic opportunity in the labor market. The labor market characteristics and operations discussed in this paper document the degree to which major cultural and institutional barriers have operated to the detriment of the

Negro worker. The results of this discrimination, based upon race, have been reflected in differential employment and income patterns. As this study demonstrates, guideposts for public and private non-discriminatory employment programs must be rooted in the labor market realities faced by Negro workers to be meaningful.

FOOTNOTES

1. *Philadelphia's Position in the Regional and National Economy.* Prepared by National Analysts, Inc., for the city of Philadelphia, Renewal Program, May, 1964. The basic aim of the study was to develop gross product data, that is, measurements of the value of the goods and services produced within a given geographic area. In the determination of the components of local gross product for 1947 to 1962, called "Basic Private Demand," both federal and local government spending have been omitted.

2. Nonwhites included other than Negroes were Indians, Japanese, Chinese, and Filipinos. Collectively these "other races" constituted 1 per cent of the nonwhite population of Philadelphia. "Philadelphia's Non-white Population, 1960," *Report Number 1, Demographic Data.* (Philadelphia: Commission on Human Relations, Nov., 1961), p. 3. In the text "Negro" and "nonwhite" are used interchangeably.

3. The Philadelphia labor market is defined by the Pennsylvania Bureau of Employment Security as consisting of eight counties, three of which are in New Jersey. This eight-county area, e.g., Philadelphia labor market, is also termed the Standard Metropolitan Statistical Area (SMSA). One of the five counties in the Pennsylvania portion of the labor market is Philadelphia County, which is equivalent to the city of Philadelphia.

4. *Overall Economic Development Program, City of Philadelphia.* (Philadelphia: Economic Development Committee, June 16, 1964). The committee, formed by the Mayor in December, 1963, is made up of thirty members representing public administrators and business, labor, education, religious, and citizen groups. John L. Culp, City Economist, was in charge of preparing this fine report.

5. "Philadelphia's Non-white Population, 1960," *Report Number 3, Socioeconomic Data.* (Philadelphia: Commission on Human Relations, Dec., 1962), p. 3.

6. "General Population Characteristics and Trends, Philadelphia and Environs," *Public Information Bulletin 8-A.* (Philadelphia: City Planning Commission, Apr., 1963), Table 3.

7. "General Socio-Economic Characteristics and Trends, Philadelphia and Environs," *Public Information Bulletin 8-C.* (Philadelphia: City Planning Commission, Apr., 1963), Tables 9 and 10.

8. *Report of the Special Committee on Nondiscrimination* (Philadelphia: Board of Public Education, July 23, 1964), pp. 16-18.

9. *Ibid.,* pp. 12-14.

10. *Ibid.,* p. 11.

11. These data, prepared by Daniel Schreiber, Director of the National Education Association, were reported on in "Philadelphia Leads Big Cities in Number of Dropouts," *The Evening Bulletin,* 118: No. 105, pp. 1, 6 (July 25, 1964).

12. *Report of the Special Committee on Nondiscrimination, op. cit.,* pp. 13-14.

13. *Overall Economic Development Program, City of Philadelphia, op. cit.,* p. 84.

14. The data on the MDTA program in Philadelphia are from the author's forthcoming study, "Urban Manpower and the MDTA: The Philadelphia Story."

15. *Overall Economic Development Program, City of Philadelphia, op. cit.,* Table 2-I.

16. *Ibid.,* p. 36.

17. "Philadelphia's Non-white Population, 1960," *Report Number 3, op. cit.,* Table 6.

18. *Overall Economic Development Program, City of Philadelphia, op. cit.,* Table 9-II.

19. *Report of the Special Committee on Nondiscrimination, op. cit.,* pp. 3-4.

20. *Ibid.,* p. 160.

21. *Ibid.,* p. 164.

22. "Philadelphia's Non-white Population, 1960," *Report Number 3, op. cit.,* p. 4.

23. "General Socio-Economic Characteristics and Trends," *op. cit.,* discussion of Table 5.

24. *Overall Economic Development Program, City of Philadelphia, op. cit.,* Tables 5-II and 6-II, and p. 43.

25. "Philadelphia's Non-white Population, 1960," *Report Number 3, op. cit.,* Table 4.

26. "Joblessness Rate of Negro Youths Increases to 25 per cent," *New York Times,* cxiii: No. 38, 928, p. 1 (Aug. 23, 1964).

27. "Jim Crow's Sweetheart Contract," *Greater Philadelphia Magazine,* 54: No. 2, p. 29 (Feb., 1963).

28. *City Contract Compliance: Progress in 1963.* (Philadelphia: Commission on Human Relations, Apr., 1964), pp. 1-2.

25

THE UNIVERSITY OF PENNSYLVANIA PILOT RESIDENTIAL EDUCATIONAL-VOCATIONAL PROJECT

Howard E. Mitchell*

With a degree of urgency in our country, we are moving toward integration rather than separation and differentiation. One aspect of this movement is reflected in our concern for a large segment of the population which cannot contribute effectively or has been impaired by "cultural disadvantage" or lack of opportunity. There is a pressing need to salvage what is good and what can make a contribution to the common good. However, we need devices and a sharp look at the processes whereby we assure greater opportunities for realizing the maximum potential for the pursuit of happiness and individual growth in every citizen. This paper presents the experimental role played and contribution made by a large urban university toward this goal. The administrative mechanism which made the program possible is discussed, followed by an over-view of the project and initial findings. Most important, focus is made upon lessons learned concerning the latent talent and leadership in the "culturally disadvantaged" youth group. This aspect of our experience is discussed in terms of the importance of making effective use of latent potential in equal opportunity program participants. The hypothesis is offered that equal opportunity programs developed and implemented by the formal public and private institutions and agencies of our society will more effectively serve the participating population, if that population is permitted to have a responsible role in policy and decision making concerning development and direction of the program.

---

*Director, Human Resources Program, University of Pennsylvania.

THE HUMAN RESOURCES PROGRAM OF THE UNIVERSITY OF PENNSYLVANIA

"Historically, a university met society's need for the fruits of learning at arm's length, through the individuals it educated and the knowledge it put on record. Today, the American university has itself become an instrument of national purpose,"[1] stated President Gaylord P. Harnwell of the University of Pennsylvania in early 1964. Such a philosophy dictates a sensitive interaction between the university and the surrounding society and culture. In keeping with this orientation, the Human Resources Program was established at the University of Pennsylvania by President Harnwell in April, 1964, as a mechanism through which student, faculty, and administrative efforts might be coordinated in the areas of education and human and industrial relations relating to social change and equal opportunity. A staff was organized responsible to the Office of the President, assisted in its policy-making by an advisory committee comprised of key faculty in education, the social sciences, law, social work, and labor and industry departments of the university.

Shortly after the establishment of the Human Resources Program its director met with members of the President's War on Poverty Task Force to explore the role of the urban university in the pending Economic Opportunity Act of 1964. Resulting from these conversations was the decision that the Human Resources Program staff would develop a proposal for submission to the Office of Economic Opportunity to operate one of the proposed Job Corps Training Centers provided for in the then pending legislation.

As the Human Resources Program staff and its advisory committee began to consider the scope of initial issues to be faced in conducting such a residential educational project, critical guide lines were needed. Search of the literature and talk with experienced personnel yielded limited opinion and few facts concerning how best to recruit out-of-school youth, effective assessment methods and their limitations, modifications necessary in traditional motivational systems and educational methods, and the anticipated problems and their handling by the resident counselor-teacher (the latter being typically of a middle-class culture and value orientation and many encountering low-income youth for the first time in an intensive living situation). Therefore a project was designed to operate a six-week pilot residential educational-vocational program,[2] including a follow-up study of its participants, in order to establish guide-lines for the larger proposed operation.

THE PILOT PROGRAM

On funds granted from the United States Office of Education, one hundred high school male dropouts spent six weeks at the University of Pennsylvania in the summer of 1964. They lived and studied in the men's dormitories and worked on vocational skill-producing projects on and off campus. Their teachers and counselors were university faculty members and college students from Pennsylvania and other institutions who lived, ate, worked, and studied with their charges, accompanying them throughout their daily activities.

The enrollees were recruited from public and private social agencies, school personnel, court officials, and neighborhood block groups. Requirements for participation dictated that these young men be 16 to 21 years of age, out-of-school, educationally and culturally deficient by the middle class standards of our society, and free of any infection, communicable disease, or addictive state. The latter requirements were established through a medical processing provided by the diagnostic clinic of the Hospital of the University of Pennsylvania.[3] Another requirement was that the participants be representative of both Negro and white youth as well as urban versus rural populations.

The original one hundred invited to participate in the six-week program were told we had no illusions concerning teaching them employable job skills in so brief a period. We offered a five-day-a-week opportunity to receive remedial instruction in reading, mathematics, and communication skills in the morning. Following expression of their vocational interests and assessment of their vocational aptitudes and interests, they would be assigned to work programs on and off the campus in the afternoons. Some would work in the university planning and printing offices, dining service, book store, building and grounds, and engineering service. Approximately 60 per cent would work on community-based construction trades programs improving two neighborhood areas by building tot lots, painting, laying concrete sidewalks and walk-ways. During evenings, educational, cultural, and recreational activities would be provided.

Provision was also made to give each enrollee a ten-dollar-weekly living allowance, which he received prior to going home for the weekend in a simulated industrial pay-line. Those trainees who completed the full six weeks were instructed that they would receive a twenty-five-dollar bonus. This was part of our search for guide lines in regard to a meaningful new system of rewards to motivate these

out-of-school youth. Throughout the program we also made use of
the fact that the program was voluntary and that approximately
eighty others had appeared the initial day asking to be admitted.
This was well known to them since a number of those who had
to be placed on a waiting list in case of a high rate of attrition the
first two weeks were their friends or relatives.

During the final week of the program, the project carried out its
responsibility for making each trainee aware of existing public
and private training and employment opportunities in the community. Leaders of such programs, as well as representatives of the
Philadelphia School District, accepted invitations to speak to the
group. The Pennsylvania State Employment Service registered each
boy during this "phase-out" week and arranged for personal interviews in its own offices.

The week concluded with a graduation ceremony largely arranged
by the student government council. This group was elected during
the second week of the program by the enrollees, who were divided
into groups of ten each and assigned to one resident counselor. The
student government council met at least twice per week throughout the final month of the program with the program director, two
counselor supervisors, and a representative of the counselor group.
This aspect of the pilot program is discussed in greater detail later
in this paper.

GENERAL FINDINGS OF THE PILOT PROGRAM

Attention was first given to a descriptive analysis of the population of out-of-school unemployed youth referred to the pilot residential educational project on the University campus. Racially the
one hundred selected were 68 per cent Negro and 32 per cent white.

A wide range of intellectual capacity and achievement was noted.
Their intelligence quotients, measured by techniques with the least
amount of cultural bias, ranged from 66 to 120. Reading and
mathematical achievement ranged from first-grade to twelfth-grade
level. In fact, 20 per cent of the group were so advanced in reading
that special provision was made to provide a widening experience
with literature and language development. Plans had been made
to have the entire group participate in a remedial reading program
using the "Words-in-Color" technique developed by Dr. Caleb
Gattegno.[4]

Judgment of the economic status of the families of the enrollees
was based upon the occupation of the parents. Information on this

factor was obtained before the program started for 82 per cent of the families. Out of this group, 92 per cent could be designated "working class." Of this number, 14 per cent worked so infrequently that they might be further classified as "welfare-working-class." This is consistent with other studies of dropouts which indicate they are usually from low-income groups, generally trade or labor occupations.[5]

The impact of the program upon the participants is seen best perhaps in the fact that ninety of the original one hundred completed the program. Of the low 10 per cent attrition rate, 7 per cent were those dismissed from the program because of infraction of the rules set by the administration. During the final week when all ninety of the trainees were interviewed by school, state, and federal agency representatives, twenty expressed interest in returning to school. Ten were interviewed for employment by the University of Pennsylvania, five expressed interest in entering the armed forces, and the others indicated serious intent to enter full-scale training programs under the Youth Job Corps of the Office of Economic Opportunity.

The main gain in reading and mathematical achievement was one grade-level. Moreover, considerable insight was gained concerning the limitations of traditional educational techniques and materials. Much of this we learned by listening to the participants and seeking their counsel and reaction as to their needs, readiness to learn, and factors influencing their motivation.

THE STUDENT GOVERNMENT

Perhaps more was learned in respect to the latent capacities of the enrollee group when they were made a part of the policy and decision-making apparatus through the establishment of the student government council than in any other program element. Equal opportunity programs, whether in an educational or vocational setting, are rehabilitative in character for those who have not learned productive employable skills and behaviors in our society. Such groups, whether school dropouts, delinquent youth, slum dwellers, racial minorities, or the unemployed, feel alienated, often sullen and unhappy. Great reliance is placed upon deriving satisfactions from the peer-group culture. The school dropout hangs out with the corner gang in the urban community, adopts its dress, language, and code of behavior. Communication from outside this network is often not trusted. For the same reason people living in "pockets of poverty" disbelieve messages from outsiders that jobs or opportunities are available outside their narrow orbit. It is easy for society to establish these opportunities, announce their availability via the usual media, and then be embarrassed by few participants or alarmingly high attrition. The argument is that early in such planning, the leadership of the participant group themselves must be identified and play a key role in such planning. The modest experiment reported here suggests that the student government group was largely capable of regulating itself and apprising the administration of program needs and direction. The council group capably dealt with such issues as (1) lateness and tardiness; (2) care and loss of equipment; (3) how best to discipline the enrollee for failure to carry out orders; (4) recognition of special learning problems in their peers; (5) the impact of a lifetime of discrimination upon the enrollee's ability to perform educational and vocational tasks; (6) how best to handle serious (versus minor) fights between enrollees; and (7) when and how to handle other interpersonal and intra-group problems as they affect living and working together.

Conceptually the point can be made that effective rehabilitative efforts must work toward a unified social system in which authorities and participants alike are devoted to one task — helping each individual to realize his maximum potential. In order to accomplish this, programs must avoid establishing the administration as authorities who serve as "rejectors," making inevitable the creation of two social systems within the program. This philosophy of operation has best been articulated in rehabilitative programs developed in Utah[6] and New Jersey[7] for the institutional care of delinquent youth.

Both programs make effective use of peer-group leadership. It has been found in both these progressive efforts that a rehabilitative system is most effective if the delinquent peer-group is used as a means of perpetuating the norms and imposing the sanctions of the system. Evidence is accumulating which suggests that the peer group is viewed by delinquents as the primary source of help and support. Although the pilot program reported here was voluntary and did not deal with court-adjudged delinquents, our experience was consistent. It is of some interest to speculate about the degree to which equal opportunity programs would be more effective in educational and vocational settings, as a function of establishing a mechanism to utilize the participation of indigenous leadership.

FOOTNOTES

1. G. P. Harnwell, quoted in "Six Weeks' Summer Session — with *A Difference*," *The Pennsylvania Gazette*, Vol. 63, No. 1, October, 1964, pp. 11-14.
2. This program for out-of-school youth was different in this respect from programs also begun in the summer of 1964 at Princeton, Yale, and Dartmouth for youth from low-income groups all of whom, however, were felt to have the potential for matriculation in college.
3. The rejection rate for physical illness or addictive states was a surprisingly low 6 per cent of the 180 examined.
4. This technique uses color groupings which illustrate the 271 combinations for the 47 basic sounds in the English language. The materials are published by the Encyclopedia Brittanica and are currently being experimented with in literary training for a variety of age-groups in the U. S. and Great Britain.
5. D. Schreiber, *Guidance and the School Dropout* (Washington: National Education Association of the United States, 1964). See also L. M. Miiller, *Reference on Dropouts*, U. S. Department of Health, Education, and Welfare, Office of Education (Washington: Government Printing Office, October, 1962).
6. L. T. Empey and J. Rabor, "The Provo Experiment in Delinquency Rehabilitation," *American Sociological Review*, Vol. 26, No. 5, October, 1961, pp. 679-695.
7. H. A. Weeks, *Youthful Offenders at Highfields* (Ann Arbor: University of Michigan Press, 1958).

PART VII

Business and Professional Jobs and Negro Leadership

26

THE NEGRO PROBLEM OF ENTREPRENEURSHIP

William Gomberg*

To assert that America is a land of immigrants is a truism. The economic study of America is a study of migrant nationalities coming over in succeeding waves, bringing with them little capital except their willingness to work. Each wave coincided with an expanding demand in the labor market for semi-skilled and unskilled workers in an industry on the verge of explosive growth.

The Irish, in the mid-nineteenth century, made up the laboring corps, laying our railroads from east to west; the Chinese coolies made up the construction gangs building from west to east; the Italians provided the construction personnel for our eastern subways and buildings; the east European Slavs went into the mines; and the Jews into the ready-to-wear garment industry and retailing.

The most energetic members of these groups strived to accumulate some little measure of capital and eventually went into enterprises of their own. They became the employers in many cases of their fellow nationals. The offspring of the original migrants were educated in our schools and colleges. In the mobile society of America, many of them found their way into business careers and professional practice, and can be little distinguished from the American mainstream into which they have been absorbed.

The Northern Negro, in a sense, is a part of a migratory wave from the South where the mechanization of cotton cultivation has displaced him from his historic job — cotton chopping. He resents the combination of restricted economic opportunity and political disenfranchisement exactly the way the Caucasians from western Europe did in their original homes. He too seeks to improve his lot by fleeing north. When he arrives, he finds that though opportun-

---

*Professor of Industry, Wharton School of Finance and Commerce, University of Pennsylvania.

ity may be better than at home, he is subject to the same kind of exploitation that every greenhorn group experienced in its beginning years.

The Negro, however, has two additional problems. One, he is entering the labor market for semi-skilled and unskilled work when for the first time in our history, the labor market for this kind of work is contracting. Second, he is saddled with permanent prominent visibility. There is little that we can do about the Negro's visibility except hope that a developing emotional maturity of our fellow citizens will cease to make this a handicap for the Negro. After all this kind of prejudice is the white man's problem. Only we can correct this kind of irrationality. There is not much that the Negro can do about our problem, mine and yours.

Now, what about this other problem? The problem of the Negro as an employee, what about his prospect as a businessman, as an administrator, as an entrepreneur? The problem of a fair share of employment for the Negro employee has been treated elsewhere.

The common explanation for the paucity of Negroes in enterprises of their own is attributed by academic scholars to a wide variety of causes.

Some of them follow:

1. The Negro culture since slavery lacks family solidarity. The family unit is loosely built. This prevents the family accumulation of capital from the earnings of its members to finance the more energetic member in starting an enterprise.

2. There are virtually no successful business members of the family group who can set an example of triumph for the youngster to emulate.

3. The Negro has virtually no business skills. He has not had the opportunity to learn business technique by either informal instruction or formal university training.

Somehow all of these reasons sound so logical and self-satisfying that they remove our responsibility for what we find, or better yet, do not find.

Harding Young and James Hund[1] have made a study of Negro entrepreneurship in the South. Given the entrepreneurial climate of the South until relatively recently, it is a miracle that any Negro entrepreneurship has shown itself. Ordinarily, skilled craftsmen are the self-starters in creating new enterprises with their technical skills as a core asset.

When slavery terminated, the Negro found himself barred from the crafts. The more ambitious, newly-emancipated slaves hoped to satisfy their drive for prestige by (1) learning Greek and Latin, (2) holding public office, and (3) becoming preachers.

The second ambition was suppressed after reconstruction and has only begun to emerge again now with the enfranchisement of Southern Negroes.

Business careers simply did not hold any attraction for Negroes as a group. What is more important is that many of the Negroes with entrepreneurial drive migrated northward.

Despite all these handicaps, nevertheless, there did emerge an active Negro business life. Negroes did create banks, savings and loan associations, and insurance companies, and this in the face of a social climate that varied from indifference to active hostility.

Negroes seeking credit from white banks that loaned on character had no character as far as white banks were concerned. The answer of the Negro was to create highly successful fiscal institutions in the face of odds strongly against them.

It might parenthetically be added that the few white institutions which were willing to assist them found themselves the beneficiaries of valuable business from which others had barred themselves.

Some 94 per cent of Negro businesses nevertheless remain in retail trades and services, where they employ from two to twenty employees. The Negro financial institutions are a source of credit to these small enterprises.

The reaction of the white financial community to this activity is most revealing. Upon the organization of a Negro commercial bank in Houston, white lenders suddenly began to make an effort to search out Negro customers for real estate loans who would make good loan risks.

It seems to me that the seething cauldron of the Negro revolt is a signal that there is much entrepreneurial drive seeking to be channeled. Wise business leaders in the white community can identify themselves with this striving and thereby both fulfill their own "good works" instincts and find new sources of business for their institutions.

After all, the secret well-spring of the growth of the Bank of America is best understood when we remember that A. P. Giannini, head of the predecessor Bank of Italy, was willing to extend credit to groups of Jewish immigrants engaged in that most chimerical speculation — the early moving-picture industry.

I, for one, reject the pat sociological apologies mentioned earlier for the status quo.

At the turn of the century, John R. Commons, foremost labor analyst of the day, explained why the Jews could never organize a successful trade union in the clothing industry. They all had the instincts of small businessmen. Yet within a comparatively few years after Commons made this statement, three of the most respected labor unions established themselves: the Amalgamated Clothing Workers of America, the International Ladies Garment Workers Union, and the Hat, Cap and Millinery Workers Union.

Is the dismissal of the Negro as an entrepreneur as superficially founded as were John R. Commons' observations about the Jews?

The Wharton School of the University of Pennsylvania is considering the establishment of a center for the specialized study of the economic problems of minority groups in our population.

In the course of surveying the area of economic activity in which Negroes find themselves, we undertook first to distinguish employment from management and then to separate those Negroes who are in administration management from those who are in the entrepreneurial management.

At first blush this may strike the reader as a distinction without a difference, but a closer look at what we have in mind and a more careful look at the myriad functions subsumed under the rubric "management" will help make the difference clear.

The primary functions of the entrepreneurial management of the autonomous enterprise may be listed as follows:

1. Creating a new organization for exploiting economically one or more ideas.
2. Reorganizing or absorbing an old organization to revamp old ideas or to infuse new ideas.
3. Dismembering and liquidating organizations, whose idea-base has become obsolete and unprofitable.

All three of these activities can be included in the term "problem formulation." They make up the basic functions of entrepreneurial management. The entrepreneur-manager takes amorphous material, neutral information and ideas and combines them in a seminal fashion into a producing, organizational structure. He thereby performs the innovating function of any economic system.

Managerial efforts devoted to supervision, control, and such forms of decision-making make up the technology of management. Such managerial functions are of substantial importance, but by the very nature of the management process, these decision-making functions are derived from and subsidiary to the basic entrepreneurial function that determines the character and the economic course of the enterprise.

The distinction between the technology of management and the entrepreneurial function of management was the subject of comment by Frederick W. Taylor. He observed as early as 1905 that ". . . there is no apparent relation in many, if not most cases, between good shop management and the success or failure of the company."[2]

Thus the generic term "management," as it is used loosely in current literature, encompasses three hierarchies of activities:

1. The entrepreneurial set of activities.
2. The administrative activities.
3. The routine supervisory duties.

We distinguish these three levels of management as entrepreneurial management, administrative management, and supervision.

Administrative and supervisory activities have received much the major portion of scholarly attention. This has not been without its useful aspect. The emphasis on decision-making has led to the examination of well-structured problems that follow in the wake of entrepreneurial creativity. However, the principal work of the entrepreneur is the formulation of what the problem is rather than the determination of a decision. The resulting decision is implicit in the way the problem is formulated. The great emphasis on decision-making, as by far the most fashionable phrase in current business literature, has obscured this distinction. Actually, close observation discloses that there is a constant conflict between entrepreneurial management on the one hand and administrative and supervisory management on the other.

This basic idea and its implications have been developed elsewhere. It does give us an adequate idea for our purpose to separate out Negroes in corporate management from those who are self-starting.

Ebony magazine serves the same purposes in the Negro community that *Life* does in the entire community: the creation of celebrities, that is, personages to emulate. The editor chooses Negro success-images in the economic life of the country. It is revealing to examine the weekly two pages called "Speaking of People," a regular feature of each issue. *Ebony* celebrates *People* who are in a success in the following government, corporate, or independent professional fields:

*Entrepreneurs	2	
Corporate professionals		In an analysis of 37
or executives	17	celebratees listed in eight
Eleemosynary professionals		*Ebony* issues, only two can
or executives	7	be even vaguely thought of
Government professionals	9	as entrepreneurs.
Independent professionals	2	

*See *Ebony,* May '62, March '63, January '64, April '64, May '64, October '64, November '64, January '65.

In other words these successful Negroes are mostly never independent entrepreneurs; they find themselves corporate professionals or occupants of political shelters such as eleemosynary institutions or government units.

Ebony published a special "festival" issue in September, 1963, the 100th anniversary of the Emancipation Proclamation, in which it celebrated Negro business achievements. These are the men who literally pulled themselves up by their bootstraps, making a contribution to the economic health of their communities and furnishing employment for their fellow Negroes. Among those listed are the North Carolina Mutual Life Insurance Company in the South and the Supreme Life Insurance Company in the North, the largest Negro-controlled insurance companies in the country. It is relatively recently that the North Carolina's president, Asa T. Spaulding, has received acceptance by the business community. Little wonder that he muses: "We had to make bricks without straw and we did it."

The efforts of Negroes to gain economic independence is not a recent development. As early as 1907 Booker T. Washington, founder of the Negro Business League, observed that Negroes organized to own and operate oil wells in Indian territory; that Negroes owned and operated a trolley car line in Jacksonville, Florida. Truman K. Gibson, Sr., another successful Negro entrepreneur, recalls the missionary spirit about Negroes' going into business and gaining economic independence. This spirit was repressed to some extent for many years but under the new political climate engendered by the civil rights agitation it is hoped that this entrepreneurial drive will once again assert itself. It is significant that the children of this middle class offer a disproportionately large part of the leadership of the Negro community in carrying on the agitation to make the 13th, 14th and 15th Amendments come alive.

To be sure, the Negro community has its dissenters. The late Franklin E. Frazier,[4] former president of the American Sociological Society and professor at Howard University, denigrates the role of these business entrepreneurs, though he does hold out hope for their children.

He refers to the myth of Negro business, whose combined assets do not attain the net worth of numerous single white corporations. He expresses his contempt for their catering to the worst in white society, with all the trappings of "society and debutantes." He rails against their lack of involvement in the aspirations of the Negro lower classes. Their highest desire is to pass in white society; they are worthy successors to their ancestors who were Negro owners of Negro slaves in colonial Virginia.

Whitney Young,[5] president of the Urban League, is somewhat more temperate in his assessment.

He is concerned about the growing social gap between the Negro middle class leadership and the masses they are called to lead. He does point out that the children of this middle class lack the drives "to pass" of their elders and have thrown themselves into the civil rights struggle.

Every minority in American history has gone through a similar development. The more ambitious are seldom the more introspective. The first desire is for recognition in the host society. The victim of discrimination seems to be the "white Negro" or "well-mannered Jew." He seldom gains this acceptance and is thrust back into the society of his minority and remains there until the entire minority gains acceptance without patronage.

The experience narrated by Frazier is his reason for persuasion; the same experience described by Young is a fountain of hope.

There is little doubt that the future lies with the young offspring of the middle class. Until the members of the Negro community gain economic strength, they will be regarded even by liberals as wards of the white society. Political recognition is coming fast, and if followed by widespread entrepreneurial activity, the day of full social parity cannot be far off.

Few people are as aware of the limitations of small business opportunities as a professor in a business school. Yet when we look backward and attempt to put ourselves in the time perspective of fifty years ago, did not independent business undertaking look to these ancestors of ours as ill-fated as it does today? How could any man survive the power of the big trusts? And yet look how many major enterprises were born in that era.

Only the future will tell.

FOOTNOTES

1. Harding B. Young and James M. Hund, "Negro Entrepreneurship in Southern Economic Development," from Melvin L. Greenhut and W. Tate Whitman, *Essays in Southern Economic Development* (Chapel Hill: University of North Carolina Press, 1964), pp. 112-157.
2. Frederick W. Taylor, *Shop Management* (New York: Harper Brothers, 1947), p. 19.
3. "The Negro in Business," *Ebony*, September '63, pp. 2-11.
4. Franklin Frazier, *Black Bourgeoisie* (New York: Collier, 1962).
5. Whitney Young, "The Role of the Middle Class Negro," *Ebony*, September '63, pp. 66-72.

27

NEGRO EMPLOYMENT IN WHITE COLLAR AND PROFESSIONAL JOBS*

Mahlon T. Puryear**

For those of us who have interest in and concern for some of the problems inherent in making greater use of the nation's manpower, this opportunity to identify, renew, and discuss our experiences is most welcome. We, of course, are grateful to the planners of today's program for making this possible.

I have been asked to talk about prospects for Negroes in white collar and professional job areas and about what the Urban League has been doing as it sought ways to implement meaningful job opportunities programs. I also would like to enumerate some of the things we might do together, in the days immediately ahead, in order that our combined efforts might have a real impact on overall expanded job prospects for all workers.

It is not always easy to approach our subject completely without emotion or subjectivity. For example, it is extremely difficult to refrain from mentioning my dismay that we find ourselves in 1964 involved in this discussion of job opportunities for *Negroes* — when, by now, we might have hoped to be able to turn our attention to *manpower needs, without regard to race or color*. We know we cannot do this as long as there exist many of the inequities in opportunities known to all of us.

In order to fully understand what progress has been made, or just how big a job lies ahead, I scanned a couple of reports we developed a year or so ago. I need not go into a full-blown story of the problems Negro workers have faced in recent years, but I would like to cite a few very significant figures to illustrate why

*A speech delivered at the luncheon meeting of the Labor Relations Conference, University of Pennsylvania, "Equal Opportunity — The Job Aspect," on November 13, 1964.

**Associate Director, Job Development and Employment, National Urban League.

we *should* devote time and energies to this important subject. Significant, also, is the fact that the year of research — 1961 — coincides with the year the Urban League moved into an era of new administration, community image, increased financial support, and commitments to expanded opportunities in jobs, education, housing, and health services.

Also, 1961 was the year in which many other groups began to review their roles in bringing about effective changes in the status of Negro Americans. They, too, entered an era of increased research, studies, and expanded efforts in trying to determine the role Negro workers play or do not play in the social, cultural, educational, political, and economic life of America.

The reports have covered a wide area. The Negro has been called a *burden on society* because he is so dependent upon welfare services and other assistance from public agencies. He has been called *socially deprived* because he has been a social outcast, having been a victim of a social system which not only relegated him to a second-class citizenship, but also used legal means, as well as customs and traditions, to deter his efforts to change his status.

The Negro has been called *culturally deprived* because he so often lived in communities where cultural activities were not available to him, or his very fight for survival often did not include the time or energy to develop interest in or taste for such activities.

He has been called *educationally deprived* and *intellectually unfit* because he has not been able to develop the background necessary to acquire the training and experience required to compete in the job market.

He has been called a *political novice* because, I suppose, a group which has so long been denied the simple right to vote could certainly not develop very much political sophistication.

The Negro has been called a *low producer* because he has worked mainly in unskilled, menial, or, in fact, disappearing job categories. He has been called *unqualified as a worker* because of the serious lack of education and experience so often required when he sought new or advanced job opportunities.

To some degree, there is truth, a lot of truth, in each of the above statements. We cannot, however, accept them as stated, for to do so is to accept the stereotype so well known to all of us.

Whatever the status of Negro workers generally, the plight of those who work in white collar jobs, or even those who aspire to do so, is even more serious. For this group of workers or aspirants includes those persons who accepted the advice of adults — teachers, counselors, parents — and stayed in school to acquire the educational backgrounds that were to lead to rewarding jobs in business, industry, government, and education. This is the group which, if working, has found entry jobs available, but upgrading, transfer, and promotion out of its reach. Included also in this group are those thousands of teachers and administrators relegated to working in inferior segregated school systems in the North and the South, and from which we have not been able to develop the kinds of students who could take advantage of newly developed opportunities for continued study or work.

The 1961 research figures reveal that Negro workers were 14.1 per cent, compared to 45.6 per cent for others, employed in skilled, white collar, and professional jobs. If you take out of the 14 per cent figure those employed in segregated school systems and colleges in the South, and those Negro professionals serving Negroes mainly, the remaining percentage is extremely small.

Speaking more specifically, we found:
- that there were 3,662 Negro accountants and auditors as compared to 463,934 others;
- that there were 233 architects as compared to 28,813 others;
- that there were 1,998 Negro dentists compared to 78,200 others;
- that the ratio of Negro physicians and surgeons to others was 4,706 to 218,904;
- that among aeronautical, civil, and electrical engineers, the ratio was 2,794 to 380,273;
- that in the area of business management, the ratio was 73,433 Negroes to 4,420,894 others — with 45,464 of the 73-odd thousand Negro managers being listed as self-employed.

These figures prevailed in spite of increased efforts by employers during and after World War II.

In the area of work in business, we find that the Negro has made his greatest contributions in businesses which serve the Negro community — insurance, banking, and personal services. He is not a substantial participant in the over-all business world because he qualifies as neither lender nor borrower of important monies. He most certainly does not qualify as an important stockholder with major firms, although he seems to make great efforts to develop and hold on to whatever he chances to acquire.

When Negroes did have an opportunity to participate in over-all economic development, they were generally not given equal pay for equal work. That this difference in income has widened in recent years is reflected in the fact that today Negro workers, as a whole, earn only 53 per cent as much as white workers, a drop of 4 per cent since 1950. Also, 62.4 per cent of Negro families earn less than $4,000, while 70.6 per cent of white families earn more than $4,000.

Among white collar workers, one finds that college graduates, as a whole, may expect to earn $9,000 per year. For Negro college graduates the figure is $5,400. This is due to the fact that most Negroes, even in white collar jobs, work at the lowest-paying levels and, so far, have not had sufficient opportunity to work in as wide a variety of jobs as have other groups.

Until quite recently, neither business, industry, government, labor, nor education could point with pride to its record in making full use of available manpower in this country. Too often our concerns were in getting the job done, with little attention paid to total contributions which might be made by those who worked.

Many persons did not realize how really serious the situation was. In business, we had produced outside the Negro community only one corporation president; fewer than eight directors on major corporation boards; fewer than six vice-presidents, and several of these dealing with the "special Negro market." Most of us here know personally all of the Negroes who hold top-level jobs in industry and business.

In government, the situation was certainly one which presented a very interesting picture. Here we have had the advantage of fair employment programs dating back 90 years. We have had state and city ordinances guaranteeing equal employment opportunities all through those years. Yet, we cannot point with pride to the fact that some four years ago, there were only three Negroes in the Southeast holding federal positions above GS-8 — except those in post office jobs or those dealing specifically with race relations. Negroes held, and still hold, few supervisory jobs in most governmental work areas.

At the state and city levels of employment, the situation was certainly no better, as politics played such an important part in the selection process. We undertook as an assignment a few years ago the task of reviewing the make-up of the various agencies which had been set up to deal with the identifiable problems of Negroes. We were amazed to note that in the large majority of instances these agencies themselves were not examples of progress. Too often they were politically conceived and were thus politically staffed and operated.

In higher education, other than Negro colleges, we have not produced one president of a college or university, not a dean, and very few department heads. There are surprisingly few Negroes holding *full* professorships in major universities. This is true in spite of the fact that Negroes have been graduating from these institutions for more than a hundred years.

The opportunity to learn, to acquire meaningful experiences, to explore, to make mistakes and recover from them, to be a part of the whole and not just a segment, to be understood as having desires, aspirations, ambitions, and feelings for America, has not typically been the lot of Negro citizens.

Fortunately we are now moving ahead, and we are making some real progress. The period since 1961, then, represents the era of greatest progress in providing expanded job opportunities for minority groups. While state and local groups were retooling, improving techniques and methods for dealing with minority group employment programs and problems, business, industry, and our national government were taking the lead.

What has been done in your business, with and without governmental assistance, is better known to you than to anyone else. Among the firms represented here can be found some of our most productive merit employment programs. Represented here, too, are firms into whose merit hiring and upgrading activities have gone sober thinking, resourceful planning, and meaningful implementation efforts.

What you have done has had telling results in a number of ways: (1) There is now closer cooperation between those who seek workers and those who offer responsible leadership, guidance and assistance to employers; (2) You are now identified with and actively participating in programs designed to narrow the gap which has for so long existed between Negroes and other citizens; (3) You have increased your support of agencies and institutions having major responsibility for the preparation of new generations of Negro Americans; (4) You have increased the number of Negroes now employed in supervisory and first-level management positions in business and industry; (5) You have increased recruiting on campuses whose student bodies are predominantly Negro; (6) You have initiated and expanded summer and part-time work experiences for Negro teachers; (7) You have expanded summer employment opportunities for Negro college and high school students, particularly in governmental departments such as Labor and Commerce; and (8) You have expanded opportunities to learn and work in major educational settings.

As an Urban Leaguer, I take some pride in knowing that we have worked, hand in hand, with many of you who have been associated with these examples of progress. For many years we have placed major emphasis on finding new jobs for qualified Negro workers. We have had a part in numerous programs related to integrating the work force at all working levels. We are known the country over for our efforts in helping America prove to itself that a more equitable use of Negro manpower is a *must* if we are to solve the problems of automation, unemployment, underemployment, and improved education.

From a pilot placement program in 1945 which placed hundreds of Negro workers in new job situations during the 1940's and 1950's, we have moved to the establishment of a reservoir, or *Skills Bank,* into which is being placed information on men and women who are available for jobs anywhere in the country. In addition to those seeking initial employment, or those struggling to leave the ranks of the unemployed, our files cover individuals who have not found promotion or upgrading possible in their present jobs.

In our national office and in 56 local *Banks* in 56 Urban League cities are more than 10,000 résumés of Negroes now qualified to do almost any job available, or possessing the necessary background and education to learn after employment. These people can work in your offices, your development centers, your personnel departments, your sales units — anywhere you need help. We welcome, in fact, we urge your making greater use of this resource, for to do so is to step up the pace of any equal-hiring program.

We have always worked very closely with the leaders of business and industry through their membership on our *Commerce and Industry Council.* In addition to providing an excellent source for counsel, advice, and assistance in developing realistic job development and employment programs, the council plays an important role in our fund-raising activities — and serves as a sounding-board for new program ideas.

Most recently, we requested and secured the council member firms' participation in a *business and industry orientation program for administrators and teachers* in predominantly Negro colleges. This project, which we expect to get under way shortly after the first of the year, is designed to provide a four-to-six-week work orientation experience for the professional personnel responsible for the education of the majority of Negro students.

In Urban League cities across the country, we are providing a variety of programs which serve to assist employers in finding qualified workers. *Urban League-industry co-sponsored secretarial training programs* are in operation in Pittsburgh, Omaha, New York, and St. Louis. On-the-job training projects, financed with federal funds, are now in operation in New York, Cleveland, and Pittsburgh — and others are to begin shortly. Urban Leagues in many cities are active participants in recruiting and referring Negro youth and adults for MDTA training programs. On December 9, 10, and 11 we are holding a conference of some 300 Negro leaders to discuss active participation in the anti-poverty program.

We are now cooperating with many companies in their management training programs. Here we believe that we can be of even greater service because we feel very keenly that our involvement provides, for both management and the Urban League, a most effective way of discussing and solving programs and problems in human relations and manpower utilization.

Management, more and more, is calling on us for assistance in developing college recruiting programs. We think this is sound, for our staff has had a long-standing working relationship with educational leaders.

Because of the respect we command in the Negro community, we play an important role in interpreting to Negroes changes that are taking place in the job market. We also serve management, on the one hand, as a screening agency in recruiting and hiring — and the Negro citizen, on the other, by helping him to attain the training and other experiences needed to find satisfactory employment.

We are also fortunate in that the Urban League's Executive Director, Whitney M. Young, Jr., has earned the respect of leaders in all walks of life in America. We who work with him sense our responsibility to constantly seek out those persons who can, and will, work with us as we move ever forward toward the goal of equal opportunity.

Yes, much has been done, but there yet remains so much more to be done.

We must first accept the fact that the solution to problems faced by Negro workers must be given priority treatment *now* if the recent gains are to be maintained and enhanced. Every force in government, labor, industry, business, and education must work as hard as humanly possible to push ahead in all positively-oriented job opportunities programs for Negroes. This means that programs of recruiting at the high school and college levels, of initial hiring, and of upgrading for those already employed, must be re-examined, re-defined, and given new emphasis in order that they have real meaning for Negro job-seekers.

Policy statements as now recorded by every leading employer in the country must be translated into practices from the corporate office to the janitor's supply room, and must apply to white collar jobs as well as blue collar jobs.

Since education plays such a vital role in the development of the work force, education processes and practices must in fact be made more democratic. Negro youth and their parents, North and South, East and West, need to see more examples to prove that staying in school to get a good education is more profitable than being a dropout or the recipient of public assistance in a new form.

Employers who have questions about the application of the Fair Employment Practices Title of the 1964 Civil Rights Act would be unwise to spend time trying to figure out how to comply *next* year. The rest of *this* year should be used to plan purposefully, to plan with diligence, and to plan productively, ways of making merit employment work — all of which will give less and less meaning to the compliance portions of that act.

Together, we must plan and implement job expansion programs which show real imagination and determination and which will give further evidence to Negro job-seekers that they, too, can have an equal share in developing our expanding economy.

28

EMPLOYMENT PROBLEMS AND NEGRO LEADERSHIP*

Roy Wilkins**

The continuing campaign for the upgrading of America's Negro minority must continue to engage the attention of the business, industrial and financial community if we are not to have serious disturbances in American life.

This is no sensational threat based upon an emotional fever. It must not be ascribed erroneously to a protest demonstration in a particular locality. It is not the consequence of the appearance, the truculent language, or the activity of self-styled "militant" leaders of the protest movement.

The serious disturbance that could occur unless more than routine remedial steps are taken has its roots in the generations of racial proscription that have operated on the Negro-white situation in such a widespread, complex, rigid, and implacable fashion as to present our country today with an explosive condition. This portent is reflected in unanswerable statistics, extending over decades, of which the erupting protests are but an inevitable symptom. To paraphrase an old, but descriptive, cliché, "The chickens of neglect, of contrived and imposed inequality, and of plain, unvarnished racial prejudice are coming home to roost."

Any student or mere casual inquirer into America's racial difficulties must be appalled at the complex interrelationship of the factors that have produced the present very real threat. Where does one begin? With education? With morality? With political democracy? With economic opportunity? With family and neighborhood life? With the stimulation of youth and the rewarding of adults?

---

*A speech delivered at the dinner meeting of the Labor Relations Conference, University of Pennsylvania, "Equal Opportunity — The Job Aspect," on November 13, 1964.

**Executive Director, the National Association for the Advancement of Colored People.

With the re-education of both races? In every area records of disappointment and despair abound.

We have just come through a nation-wide election campaign in which one of the principal proposals was that this whole area of redressing the acknowledged racial inequities in all aspects of citizenship be left to the local and state communities, with emphasis to be placed upon voluntary action, upon the "minds and hearts of men." Federal action to delineate, protect, and enhance constitutional citizenship rights was denounced by the nominee and by the thinkers who took over the Republican party. This view, fortunately for the nation as a whole, was emphatically repudiated on November 3.

As in every election, many ingredients shaped the repudiation, but few will discount the potency of the civil rights issue. It seems undeniable that the states of Mississippi, Alabama, South Carolina, Georgia, and Louisiana registered their totals on the basis of the Republican candidate's stand on the civil rights issue.

It may be a kind of encouragement to the optimists that the recorded support for a stand-pat, or at best a very slow movement, was limited to a majority in only five of the fifty states. Realists, however, are sobered by the fact that the obdurate attitude which has brought us this far toward disaster, has persisted in such a virulent fashion into the 1960's that segments of five states can still hark — officially and openly — to slavery time and to the vicious rear-guard roadblocks of the post-Civil War century.

Despite the warnings and the crusading of Negro civil rights groups since 1910, despite the steady alterations of the legal status of the Negro citizen, despite growing Negro political influence in non-Southern urban areas since 1930, white America continued its laissez-faire racial policy until jarred by the public school segregation ruling of the U.S. Supreme Court in 1954 in the *Brown v. Board of Education* case.

So deliberately did the nation react that the Southern rate of compliance was less than one per cent a year. The North sympathized with the Southern plea for "more time." It agreed with Dixie that the Negro was "going too fast" — at 0.9 of one per cent a year! The Northern attitude towards its own ghetto schools ranged from forthright action by a few cities through patchwork programs in many to incredulous denial and flat refusal to budge in others.

The attitude on school desegregation, embodying, it seemed to the Negro population, the whole frustrating concept of racial segregation and discrimination in American life and the determination to maintain it at all costs, led to the direct action protest activity. This began on a pilot basis in Oklahoma, Kansas, and Missouri in 1958 and 1959, caught on in North Carolina in 1960, and swept the nation thereafter.

American businessmen have a stake in the Negro's struggle for equality. Failure to redress his just complaints in this area could harass the economy, could spark upheavals in production, distribution and sales, and could, also, speed the creation of a permanently-unemployed Negro class, which would constitute an expanding financial burden upon the economy and a restive and potentially explosive cadre in every urban community.

Why are the Negroes so shrill in demanding jobs? Why did we have picketing of construction projects in Philadelphia and other large cities? Isn't the country in a boom period? Cannot one observe the increase in Negroes in white collar and technical jobs? Isn't the nation affluent? Isn't the fault really with the Negroes who, somehow, don't "measure up" to their opportunities?

Perhaps the most exhaustive study of the current economic status of Negroes in the United States has been made by Herman Miller of the Bureau of the Census. This report was presented before the 1963 hearings of the Subcommittee on Employment and Manpower of the Committee on Labor and Public Welfare of the United States Senate. Miller states flatly, "the Negro still ranks among the poorest of the poor and his economic status relative to whites has not improved for nearly 20 years." Miller asserts that it is valid to state that for the country as a whole Negroes have raised their occupational levels in the past 22 years at a faster rate than whites. But, he contends, the improvement in the occupational status of the Negro since 1940 is due only to movement from the rural South to urban industrial areas. Negroes who once were highly concentrated in sharecropping and agricultural labor have moved up to urban service jobs or to unskilled and semi-skilled factory work, and some few have moved into white collar employment. But there has been a parallel upgrading of jobs held by whites.

Moreover, during the past decade there has been no change in income differentials between whites and Negroes, according to the report: "In 1947, the median wage or salary income for non-white workers was 54 per cent of that received by the whites. In 1962, the ratio was almost identical (55 per cent)."

The concentration of Negro labor "in low-paid occupations such as laborers and service workers" is a fact not to be ignored. A Negro man who has not gone beyond the eighth grade has little chance of being anything other than a laborer, porter, or factory hand; 8 out of every 10 Negro men with 8 years of schooling worked as laborers, service workers, or in other unskilled jobs — compared

with only 3 out of 10 whites with the same amount of schooling!
The lifetime earnings of nonwhite elementary school graduates is
about 64 per cent of the white total. Among college graduates nonwhites have only 47 per cent of the white total. The fact of the
matter is that the average nonwhite with four years of college can
expect to earn less over a lifetime than the white who did not
go beyond the eighth grade.

Miller's presentation was strikingly confirmed in a recent study
made by Dr. Vivian Henderson, professor of economics and business administration at Fisk University. The issue is not whether
Negroes have made any progress, but whether it has been rapid
enough to enable the Negro to adjust to an economy whose rate
of change is cumulative and intense and undergoing revolutionary
changes in the mode of production.

The truth is, as Professor Henderson points out, that "Negroes
are on a treadmill and time is in reality 'running out' on them as
a group, in their pursuit of parity with whites. The group has to
run exceptionally fast in order to stand still." They continue to be
confined to the lowest occupational categories. More than twice
as many Negroes as whites are in the lower income brackets.

Henderson states: "Whites are acquiring the highest paying jobs
in the higher occupational classifications. The benefits of general
economic expansion and technology, therefore, have only 'trickled
down' to the Negroes, putting more of them into wage and salary
jobs. These benefits automatically produced high acceleration in
the income change, but were restricted tightly to lower occupational
classifications."

The need for unskilled labor has drastically declined, while
highly skilled labor in a variety of crafts finds more employment.
The very slow pace of manpower change and development among
Negroes means that the colored worker is in an unfavorable position
in relation to the requirements of the labor market. Excluding
government, the areas of growth in employment generally are not
the areas in which Negroes have traditionally found employment.
Automation means there will be a further sharp decline in the need
for semi-skilled and unskilled workers.

In 1960-61 in Chicago, Negroes were 20 per cent of the total labor
force, but made up 43 per cent of Chicago's unemployed. The
Negro unemployment rate was 11.5 per cent but the white unemployment rate was only 3.5 per cent.

Negro unemployment in Chicago has not changed for the better
since 1950, and the concentration among Negroes has remained
constant. Labor force projections indicate that there will be 450,000
more workers in Chicago's metropolitan area in 1970 than there

were in 1960. One-third of these will be Negroes. Yet the trend of employment potentiality indicates that only 150,000 new positions will be created by 1970.

The entire Negro community throughout the United States is today faced with a crisis of unemployment. What for the white worker has been a mild or temporary recession has become for the Negro worker a major depression.

The U. S. Department of Labor, Manpower Report of the President for 1964 puts this grave matter in a capsule paragraph: "In 1963, there were more than 22 million nonwhites in the United States, most of whom were Negroes. Nonwhites comprised 11.7 per cent of the population, 11 per cent of the work force, and 21 per cent of the unemployed. These stark figures serve to dramatize the disadvantaged status of Negro workers, for their disproportionately high rate of unemployment is essentially the climax of all the discriminatory forces shaping the lives of Negroes . . ."

The *New York Times* has added its estimation: "Unemployment of these proportions were it general, would be a national catastrophe."

The challenge to business and industry management is nowhere better stated than by George Schermer of Philadelphia in his recent article in "The Personnel Job in a Changing World": "Those who possess some imagination and a broad grasp of economics will have no difficulty recognizing that the 22 million plus nonwhite Americans have the potentiality of becoming either a tremendous asset or an economic liability. The nonwhite population of the United States is larger than the total population of Canada. With adequate education, training, and opportunity, it can be a major force for productivity and an extremely lucrative market for goods and services. Without training and without opportunity, it is certain to become both a burden and a threat to the safety and welfare of the nation."

There will be efforts by minority groups to utilize the new Civil Rights Act of 1964 and the new anti-poverty legislation, as well as to renew their efforts under the National Defense Education Act, the Manpower Development and Training Act, the Area Redevelopment Act and the Public Works Acceleration Act.

They have found, in many instances, that the old patterns and handicaps are restricting their benefits under the various federal laws. For example, more than 40 per cent of the Negro trainees in the MDTA program were in the service category in June, 1963. There were but three Negroes out of 263 electrical, plumbing, and carpentry trainees.

Many applicants were hampered by lack of education and others by lack of working experience in the fields in which they sought additional training. A small ray of hope is contained in a spotty survey by *The Wall Street Journal* in early October, 1964, which reveals that some industry at long last is reaching for categories of persons long idle in the boom period, including the unskilled, teen-agers, women, the less educated, and the Negroes.

But the Negro position as to employment remains desperate. It is entirely valid to assume that much of the post-election activity of civil right groups will be directed toward opening up new employment opportunities, getting more jobs, getting more training for jobs, and winning promotion to better-paying categories. Employment discrimination along with that in housing and in public education constitute the targets, in the North, of all civil rights workers. If they are smart they will publicly assign no priorities, but privately they will concentrate on jobs, with schooling but a half-step behind and ghetto housing but a half-step farther back.

They will use every possible tactic and pressure, for they have the feeling, buttressed by the statistics, that they have been cheated these many years. They feel they will be shut out, with only infuriating tastes of the good life, unless they can institute a crash program in behalf of their millions of deprived adults and of oncoming millions of their youth.

Where negotiations fail or where agreements are not kept, where loopholes in the law are invoked, where hard noses meet the hard fact of discrimination, demonstrations undoubtedly will be employed. If the situation is an aggravated one, these demonstrations could get out of hand.

Undoubtedly, also, selective buying techniques will be called into play. Businesses, particularly consumer businesses, which accept Negro customers but refuse Negroes jobs will feel the outrage of the community. In contrast to demonstrations, these buying (or non-buying) campaigns are apt to be orderly, well organized and disciplined. Philadelphia Negro ministers have conducted extremely successful campaigns on the retail level and have won hundreds of new jobs. Similar campaigns in Savannah, Georgia; Jacksonville, Florida, and a dozen other cities have been successful. There are signs that this type of action will spread from consumer outlets to manufacturing and distributing firms if results should not be forthcoming in response to present efforts.

Management must meet the legitimate demands of the Negro community with a recognition, first, of their justice. It should anticipate the situation by assembling information about Negro employment in the localities concerned, about schools and training, about informed and responsible groups in the Negro community, and about the applicable municipal, state, and federal laws and regulations.

Sometimes a group of Negro ministers will be the key, sometimes one or more of the regularly organized civil rights groups, sometimes an ad hoc committee of persons new to negotiating, but sincere in their zeal and in their requests.

The George Schermer article, referred to above, goes into considerable detail on the handling of civil rights delegations and negotiations by management, stressing, correctly, that these are often less sophisticated and less disciplined than similar organized labor negotiators.

Sophisticated or not, the Negro and the problem are here, forced up from their burial below by the march of history. One hundred and one years have passed since the Emancipation Proclamation. Nearly two-score African nations have emerged as free people since 1957. Technology, transport, and communications have changed the world.

The United States cannot brush aside any longer the differential treatment accorded twenty millions of its citizens because of skin color. The evidence is in that the nation does not desire to stage a brush-off and will take positive steps. The court decisions, the executive action on the federal level by Presidents Roosevelt, Truman, Eisenhower, Kennedy, and now Lyndon Johnson, reinforced by the legislative concurrence of the Civil Rights Act of 1964, all signal a turn from the past to a new way.

The manner in which Southerners have begun, often reluctantly, to change, argues that despite the five-state minority of November 3, the clear trend is to non-discrimination as a working national policy. Business, which played a strong role in many a desegregation change in the South when politicians stubbornly postured and moralists abdicated, can lead the way now to folding the Negro into the economy and thus developing the strength that the economy — and the nation — must have to survive.

As must be apparent in today's world, that survival strength is only in part economic; in substantial, even determining measure, it is spiritual, a vindication of the dream of 1776, which every American carries in his heart.